Black Comedians on Black Comedy

Black Comedians on Black Comedy

HOW AFRICAN-AMERICANS TAUGHT US TO LAUGH

Darryl Littleton

APPLAUSE THEATRE & CINEMA BOOKS · NEW YORK

Black Comedians on Black Comedy
How African-Americans Taught Us to Laugh
By Darryl Littleton

Book design by Mark Lerner

Library of Congress Cataloging-in-Publication Data

Littleton, Darryl
 Black comedians on Black comedy : how African-Americans taught us how to laugh / by Darryl Littleton.
  p. cm.
 ISBN-13: 978-1-55783-680-9 (cloth)
 ISBN-10: 1-55783-680-9 (cloth)
 1. African American comedians—Interviews. 2. African American wit and humor—History and criticism. I. Title.

 PN2286.L58 2006
 792.702'8092396073—dc22
 [B]
            2006018071

Applause Theatre & Cinema Books
19 West 21st Street
Suite 201
New York, NY 10010
Phone: (212) 575-9265
Fax: (212) 575-9270
Email: info@applausepub.com
Internet: www.applausepub.com
Applause books are available through your local bookstore, or you may order at www.applausepub.com or call Music Dispatch at 800-637-2852

SALES & DISTRIBUTION
North America:
Hal Leonard Corp.
7777 West Bluemound Road
P. O. Box 13819
Milwaukee, WI 53213
Phone: (414) 774-3630
Fax: (414) 774-3259
Email: halinfo@halleonard.com
Internet: www.halleonard.com

Europe:
Roundhouse Publishing Ltd.
Millstone, Limers Lane
Northam, North Devon EX 39 2RG
Phone: (0) 1237-474-474
Fax: (0) 1237-474-774
Email: roundhouse.group@ukgateway.net

CONTENTS

Introduction by Dick Gregory vii

Preface ix

Special Thanks xi

Thanks to All the Comedians and Industry Talent xiii

Chapter 1 **Take My Overseer, Please!** 2

Chapter 2 **Is This Absolutely Necessary?** 12

Chapter 3 **Blackface on Black Face Crime** 18

Chapter 4 **Two Coons Were Better Than One** 28

Chapter 5 **If It's a Clark Gable Movie, I'll Do It** 38

Chapter 6 **"Sure Sounds Black to Me"** 50

Chapter 7 **You Call That Reception?** 54

Chapter 8 **Not You Too, Bugs** 60

Chapter 9 **I'll Make My Own Damn Image** 66

Chapter 10 **Pass the Corn Liquor, I'm a Vegetarian on the Chitlin' Circuit** 74

Chapter 11 **How Low Can I Go?** 82

Chapter 12 **Git In Where You Fit In** 92

Chapter 13 **So This Is What They Mean by "Colored TV"** 112

Chapter 14 **The True "King" of Comedy** 124

Chapter 15 **The Heir to The Throne** 152

Chapter 16 **Down Home Blues** 166

Chapter 17 **The African-Americans Are Coming!! The African-Americans Are Coming!!** 186

Chapter 18 **Lend a Def Ear** 194

Chapter 19 **A View from Behind** 204

Chapter 20 **A Different Shade of Black** 224

Chapter 21 **And the Nights Got Darker** 236

Chapter 22 **Mo Money, Mo Money, Mo Money** 254

Chapter 23 **When We Were Kings and Queens** 274

Chapter 24 **Jerry Lewis Never Heard a Sister** 290

Chapter 25 **From Hambones to Hummers** 298

Sources and Photo Credits 325

Index 327

INTRODUCTION by Dick Gregory

Darryl Littleton has captured the history in progress of the contribution of black comedians in his first book *Black Comedians on Black Comedy: How African-Americans Taught Us to Laugh.*

This work of passion is not only entertaining, it is our *history!* Littleton's work presents us with the authenticity of who we are as a people and how the gift of laughter became a profession for black comedians to provide for their families and a way to endure in an unjust white racist insane system that had more respect for animals than black human beings. Momma always told me the best medicine to deal with the illness of society was through laughter and God knows we as a people chose laughter throughout the history of discrimination and inequality.

This book is a celebration of gratitude, forever applauding the genius of all black comedians of yesterday who throughout history have contributed to the world of entertainment. This work also presents the black comedians of today who not only have taken care of their families but who have begun owning their own work and media production houses, and who are contributing to the economic growth of this country.

Today is a new day but yesterday cannot be forgotten. *Black Comedians on Black Comedy: How African-Americans Taught Us to Laugh*, will allow this history to be passed on from generation to generation. Darryl Littleton is a funny writer; reading this book you will know he's also a funny comedian. If he were born 100 years ago he would not have been mentioned in this book. There was no avenue for this type of work.

The history of comedy as it relates to the roadmap used by African-Americans must be told because it captures so much of who we are. Laughter was very powerful in our history even under the worst human conditions. This work demonstrates how for every black comic who made it, tens of thousands went by the wayside. We just didn't become Richard Pryor or Bill Cosby. We had figures like them at the dinner table or sitting in the living room telling stories. There just wasn't a stage for them and now there is.

Now you can go into the bookstore and see a black section displaying books by black authors for adults and children. Change has happened. And at this point in our lives there are numerous Black comics recognized all over the world representing all facets of the black experience. For example, Paul Mooney is one of our most conscious black stand-up comedians and acclaimed comic writers of today using the stage and the media to keep the black consciousness alive through laughter.

We have to stop and say thanks to Hugh Hefner. The world is not aware that Hugh Hefner is and always has been a courageous, fearless, loving, and unselfish human being. He feared not the racist mentality and behavior of the oppressor by opening the door of White America to the genius of black comics. It was Hugh Hefner who gave me the opportunity of becoming the first Negro comedian to perform in his Playboy nightclub located in downtown Chicago. This was a *FIRST*! White comedians such as Bob Hope and Red Skelton always walked out on stage as human beings first and then as a comic. There are few people who know that Hugh Hefner single-handedly broke the color line by allowing me, a black man, to integrate his club by performing my stand-up comic routine; but if Hugh Hefner had had a policy of not letting Negro's come in his club as patrons, whenever they talked about Hugh Hefner, they would have mentioned he operated a segregated Playboy nightclub. Nobody would have ever praised him for operating an integrated nightclub. His decision to give me this opportunity and platform to perform on stage with no rules and no restrictions opened the national door to a new generation of black comics. I will always say "thank you" to Hugh Hefner because without that experience the rest would not have happened.

This book is a teachers' guide for all Americans to tap into the culture of the relationships of blacks and whites showing what the struggle was all about in the world of entertainment as well as the various styles and choices black comics used to express themselves in their work. It's not about turning on the TV and seeing Denzel Washington or Dave Chappelle. This work brings you directly to the pain, choices made, suffering and successes we as a people experienced on the journey of honing our craft as black comedians throughout history. This book is a celebration of and tribute to black comedians of yesterday and today for the laughter provided to our families through the good and hard times.

Black Comedians on Black Comedy: How African-Americans Taught Us to Laugh is written in a powerful style intertwined with comics of today sharing their personal stories, styles and accomplishments. I am delighted to introduce this work. This book is a must read! Comedy is an art form and Darryl's experience as a comedian and writer captures the true works of our black comedians' journey from our ancestors to the 21st century. Darryl Littleton is a gifted comic who knows how to write and that's very very rare; there are brilliant black comics out there but most are not writers and you have brilliant black writers who are not comedians.

Thank you Darryl for working so hard to capture our history. You make us all proud.

This work is truly another roadmap that leads us in the right direction of understanding where our comedy came from, how it materialized in the minds of the comedians, and how laughter supported the family as well as kept the family together.

PREFACE

Stand up comedians always state their influences. Mine was my father. Though not a comedian himself (the guy really didn't have much of a sense of humor, but a great disciplinarian backswing) he introduced me to Dick Gregory then Richard Pryor through the recordings he'd play over and over until the curse words slurred. I later stumbled upon Redd Foxx and Rudy Ray Moore and I was hooked. As soon as I got of age I remember taking my fake ID, getting into the Comedy Store in Hollywood and being cursed out by an amateur comedian for heckling. Fonder memories I have yet to find.

It wasn't until I got married and needed an excuse to get out of the house at night that I ventured into this arena of fools myself. My appetite was insatiable. I couldn't get enough of hearing people laugh; especially since most of my early shows were scud missions with me bombing on just about every stage I was kicked off of. But with time, patience and an obscure joke book, I developed my act, my style and was called upon to write for DJ Tom Joyner. Next was "The Black Comedy Boom" where I appeared on HBO's *Def Comedy Jam*. That show could make a career in the early days and I was on the road in no time. Besides learning what names not to call the locals if you wanted to avoid a beat down, I polished my skills across this country, came back and put those talents to use writing jokes for other comics on BET's *Comic View* (D.L. Hughley, Cedric the Entertainer, Sommore, and Don "DC" Curry). I went on to produce and act on that same show.

I never thought I'd love anything that didn't bear my name as much as I do comedy. It's made me a living and given me a life. So in my opinion a celebration by those who made and continue to make that history is long overdue. It is my hope that this book will be enjoyed for generations and if not it should be just thick enough to balance an uneven coffee table.

SPECIAL THANKS

My only wife, Alicia, for sticking and reminding me to sleep.

My only daughter that I'm aware of and my constant muse, Darina.

June Clark, my wizard of an agent and the best tour guide a first time author could desire.

Jeff Silberman, my manager with impeccable timing

Rose Mitchell of the A. C. Bilbrew Library for hipping me to public domain.

Jamie Foxx, for being cool enough to say "sell it" and getting the ball rolling.

Michael Messina, a great publisher with the insight and moxie to say, "buy it."

And to all those who provided introductions and source material. Without your assistance this project would have never come about:

Ajai Sanders, Andre Lavelle, Angela Means, Brad Sanders, Charlie Murphy, Damon Williams, Darren Carter, Daryl and Dwayne Mooney, David Damas, Eddie Murphy, Edwonda White, Hope Flood, Laverne Thompson, Luenell Campbell, Michael Ajakwe, Reynaldo Rey, Richard Stanfield, Shang Forbes, Tom Dreesen, Toure Mohammad, and Lillian Smith.

This book is dedicated to my mother, Theresa Littleton, who loved and stood by a guy like me above and beyond the call of maternal duty; to my father, William Littleton Jr., whose advice has stood the test of time and is more relevant in death than the dribble I get from so-called "live" people on a daily basis; and to all the talented comedic performers that time and space would not permit within the text whose camaraderie, abilities, and unpredictability help create a sub-culture that is beyond living.

THANKS TO ALL THE COMEDIANS AND INDUSTRY TALENT

A. J. Jamal
Adele Givens
Affion Crockett
Ajai Sanders
Al Toomer
Alex Thomas
Alonzo Bodden
Andre Lavelle
Angela Means
Arsenio Hall
Bernie Mac
Bob Sumner
Brad Sanders
Brandonn Mosley
Buddy Lewis
Cedric The Entertainer
Charlie Murphy
Chris Rock
Chris Spencer
Cocoa Brown
Curtis Arceneaux
Damon Wayans
Damon Williams
Dannon Green
Daran Howard
Darrel Heath
Darren Carter
Darren Fields
David Arnold
David Banks
David Damas

David Drozen
Deon Cole
Derrick Ellis
Dick Gregory
Doug Williams
Earthquake
Eddie Griffin
Eddie Murphy
Edwonda White
Eric Rhone
Evan Lionel
Franklyn Ajaye
Geoff Brown
Gerard Guillory
Guy Torry
Honest John
Hope Flood
Ian Edwards
J. B. Smoove
James Hannah
Jay Lamont
Jay Phillips
Jemmerio
Joe Blount
Joe Torry
Joey "J-Dub" Wells
John Witherspoon
Joyce Coleman
Katt Williams
Keith Morris
Kevin Hart

Kool Bubba Ice
Kym Whitley
Lamont Ferrell
Laura Hayes
Lauren Bailey
Leslie Jones
Loni Love
Luenell Campbell
Marc Howard
Mark Curry
Mark Prince
Marla Gibbs
Marquez The Greatest
Marvin Thomas a.k.a. Madd Marv
Melanie Comarcho
Michael Ajakwe Jr.
Michael Blackson
Michael Williams
Mike Bonner
Mike Epps
Mystro Clark
Nick Cannon
Norman Mitchell
Paula Jai Parker
Pierre
Red Grant
Reginald Ballard (Bro Man)
Reynaldo Rey
Richard & Willie
Ricky Harris
Robert Townsend

Rodman
Rodney Perry
Roger Rodd
Royale Watkins
Ruben Paul
Rudy Ray Moore
Rusty Cundieff
Sandy Brown
Shang
Shaun Jones
Shawn Wayans

Sheri Shepherd
Shuckey Duckey
Sinbad
Smokey Deese
Sommore
Spanky Hayes
Speedy
T. Faye Griffin
T'keyah "Crystal" Keymah
Talent
The Mooney Twins

Thea Vidale
Timmie Rogers
Tom Dreesen
Tommy Chunn
Tony Rock
Tony Spires
Tony Tone
Vince D
Willie Brown & Woody

Take My Overseer, Please!

CHAPTER 1

"Did you hear the one about the master that got his throat slit while he was asleep?"
— MYSTRO CLARK

It would be foolish of us to assume that slaves didn't poke fun at their masters. Needless to say there was plenty of time to do it. The first recorded slaves were brought to North America in 1619 and the lowly practice continued until 1863 (that is unless you were in Texas; in which case you didn't discover you were free until two years later).

> **Comedian, Spanky Hayes:** "If I had found out slavery had been over two years before they came and told me, I probably would've robbed them of their carriage and moved to Detroit."

Initially indentured servitude included Irish and Indians, but since white men, like the Indian runaway, could blend into an accommodating environment and thus avoid detection, the non-blendable African was left holding the bag...and rake and dustpan. Not only were blacks the race of easy identification, it was highly unlikely there'd be confrontation from kinsmen raising a ruckus in attempts to reclaim the involuntary workers.

> **Comedian/Actor, John Witherspoon:** "I don't know about me being no slave ever because I would've always devised a plan to get the f*#k out of there."

It must also be remembered that slaves were not of the same tribes and cultures and thus dance, music, and mimicry were their only forms of communication. This behavior of course amused the slaveholders, who often would entertain their visiting European guests with viewings of the Negro antics—antics that were regularly rewarded.

Musical humorist, Jay Lamont: "Maybe the master would've invited me to one of his little parties to do a show for them. I probably would've done it too. I would've found a way to get up in that house."

Many a slave was treated with favor for putting a smile on a master's face. Masters would in turn send that slave off to a neighboring plantation to amuse another family, as well as show off the talented darkies the sender possessed.

Comedian, Madd Marv: "To be honest with you I probably would've been the type of guy to tell all-black jokes. You know, derogatory Negro jokes. I would have told master-friendly jokes. And now I would have been in the house with the master eating pancakes and pudding."

Well, with all this eating, smiling, dancing, and singing going on, the slave master was still perplexed as what to make of the African cargo he'd purchased. One major problem was the seeming lack of respect for work or the tools with which to do it. Slaves would destroy property as though they were children. They had to be prodded into doing the most rudimentary of tasks and by the highest bidder's estimation, this spelled the mind of a stupid, lazy race.

Comedian/Filmmaker/Actor/Writer/Producer, Robert Townsend: "I would probably be breaking up stuff in the house and messing with his daughter on the side and making jokes about what he don't know."

What the slave owner didn't know was that this was actually the behavior of those who chose and managed to survive in this strange new land with its even stranger circumstances. Many a potential slave had met their end in the grueling Middle Passage. The three month journey, lying tight-packed in the prone position in one's own waste and the residual filth of others, provoked understandable violence which was met with immediate death or a slower dunking in shark-invested waters.

Comedian, Evan Lionel: "I would've been killed. I would've been like, 'Slavery is wrong. Y'all really don't have to go for this. Y'all need to learn how to read.' It'd have been ridiculous. They'd have killed me when they found out what I was doing."

Among the survivors, some decided upon their arrival that this new life was not one they chose to live and either killed themselves those first few dreadful nights or forced their masters to do it by imposing the threat of physical harm upon them and their loved ones.

Talented slaves were often sent from the plantation to entertain neighbors and sometimes even troops whose sworn duty was to preserve slavery.

Comedian, Dannon Green: "I'd have got killed the first day off the boat. Seriously. I would've said, 'Look at that white woman's ass' and they would have shot me."

Then there were those who resigned themselves to survive at any cost. The one unspoken condition was that that cost would be paid on their terms. The kidnappers might have had their bodies, but they'd never inhibit their spirits.

Comedian, Marc Howard: "Well, looking at the color of my complexion I probably would've been a happy slave. I probably would've been talking about how good the master was."

Comedienne, Leslie: "I would've been in the field because I'm a black muthaf*#ka, so I wouldn't have been able to have been no house slave. I think I would've talked about how the master's wife was f*#kin' all the brothas."

Though most had been sold out by rival tribes prescribing to the motto of "the enemy of my enemy is my friend," only to discover belatedly as the boat backed to the shore to load up their family that this wasn't necessarily true, they were determined not to break the chain of their people. And though by the very action of enslavement billions of future Blacks in America would grow up never knowing their real last name, only the surname thrust upon them by their purchasers, they remained diligent.

Comedian/Actor, Sinbad: "You can't judge it if you didn't live in that era. I mean people come up with what they would not do. Some people say, 'If I was a slave I'd have...' Yeah, right! You'd have what—run? You don't know what you would've done."

Slave owners and their families loved to check on their holdings, giving the slaves something to observe as well.

We do know that the need to appear dimwitted and slow was a tactic to appease the master. Attempts of equality or independent thought were met with a cracking whip.

Comedian, Shuckey Duckey: "I know I couldn't handle those whips. I would have punked out. I would've had a name like Toby Jr."

Comedian/Actor, Bernie Mac: "I'd have been like, 'Them whuppins hurt so don't hit me on my ass, master. And whatever you do—don't go to sleep."

The old saying, "if you can't beat them join them," wasn't a viable option so the slaves rewrote the latter part to the tune of "fool 'em." Of course it wasn't long before this public persona of infantile mentality began to have a double-edged effect. Slaves were viewed as fools, which didn't help when they mispronounced commonly used American words and phrases to disastrous results. Their once cute behavior was now ridiculed.

Slave owners constantly wrestled with such issues. Outwardly they viewed their captives as innocent and childlike, but at the same time were fully aware of the image they carried from Africa of wild, savage natives on the rampage. This latter viewpoint was discouraged as popular perception in America because of the panic it might cause, but more importantly because it might interfere with trade if genteel slave purchasers took more than a moment to consider what would happen to them in the middle of the night if their newly acquired property got loose.

Angry comedian, Al Toomer: "I probably would've been dead."

Another weight on the knowledgeable slave owner's conscience was treating blacks as property and referring to them as chattel, similar to a cow or a horse, but then slinking out in the cover of darkness and bedding down the females of this so-called subhuman race. Could it be that the offending slave owners were wrong and the slaves were humans such as themselves or were the slaveholders right about their holdings and thus practitioners of bestiality?

Comedian/Filmmaker, David Arnold: "I would've been cracking on the guys whose slave wives were getting popped by the master."

WHAT WOULD YOU DO WHEN MASTER HAD SEX WITH YOUR WOMAN?

Comedian, Tommy Chunn: "I'd joke on how he looked trying to f*#k my wife. 'Look at you. You can't f*#k.'"

Comedian, Talent: "I would've got my ass beat. My reflexes would've gotten me f*#ked up. I'd have jumped up, 'Hey, get your hands off my woman, white cracker' and then quick cut to Toby getting his foot cut off."

Comedian, Norman Mitchell of Arceneaux & Mitchell: "I wouldn't have been able to take it. I would've been the brotha with two stumps, no legs and no arms. They would've had to roll me out in a wheel barrel."

Comedian/Documentary Filmmaker, Deon Cole: "After he had got up and left I would've told her to wake up and I'd have been like, 'Check this out. I see that this is a pattern going on and since it's going to keep happening we're gonna blackmail this muthaf*#ka for more chitlin's and shit.'"

This confusion in the whip holder was also not lost on the slaves who used this lack of knowledge about them to even greater advantage. They viewed their masters as self-important, pompous, and none-too-bright. Thus their humor centered on making fun of their captors without being detected, and they incorporated the many comedy traditions commonly used in Africa.

Comedian/Impressionist, Tony Tone: "Being an impressionist I probably would've been impersonating the master. Imitating him and having all the other slaves laugh and then he'd hear me doing that and I'd take my butt whooping."

Comedian/Actor/Writer/Producer, Brad Sanders: "I probably would've imitated the way he talked. I think the word *honky* came from the 'honk, honk, honk'—the way they talked. I know I would've had to imitate the way they talk because I do it now, in my present slave state. So if I was a slave then as opposed to now, well let's see, I'd imitate the massa, I'd ridicule him, but I'd do everything I could to be like him."

The practice of talking about somebody else, also known as "baggin," "ranking," "signifying," "capping," "the dozens," or whatever it was called in your neighborhood all go back to the tribes of the Motherland. And yes—mama jokes also originated in Africa from groups such as the Dogon, Yoruba, Efik, and a number of Bantu tribes.

Comedian/Writer, Jay Phillips: "I probably wouldn't have been able to get out too many of them, man. I don't know how many of them jokes I could have got off before I ended up saying something that would get me up on one of them trees."

Blacks employed many comedy mainstays in America: misdirection, making things appear one way when they were clearly another; broken dialogue where only the in-the-know listener knew what was really being said (something commonly done currently with TV censors); voice inflection, so the tone of a phrase could distinguish it from being run-of-the-mill verbiage or a biting insult; and innuendo, where subtlety was paramount in talking about somebody without their knowledge.

Another aspect of African humor was the historian, known as the *griot*, who carried the additional skills of musical talent with poetry to blend their own distinctive style. These early entertainer models could not only sing, dance, do spoken word, trickery, and pantomime, they could also lay out the rest of the village with hilarious banter about whatever loincloth you were wearing that day. Like their European counterparts, African kings were known to have several griots around to keep the mood upbeat and entertain visitors.

Unfortunately, those days would never be seen again and the importance of having a sense of humor became crucial in such a mind-boggling situation. This was especially true for the early slaves whose connection to their native land was vivid. Their memories weren't based on a passed-down story or some small preserved trinket that had managed to be hidden and shared. No, theirs was the full shock of going from building a life in the land of their birth to toiling for people who called you out of your name and expected a negative reaction.

This brings us to the word *nigger*. Lest we not forget this was the era when the N word was invented and precious man-hours devoted to instructing the slaves they were being insulted when this word was uttered. It was supposed to mean a person who is lazy, stupid, and good-for-nothing; this came from the slave owners who said it as they were sitting on their asses watching others do their work for them. Obviously the black slave didn't create it and popularize its use the way rappers did in the 1990s. These two syllables were put together by an Anglo Saxon with the intent to do psychological harm on those it would be directed towards.

Comedian, Smokey Deese: "Nig-ger! It's pretty much like the fire to a wick to violence as far as I'm concerned because I've never heard a black person use that phrase unless they were saying it like a white boy says it. The word *nigger*— yeah, that's a way to get your butt kicked right there."

Comedienne/Actress, Thea Vidale: "When I say 'nigga' I mean that nigga over there that owes me $20. When you say 'nigger' you mean all of us and I ain't that nigga."

The spelling of this most offensive of words dates back to the year 1786, although the word itself can be traced back to the sixteenth century. The old spelling of *niger* first appeared in 1574. It's Latin and means "black." The root of this word was *negro*, which dates back to 1555. Initially this word was not used in derogatory terms—in 1700 Judge Samuel Sewall used it to denounce slavery—but as we all know, that changed.

Comedy legend Dick Gregory points out how literary legend Mark Twain was a genius when dealing with this word in *Huckleberry Finn*:

> "What he did for white folks without them knowing it, he gave 'nigger' a face. Nigger Jim. And because of that he was able to have two human beings talking as two human beings. That's how clever and brilliant he was. And when they would go fishing, Jim wasn't putting bait on the white boy's hook and Jim wasn't saying to him, 'Hey look, when you catch your fish I'll clean them for you.' They were out there fishing as two human beings. Whites had never been able to read a black and a white talking as human beings."

The slaves being sold to the Americans were being done so by Portuguese slave traders. That's how the Spanish terminology came to be, but make no mistake—it was the slave owners themselves who came up with the name Nigger. They were attempting to call them a name from their African region of Niger, but poor white trash being what it was in those days the geographical significance lost its way.

The French were also involved. Niger became *negre* and later *negress*, which meant a black woman. In the early English writings the word was put down on paper as "negar," "neegar," "neger," and "niggor." There's a theory that "nigger" is simply the Southern whites' mispronunciation of the word *Negro*.

The problem was that every race had names hurled at them for the purpose of offending them, but none more than blacks. Not only was the word *nigger* made exclusively for descendants of and actual slave Africans themselves, but other titles came into the lexicon to make sure derogatory epithets never ran short. There was "coon," "spear-chucker," "jigaboo," "burr head," "jungle bunny," "buckwheat," "spook," "tar baby," "picaninny," "boot," "shine," "darkie," and of course, the most popular one of that era—"Sambo."

WHAT DO YOU THINK ABOUT THE WORD "NIGGER"?

Comedian/writer/actor, Alex Thomas: "Nig-ger. Yeah, yeah—the E R hurts. 'Nigga,' we use that as a term of endearment.

'Nigga, what's up?'

'My nigga.'

'How was the party?' 'Niggah!'

'Were there any girls up there?' 'Nig-ga.'

Now as far as Nigger, yes! If a white man says 'nigger' in my face I feel to this day I would have problems."

That's because when whites of the day used the word it was almost always negative no matter how many meanings they put on it, and they had a bunch of them.

For instance:

Niggerish: Acting in a lazy and irresponsible manner.

Niggerlipping: Wetting the end of a cigarette while smoking it.

Niggerlover: Derogatory term aimed at whites lacking in the necessary loathing of blacks.

Nigger luck: Exceptionally good luck, emphasis on undeserved.

Nigger heaven: Designated places where blacks were forced to sit in an integrated movie theater or church. It was usually in the balcony.

Nigger knocker: Axe handle or a weapon made from an axe handle.

Nigger rich: Deeply in debt but flamboyant.

Nigger shooter: A slingshot.

Nigger steak: A slice of liver or a cheap piece of meat.

Nigger stick: Police officer's baton.

Nigger tip: Leaving a small tip or no tip in a restaurant.

Nigger in the woodpile: A concealed motive or unknown factor affecting a situation in an adverse way.

Nigger work: Demeaning, menial tasks.

The N word has also been used to offend non-black racial groups. Jews have been called white niggers; Arabs, sand niggers; and Japanese, yellow niggers. As long as you were some type of nigger you knew where you stood as far as white America was concerned. The country was divided into two halves: whites on top, blacks on the bottom.

The real tragedy lies in the fact there are few examples of actual slave humor because the really good stuff was only said among fellow slaves and of course, never documented. One can only guess at the mockery and fierce insults levied at the masters and their kin, but why dwell in conjecture when we have comedians?

IF YOU'D BEEN A SLAVE WHAT KIND OF JOKES WOULD YOU HAVE TOLD ABOUT THE MASTER?

Comedian, Speedy: "Quiet ones."

Comedian, A. J. Jamal: "If I would've been?! I am a slave. What you talking past tense for? Do you know who the president is? If I was a slave...y'know the darker you are the farther you were from the slavemaster's house. We didn't even know there was a house on the plantation. As a matter of fact we were two feet from freedom. If we had stepped two feet to the right we'd have been free."

Comedian/Actor/Producer, Eddie Griffin: "What does the master say after I left his wife's bedroom? Baby, get that board and strap it across my ass. I'm about to fall in."

Comedian/Actor, Mark Prince: "I'd have been dead. It would've been one show only. It would have been a sold out event and after that I would've been hung and castrated and burned at the stake. I would've been brought back to life just to be murdered again for the shit that I would've said."

Comedian/Writer/Actor/Union Rep, Buddy Lewis: "I probably wouldn't have been telling jokes. I'd have been doing Miss Betty. I'd have been Timbuck, the Wonder Slave."

Comedian, Derrick Ellis: "I would've told the master, 'you suck my dick you dirty muthaf*#ka.'"

Comedian, Marquez the Greatest: "It depends. If you wanted to go in the house you'd tell a joke that said something about where the slaves were going to meet."

Comedienne, Melanie Comarcho "I'm sure it would have been something about my dark complexion because I would've been in the fields or whatever. I wouldn't have been no house nigga. I would've been probably telling jokes about how you had to be hi-yella to get the master to do anything for you."

Comedian/Writer, Vince D: "Oh, I would've been a house nigga. I would've told no jokes. I would've told nigga jokes to the master."

Comedian/Filmmaker, Red Grant: "First of all if I was a slave I would be a little darker now. I would've been in the field. I'm tired of people saying light skins would've been in the house—no. We were in the fields too, getting black like everybody else."

Comedian/Writer/Actor, Shang "How his wife makes different noises with me than she does with him."

Comedienne/Actress, Sandy Brown: "I'd have said, 'I'm going to tell the kids that you're their real daddy.'"

Comedian, Gerard: "I probably wouldn't have made it of age to be a comic because I would've told all the jokes about the master. It would have been everything that was going on in the house."

Comedian/Writer, Ian Edwards: "I'm a punk. I would've told none."

Is This Absolutely Necessary?

CHAPTER 2

"I'm half white and half black. That means I get the worst of both worlds: bad hair and a little dick."
— SMOKEY DEESE

By the early nineteenth century the humor of black Americans was rooted in its unique physical and vocal rhythms. Satire was also practiced; along with callbacks, call and response, misdirection, and many other subtleties frequently used by today's performers. Of course the need to stay welt-free dictated that there be no poking of fun at the slave master in his face, but when the brothers and sisters were alone the barbs flew full throttle.

Renowned African comedian, Michael Blackson: "Like how when it rains on him he smells like a wet dog."

Oddly enough, this bemused posturing and imitation of the plantation owners inadvertently inspired the blackface minstrel era. The portrayal of the stereotypical coon came from the slave's portrayal of their high-falutin' white masters. Thus minstrel antics were whites imitating blacks who had been imitating whites. Get it?

Talk about backfiring—'minstrelsy' swept the country as white performers played to white audiences who deemed it the most hilarious thing in entertainment.

Marc Howard: "Funny in a most ignorant way; because it's so funny that white folks want to see blackface, but they don't want black bodies doing it. How ignorant can you be? And it's not just a couple who decided to do it; people all over the country enjoyed this type of so-called entertainment, where people were acting like they were black. 'We want to see some niggas and we'll paint our faces black. Make the lips up nice and red and talk like, Yowsa, yowsa, yowsa'; that's to entertain you, but you can't have a black person nowhere near the place; because you hate 'em, but you want to look at a black face on stage. That is the most...I can't even explain where that mentality comes from and how it could even be festered."

It also gained popularity in Australia (where it thrived up until the 1950s) and parts of Europe. This is not too surprising, for back in the day on European stages blacks were below women in status and like females had to be portrayed by true thespians, meaning white males. By the 1820s in America, the blackfaced buffoon became the national laugh-getter and the job those men were lining up to take.

Al Toomer: "I have no problem with that. Any time a white man will alter himself to come down to try and be a nigga to get over in life I think that's a victory for us."

Initially the minstrel movement began with a few local street entertainers, like the singing, clowning and black John "Picayune" Butler, and a white New Orleans vendor, Signor Cornmeali, who performed while he sold Indian cornmeal out of a horsedrawn cart. Neither one of these "pioneers" performed in blackface.

However, white entertainers such as Edwin Forrest couldn't wait to burn cork, smear the residue on his face and make fun of Negroes. Ole Ed was a method actor, who'd darken himself up and stroll into the black areas to mingle—testing his acting skills and character credibility. There was also the Englishman Charles James Mathews. When he toured America in 1822, he not only impersonated blacks, but every other race native to the continent at that time. Makes you wonder if they ever got busted and suffered a stern, well-deserved ass whooping.

Comedienne, Cocoa Brown: "I have a problem with a white comedian trying really hard to be black. Now if you grew up in a black neighborhood and that's all you know, fine; but if all you've done is infiltrate yourself into the black community and you picked up everything that you've seen us do and then you go on stage and make a mockery of that then I have a problem."

Well, both of these gentlemen cooned for their audiences and presented an over-the-top version of African-Americans, which was fine with the audiences who had no idea of the inaccuracy. Most blacks were still slaves and what type of free black man was going to go to the minstrel show around nothing but whites who would surely have asked him to join the

London's Surrey Theatre poster for the era's most popular white minstrel, Thomas "Jim Crow" Rice (1836).

other "Negroes" on the stage? Quite simply, Forrest and Mathews claimed their portrayals were the real deal and the public went along with it.

Gerard: "It was entertaining at the time and again that's how we were looked at."

Naturally a new industry meant anybody with a face to blacken could seek their fortune. Clowns of the era included George Nichols, Bob Farrell, George Washington Dixon and Thomas D. Rice, who claims to have introduced the tune "Jim Crow" (even though some historians credit it to Nichols). According to the Rice tale, he observed a crippled black stable hand dancing a jaunty little dance and as the man worked he sang, "Every time I turn around I jump Jim Crow." Rice imitated the routine, raggedy clothes and all. To avoid any confusion, Rice dubbed himself "Jim Crow Rice," eclipsing Nichols and anybody else and becoming one of the country's most popular comics.

YOUR THOUGHTS ON WHITE MINSTRELS

John Witherspoon: "I don't give a f*#k. Muthaf*#ka got a job, didn't he? I don't care if he put on blue face or purple face. While that man is putting on that stuff and got his eyes closed I'll steal his car and his shoes and his wife."

In the 1830s the minstrel touring troupe known as the Ethiopian Delineators consisted of all white men: Nichols, Dixon, Farrell, J. W. Sweeney, and Ben Cotton. This was considered an authentic Negro representation.

Comedian, Ruben Paul: "It just doesn't seem authentic from a bunch of them. They might've had one black friend."

Shows of the day were variety excursions featuring a play, juggling, dancing, singing, acrobatics, and finally—blackface. The minstrel portion of the show incorporated a three-act format. The performers were situated in a semi-circle with the Master of Ceremonies, known as the "Interlocutor" placed smack dab in the middle. On either end were seated two characters referred to as "Mr. Bones" and "Mr. Tambo." They were called the endmen and provided most of the humor.

The interlocutor, though in blackface himself, was supposedly the intelligent one of the gathering; which meant he was the whiter of the three (in behavior, not pigment). It was the interlocutor's function to get the two silly buffoons back on track. A number of the jokes from that era are still used today. "Why'd the chicken cross the road?" and "Why do firemen wear suspenders?" were created by endmen.

Then in 1842, the Virginia Minstrels were formed by four down-on-their luck minstrels who decided blackface should be the main focus. They concentrated on their coon antics, exaggerated black dialect, then made their debut in 1843 and were a smash sensation. It was said that the black makeup allowed this minstrel troupe to abandon all Anglo-Saxon inhibitions and cut loose as true Negroes were known to do.

Comedian/Actor, Cedric the Entertainer: "White people were putting themselves in blackface to try to entertain or to try to free themselves of the inhibitions they had about themselves. So it's easier to make yourself look like a black man if you want to do something that was silly or different or that wouldn't be acceptable to the white world."

Comedian, Keith Morris: "They wanted to be black so they could get more women."

Ham-boning, shinning, grinning, shucking and jiving, hollering, thick dialects, and body contortions were all part of the package. Oh, and did I mention eye bucking?

WHO WOULD HAVE MADE A GOOD MINSTREL?

Madd Marv: "Chris Tucker. Big old eyed, Michael Jackson dancing in the middle of the street ass nigga."

Thankfully, the Virginia Minstrels' tenure was brief, but by the late 1840s countless minstrel troupes roamed the countryside: the Christy Minstrels, the African Melodists, the Ethiopian Serenaders (who performed for President Tyler), Bryant's Minstrels, the Congo Minstrels, and the Ethiopian Mountain Singers. Colorful names for groups where the only black faces were the ones they painted over their white ones.

Spanky Hayes: "Michael Jackson's doing it right now. He's just got a white face. He's doing it in reverse."

WHAT DO YOU THINK OF MINSTRELSY?

Comedian, Mark Curry: "White America, as usual, was trying to imitate us. They weren't funny enough so they tried to imitate us. So it was basically a form of flattery."

Deon Cole: "That shit was horrible."

Comedian, Joey "J-Dub" Wells: "It's almost the same thing now—they talk about us and act like they don't want to be around us, but they still deep down want to be us. They want to imitate us which they're still doing to this day, it's just now instead of the face painting now it's the baggy jeans and all the urban gear that we wear."

Comedienne/Actress, Sommore: "They have this place over where I live called Want-to-do-City, whereas kids can go in and dress up like a firefighter and they pretend like it's a real fire and you get on the truck. If they had such a thing where you could dress up and be black for a day...I mean it's like a whole world; they would honestly pay to go; just go in and be black. And I'm telling you—if somebody wants to make millions it would sell. They're crazy."

Blackface on Black Face Crime

CHAPTER 3

"You're so black you bleed smoke."
— JOE TORRY

From 1861–1865 minstrel shows took a back seat to killing thy neighbor. During the Civil War, with the white minstrel boom subsiding, the long debated thought of using authentic Negroes resurfaced. Although to satisfy a jaded audience, they'd have to be even more outlandishly minstrel than the whites, and would also have to wear blackface no matter how dark they actually were.

> **David Arnold:** "People did what they had to so they could take care of families and if I had to go and put on blackface and be humiliated to make sure that my daughter had something to eat I would probably do it too."

Fact was, it was work for hire, meaning the minstrels did get paid for the gig and this was completely new to black men. Prior to the Civil War very few African-American freemen wrote down "entertainer" as their profession. Of those who did, only a couple of black performers were known to have had the distinction of performing in blackface minstrel shows alongside white performers. One was William Henry "Juba" Lane, who many historians consider to be the father of tap dancing. Another performer was the dwarf Thomas Dilward, known as "Japanese Tommy" even though he was black.

The first black minstrel troupe debuted in 1855, but it wasn't until 1865 when Brooker and

Billy Kersands proudly displays his gaping chasm in this poster from Callender's (Georgia) Minstrels, Virginia, circa 1870.

Sheet music cover for "James Bland's 3 Great Songs," 1879.

Clayton's Georgia Minstrels (blacks managed by blacks) hit the scene and were widely lauded that others followed suit. By 1875 most had either been run out of the business or gobbled up by white owners, men like J. H. Haverly, known as "the greatest minstrel entrepreneur." His shows were full "plantation extravaganzas;" he even built a replica of a plantation complete with all the trimmings—overseers, hound dogs, and of course a plethora of slaves.

White as well as black patrons packed these presentations with the Caucasians in one section and the Negroes seated in another: their own little area of the theater affectionately known as "Nigger Heaven." White or black—as far as Haverly was concerned it was all for the green and he purchased the hottest minstrel group in the land to make sure it kept rolling in. The group combined the talents of Charles Hicks, Bob Height, and the legendary Billy Kersands, a man with a mouth so big it was said he could put a cup of coffee with a saucer in his gaping chasm, even though his usual jaw filler was pool balls.

BILLY KERSANDS

Kersands was born in 1842, started performing around the time of the Civil War and worked with just about every major minstrel troupe that toured. His facial contortions and agility made him a hit with white audiences as well as black. Not only could Kersands sing and dance, he was a consummate comedian, who regrettably loved the adulation so much that when other performers of his ilk had long since abandoned blackface to do what were known as urban shows (which didn't utilize a plantation backdrop), Kersands would still break out the burnt cork. He felt that since his fortune had been made in the South, he would be disloyal to turn his back on those folks. It also gave him a sense of home and he worked until his death in 1915.

Another popular minstrel was the talented composer James Bland.

JAMES BLAND

Billed as "The World's Greatest Minstrel," James Bland was born in 1854, grew up in New York and left his studies at Howard University to become a minstrel after getting a glimpse of the white minstrel George Primrose. Bland started his own troupe and was one of our first recognized comic ad-libbers, known to talk about whatever went across his mind, but it was his songwriting ability that truly set him apart. Writing as many as seven hundred songs, including "Carry Me Back to Old Virginny," he specialized in the same degrading minstrel tunes the white composers were penning so he could get his songs published. At his peak he earned up to $10,000 per year touring in Europe. Unfortunately for Bland, he became too associated with those tunes and by the 1890s when they were passé so was he, which led to alcoholism. In the year 1911 James Bland was buried near Philadelphia in an unmarked grave because the authorities had no idea who he was.

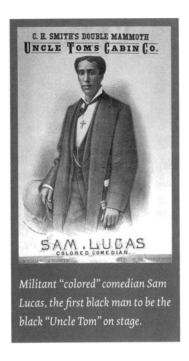

Militant "colored" comedian Sam Lucas, the first black man to be the black "Uncle Tom" on stage.

Not all stories are so tragic. Take Sam Lucas, for instance. If there were a minstrel Hall of Fame he'd have been inducted right alongside Kersands and Bland.

SAM LUCAS

Known as "the Grand Old Man of the Negro Stage," the multifaceted, militant Sam Lucas was the true transitional minstrel. Born in Ohio in 1850, he played his guitar and sang on the boats going up and down the Ohio River soon after the Civil War. Bland was fond of inserting lyrics in his stage act that downplayed the happy-go-lucky Negro image and celebrated the joys of Emancipation, but like many a comedian, he also wanted to be recognized as a serious actor.

In 1878 he got the role as the first Tom in the Frohman Brothers' stage production of *Uncle Tom's Cabin*. Ironically in 1915 his career went full circle when he starred in the film version of *Uncle Tom's Cabin*, only to die on January 15, 1916 of an illness contracted while making the film.

You might have noticed a pattern of performers working up until death. As a matter of fact most comedians who make it to old age seem to stay active in the profession until they take their last breath. For some reason throughout history, comedians either die at an early age from abuse or under tragic circumstances, but if they make it past forty they usually survive beyond their sixty-fifth birthday. At that juncture in life retirement barely ever enters the picture.

> **Comedienne/Actress, Loni Love:** "The nice thing about stand-up is you don't have to retire. As long as you can get up and get on a stage and talk you're fine. Retiring from comedy?! There is always something to say."

> **John Witherspoon:** "Naw, no—black folks can't retire, brotha. Retire?! They just wake up and a nigga's dead."

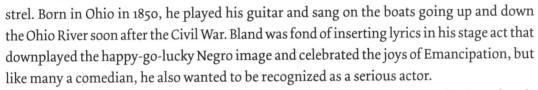

Lesser minstrels also made their mark. Bob Height, Charles Hicks, Tom McIntosh, Tom Fletcher (who wrote *100 Years of the Negro in Show Business*), and Billy McClain each performed in all-black troupes that were commonly referred to as "all-black nigs," "genuine plantation darkies from the South," "great delineators of darkie life," and "slave troupes"

An illustration from Harper's Weekly, New York, 1876.

and they always had to be "on." Since whites viewed the minstrels with a certain amount of amusement, the minstrels had to stay within the confines of that role, which meant from the time they hit a town until they left it was all smiles and jolliness. If not they placed themselves in serious jeopardy.

Sinbad: "These brothers did what they had to do to survive and to be entertainers."

Following Emancipation, newly freed blacks perceived to be different from the image whites had conjured up of being simpleminded and childlike were labeled "uppity" and dealt with appropriately. African-American congressmen and senators were relentlessly mocked during the Reconstruction Era as minstrels imitated them strutting around, popping suspenders and spewing ignorance as fluid as a waterfall. America was scared because for the first time blacks were voting; electing African-American Senators, treasurers, and lieutenant governors who were making changes that affected black and white Americans, who for the most part wanted nothing to do with ex-slaves telling them what to do or how to live.

Comedian/Actor/Writer, Chris Spencer: "When it comes to voting I really don't know what's going on. I just kind of jump on the bandwagon, or Escalade, or whatever brothers are jumping on at the time. They've got so many propositions and amendments that they could've brought back slavery and I wouldn't have known. There would've been three hundred thousand brothers marching up Crenshaw in shackles (sweating and breathing hard).

I'd be like, 'Where y'all going?'

'They brought back slavery. You didn't vote?'

'Naw.'

'Nigga, we lost by one.'"

The backlash was immediate. Enter the "Jim Crow" laws, meant to protect the citizenry from the possible reckless and uninformed behavior of the recently freed Negroes. They were put in under the guise of aiding the blacks in their transition into polite society. What these laws really did was open the door to segregation, voter intimidation, legal castration and redlining in housing and the workplace. In many regions, blacks needed to get written permission from some white person to leave the area.

Then of course there was the ultimate deterrent for any black who felt America had their best interest at heart—the KKK, started in May of 1866 by some bored ex-Confederate soldiers whose initial purpose was just to get out of the house at night for some rowdy shenanigans. This "circle of brothers" used the literal Greek meaning *Kuklos Adelphon*; translation—Ku Klux Klan.

They were nothing but a small-time social club that wore silly outfits and engaged in made-up rituals to add to the backwoods mystique of this brainchild of bumpkins. Unfortunately bumpkins can cause harm and "maintaining white supremacy" replaced rambunctious rabble-rousing as their new credo.

Since blacks weren't toiling anymore—what good were they? Membership boomed and terror reigned. It got so bad that even one of the knuckleheaded founding fathers was compelled to write an open letter expressing his regret for the perverse turn the once fun-loving group had taken and his sorrow that it had ever been heard of in the first place. Join the club, anus.

WHAT DO YOU THINK ABOUT THE KKK?

Deon Cole: "It's a horrible organization and they need to jump in front of a truck and kill themselves."

Thea Vidale: "It exists. It's in the White House. What's new?"

Mark Prince: "I love the KKK because you wear a big white uniform therefore you are a target to me. The fear of the KKK is that the minorities will take over

Sheet music cover for "We Are All Loyal Klansmen," 1923.

this here United States and it won't be the place that they stole."

Comic/Impressionist, Kool Bubba Ice: "Don't have to worry about them no more. We got to worry about each other. I mean, you see some Ku Klux Klan walking down the street and you see some thugs walking down the street, who you gonna be scared of?"

Joey "J-Dub" Wells: "They're cowards and most of them are idiot cowards. I don't think most of them probably have a GED. That's why there's only one of them that leads because the rest of them are third grade idiots. You take that one good GED dude out of there and the rest of them are like, 'what are we supposed to do now?'"

Keep in mind, not everybody was a Klansperson. For the less extreme of the era there was the knowledge that they could go shuck off their worries and have a few pints of ale at the neighborhood darkie show. So white enthusiasm and support for minstrelsy was understandable, but what did black people find so funny? Why did they attend this obvious attack on their culture? Would the Chinese go to a show where they were building railroads, causing road rage, and gardening? Could you picture Mexicans flocking to a presentation showing them crossing borders, reproducing in mass quantities, and gardening? No! And you can best believe that the organizers of such a show would've been run out of town or at the very least ignored. Well, for some reason blacks not only patronized these shows, they kept them going long after whites had tired of them.

The likely reason was that African-Americans from that era understood that minstrelsy was based on stereotypes rooted in distorted fact and perception. They wanted to see other blacks perform and didn't care what white America thought when it came to what made them laugh. Blacks were well aware that there were lazy, trifling, slow-witted black people as well as upstanding citizens, but frankly, who's going to laugh at the antics of a black mathematician?

They knew a joke when they saw one and felt like the black makeup used was similar to the makeup of a circus clown, a mime, or an operatic stage performer. Besides, minstrelsy had made stars of Kersands, Lucas, and McIntosh. They were the first ghetto-fabulous celebrities and like it or not, these made-up buffoons were early role models; evidence that there were opportunities beyond the horsedrawn plow and the blacksmith's stable.

SO DO YOU THINK MINSTRELS HAD GROUPIES?

Shang: "If so they were women with real low self esteem."

White comedian, Roger Rodd: "If so, they were white girls."

A. J. Jamal: "You got a black face, you got a white woman. I don't care. White women wanted that black face. Sometimes I put blackface on just to get the white girls."

Mystro Clark: "I'm sure minstrels had groupies, but probably when they took off the make up some of them lost the deal. Or you take off that makeup and you have a white dude. 'Good luck. I'll wait until you're black again. I can f*#k a white dude anytime.'"

Michael Blackson: "I'm sure they did, but it was hard to recognize them without the f*#kin' face. There were probably other guys who came up talkin' about, 'I'm that muthaf*#ka without the mask. This is what I look like.' Dumb ass bitches fell for it."

Melanie Comarcho: "Yes. If they think that you're making money, then yes, there's someone who will want to be your girl...or boy."

Joey "J-Dub" Wells: "Hell yeah, as soon as they finished their minstrel show there was somebody waiting in the back, 'I sure liked your show. You was funny, Bubba.'"

Comedian, Damon Williams: "I'm sure they did—shufflin' hos."

Speedy: "Somebody had to put the makeup on."

Marc Howard: "They probably had groupies that was dressed in blackface"

Al Toomer: "Sure they did. I mean, c'mon—some of the guys we have in this business who shouldn't be getting any sex—of course they had 'em."

Comedian/Writer, Rodney Perry: "C'mon, Buckwheat had bitches"

Evan Lionel: "Let's be real—Stepin Fetchit..."

Comedian/Actor/Writer/Producer, Kevin Hart: "Everybody has groupies. The head guy at a laptop company has groupies."

Ian Edwards: "I hope they had something for selling out like that."

Norman Mitchell: "Yeah, after they left town you had all these white women walking around with little curly-haired babies."

The decline of the pitiful art form of minstrelsy was so slow that historians are at odds as to when the final nail was driven into the coffin. Some say it died in the 1880s, only to be replaced by a barrage of jokes about eating fried chicken and watermelon (popular foods with all races), smelling funny (obviously the anti-deodorant races had not yet been introduced into society), big lips (the kind Melanie Griffith would die for), laziness, shiftlessness, lustfulness (oh yeah—blacks are the only race who like sex), and cowardice (true, we don't let bulls chase us for fun, but that's hardly the sign of a wimp). These traits became the things whites remembered. Let's face it—if you didn't own a plantation and watch blacks work from sun up to sundown—the minstrel image was really quite a comfortable one to live with.

Others point to traveling minstrel troupes performing through the countryside in 1928, and there's evidence that a group of local minstrel groups put on shows as late as 1970. Now if a single individual can be considered a minstrel show, white actor Ted Danson last revived the art form wearing blackface in 1993 at a Friar's Club roast at the behest of his then-black lover and social advisor Whoopi Goldberg (who only wore makeup from Max Factor on that occasion).

> **Deon Cole:** "He did that because it was okayed by a black person. So he didn't think it would be harming anything. But when he caught the backlash of it it was more like, 'wow!' And Whoopi needs her ass whooped for that. My thing is, yeah, I understand that yawl felt like there's no color with us and you're white and I'm black and we're together, but there's still the world that you have to deal with, y'know."

It seemed the world was also into blackface. The BBC broadcast *Sterling's Black & White Minstrel Show* from 1958–1978 in full blackface Technicolor splendor. Once the show was canceled, the British had no qualms staging annual reunions for fans to enjoy the huckle-bucking and washtub tunes of a period their country watched from afar. The last known re-gathering of the cast was in 2005. The antics and songs were still the same, but done in the fleshy skin tones of the performers. The changing of the times dictated that not a single cork be burnt in the making of the production, but they got away with it on TV until 1978.

Now naturally when minstrelsy finally ended in the States attempts were made to explain why it existed in the first place. Considering the temperament of the times it's not surprising it was such a huge success. Of the few white writers who detailed slave life in those Antebellum days, the portrayals were of happy blacks and even happier slave owners. In their works the sun hung high in the cloudless sky, the birds joyfully chirped a sweet ditty without a single dropping hitting massa's lapel, as he wiled away the hours relaxed under a shade tree or parasol with a smiling darkie shining his boots. Mammy kept the ice cold lemonades and mint juleps coming as the coons in the field hummed and sang all day long for the amusement of their betters. Ah, why did those days ever have to end? Because there's a God—that's why!

Two Coons Were
Better Than One

CHAPTER 4

"Honey, that old man couldn't keep no kinda job. That's the only man I know that ever went to the unemployment office and lost his place in line."
— LaWanda Page

By 1890 minstrelsy, in its plantation backdrop form, was practically dead and the minstrels of yesteryear were gaining acceptance in carnivals, road shows, circuses, variety shows, vaudeville, and tent shows. There the comedians had an arena of expression not available to them in the minstrel shows many had been weaned on. All the audiences were black, and away from the preconceived notions of whites these comics could do humor closer to what blacks organically thought was funny. True, some were still putting on burnt cork, but the eye bucking was minimized and the minstrel gait was replaced by pantomime. These road shows were the genesis of modern stand-up.

America didn't truly understand black humor; they just knew they liked watching it and dancing to the cakewalk (see page 31), ragtime, and "coon" songs. The latter were songs written by white men whose only frame of reference regarding blacks was to poke fun at them. In these uplifting tunes, the black man was lazy, cowardly, or wanted to be white. On any given night you could pass a bar and hear the strains of a tune like *Those Chicken Steal-*

ing Coons, *I'm the Luckiest Coon in Town*, or the most popular of these ditties, *All Coons Look Alike to Me* (a love song). Don't tell me you don't remember that one. This cut was credited to a black man, comedian and songsmith Ernest Hogan, who allegedly ripped it off from a piano player for a few shots of liquor. Let's take a look at what this big spender got for his investment. It went a little something like this:

ALL COONS LOOK ALIKE TO ME, by Ernest Hogan, 1896

Talk about a coon a having trouble
I think I have enough of ma own
It's alla bout ma Lucy Jane Stubbles
And she has caused my heart to mourn
Thar's another coon barber from Virginia
In soci'ty he's the leader of the day
And now ma honey gal is gwine to quit me
Yes she's gone and drove this coon away
She'd no excuse to turn me loose
I've been abused, I'm all confused
Cause these words she did say

Chorus: All coons look alike to me
      I've got another beau, you see
      And he's just as good to me as you, nig!
      Ever tried to be
      He spends his money free,
      I know we can't agree
      So I don't like you no how
      All coons look alike to me

Never said a word to hurt her feelings
I always bou't her presents by the score
And now my brain with sorrow am a reeling
Cause she won't accept them any more
If I treated her wrong she may have loved me
Like all the rest she's gone and let me down
If I'm lucky I'm a gwine to catch my policy
And win my sweet thing way from town
For I'm worried, yes, I'm desp'rate
I've been Jonahed, and I'll get dang'rous
If these words she says to me

Repeat Chorus

Now let's meet this composer of the first order.

ERNEST HOGAN

Billed as "The Unbleached American," Ernest Hogan was born in Bowling Green, Kentucky, on April 17, 1865. In 1895 he composed what could be the first ragtime song, *La Pas Ma La*, then had a hit with *All Coons Look Alike to Me* and became a famous New York comedian, going from minstrelsy road shows to black musicals to vaudeville, where he pantomimed gobbling down a watermelon while the band played *Watermelon Time*...in blackface of course. So it is of little consolation that he decried the "coon" reference right before his death, after collapsing while working on his production *The Oyster Man* in 1909. For all we know he could have been going through dementia brought on by all those undigested watermelon seeds.

Enough of Mr. Hogan. During that same era two of the most renowned and respected performers of their day lived and breathed. One went on to be known as the greatest comedian of all time.

WILLIAMS & WALKER

In 1893, when dancer/singer/composer/comedian Bert Williams met up with the flamboyant singing, dancing, comedian George Walker (born in 1873) in San Francisco, they started a relationship that would change black entertainment. They billed themselves as "The Two Real Coons" since so many white acts were still working the circuit in blackface, and played vaudeville, then toured in their own show, *A Lucky Coon*. They were the first black performers to star in a motion picture in 1901 (where Williams' classic pantomime routine "The Poker Game" was caught on camera), but the times regulated Williams & Walker to the stage, where Walker played the prancing dandy to Bert Williams' shiftless darkie. They had classic hit songs, started a national dance craze in 1897 with the cakewalk (the winner of the dance contest receiving a cake), and produced groundbreaking shows: *In Dahomey* (the first full-length black musical on Broadway and then in London amid critical acclaim) and the legendary hit *Bandana Land*.

In 1909 George Walker suffered a stroke and was put in a resort to recuperate. His wife, Aida O. Walker, a noted performer herself, often dressed up in his costumes and played his role in *Bandana Land*. Meanwhile Williams studied the art of simplicity with the famous French mime, Pietro, and in 1910 embarked on his solo career with the Ziegfeld Follies. In 1911 George Walker passed away at the age of 37.

BERT WILLIAMS

Egbert Austin Williams was born in the Bahamas in 1874 and grew up in Riverside, California. He was a sensitive man—comedy great W. C. Fields called him "the funniest man I ever saw and the saddest man I ever knew." The press of the day also acknowledged his artistry, stating "it is single justice to say that our stage has no white comedian as good as Bert Williams." Eddie Cantor said, "Whatever sense of timing I have, I learned from him." On another occasion, Cantor stated that "he was far superior to any of us who put on burnt cork." Even Booker T. Washington said that Bert Williams had done more for the Negro race than any other black of his period.

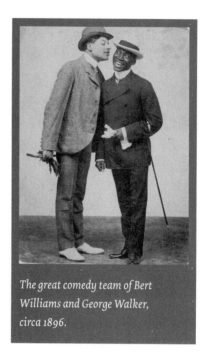

The great comedy team of Bert Williams and George Walker, circa 1896.

> **Robert Townsend:** "Back in the day Bert Williams was like Richard Pryor or Eddie Murphy. He was at the top of his game and he was one of the highest paid performers at the Zeigfeld Follies. So he was a genius, but you play to the room. The room loved comedians that played the shuffle because that's the only thing they knew; black people with shuffling feet, using words wrong and not being able to enunciate—that kind of stuff. So he was brilliant, but that's all the material that he could do."

It also irked Williams that white audience members only adored the dumb darky on stage that he had perfected, not the black man standing amongst them. At first many of the white performers in the Follies threatened to protest and leave if he joined the cast. Florenz Ziegfeld hired him anyway, but under one condition. Williams insisted that he would not share the stage with any white female performer. He did not want to have a riot started by an audience member assuming that a black performer would be in close contact with a fair-haired chorus girl of white womanhood.

> **Evan Lionel:** "You realize how great this man was because he had to do it in blackface in front of white audiences that wanted to kill him because he was black. And we think we got stress doing a show."

Williams felt that the true comedian is the one who can take the brunt of this laughter upon himself—which is exactly what he did in his routines. But the nagging contradiction of his stage persona and his real personality (a refined gentleman) eventually caught up with him, prompting Williams to become a heavy drinker in his later years. He became bitter with a public that refused to let his talent give him the peace of mind shared by so many of his white contemporaries. At the time of his death in 1922 Bert Williams was the highest paid performer in the Ziegfeld Follies.

> **Manager/Filmmaker, Tony Spires:** "Unheralded by the modern powers that be, whoever those persons are who say who was great. He's overlooked. He was a legendary pioneer, a trailblazer, a genius. It blew me away all this brother had to go through. I mean, what Jackie Robinson went through was nothing compared to what this brother went through. And he was heralded by the white comics of the day, the Eddie Cantors and all of those guys, as being much better than them. Al Jolson said, 'I bow down to this guy' yet we don't even know who the hell he is."

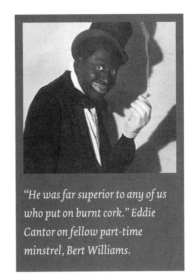

"He was far superior to any of us who put on burnt cork." Eddie Cantor on fellow part-time minstrel, Bert Williams.

Another team to advance black comedy was Cole & Johnson.

COLE & JOHNSON

Well-to-do Bob Cole could compose, sing, dance, write dramatic plays, act, and was one of the first black comedians to do a monologue. He first teamed up with writer/producer Billy Johnson in the late 1890s and when that partnership dissolved in 1901, Cole aligned himself with another Johnson—singer/composer J. R. (no relation to Billy). The new team of Cole & Johnson worked the vaudeville circuit, then wrote and produced musical comedies on their own, moving black entertainers from traditional plantation humor to the stage performances we're more familiar with today. Unfortunately, like a lot of early show business personalities, Cole's career ended tragically in 1931 when he had a nervous breakdown and several months later drowned.

These performers were rare exceptions, since most blacks initially were shunned on the vaudeville circuit. The promoters worried about mixing black audiences with white audiences in an arena they wanted to stay pristine and clean. Also, white performers, even the ones in blackface, complained about performing with black minstrels. The kettle pretended to be better than the pot, but knew better because they also had concerns about following strong black acts. Nevertheless, a number of African-American acts did make it through and became famous on the vaudeville circuit: performers like Miller & Lyles.

MILLER & LYLES

Aubrey Lyles partnered up with Flournoy Miller at Fisk University in Nashville. They performed in Chicago and introduced the comedy style of "mutilatin'" the King's English at the turn of the century (twentieth, that is). In 1921 they wrote, financed, produced, and starred in *Shuffle Along* on Broadway, and ushered in the era known as the Roaring Twenties. They not only had the writing team of Eubie Blake and his partner, singer Noble Sissle—the "Dixie Duo" with Blake on ragtime piano and Sissle singing without blackface—but also Josephine Baker and her invention of a chorus line with a sense of humor, as well as the timeless hit *I'm Just Wild About Harry*, among others.

The lovely Shuffle Along *showgirls and singer Noble Sissle, 1921.*

Miller & Lyles continued their winning ways with the show *Runnin' Wild* in 1923 and got so hot they were approached to do their own radio show. They came up with the idea that later became *Amos 'n Andy*, but the sponsors pulled the plug when they found out that the comedy team were actually black men and not men with black faces. That same station gave the idea to the white duo of Gosden & Correll when they made a similar pitch. White men in black faces were a better fit for audiences of that era.

In 1932, while filming *Midnight Lodge*, Lyles became ill and died. Miller went on to work with Mantan Moreland and later Johnny Lee. In the late 1930s F.E. Miller traveled to Hollywood and wrote for independent black films and mainstream movies, starring in many of the productions. Miller insisted on the dignified treatment of black performers and in the 1940s he put pen to paper for the radio version of *Amos 'n Andy* and made the transition to the television incarnation in its 1951 debut. Flournoy Miller enjoyed the reputation of an elder statesman until his death in 1971.

The comedians of the day, though still in minstrel attire in many cases, were moving more toward authentic black humor while simultaneously keeping white audiences comfortable with the familiar image of the coon. A radical departure would've put an end to future bookings, but it didn't stop them from making adjustments. As George "Bon Bon" Walker had stated, the only way to separate from the white who put on black-face was to capture the style and coolness of true black behavior and movement. In his opinion whites overdid what came natural to the blacks.

African-American artists were discovering a new-found freedom to experiment within the confines of the traveling show structure. Individuality became more the norm than the exception.

Ventriloquist, Willie Brown (& Woody): "There was a black ventriloquist named John W. Cooper who was known as the polite ventriloquist. He used to do a routine where he would be like the barber and he'd be cutting the dummy's hair. The dummy would be sitting in a barber chair. He was one of the first ventriloquists to hit the vaudeville circuit back in the day, but he was a black man so he really never got the credit."

Hollywood was about to dramatically, in this case comedically, change all that. The times ahead would be a place where the black man would not only be needed, but where that performer would finally get some recognition, whether he liked it or not. Unfortunately, image control was never placed in the hands of the black artists of the day and a lot of times it is still not under the control of current performers as well, but the question must still be asked.

HOW DO YOU WANT TO BE REMEMBERED?

Sommore: "Well, I made a conscious effort to say, okay, I was raunchy. I said raunchy things because that's what I do. That's what I like, but I'm intelligent and the problem that I have with a lot of people with comedy, especially when they listen to women, if you can get past the fact that we are cussing; listen to the message. My father used to always tell me people hear what they want to hear. And when people come up to me and say, oh my God you were so nasty, you were so filthy. That lets me know that you're narrow-minded because you didn't hear the whole message. You just heard the cussing. I just want people to know that I gave it my best and I intend to make a difference and that I'm intelligent. Intelligent and funny."

Adele Givens: "I want them to say, 'She owes you too? That bitch owes me money too.' I want them all to say it. Ain't nobody ever gonna to be broke as long as I owe 'em."

Nick Cannon: "I want to be remembered as an entertainer, y'know what I mean? An entertainer and somebody who was down for the people and with the people, y'know what I mean? That's what I'm always going to try and be, whether it's music, comedy, or acting. I'm just trying to entertain and give the people my best."

Earthquake: "I just want to be remembered."

Sinbad: "As far as Hollywood I could care less how they remember me. I had a higher power and I think there was a period of time where I had forgot about that higher power because you get caught up trying to do your thing and you forget it's never gonna get better; even when it looks like it's better. So I just want to be remembered as a guy who worked hard, but as far as Hollywood I don't know what they'll remember me as. I don't even know how they see me and as I get older I care less and less."

Robert Townsend: "I guess I want to be remembered as an original; an original comedian with a lot of different layers that made people laugh, cry and made them think, more importantly. So when people look back and they say, 'he was an original.' Y'know you can't say, 'well, he did so & so's stuff' or whatever. My stuff will always be unique."

Comedian/Talk Show Host/Actor, Arsenio Hall: "If black comedy was a building and we were all getting to put in a brick I'm just happy I got to put a brick in that institution; or in that monument of black comedy. There are twenty bricks in there for Richard and ten bricks in there for Eddie. If there's just one brick in that black comedy monument that belongs to me, history will look back and say, 'He was there.'"

Marla Gibbs: "I want to be remembered as someone who cared and someone who shared."

If It's a Clark Gable Movie, I'll Do It

CHAPTER 5

"I can either play a maid for $200
or be a real one for $21."
— HATTIE MCDANIEL

Little did Thomas Edison know when he invented motion pictures and opened his studio in Orange, New Jersey, that men like D. W. Griffith would lead the artistic charge. Thanks to his 1915 epic *Birth of a Nation*, based on Thomas Dixon's novel *The Clansman*, which portrayed the Ku Klux Klan as white knights riding in to save the day, KKK recruitment hit record numbers and the coon image was cemented in the American consciousness via film. When certain segments of society dared complain, those voices were initially muted when Dixon, a white supremacist, simply made a call to an old college friend, President Woodrow Wilson. The leader of the free world also shared Dixon's sentiments and viewed Griffith as a national hero.

For some reason, though, blacks never got around to hoisting old D. W. upon their shoulders and parading him around amongst falling ticker tapes, but instead greeted the film with hatred and resentment. This reaction allegedly confused and perplexed Griffith, who'd been raised in the South and insisted he had no problem with the Negro. He stated he'd met good ones and bad ones and to him what he put in his film was a realistic depiction of the black man in America (though the blacks were, as usual, white men in blackface).

An exuberant D. W. Griffith (second from left) along with United Artists co-founders Douglas Fairbanks, Sr., Mary Pickford, and Charlie Chaplin, circa 1920.

Ever hear of a movie called *Nigger in the Woodpile*? The audiences in 1904 did. Films like this were all the rage. They showed untamed blacks stealing chickens, philandering, and gobbling down watermelons. *The Interrupted Card Game* used posters showing blacks being lynched with ads saying things like, "Hear his moans and groans, price one cent." So it's easy to see the climate in which *Birth of a Nation* was made.

What was so insidious about *Birth* was that it was so well done. The film was packed with film "innovations" credited to Griffith that had actually been used previously by European directors the average American filmgoer knew nothing about.

Birth also unwittingly became the model for future filmmakers looking to slant the image of other races (Native Americans, Chinese, etc.); even the African in his homeland assumed a typical Uncle Tom posture when Tarzan swung by hollering at the top of his lungs. Who was going to stop it? Just how many minorities do you think were sitting in the boardroom when filmmaking decisions and script approvals were being handled? Those writers were content to rely on old stereotypes, finish the movie, and get their checks.

However, in order to keep making trips to the bank Hollywood had to back off from its tactics of glorifying melon-devouring and ropes around people's necks. For the stereotype they could get away with they decided to go with the servant, and the favorite domestic of all was the mammy. She was loyal, faithful to her mistress, and lambasted any black man who came around with the leering eye.

Thea Vidale: "Mammy ran the house. Mammy knew everything that was going on in the house and Mammy was the only one who could step to master and tell him that he was wrong. She might have to tread lightly, but Mammy had a way about her. Mammy was the Henry Kissinger of her time."

Even more than that, mammy was not sexy and thus white audiences could go as families and enjoy her jovial antics without any hint of the white male lusting for her. The mammy role reached its peak in 1939 when Hattie McDaniel won the first Academy Award for an African-American for her supporting role in *Gone with the Wind*.

Thea Vidale: "If they ever did a remake of *Gone with the Wind* I'd want to be Mammy."

"Hi-hat Hattie" McDaniel in her earlier years.

HATTIE McDANIEL

Hattie McDaniel was born in Wichita, Kansas in 1895 and began her career performing in minstrel shows as a teenager. She sang in clubs, theaters, and vaudeville then moved to Los Angeles in 1930 and discovered that her forte was mammy/maid parts, but Hattie took a lot of latitude with them. She'd make rude comments and outright "sass" her employers, their "friends," and any visitor who lacked proper manners. But following her Academy Award win for *Gone with the Wind* (she and Butterfly McQueen weren't allowed to attend the premiere in Atlanta because of racial politics), the good folks (white) in the South felt the "uppity maid" Hattie portrayed should've stayed in her place more and Hollywood received a number of complaining letters (some surely signed with an X) and her outspokenness on the silver screen was minimized.

Sommore: "She opened doors, but again she wasn't able to make a difference. She did it, but what could she do?"

Joey "J-Dub" Wells: "That was a role she played, but when she accepted her Oscar she was a totally different woman. You got people saying, 'I wouldn't have played no Aunt Jemima maid,' but did you see her accept the award? Now if she had walked up there saying, 'I wants to thank everybody for this here award. I shore appreciate youse white folks.' No, she just went up and said, 'Thank you, very much.'"

McDaniel starred on radio's *Beulah* from 1947 until 1951 then moved with the show to television, but she was stricken during its run. Hattie McDaniel died in 1952.

Thea Vidale: "One of the bravest black women who ever existed."

Meanwhile D.W. Griffith struck again when he twisted the image of the man servant into that of a coward. They had just the actor to play this new Negro.

Tony Spires: "A paradox, a conundrum; but again, a pioneer, very talented, a very smart man and a successful businessman, a land baron. Beyond that, if you watch him closely he was a genius. He was a genius in what he did with what was available."

STEPIN FETCHIT

Lincoln Theodore Monroe Andrew Perry was born on May 30, 1902 in Key West, Florida and studied the blackfaced minstrels when they came through town. Originally part of a team known as "Step n' Fetchit: The Two Dancing Fools from Dixie," he went solo because his partner was so lazy he'd often miss gigs. Perry claimed to be not much better, billing himself as "The Laziest Man in the World," and claiming that he was so damn lazy when he did his stage act he'd have another man come out and wave his hand good-bye to the audience. That act consisted of him going on stage, scratching his head, looking lost, then breaking into a virtuoso dance number complete with a knowing smile showing that all along the dumb act was just that—an act. When he'd finish his dance the dumb character would return like nothing had ever happened (reminds you of the Warner Bros. singing frog, doesn't it?). That bit of acting strategy got him a six-month contract with Fox Studios, making him the first black movie star, as he often claimed.

Perry used the old slave trick of behaving dumber than one was to avoid unpleasantries. He cultivated the myth that he was ignorant and not a savvy businessman. He'd have to consult with his non-existent manager, "Mr. Goldberg," then Perry would consider an issue without pressure and render the decision "Mr. Goldberg" suggested. He didn't even want people to know he could read. That way all a director could do was tell him to be funny and helplessly watch him steal scenes so many times that other actors refused to work with him. So he worked with his old vaudeville friend Will Rogers in four films from 1934–1935. In return, Rogers' on screen character would scold, belittle, and even kick Fetchit in the ass.

> **Al Toomer:** "Yeah, he was a spook and a coon, but that's the way a nigga had to act every goddamn day of the week back then. Just living your life you had to act like that, so why not get paid and he was a millionaire."

Between the years 1927 and 1936, Stepin Fetchit made almost thirty movies and amassed over one million dollars, with a lifestyle that included Asian servants and the best of everything, but by the late 1930s black civil rights groups said he was an embarrassment to his race. His protector Will Rogers had died in a plane crash, and Perry had blown most of his dough. He filed for bankruptcy in the '40s; couldn't get much stage or movie work in the '50s, but in the '60s there was a ray of hope. He was set to have his own show playing comedian Flip Wilson's father; that is, until CBS aired a segment in 1968 on the series *Of Black America* which portrayed Perry as a crap-shooting, chicken-stealing idiot and which proclaimed that he and his ilk were the problem with black images.

WHAT MOVIE PART WOULD YOU NOT PLAY?

Eddie Griffin: "I ain't gonna play a bitch."

Thea Vidale: "I don't think I could ever play a sell-out."

Joey "J-Dub" Wells: "I wouldn't play a role where the dude's gotta kiss the other man."

Comedian, Shaun Jones: "A flamboyant gay character or a *Roots*-like slave."

Mark Prince: "A black gay man, but I would play a white gay man."

Deon Cole: "*Six Degrees of Separation*—I don't think I would've did that one, dawg. I would've been like 'hell naw' and then he'd (Will Smith) have did it and blew up and then I'd be looking for gay roles."

Perry made a couple more films: *Amazing Grace* with Moms Mabley (1974) and *Won Ton Ton the Wonder Dog* (1976), but mainly spent the rest of his healthy days trying to convince everybody that he really wasn't a coon.

Comedian/Filmmaker, Rudy Ray Moore: "He was in Las Vegas working over on the North Las Vegas side in the secondary casinos. He was still getting some jobs over there. The whiteys liked him."

At the age of 74, Perry became partially paralyzed when he suffered a stroke while reading an article once again blaming him for the negative image of blacks in his era. The man known as Stepin Fetchit died in 1985 at the Motion Picture Country Home and Hospital in Los Angeles.

Comedian/Writer/Actor, J. B. Smoove: "I can respect him because I can get a sense of what he did for black comedy and what he did for the comedy world through someone else. If Bill Cosby says he inspired him and he inspires me it all plays a part in where I'm going."

A less polarizing image of blacks came from quite an unexpected place: the Hal Roach film shorts known as the *Our Gang* series, which ran from 1922–1944. The shorts featured children of different races and backgrounds (most notably an innocent, adolescent Robert Blake) and at a time when it was hard for a black actor to attain any type of work, these productions employed four young black actors. The first was known as Sunshine Sammy, whose real name was Ernie Morrison. He worked on the *Our Gang* comedies from 1922 until 1924. The next to step up to the plate was Alan "Farina" Hoskins. He appeared in 105 of the comedies and went on to make feature films.

Joe Blount: "Farina was pre-Buckwheat so he never really got his real propers. They had this one scene where he was real hungry and he went over to this white kid's house and he asked the white kid did he know that ham and eggs could talk and the white kid didn't believe him and so he told him he had to put it in the skillet and they started cooking and he did some old nigga shit, 'They sure is talkin' now.'"

Another BB (Before Buckwheat) was Matthew "Stymie" Beard, who worked on the series from 1930 until 1935. He later had a serious drug addiction, but recovered and revived his career.

Ernie Morrison (Sunshine Sammy), Jay R. Smith, Allen Clayton Hoskins (Farina), Mickey Daniels, and Joe Cobb in 1922.

Then there was Buckwheat, the most famous of the black *Our Gang* kids. William Thomas Jr. made his debut in 1934 and appeared in ninety-eight of the movies.

Deon Cole: "They loved Buckwheat. They wasn't kicking him and spitting on him and hitting him with rocks and hanging him. Buckwheat was raw. They couldn't have the gang if it wasn't for Buckwheat."

Eddie Griffin: "I used to watch it. Quite some inventive young kids, entrepreneurs. They never went to their parents and asked for money. They always put on a show. Some of the kids could learn something from that today."

Thea Vidale: "They were fun and we should be so lucky to have children who played like that. Our children don't play. They create trench coat Mafias and gangbangin'."

Our Gang was later reissued for TV as *The Little Rascals* due to the street gang climate at the time of its re-emergence in the 1970s.

Hal Roach had given the world a welcome relief from coondom, but the rest of Hollywood was still having trouble supplying any textured image of blacks. True, the *Christie Comedies* and the rival *Florian Slappery* series each utilized black consultants (Spencer Williams and Buck & Bubbles, respectively), but this merely provided a slightly less coonish depiction. What was needed was balance. So they gave us a running, cringing, super eye-bucking actor who was the energetic answer to Stepin Fetchit's slow man approach.

Eddie Griffin: "He had some talented eyeballs. Not many people have that kind of muscle control over their eyes."

MANTAN MORELAND

Mantan Moreland was born in Louisiana around 1900 and began his show business career when he joined the circus at 14, then toured with a minstrel show. His trademark film traits became the rolling eyes, quick double takes, and signature lines like, "Feets, don't fail me now!" These devices of buffoonery in no way downplayed the fact that Mantan was a consummate actor. During the late '30s and early '40s, he played Birmingham Brown, the chauffer and valet in the Charlie Chan film series and appeared in over 300 films. However, his screen image was not one that endeared him with his people.

> **Rudy Ray Moore:** "When he went to (perform in) nightclubs he was not totally well appreciated and accepted."

In the last couple of decades or so of his life, Moreland worked the Los Angeles chitlin' circuit: the California Club and different clubs on the Westside of L.A.

> **Rudy Ray Moore:** "He had lost that power of getting anything that was worth anything after the movies. I think *Cabin in the Sky* was the last big movie he'd done."

Moreland died in 1973 of a cerebral hemorrhage.

> **Mystro Clark:** "That was an underrated brother now that I think about it. He was one of the highest-paid entertainers of his era and not even being able to stay in the hotel with the other white performers. Yeah, he was a tough dude. I respect that."

A tough female and the small-boned gatekeeper of stereotypical behavior was a comedienne with a name that could have been originated by Scottish hippies. Butterfly McQueen, with her high-pitched, squeaky voice, was the domestic who made you wonder how she got the job in the first place. After gaining acclaim for the part of Prissy in 1939's *Gone with the Wind*, McQueen worked through the 1940s, did *Beulah* in the early 1950s, then found herself working as a real life domestic to pay the bills. She later managed to get TV work and appeared in *Amazing Grace* with Moms Mabley in 1974. On December 22, 1995 in Augusta, Georgia, she died from burns sustained when she attempted to light a kerosene heater and it exploded and burst into flames.

Domestics were the roles Hollywood demanded of their blacks and many a male actor brushed up on his best, "Yassur" delivery. There was Dudley Dickerson, a gifted comic and physical humorist who ran through doors, outran moving vehicles, and got hit over the head with an anvil and took it all in stride. Nicodemus Stewart was another who toiled in the trenches throughout the 1940s until he finally got his big break playing Lightnin' on *Amos 'n Andy* for TV. Hattie McDaniel's brother Sam played servants as well, as did Fred "Snowflake" Toones. Mr. Toones specialized in playing coons. He was like Stepin Fetchit lite. However, he was outdone in the cooning department by the actor Ben Carter. His take on the head scratching, dumb-as-dirt character was so backwards that he was an embarrassment even as an Uncle Tom.

WILLIE BEST

However, this quintessential Stepin Fetchit clone was so convincing in his roles that the real world often thought he must truly be the way he behaved on camera. It became so bad for him that even after he'd gotten over and was rich beyond his wildest dreams, he still couldn't go out for a quiet game of golf like most celebrities. He was a black celebrity, which meant if he wanted to shoot a few holes it would be while carrying the bag of a white Hollywood star, such as Charles Winninger. (Who could forget that box office titan?) How irksome it must have been to hear, "I'll take a five iron, Willie," from a lesser performer, but that was the fate of Willie Best.

Best was born in Mississippi and was discovered walking down Central Avenue in Watts in 1927. He was pursued by a white man in a car, and when most brothers see white men following them (especially in the 1920s) they run. Best was black and got to getting. The white man caught him and offered him a future in movies (a fate a lot of black men wish had been the case as opposed to the invitation to try on a noose to see how it fit).

They dubbed him "Sleep 'n Eat," but in one of his movies his character's name was actually "Sambo." He'd mastered all the coon antics: drooping jaw, bucked eyes, and the ability to run as though your life depended on it. Best was well aware he was being used, but also aware that if he didn't do it somebody else would so he cooned in films until 1947, when he moved on to television, playing minor roles in *The Stu Erwin Show* and *My Little Margie* in the 1950s. Willie Best died in 1962.

The roles black actors portrayed were of course the only parts available under the Hollywood studio system, but after a vigorous protest was waged by the NAACP, actors/writers/producers Spencer Williams and Clarence Muse and several black newspapers, the pressure became too much and the options, the way the movie moguls saw it, were too few. The result was that the Negro image, negative or otherwise, took a prolonged break from the big screen altogether, forcing many black talents to find work elsewhere.

HAVE YOU EVER WANTED TO JUST QUIT AND GET A REAL JOB?

Leslie: "Every day. I'm filling out applications right now as we speak."

Comedian, Geoff Brown: "A number of times, but that's not who I am. I had to realize I'm in love with a whore. Her name is comedy. I love her, but she doesn't love me."

Comedian/Actor, Katt Williams: "There's nothing for me to quit because I've already seen the worse part of stand-up. It's the best part that I haven't seen yet."

Buddy Lewis: "Several times. If comedy doesn't treat you like a down-and-out whore—you're not doing it right."

Bernie Mac: "No; other people wanted me to, saying: 'Get a real job' or 'You ain't no Richard Pryor.' I was always compared to whoever was on top at the time."

Al Toomer: "Nope. My worse days in this have been better than my best days on a job. I've been in some relationships where some goddamn woman wanted me to do that, but that's when the relationship normally ended."

Smokey Deese: "Not once. My wife has thought that for me, but I, myself—never."

Comedienne/Actress, Sherri Shepherd: "Those times when I bombed, 'Get the f*#k off the stage!' You just want to go back to a job where nobody is going to be cursing at you."

Evan Lionel: "I think about that all the time now since I became a father. You be like, 'maybe I could be the entertainment director on a cruise ship or sell drugs on the side.' All kinds of stuff because you want your kids to have the best advantage."

Rodney Perry: "At some point you got to work without a net. As long as you got to be at a place in the morning, your creative energy's not the same. A low-end comic, you ain't never heard of, if he's a hustler—he can make rent. You can take care of your family. Niggas in L.A., they claim they can't make no money, they not working hard enough. I got five kids, a wife and two baby's mamas. If I can make it..."

Comedienne/Radio Personality, Hope Flood: "A woman came up to me after a show and said, 'Today was my birthday and nobody called me and wished me a Happy Birthday. I decided after I finished treating myself I was going to go home and kill myself. And you made me laugh and gave me my will to live back.' This is why you do it."

Kool Bubba Ice: "The money's too good that I make on the road to go get a regular job. And the amount of hours I'd have to work to make what I make in one night is ridiculous so I might as well just stick it out and do what I do."

Angela Means: "I'm thinking about it right now."

Ajai Sanders: "I quit a million times, but there's a difference of quitting and giving up."

Shang: "We're hustlers. We're gonna get a gig. So I don't ever think about that."

Willie Brown (& Woody): "Every time I try to quit I start getting calls for work."

Jay Phillips: "I've done that before; go get the paper, get all pumped up, start looking through the paper and next thing I know somebody will call me and say, 'Hey, we got a job for you for one thousand dollars next week—wanna do it?'"

Damon Williams: "Yeah man, I went in for an interview and they called me back and the night before I was due to go in I ran into Deon Cole and I told him and he says, 'Man dude, they say once people get them jobs they don't come back to the mic.' So I woke up the next day and it was time for me to go to that job and I couldn't go."

Melanie Comarcho: "If I was to go back and get a real job I would still want to stay in the entertainment business, but I'll never stop 'til I reach the top."

Alex Thomas: "My saying is: I don't have a Plan B. There is no, 'If comedy doesn't work out I can always go back to fulfilling my lifelong dream of becoming an astronaut.' No. If this shit don't work out I may be robbing your house or doing adult films, sponsored by Magnum condoms."

Sommore: "Yes. Yes, I have because you get frustrated. I've gotten frustrated at times when trying to get to that next level becomes so frustrating, but it's always the work and the stage that draws you back."

Adele Givens: "Hell naw—no matter how bad it got. I've had real jobs. I know how it go out there. Somebody who wished they could just quit and go to a job, they either somebody who just can't do their shit on stage or they ain't never had a real damn job before."

Mike Bonner: "Comedy is a marathon, not a sprint so you got to run your own race."

Brad Sanders: "Hell naw, shit no. I never wanted to quit comedy and go to work because see, by the time I became a comedian I already knew I didn't want no job. I didn't mind working, but I didn't want no job. The one thing about a job is you will never be rich because you will never accumulate enough money working for somebody else to become wealthy. I did not want to be poor and I decided that I was not afraid to be rich; most people are not wealthy because they choose not to. They don't want the responsibility of handling that wealth and dealing with the emotional challenges of how people relate to you of you having wealth and them not having it or them needing something from you and all that, whatever. I decided that I would be willing to handle it."

"Sure Sounds Black to Me"

CHAPTER 6

"I was with a girl so ugly she was the reason they invented light switches and doggie style."
— GUY TORRY

Radio was an alternative for black performers that offered a ray of hope; a ray that vanished as soon as white minstrels started doing black voices to extend their dying careers. Black-face performers were all over the airwaves on shows like *The Burnt Cork Review*, *Plantation Party*, and *The Dutch Master Minstrels*. It makes one wonder if these acts wore the actual blackface while they yukked it up in front of the microphone; y'know, to get them into the right cooning mood. Remember, these were the days when *Amos 'n Andy* got their start.

That now-notorious duo was the alleged brainchild of Freeman F. Gosden and Charles J. Correll, two small-time white musicians who claimed to have brought the idea of a black comedy show (with whites being the blacks, of course) to Chicago station WGN. However, there was always some thinly veiled dispute as to whether they actually took the notion to the station or if WGN simply gave them the Miller & Lyles idea the station had previously reneged on when the sponsors discovered Miller & Lyles were real blacks, not actory blacks. Either way—the white Gosden and Correll were the New Negroes.

Sam 'n Henry made its debut in 1926 and lasted for two years, six days a week. Once their contract expired with WGN, they skipped over to station WMAQ (also in Chicago). On

March 19, 1928, *Amos 'n Andy* was officially born. The names had been changed for legal reasons, but one character was still naïve, and the other ignorant yet conniving. The fifteen-minute show was such an unprecedented hit that during movie showings, when the now-NBC program aired, the speakers from the movie would go dead and the radio show would be piped in for the sacred quarter hour. At its peak in 1930 the show had forty million listeners. In short, the country adored *Amos 'n Andy*, stereotypical dialects and all.

> **Dick Gregory:** "I knew those were white folks. They didn't have the first Amos 'n Andy African-Americans until they were on TV. And they were funny, but it wasn't nothing that, I mean…out of 500 people I bump into in a week I ain't never heard nobody talk like that."

But as the nation came creeping out of the Great Depression, the last thing they wanted to be reminded of were those soon-to-be-over hard times. That had been a major component of the program's charm: its ability to connect to the immediate problems of the average citizen. So acknowledging they were in trouble, Gosden and Correll (who did all the voices) hired on other actors (black as well as white) to provide additional voices, started using live audiences, and expanded to a half-hour format. The ratings climbed back up, but it was now more or less the Kingfish show. Other characters like Lightnin', Stonewall, and Sapphire (Kingfish's wife whose name became synonymous with the shrill, browbeating, nagging black woman) were funny, but the Kingfish was the true ruler. His slick ways and trickster mind kept audiences coming back week after week until 1954 when the show became *The Amos 'n Andy Music Hall*. That homogenized version saw its last day on November 25, 1960.

> **Comedian, Tom Dreesen:** "Back then everybody in my neighborhood, even black folks, listened to *Amos 'n Andy* on the radio. I grew up around black folks and there was nobody in my neighborhood like the Kingfish. To a white boy like me who was raised around black folks he'd know right away that that's people doing an act. To a kid in Omaha, Nebraska who's never met a black person in his life, or in Utah, then he's going to think Kingfish and all black folks are like that."

Though *Amos 'n Andy* did come to represent negative stereotypes blacks chose to bury away, the show offered a better image than many others. Most radio situation comedies gave black performers little more to do than use a mop, a bucket, a sponge, or a washrag—just clean up. That's your job, black actor. Oh, and make it funny. Butterfly McQueen, Pigmeat Markham, Mantan Moreland, and others all did a radio stint, but the most famous of all was a houseboy who started off as a porter.

EDDIE "ROCHESTER" ANDERSON

Eddie Anderson was born on September 18, 1905 in Oakland, California to vaudevillians (minstrel father, tight rope-walking mother) and began performing at the age of 8. He and his brother Cornelius toured as a two-man song and dance team, but he got his big break when asked to play a Pullman porter named Rochester on the Jack Benny radio show. A one-time shot turned into a long-term career once Anderson breathed life into the part with his trademark gravelly voice. In doing so Anderson became the first black performer to obtain a steady job in radio.

Rochester was a typical servant, kowtowing, saying very little in the way of backtalk, but when he was away from his job he'd lose things in crap games and blow his cash on the company of young ladies. That changed, thanks to the NAACP. Next thing you know Jack Benny's apologizing for the stereotyping and a revamped Rochester received the same carte blanche as the rest of the cast to make fun of his employer's stinginess, lack of musical talent, and over-inflated ego. Thus Anderson made history as being the only black man in radio or motion pictures talking back to a white man. Work poured in: *Jezebel* with Bette Davis in 1938, *Gone with the Wind* with Clark Gable in 1939, and 1941's *Birth of the Blues*. He was also featured in several "race" films including two 1943 classics: *Stormy Weather* with Lena Horne and *Cabin in the Sky* with Ethel Waters.

Anderson had gotten so popular he got star billing along with Benny, but blacks still resented the fact that he was a servant and Southern whites were perturbed because he was an "uppity" servant; running his mouth when he should've just done as he was told and be glad he had a job. Oh, yeah, that would've been real funny. Other radio programs that utilized black characters tried that formula and they were all canceled.

Jack Benny's show lasted on radio until May of 1955. Benny had taken the entire radio cast into the TV world with him in 1950 and the radio and TV shows ran simultaneously for five years. *The Jack Benny Show* on TV ran until the mid-'60s, making Rochester even more of a household name. In 1963 Anderson co-starred with every other working comedian at the time in Stanley Kramer's *It's a Mad Mad Mad Mad World*. He worked with Benny until 1964 when Anderson retired due to health problems. Anderson passed on February 28, 1977 in Los Angeles, California and was posthumously inducted into the Radio Hall of Fame in 2001.

Mike Bonner: "He had to shuck 'n jive back then. He shucked 'n jived with grace."

The problem most black performers had on radio was not sounding black enough. Since white actors had laid the groundwork for the Negro dialect, that way of speaking and only that way was accepted. Many a black actor had to learn this method of speech—some blacks even had to go to white vocal coaches to get just the right inflections. So a number of African-Americans lost their jobs being black because they just didn't have the vocal credibility.

You Call That Reception?

CHAPTER 7

"Pregnant women who use vibrators
need to get kids who come out stuttering."
— SHANG

As radio declined television became the medium of the masses. The flickering box began its journey in 1920 with low-quality airings in New York and England, but by 1948 it saw a major expansion across the United States with radio comics defecting to join the TV brigade, and blacks welcomed in the mass march. Pearl Bailey, Sammy Davis Jr., and Pigmeat Markham appeared regularly on shows hosted by Milton Berle and Ed Sullivan (both staunch advocates of exposing deserving black talent). Ethel Waters made history as the first black star of a sitcom when she played the role of *Beulah* on ABC in 1950.

Then in stepped the middle-class Negroes, who felt that maid and servant roles on this new medium was history repeating itself. How long before TV would spin *Birth of a Nation* off into a weekly series? Something had to be done, and as usual protesting was the solution. In response the industry came back with a tried and true show beloved by all Americans— *Amos 'n Andy*. It had pulled the country together during the Great Depression, so surely it could do the same during a Cold War.

The show employed blacks in front of and behind the camera, including Flournoy Miller as consultant on racial matters. Initially Gosden and Correll were going to play the leads

White minstrel in blackface.

themselves (as they had on film in the 1930 debacle *Check, Double Check*, where they appeared in blackface to the dismay and revulsion of whites and blacks). Instead they wisely opted to use Spencer Williams as Andy, Alvin Childress as the good-natured Amos, and Tim Moore as the constantly scheming Kingfish.

Once again the show hit pay dirt and within a week the NAACP was calling it an affront to blacks. With the embarrassing character of Lightnin' (who was nothing but a Stepin Fetchit take-off) and the degradation of black women through Kingfish's harpy wife Sapphire and his interfering mother-in-law, the show was still accused of presenting a narrow portrayal of black sensibilities. The NAACP even compiled a top ten list of why the show should be removed from TV and radio, and as we all know you can't fight the NAACP. So the only show in the TV universe to ever present an all-black world of not only stereotypical characters but upright black citizens as well, was cut off at the knees and only ran from 1951 until 1953.

'Thing was, most blacks liked *Amos 'n Andy*. They understood that the purpose of comedy is to make you laugh, of drama to make you cry, and of satire to make you think, but were the stereotypes going too far for their stated purpose?

WHAT DID YOU THINK ABOUT *AMOS 'N ANDY*?

Dick Gregory: "I mean, I see nothing wrong with *Amos 'n Andy* being on TV now, when you got other people you can look at. It's when you didn't have anything to look at but him and he represented us. So when you think about where we've come from a lot of things that would've made sense ten, fifteen years ago don't make sense now. How *Amos 'n Andy* gonna damage us and we got a woman Secretary of State? Two of the most powerful magazines in the world, *Time* and *Newsweek*, are run by black men. American Express is run by a black man. We've seen intelligent black people all our life; white people had never seen them."

Sinbad: "We've got brothers doing *Amos 'n Andy* now. They just don't realize it."

Ventriloquist, Richard Stanfield of Richard & Willie: "I didn't see anything wrong. *Amos 'n Andy* to me was like the *Beverly Hillbillies* of black people. It wasn't offensive to me because I knew that's not the way that I acted or black people in general acted. It was a comedy. I know most white people are not *Beverly Hillbillies*. They're not that stupid. Give me a break, but I think sometimes as a people we get overly sensitive. I hope they'll bring it back one day."

The fledgling networks were confused. They gave black people what they thought they wanted, but they didn't want it. So obviously comedy was out until they could figure out what black people truly desired. Let's try music, they thought. Sure. How about Nat King

Cole? Everybody loved musical Negroes and Cole was one of the best, but when Nat King Cole, a major star with hit records under his belt, got his show on NBC in 1956, it died a death as mysterious as Jimmy Hoffa's. Nat King Cole might've been welcome on radios and jukeboxes, but he obviously was not the type of individual America was willing to let into their living rooms on a regular basis.

> **Rodney Perry:** "They didn't want Nat King Cole. That's how bad racism was."

TV, huh? Big-name black comics were given such strict censorship rules to follow that the networks might as well have hired somebody else. It was a chap-lipped kiss of death for black performers on television for almost two decades. Many of the artists of the era survived by playing the chitlin' circuit, others did touring plays and some found work in low-budget films. They made do without the glamorous medium of television and did whatever they had to so they could continue to entertain. Makes you wonder…

WERE COMEDIANS FROM THE PAST MORE DEVOTED TO THEIR CRAFT?

> **Bernie Mac:** "YES! Hell yes. No question, without a doubt, absolutely, SHO' you right, you know that!"

> **Jay Phillips:** "It depends on how far back you go."

> **Mystro Clark:** "Yes, because comedians started back in history as the town crier, the guy who told all and he could talk about the King and all that stuff, but if you made it funny you wouldn't get your head chopped off."

> **Al Toomer:** "I wouldn't know because I wasn't back then, but how hard do you have to practice to buck your eyes and fall around and do all that other shit?"

> **John Witherspoon:** "Well, comics from the past had to do their homework and had to pay their dues. A lot of comics today ain't never paid their dues. A lot of people look at BET (Black Entertainment Televsion) and steal the other guy's act and go out there and do that. Plus there's not many places where these dudes can work anymore. Most of these comics ain't doing no work anywhere. They got BET, but that ain't paying no money. You see them on BET dance up and down, but where they gonna go from there? You got to be able to work these clubs and to work these clubs you can't be doing all somebody else's act 'cause it ain't gonna work. You will never be a headliner if you are doing stuff from *Comic View*. You tell me where they're working at."

> **Hope Flood:** "Oh, definitely. Now, everybody says they can be a comedian. When people say, 'I want to be a comedian. Hope, can you give me some advice?' I say don't do it. I got a memo the other day that said we don't need another goddamn comedian."

> **Edwonda White:** "There was too much going on with the racism back in the Moms Mabley days and I wouldn't have been able to take it. I would've been like— forget it. I'm not going through the kitchen door and all that. I don't want to go

through that, but I really admire those who paved the way for us; to where we can have black clubs and we can have different things. And if it wasn't for those people who went through the back door and who was called the black Sambos this and that; a lot of those filthy names, all in the name of entertainment; if it wasn't for them then we wouldn't be able to do *Comic View* or VH1 or do Comedy Central and do these shows."

Alex Thomas: "I would say the guys in the past did it more for the love. In our era we know it's a very lucrative sport. I'm pretty sure a guy starts out nowadays going, 'Yeah, I love it, but nigga I'm trying to make a million dollars in the next couple of years.' I've been doing this shit for thirteen years. If I did it for the money I wouldn't still be doing it."

Talent: "Yeah. Everything in America today I call it microwave days. Lazy muthaf*#kas don't want to cook. He wants to put it in there, press a minute and eat and that's how everybody is. There's nobody who starts comedy like, 'Okay, I'm going to go in and put my twenty years in. I'm going to be the shit in twenty years.' Nobody's thinking like that. Everybody's like, 'In about a year I'll have my TV show' and that's crazy."

Rudy Ray Moore: "The comedians today, those kids today are saying something out there that may go across because it has no story to it. It's just something they can think of, 'Well, my grandma used to beat my behind' and shit like that, y'know. You know what I'm talking about. They come out with that shit which is not an act."

Speedy: "Comics back then—the agenda was to just become funny comedians and then actors and then famous. Most comics now want to be famous the next day. They're like, well, I'll go up tonight, but then I don't really need to go up the rest of the week. Well, we were trying to go up any and everywhere. Whether it was two people or twenty. We were dedicated to going up, getting that stage time and working out our craft to be ready when they came to see you and it was your night to shine."

Robert Townsend: "With every group of comedians from old school to new there are those that are dedicated more than others. You can look at Eddie Murphy, then you can look at Dave Chappelle. You could look at Sinbad and then you could look at Chris Rock. I mean, there's different cats; everybody dedicated from different times."

Melanie Comarcho: "I think we're more clever than they were. They did a lot of what we call 'stock jokes' now. So I think we've evolved."

Richard of Richard & Willie: "I think the ventriloquists don't put the time and practice in that I put in. I did seven hours a day, seven days a week. My hands would almost bleed, but it was because of great determination that I'm gonna make this thing work. I mean I gave up a lot for that; my family. I gave up time I wanted to be doing other things, but it was like a great determination. You have to put in the time. You have to."

Cedric the Entertainer: "The comics of the past had to be. I come from the end of that era where the goal was to be a headliner; become the person everybody came to see; do stand-up. Now with the heightened degree of television, cable specials, and movies, it seems to be that people only use comedy as a vehicle to become famous to do something else and so I definitely would say that the old school comics cared about and worked on the craft of and art form of stand-up comedy a lot more than the guys do today."

Leslie: "Entertainers period were more devoted to their craft and their art—period! Not just comics—singers, everybody. It's so funny because you look at the performers back in the day, everybody could do everything. Sammy Davis Jr., he could sing, dance, tell jokes, he could do all that shit, y'know? Everybody was trained to know how to do everything because it wasn't just about one aspect of performance; it was about being an entertainer."

Keith Morris: "Yes, because a lot of them get into different areas now and singing and all that and forget about where they come from."

Comedian/Actor, Honest John: "No. It's how people work at it. I'm sure in the past some people got into comedy just to get a sitcom or series or whatever. There are other people who are true stand-up comics, you just know they are. They're into it for life."

Comedian, Daryl Mooney (The Mooney Twins): "Back then it was a do or die. They were paving the road for what we're doing today and it was just more serious, man, because there was less opportunity for folks who could come through the door."

Comedian/Actor/Filmmaker, Pierre: "Sure. By leaps and bounds. It's like comedy is kind of like sugar now. People just go for the instant BANG without the substance. It's almost like chasing a fast buck. Your friends tell you you're funny, you go down to the comedy club and try to be a comedian. Where years ago I think more people tried to take the steps to be a good comedian. Now it's just, let me go after the money. You got cats making five to ten thousand a show—I want that money. Before that it wasn't about money so you had to be doing it for a reason; because you wanted to do it for the love of it and you really thought about, maybe I can build a set and wind up touring; doing comedy clubs. It wasn't as glamorous as it is now, but it was just something you wanted to do."

Writer/Producer/Show Creator, T. Faye Griffin: "Yeah, I do in the sense of they looked at it as a craft and not a hustle. For so many comics today it's a hustle. Richard Pryor, Godfrey Cambridge, Dick Gregory—it was a craft. It's art. Bill Cosby...even Chris Rock; it's a craft. It's an art form, not a hustle."

Not You Too, Bugs

CHAPTER 8

"Daffy Duck was black. Look at the way
they were always whooping his ass.
He was the Rodney King of cartoons."
— D'MILITANT

Despite the meddling of pressure groups and the protestations of the upper elite, Hollywood broadened its scope by making fun of black Americans without the concern of their participation—in the world of animation, where a black character could be given the most preposterous, outrageous facial expressions and physical tasks to perform without the stigma of a live-action black actor balking about it or worse, not being able to perform the antics. It was perfect.

Mystro Clark: "Bugs Bunny was black, for one he was cool. He never got flustered and he was always giving it to the man."

In the case of *Fresh Hare* the man was Bugs Bunny's arch nemesis, roly-poly Elmer Fudd. Producer Leon Schlesinger over at Merrie Melodies spared no black ink when he made this animated short featuring Fudd as a Royal Canadian Mountie on the trail of the "wascally wabbit" only to be blown to smithereens, stripped down to his shorts and corset by Bugs in the snow, slammed headlong into a tree while giving chase to a rabbit whose ears miraculously split apart and went around it, punched in the face, kissed in the mouth, and duped into running smack-dab into a solid rock. But the coup de grace came in the final moments when Fudd has taken Bugs back to the fort to be executed by a firing squad. Elmer said to the blindfolded, carrot chomping rabbit, "Before you die you can make one last wish."

Bugs pondered then begins singing, "I wish I was in Dixie. Hooray, Hooray."

The scenery suddenly went from a Canadian fort to the old South and all the Mounties, as well as Bugs (strumming a banjo) and Elmer (playing a tambourine), turned into black-faced minstrels and broke into singing "Camp town ladies sing this song. Doo-da, doo-da." It's a classic example of how any bad situation can come out all right if you just coon.

> **Rodney Perry:** "I always pictured Bugs Bunny as a black dude, too. He was cool with me."

Well, Mr. Cool was at it again in 1942 in *Any Bonds Today?*, and he was definitely a black dude—parodying Al Jolson in blackface, the movie minstrel's trademark.

That was nothing compared to how they drew the brothers and sister from the Motherland. In *Jungle Jitters*, featuring grinning, happy-to-be-alive natives, the opening scene consists of the locals beating the drums (one drummer is even wearing a top hat, obviously the remains from a previous meal), dancing around huts with spears hoisted high and lips flapping wildly. One clever drummer even embellishes on his beats by slapping his own behind as another native jumps rope using the ring in his nose. As far as language, the native tongue that stretched all across the vast continent of Africa was pared down to "ugum bugum."

The inhabitants of cartoon Africa also seemed to have a never-satisfied taste for animated, talking animals. No matter how many times Bugs Bunny, Porky Pig, or even the aptly named Daffy Duck would get caught up in a scrape and end up in the tribe's giant pot, our "heroes" always managed to outsmart the tribe's people. These were obvious descendants of the native folk who let Tarzan move into their neighborhood.

> **Brad Sanders:** "Daffy was too damn goofy to be black. You can't be that goofy and black and live."

> **Rodney Perry:** "Daffy was a nigga."

Animators pushed the racial envelope for all it was worth, but whenever such blatant disrespect occurs there's a protest, and with every protest the powers that be throw up their hands and eliminate blacks from the landscape altogether. This time was no different. From then on other races would see their flaws and human foibles ridiculed. Native Americans, Asians, Mexicans, and the ever-nose-rubbing Eskimo were lampooned, and blacks for the most part became completely absent from the world of animation.

But did the Negro really leave or did Hollywood simply disguise 'em?

WHICH CARTOON ANIMALS WERE SUPPOSED TO BE BLACK?

J. B. Smoove: "Heckle and Jeckle were definitely two black dudes. They were always trying to get over; always scamming and always getting shot at."

Mystro Clark: "Wile E. Coyote, his little schemes always broke up at the last minute, like being thrown off the cliff or whatever, but he was a brother with ingenuity. It said so on his mailbox. Resident genius."

Jay Phillips: "Foghorn Leghorn for sure, because he had so much flavor. That was the coolest cartoon dude on the planet. Him and Snagglepuss. They were damn near pimps."

Norman Mitchell: "Heckle and Jeckle were black. They really had nothing to do and they always conned their way through. Neither one of them had a job; just lazy birds that basically did nothing. Foghorn Leghorn was representative of the black preacher. He'd walk around with his chest poked out like he ran the yard, but he really didn't run anything because whatever problems came—like the preacher—he hid. And then when the problem was over he came out, 'See how we worked this out.'"

Kevin Hart: "Mickey Mouse because sometimes Mickey got lazy and Mickey just took off. Like Mickey would just pop up on cartoons, 'Hey, it's Mickey Mouse' and everybody would be happy and then Mickey'd get lost. That's some black shit. You jump in when you want and then go on about your business."

Vince D: "I'm sure the homeboy in the trash can was black."

Mark Prince: "Tigger from Winnie the Pooh. Tigger, Tigger the magic nigger. That's what he was: bouncing through life, couldn't talk right and all that old stupid bullshit."

Brad Sanders: "The Bears. Anything brown."

Joey "J-Dub" Wells: "Yeah, those Hanna-Barbera bears—I think those were niggas."

Joe Blount: "Yogi Bear had the whole nigga style. Always trying to get some free shit."

Alex Thomas: "Popeye had some nigga characteristics to him: big ass forearms, a big ass, a pipe, and a little tattoo that said Crenshaw & Slauson."

Willie Brown (& Woody): "I think a lot of them cartoon characters were gay, like Casper the friendly ghost; too damn friendly. And that lion, even: Snagglepuss, always saying 'Heavens to murgatroid.' Those two little chipmunks were gay. Pepe LePew, I don't know. He was always hugging and kissing on somebody."

This animal transmutation also extended to the X-rated animation genre in the guise of Ralph Bakshi's *Fritz the Cat* and its follow-up, *The Nine Lives of Fritz the Cat*, where crows with enormous breasts were clearly meant to be black harlots looking for nothing but a good time from cool, white Fritz and the males were pimps and hustlers out to part Fritz from his

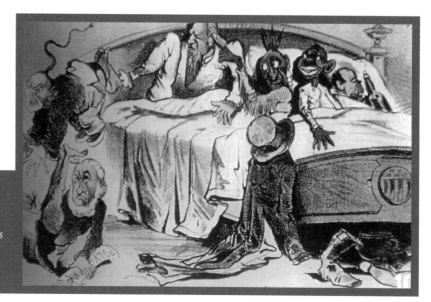

Harper's Weekly *cartoon demonstrating America's dilemma of dealing with its ever changing bedfellows, 1876.*

hard earned money. These theatrically released feature cartoons were quite successful in the mid-'70s, but in no way portrayed blacks as anything more than street rabble.

It took a star with the clout of Bill Cosby to reintroduce black animation back into mainstream homes when he mounted the *Cosby Kids* on CBS from 1972–1984. This was after NBC had rejected an ongoing relationship following the airing of the special *Hey, Hey, Hey—It's Fat Albert* on November 12, 1969, due to Cosby's intent to throw education into the cartoon mix. His cartoon characters taught lessons, sang, and got into all sorts of mischief. America loved it, but after Cosby, the pickings were slim.

One of the few bright spots occurred when African-American cartoonist Morrie Turner's nationally syndicated and racially integrated comic strip known as *Wee Pals* was adapted for television under the name *Kid Power* on ABC in 1973. Its popularity on TV and the comics ushered in a new era of ethnically driven artists, including *Boondocks* by Aaron McGruder, which went from print to TV in 2005.

There were attempts in later years to appease blacks by transforming previously white characters into black ones, like replacing white icon The Green Lantern. This super hero had been fair-skinned for decades, then all of a sudden he was a brother. No explanation, just *voilà* instant Negro. I guess the tanning booth at the Justice League went haywire.

There was another such black super hero that was simply manufactured. He also made his appearance on Saturday mornings and had a funky hairdo. He rode a hover board and was a teenager. Do you know who I'm talking about? Of course not and they don't want you to know; that's why they never do commercials with this character and he's rarely ever mentioned. How many kids do you know go around talking about the black super hero with the funky hair style?

I'll Make My Own Damn Image

CHAPTER 9

"If you keep doing what you always did,
you'll keep getting what you always got!"
— "Moms" Mabley

Studies have shown, like the one conducted by psychologist Samuel Janus, that a large percentage of comedians "came from families in the lowest socio-economic class." In addition to blacks, this was also the case with the Jewish and the Irish. Seemingly people from poverty have quick minds and more adaptability to various situations. They also have a burning need to prove themselves not only to themselves, but to the world at large.

This might explain the mentality of the stand-up comedian, for stand-up comedy was never a natural art form. This is probably why its evolution took so long; especially for black performers. The early days were of minstrelsy, with its three-act format featuring the interlocutor and the two endmen. This was a comfortable arrangement for white audience members because true stand-up is a dialogue between a performer and his or her audience, and no white audience was going to talk to some black minstrel.

It was unheard of for a Negro to look out among the sea of white faces in the audience and speak directly to its membership. For a black man to open his mouth and ask a question of the audience as a whole—or heaven forbid, of an individual—would have been considered the height of uppitiness and too much of a stretch to social equality. So the males would always confine their conversation to whoever was on stage with them at the time. Thus stage antics between two males were one-on-one exchanges and the audience derived the humor from this presentation. It was clearly a case of laughing *at* the performers and not *with* them.

Once women were added to the mix, the dynamics were slightly altered. Since black women were considered less of a threat (physically and mentally) than their male counterparts, they not only didn't have to wear blackface (which the males continued to don, in some cases up until the '40s), but females could also address the audience and actually make eye contact. The black woman was almost their voice, as she tried to either straighten out the black male comic or understand what predicament he'd gotten himself into this time.

Stand-up was, however, being done by white comedians soon after World War I. Good ole boy Will Rogers (though half-Indian) was talking directly to the people. He discussed politics and regularly lambasted the current president and whatever hairbrained policies he might've had. Will twirled his lasso and rambled on about anything he wanted. Some consider him the very first true stand-up. He was followed by other palm-colored comics such as Jack Benny, Fred Allen, and Milton Berle. A black comedian in this era could only scratch his head and wonder what such freedom must've felt like. That performer might have technically been a free man, but was still enslaved when it came to what left his mouth. The shackles he was forced to endure were restraints of the mind.

Nevertheless, some refused to acknowledge any verbal boundaries. These brave souls remain largely nameless, as far as popular culture is concerned. They bucked the status quo and said what they wanted to in front of their own people, choosing to be happy in their art at the sacrifice of greater fame, money, and ultimately, work. Two of the earliest pioneers were the team of Feet and Brains, consisting of Leonard Reed and Willie Bryant. Reed was a former Charleston dancer, so he was Feet; and though Bryant could dance, by default he became Brains. They worked black theaters and cabarets and went completely unnoticed by mainstream audiences.

Allen Drew was more in line with what modern audiences are accustomed to as far as comedy presentation. Many from his era dubbed him the best black stand-up comedian of all time, some say the best of any race. He played the black circuit from the 1920s up until the 1950s with his acerbic brand of unflinchingly raw material.

Drew wasn't a theater comic because he was too dirty for polite society. He was a product of nightclubs, where he could let the profanities fly. He was quick as lightning in his delivery and was the envy of his peers. He was also one of the most ripped-off comics of his day. White comedians, including the famous Milton Berle, would go uptown to not only watch and admire Drew's artistry, but to jot down jokes and key bits which could be incorporated into their own acts downtown.

WHAT DO YOU THINK ABOUT JOKE THIEVES?

Alex Thomas: "I hate them. A joke thief is like taking food off your table. There's guys out there, take like an Arnez J, who is the P. Diddy of stand-up. He will take your joke and remix it. It's just lazy. It's not cool and I think they should be prosecuted."

Sommore: "Wow! And I used to worry about that, but you have to just keep making more. Because if you sit up and argue over one joke you could've written five others by now."

Thea Vidale: "Some of the ones that make the most money think that that gives them the right to steal. That ain't how the game is played. There's niggas out here going loopty-loopty."

Keith Morris: "Hate 'em!"

Derrick Ellis: "Joke thieves are cowards."

Deon Cole: "Joke thieves need to go in a pool with lead boots and drown themselves."

Melanie Comarcho: "They say that's supposed to be a compliment, but I feel—write your own shit, and if you've got to steal be clever enough to flip it. Use the premise, change the punch. Make it seem like it's yours. Don't just do the joke verbatim."

Joe Blount: "They can all go to hell."

Joey "J-Dub" Wells: "I think they should burn their toenails. I don't think we should kill 'em—that ain't cool, but it should have to hurt because it's some bullshit."

Marquez the Greatest: "Joke thieves should be dealt with the way thieves are dealt with over in the Middle East; the way that Saddam Hussein did it, but instead of a hand it should be maybe like some teeth the first couple of times. Just pull 'em out and maybe a tongue if it's perpetual. It should be severe—that's what I think."

Eddie Griffin: "Like any other job where they steal your tools—whoop their muthaf*#kin' ass and lock 'em up."

The tragedy of Allen Drew was that even though he was known as the fastest comic alive and was a comic's comic—the poor guy couldn't get booked enough. His style and insistence on talking directly to crowds pushed him to the outer edges of show business and forced an early retirement from a true trailblazer. Drew gave up stand-up in the late '40s, moved back to Chicago and became of all things—a cop: going from a job where people loved you to one where they hated to see you coming.

Unfortunately that was the state of stand-up comedy in its early years. The major problem was reluctance on the part of society to accept any type of political or social critiques from a black comedian. That simply went against the grain of the buffoon and coon images so long perpetuated. Oh, it was all right for a Will Rogers to read the paper and bring his unique insights to what he'd digested, but if you'd told somebody that a Negro was doing the same the first thing they'd do is accuse you for lying about a Negro even reading a newspaper.

Ironic as it may seem, D.W. Griffith is responsible for the black film industry. *Birth of a Nation* pushed the black community into a position of examining their cinematic images and addressing what they felt was a gross misrepresentation. "Race" films were born—black films made by blacks for blacks, although many turned out to be dusted off white scripts supplanted with black actors. Emmet J. Scott got backing from the NAACP and after three years of delays was finally able to release *Birth of a Race*. The film bore no resemblance to the masterwork that Griffith had presented; it was critically panned and soon forgotten.

The best examples of genuine black comedy from the "race" movie era were the "shorts" that caught black comedians' stage performances: filmed stage bits of Dusty Fletcher, Stepin' Fetchit, Pigmeat Markham, Mantan Moreland, Nipsey Russell, and other great black stars.

As the nation crept into the mid-'50s, the whole idea of a "race" film was seen as obsolete. At this time the Negro was trying to integrate, not segregate, so the notion of fighting for not only the right to drink from the same fountain and use the same smelly bathroom as whites, as well as stare up at the same theater screen, would seem stupid if the movies catered to a specific race (even though most Hollywood movies still do just that).

WHAT'S THE WORST PART ABOUT STAND-UP?

Sherri Shepherd: "Bombing."

Sinbad: "Being told who I was and what I was not. And not just by white Hollywood, even black Hollywood decided who I was and what I was not."

D'Militant: "No good, lying, two-faced, rat bastard, sonofabitch ass promoters."

Derrick Ellis: "When you think you're going on the road and they cancel on you."

Comedienne/Actress, Kym Whitley: "People make jokes that I came in through the back door of comedy. Because I didn't have to do four or five nights of stand-up, live in my car, and do all this stuff and struggle. I got in as an actress and y'know what? I'm an actress who's going to act like a stand-up."

Comedian, Darren Carter: "Being put in a hotel room in the middle of nowhere."

Geoff Brown: "Using real world rules in stand-up. If you're a lawyer you went to college, law school, pass the bar—you're a lawyer. Comedy's not like that. You can bust your ass for twenty years and some new kid will get a deal because he has a hot seven minutes."

Al Toomer: "The perception that all comedians are clowns and buffoons."

Mystro Clark: "The uncertainty of not being able to plan out your life and your money in advance. Like our friends admire us because you're your own boss and whatever. I admire them because of a steady check every two weeks."

Sandy Brown: "Arrogance and theft."

Ruben Paul: "When people steal your material."

Angela Means: "When you start off with an idea and you work it, you work it, you work it, and it turns into your baby. And then somebody comes and kidnaps your baby."

Eddie Griffin: "Joke thieves. Non-original muthaf*#kas biting your material."

Talent: "The average Joe Schmo not really giving us the respect of having a real job."

Evan Lionel: "People don't want to pay us for what we do. They want to charge people fifteen, twenty, twenty-five dollars to get in at clubs and then they're sold out and they give you a fifteen dollar check."

Honest John: "Sleazy promoters. A little stronger—sleazebag muthaf*#kas!"

Rodney Perry: "A white comic can go his whole career, never make a black person laugh and make millions of dollars. For me to make millions I've *got* to make whites laugh."

Hope Flood: "People not having your money and thinking that we as comedians are just, no pun intended, a joke."

Edwonda White: "Trying to be a mother, a wife, and still doing comedy."

John Witherspoon: "Ain't nothing bad about it when you're working all the time. If you're working all the time it's good; there is no bad part of it."

Leslie: "Not getting paid."

Speedy: "The fact that if you're black it takes a lot longer to make it."

Shang: "We'll go rip a room and they still don't pick us, but some corny white boy will get put on and he's funny as throat cancer."

Alex Thomas: "Going a few years in the beginning without getting paid."

Smokey Deese: "The politics of it, I can't win because I'm not willing to play."

Tommy Chunn: "Getting booed and then having to walk through the crowd to leave."

Luenell: "Getting off the stage."

Willie Brown (& Woody): "Dealing with shady ass promoters."

Damon Williams: "Missing family events."

Comedian/Writer, James Hannah: "Getting passed over or not getting shots at all."

Comedian, Mike Bonner: "When you can't pay your bills and then you got to deal with these crackers who don't want to book you in their clubs because you're black."

Buddy Lewis: "When Negro promoters want to take you to their mama's crib, their friend's clothing store, the local barbershop. Man, stop promoting me like we're boys and friends. Take me to my hotel. I'm tired."

Katt Williams: "There is no worst part for me because what I don't like has nothing to do with stand-up. Stand-up is everything I could ever want it to be. If you're a control freak like most of us comics are, then comedy is the game for you because you're always in control. Stand-up in and of itself it's always good. Stand-up is of the gods."

Mark Curry: "Just wish I didn't have to get on the plane; the plane and the hotel."

Adele Givens: "The business aspect. We live in a world where people just don't want to do what they're supposed to do. The only time you get somebody to do their job is when they're filling out an application. They'll make that bitch look like I don't know what. You'll be like 'I got my man for this job.' That bastard will get on the job and be stealing you out of house and home and won't do shit. Put somebody on hold and talk shit about how he got this person on hold."

Sommore: "The more you learn about the business of things, you really take away the fun of it. If I could just leave my house and walk straight on stage my life would be so much easier. But it's all the stuff in between that gets you frustrated."

Marquez the Greatest: "The treatment of the stand-up comedians by the presenters, exhibiters, producers, and users of the craft. They treat stand-up comedians like crackheads while they continue to thrive and make millions of dollars. If the comics just set a standard, muthaf*#kas would be earning more than what Redd Foxx was earning back in the day and they were earning more than the average comic is earning now, which is f*#ked up."

Pass the Corn Liquor, I'm a Vegetarian on the Chitlin' Circuit

CHAPTER 10

"The biggest challenge for a black comedian
is not to become bitter."
— Brad Sanders

With Hollywood effectively closing the door to blacks on the big and small screen, most acts found work on the infamous "chitlin' circuit." This was the run of clubs around the country that catered primarily to African-American patrons and performers. Be you a musician, comedian, magician (black ones never got any cooperation because nobody from the audience ever volunteered their wallet for the trick), or novelty act—this is where you probably played and struggled to get paid after the gig.

Those artists received a tremendous boost in 1907 when the TOBA (Theater Owners Booking Association) was started by theater owner F. A. Barrasso for the purpose of insuring that performers were paid for their services. He formed theatrical tours with black entrepreneurs to guarantee steady employment, but acts still had to contend with shabby venues, "pay and rooming accommodations only" gigs (the acts had to handle their own travel arrangements), and non-tongue-biting bigots.

TELL ME ONE OF YOUR WORST ROAD STORIES

Alex Thomas: "I did a show in Jekyll Island, Georgia. I did a comedy show down there and I stayed in a hotel and the KKK was having their annual biker convention. I didn't think I was going to make it out of there. I'm from South Central L.A. I've only heard of the KKK. I didn't know the shit was alive and kicking, let alone them being on Harley Davidsons with white sheets. No helmets—sheets. I found out they're not blatant where they'll just kill a nigga out in public. Obviously they don't like us, but it was a one night gig. I still did my gig and left the next morning, but what I did was I wore a white hood myself. I just happened to have a white hood and I had like some jeans and it happened to be really cold so I had gloves on and a beanie so they really couldn't tell if I was white or black. If it was summer that would've been a problem. There would have been no way to disguise myself. I did my gig and was out. I did not leave my room. I didn't order room service. I was just terrified. They had the Confederate flag on their bikes that said KKK Biker Convention."

The TOBA boasted many now forgotten comedy teams: Buck and Bubbles, Crackshot and Hunter, Midnight and Daybreak, Step 'n Fetchit, Chuck and Chuckles, Stump and Stumpy, Moss and Frye, Pen & Ink, and Pot, Pans & Skillet; not to mention the odd pairing of Leonard Reed (also of Pen & Ink) and ex-heavyweight champion Joe Louis, where Joe engaged in a hilarious mock boxing routine. The tour also created many enduring stars. One was a man known for a classic routine and a strange name.

PIGMEAT MARKHAM

Dewey Markham was born in Durham, North Carolina on April 18, 1904. Because much of the comedy in his era involved heavy sexual overtones, Markham's stage name "Pigmeat" was suggestive of something not found in a jar on a liquor store counter. His career began in 1917 as a dancer for Bessie Smith on the Southern "race circuit." He went on to perform with the likes of Milton Berle, Eddie Cantor, and Red Buttons in burlesque shows and worked on the Andrews Sisters' radio show as Alamo the cook.

Markham stayed in blackface until public pressure forced him out of it after World War II. Turned out he was darker than the makeup he was using. Since dark brothers weren't "in" back then, maybe this was Pigmeat's way of "lightening."

He played the Regal in Chicago, The Howard in Washington, D.C., and the Apollo in Harlem, and became a king of comedy in the 1950s. Markham made numerous appearances on Ed Sullivan's *Toast of the Town* variety show, but it was his recording of *Here Comes the Judge* that would secure his place in comedy history. It became a top twenty hit for the Chicago blues record label Chess, and thanks to Sammy Davis Jr., he did guest cameos on NBC's hit *Rowan & Martin's Laugh-In*. Comedian/Writer Brad Sanders met Markham in the '70s.

"I saw him at the Regal Theater—live, then later on when 'Laugh-In' came on and Sammy Davis Jr. gave him that break, I went backstage and watched him and he seemed like a very, not sad, but very no-nonsense kind of guy. You weren't going to come back there playing, rapping and joking with him. I was going to talk to him. I spoke to him and the way he spoke to me let me know don't be bothering him."

Pigmeat Markham died on December 13, 1981.

Mystro Clark: "Another brother, who back in the day had to go through a lot just to entertain people. Anybody from that era, who made it and we're still talking about them to this day did twice as much as we did. So I credit him."

Within three years of the stock market crash of 1929 the TOBA was over. Soon thereafter in 1935, businessman Frank Schiffman merged with then-Apollo Theater owners Morris Sussman and Sidney Cohen and made the place the top spot in Harlem for talent. The Amateur Night became an institution: a performer would rub the Apollo "good luck" log, hit that stage, and more than likely suffer through a room filled with black folks cupping their hands and simultaneously letting out a wave of disapproval. The Apollo crowd loved to boo wannabes at the first whiff of neophyte aroma.

Comedian/Actor, Ricky Harris: "The audience warmed up on their booing before the act got introduced. The second you opened your mouth, it was like, 'Boo! Boo! Boo, you, nigga—boo!'"

Similar to the Keith-Orpheum circuit (started by theater owner B. F. Keith in association with Martin Beck's Orpheum Circuit in 1893 to supplant minstrelsy with vaudeville and organize the run made by black performers), Schiffman also imposed language restrictions on his comedians. There would be no foul language. This was a family theatre. No "damns." No "hells." And if you said "ass" you better be talking about a donkey.

TELL US ABOUT YOUR APOLLO EXPERIENCE

Richard of Richard & Willie: "The first time I moved to the 'A' circuit my manager called me to say, 'Richard, you're going into the Apollo with Nancy Wilson, Cannonball Adderley, Joe Williams, and Roberta Flack.' These were all heavyweights. I'm a nobody just working in the local nightclubs. So they had a meeting at the hotel to decide how they were going to open the show. So I learned when you don't know what's going on keep your big mouth shut. So I sit there, didn't say a word during this meeting with all these heavyweights. Cannonball Adderley sits there and asks my manager in front of me, 'Why is this guy here? He ain't contributing a damn thing. Maybe he shouldn't be here.' He was serious and I'm thinking this fat sucka done put me down in front of my manager and my manager had never seen me work. I'm there on reputation. Oh, I hated him. So the night of the show I said to myself, I said I'm going to show them why I'm here. I'm going to have the show of my life. So I did. On the way out, guess who's the first person to wink at me and hug me? It was Cannonball. He said, 'I see why you're here. You and that dummy's a muthaf*#ka.'"

In the early years, the Apollo was home to many comics: from the bigger names—Mantan Moreland, Pigmeat Markham, Dusty Fletcher, John "Spider Bruce" Mason, and Tim Moore; to the middle names—Leonard Reed, Ralph Cooper, and Willie Bryant; to the names only aficionados know—Crackshot Hackley, Johnny Lee Long, John "Rastus" Murray, and Spo-Dee-O-Dee. And then there was the one who bridged the traditional black character stage persona with the loose cannon, with more to say than time allows.

Madd Marv: "The funniest black female comedian ever and there has yet to be another black female comedian to touch what she was capable of or what she did."

Joey "J-Dub" Wells: "I'm still actually trying to find more stuff that I can sit down and listen to and appreciate her on my own. Y'know what I'm sayin; in my house. I've only seen some clips of her on TV and I think she's brilliant. She walked on that stage and told that story dressed like that and Moms Mabley wasn't a looker, but by the clips that I've seen she walked out there and commanded that stage and did it. So I respect her game and I want to know more about her."

JACKIE "MOMS" MABLEY

On March 19, 1894, Transylvania County's Brevard, North Carolina gave birth to its funniest citizen, Loretta Mary Aiken. One out of eleven children, she was eleven years old when her father was killed in an overturned truck explosion. Her mother died later after being plowed into by a mail truck. Before she was thirteen, little Loretta had been raped twice, one of her attackers the white sheriff of her beloved hometown. As lack of luck would have it, each rape resulted in children that she left with her grandmother to raise. She went off to Cleveland, Ohio to live with a minister's family; the minister seemed to manage to keep his hands to himself.

It was during this period that she learned how to sing and dance, and she met the man who literally gave her his name, her boyfriend, local entertainer Jack Mabley. She was content to give Mabley a hard time, as their relationship was a rocky one; but after her brother complained about her newfound profession as a "comedienne," she took Mabley's name as hers for the stage. The origin of "Moms" is unknown, but assumed to be from her tendency to mother the young males of other vaudeville revues.

She was discovered by the husband and wife team of Butterbeans and Susie and toured with them in 1921, did *Miss Bandana* in 1927, brought *Fast and Furious: A Colored Revue in 37 Scenes* to Broadway along with writer Zora Neale Hurston in 1931, and made her film debut in 1933's *Emperor Jones* (where she temporarily abandoned the old woman persona).

Moms became a solo female stand-up act when such a thing didn't even exist. At the time they called it monologue humor.

Mark Prince: "She would be one of those ones who would just sit back and talk endlessly. The jokes were joke-jokes, but she didn't say them in a joke-joke manner."

Mabley played the part of an older woman long before she herself was actually out of her twenties. It was this appearance and its broad acceptance that enabled her to spew some of the most insightful material of her day. That persona gave her license to broach subjects that would be considered too highfalutin' and sassy for a younger woman.

Between the years of 1939 into the 1960s Moms appeared on the Apollo stage more than any other performer and earned up to ten thousand dollars per week. She became so successful she performed at famed Carnegie Hall and took her career to another level when she began recording "party records" for the Chess label.

Fuel 2000 Records CD cover of Comedy Ain't Pretty *by the incomparable, first lady of black stand-up, Jackie "Moms" Mabley.*

Rudy Ray Moore: "She did rise up after Chess Records out of Chicago recorded her."

Her 1960 debut LP, *The Funniest Woman in the World*, went gold; her next, *Live at the U.N.*, made Billboard's Top 20. She cut an LP at the Chicago Playboy Club in 1961, entitled—what else?—*At the Playboy Club*. She appeared in the movie *Amazing Grace* in 1974 and just when it looked like she'd go on forever Jackie "Moms" Mabley passed away, on March 23, 1975 in White Plains, New York.

Richard of Richard & Willie: "I was on a show that 'Moms' was on and Moms was in the latter part of her career. She was pretty old. So they left me on the bill. I did like thirty-five, forty minutes, Moms did fifteen minutes, because that's all she could do; sit down and do that, but she drew the crowd, but I was able to warm them and she'd do her bit. I think she passed away about six months later, but the woman was still funny."

LAS VEGAS

Las Vegas in the 1940s held such hope and promise that it embodied the old adage: if it's too good to be true, it is. The "Mississippi of the West" was nothing more than a hick town inhabited by the same mentality that still brooded that the Confederacy had lost. Talk about segregation—the blacks who actually lived in Vegas, in other words the maids, janitors, and porters, were restricted to residing in Westside with its outhouses, shacks, and dirt roads. Visiting show folk bunked down there as well. Where else? This was the town that had an entire swimming pool drained because Sammy Davis Jr. had taken a dip in its sparkling pure water. And even though Sammy and many other black entertainers like him had made the place a bundle of money by attracting the "suckers" long enough to clip them of Junior's college fund, a star at the magnitude of Nat King Cole could still be turned away at the front entrance with a biting string of epitaphs ending in the N word. Not to mention the fact they had to stand outside until it was time to perform, since there were obviously no dressing rooms for coloreds.

Vegas was showbiz timed to the last nanosecond: pour free booze to prep 'em for the fleecing, provide cheap steaks so they won't feel the sting of a meal tab, then shuffle the hicks into a showroom for a break from the gambling so they don't stop to think how they have to take out a second mortgage as soon as they get back to their home in suburbia. Once this formula was in place, nobody, especially the components of this sophisticated pick-pocket operation, could meddle with it.

> **Comedian/Writer/Actor, Franklyn Ajaye:** "I remember the first time I opened up (for the Pointer Sisters) and I ran a couple of minutes overtime and the people at the casino set me straight. They put a gun to my head and threatened to blow my brains out if I did that again...no, just joking. No, but they did let me know that that was unacceptable because they had those shows programmed to get those people in the casinos. You have got to hit it right on the money. So I said give me a minute warning and I'd wrap it up wherever I'm at because it's not about the show. It's about the gambling."

When it comes to the subject of Vegas integration, the much-maligned Sammy Davis Jr. deserves a great deal of credit for getting many things changed in Vegas for blacks, along with his hammer-carrying friend Frank Sinatra, a veritable icon of the town and one who refused to play places that banned Davis. The Will Mastin Trio, consisting of Sammy, his play "uncle" Will Mastin and his real father, Sammy Davis Sr., were able to bunk up with gambling privileges at the Last Frontier in 1955. Soon other stars were getting similar treatment.

Harry Belafonte also helped integration by jumping into pools, placing bets, and charming gamblers until the racist casino bosses finally realized that a bonafide superstar roaming around made people want to spend more, to have illusions of living the good life like the star they were trying to impress did. If they'd only known.

Segregation ruled the day in Vegas until the Moulin Rouge Agreement. This document, drawn up between city officials and the heads of the NAACP, destroyed the long-standing racial barriers that divided that city by skin color. A mass protest march was strategically planned for March 1960 during the Rat Pack Summit. With Sammy, Frank, Dean Martin, Peter Lawford, and Joey Bishop descending upon the town, casino owners knew when they were in a tight bind. It was either relent, giving blacks the same access whites had to the full casinos, or let millions slip through their fingers, as liberals would undoubtedly view casinos keeping niggers in their place as a bad thing.

The agreement itself was named after the first integrated hotel and casino in Las Vegas. Erected in 1955 near Westside under the ownership of an East Coast Jewish syndicate and the former boxer Joe Louis, whites and blacks were able to see the same acts at the Moulin Rouge that appeared on the Strip after they'd finished working. All the black headlining acts hung out there out of necessity and camaraderie.

Sammy Davis, Jr. with the Luscious Dancers (left to right: Alicia Parks (Littleton), Lupe Ladino, Lua and Stephanie Parks (Nweke) at the Hollywood Palladium in 1982.

That paradise lasted six months—done in by poor management, underfunding and a hostile local climate. It reopened a year later under new ownership and reclosed because blacks were being charged more for drinks at the bar than whites. Time to go.

WERE YOU EVER RUN OUT OF A CLUB OR A TOWN?

Keith Morris: "No, I kick myself out of them."

Leslie: "I got kicked out of a hotel for smoking weed."

Jay Phillips: "Not to my face."

Dannon Green: "I got kicked out of a club for punching somebody in the face and the police were getting ready to come get me and I had to roll. He called me a 'nigga' on stage and I was too new to understand how to handle it so I cold cracked him."

Smokey Deese: "I've been kicked out of a club and I had to run out of a town because I had a warrant."

Gerard: "Yeah, I'll be working at the Cleveland Improv this week for the first time in like four years. I was banned from the club. I can only be in the club as long as I'm on stage and when I say, 'Good night,' I have to leave the club."

Al Toomer: "It happened at Luna Park in West Hollywood, a white waitress I was about to get with; one night her damn boyfriend was there, but he didn't hear me pat her on the ass and say, 'What's up, baby?,' but she tried to play it off by telling the owners that I was harassing her. Next thing I know two white boys come up asking me to leave and never return. I didn't just walk out I was escorted out under both elbows."

How Low Can I Go?

CHAPTER 11

"Why do we have hair in the crack of our ass
and we don't need it there?"
— AL TOOMER

It had been established early on that blacks and whites had different comedic tastes.

Comedian, Jemmerio: "A black audience is harder and you've got to come more real with them. A white audience, they're simple. You can spit at them and it's funny."

Not to mention, whites were at ease with the stereotypical black image and of course most blacks found the exaggerated coon repulsive and loathsome.

Comedian/Actor/Writer, Reynaldo Rey: "I guess it was the way they talked and looked at that time, but that old eye-bucked, greasy, inarticulate, quiver-lipped, oh, Lawd. That Sambo shit; I couldn't handle it."

This became a problem for live shows in mixed settings; blacks would often laugh in places whites found poignant. So theaters with segregated seating adopted a policy where blacks (who were placed in the rear), were told not to laugh until they heard some sign of acceptance from Caucasian patrons.

Gerard: "They don't laugh like they should. They clap a great deal, but they don't laugh. They're used to clapping and showing appreciation a whole other way."

Ian Edwards: "They'll never just get out of their seats and run around the room."

Because of this divide in what was deemed funny, black record labels were established to give that audience authentic black humor and make a niche audience buck to boot.

Okeh Records was started in 1921, catering specifically to Negroes with the boast of having "Original Race Records" (not the coon songs with the offensive lyrics altered). But it was music publisher Harry Pace who founded the very first black-owned label, Black Swan Company. Soon Paramount, Victor, Pathé, Emerson, and Columbia jumped onto the trend and vaudevillians Butterbeans and Susie were recorded. The bickering, earthy husband and wife team put out records such as *I Need a Hotdog for my Roll* and *A Married Man's a Fool If He Thinks His Wife Don't Love Nobody but Him.*

Comedy got its real push in blues recordings, mainly because things could be sung that would make most decent folks blush if they were said.

John Witherspoon: "Black people say, 'Now wait a minute, nigga. What the f*#k you talking about?' White folks ain't gonna laugh at it to begin with, but black people give you at least five minutes before they say, 'Get the f*#k out of here, muthaf*#ka.'"

Black Swan Records was sold to Paramount in 1924. From there recorded "comedy" came from bandleaders: Cab Calloway and piano player Fats Waller in the '30s; Louis Jordan in the '40s. Then in the '50s a no-name musician/singer made the move to full-time comedian and recorded for Dooto Records, opening the door to what would come to be known as "party records."

Jay Phillips: "Redd Foxx is one of my Kings of Comedy, man"

Deon Cole: "Anybody doing anything right now, they're doing Redd Foxx."

REDD FOXX

Born December 9, 1922 in St. Louis, Missouri, John Elroy Sanford was raised by his mother and grandmother in Chicago, Illinois after his electrician father, Fred, ran off and left the family when little Elroy was only 4 years old. He quit high school, after attending for a year, to play in a washtub band, and moved to New York in 1939. Rejected by the military, he performed in a tramp band act at the Apollo Theater with Jimmie Lunceford. For a while he was even a porter working alongside Malcolm X. He was known by his co-workers as "Chicago Red" and Malcolm was "Detroit Red." From 1947–1951 Foxx teamed up with comedian Slappy White, and in 1956 he recorded his first "party record" for Dooto.

Tom Dreesen and Redd Foxx backstage going over Redd's new clean jokes for "A Night Under the Stars" at Caesar's Palace in Las Vegas, 1978. (He bombed and reverted to his dirty material midway through the set as the offended audience walked).

Rudy Ray Moore: "In the early '50s I was starring over Redd Foxx until he got his break. And Dootsie Williams of Dooto Records recorded him and then he blew up and then he went down to Las Vegas and worked down there until he passed."

But before springing from his mortal coil Foxx recorded fifty such albums.

Roger Rodd: "I was in eighth grade, and he was such an underground comic back then he couldn't get any regular work because he was so quote unquote dirty. And if you listen to the stuff he said now it's tame by today's standards."

Foxx had more to worry about beyond public perception.

Rudy Ray Moore: "(Dootsie) didn't pay Redd Foxx. Redd sued him. He owed Redd somewhat of a million dollars. When he got through with the trial he had seventy thousand dollars and that was the end of it. Redd took that and went on about his business."

1964 found Redd on *The Today Show* with Hugh Downs in the morning and on *The Tonight Show with Johnny Carson* late at night, but despite this success, Redd loved talking dirty. This, coupled with an ill-informed public image of a slick city Negro brandishing a razor in one hand and a pistol in the other, forced Redd Foxx back into nightclubs; opening up his own spot, the Redd Foxx Club on LaCienega in Los Angeles in the late '60s.

Then in 1969 he played Uncle Bud, a junk dealer, in *Cotton Comes to Harlem* and life changed. That character was the genesis for Fred G. Sanford and *Sanford and Son* ran on TV from 1972–1977. Foxx had finally made it and why not? In the previous decade America had experienced riots, assassinations, a full-scale civil rights movement, anti-war demonstrations, and KKK resurgence. So who cared about a scary black man on TV?

> **Mystro Clark:** "One of the first black comedians besides Flip Wilson that I remember looking at on a TV show. It was good to see black men on TV doing something that we could relate to in the '70s."

The show was an instant hit, but there was soon trouble in paradise when Foxx felt slighted by the network, NBC, and his producers. Why was white actor Carroll O'Connor's (Archie Bunker on *All in the Family*) dressing room bigger than his? How come his dressing room didn't have a window? Confrontations such as these were either quickly resolved or Redd Foxx would be missing a few days of work until they were.

No protest lasts forever, and as time marched on ratings met their inevitable slip and the show was canceled. That cancellation was premature and the network sucked up their frustration with Foxx and offered him the spin-off, *Sanford* (3/15/80–7/10/81), but like his interim effort *The Redd Foxx Comedy Hour* (half a season) in 1977 and *The Redd Foxx Show* (12 episodes) in '86 (both on ABC) nothing else seemed to work. In 1983 Foxx filed for bankruptcy. His free-spending ways were legendary and his attitude about putting cash away for a rainy day or leaving it for his kids was a simple one.

> **Tom Dreesen:** "He said, 'I came into this world broke. I'm going out broke. I'm spending every goddamn dime I make. Ain't gonna be no fighting about who gets the car? Who gets the house? Ain't no f*#kin' car. Ain't nobody give me no f*#kin' house.' And he did it."

The IRS seized his Las Vegas home and many of Redd's personal belongings in 1985 claiming he owed the agency in excess of three million dollars. Redd Foxx died of a heart attack October 11, 1991, on the set of his CBS show *The Royal Family*.

> **Keith Morris:** "Hollywood killed him, not Hollywood; the Internal Revenue killed him."

Dooto Records had been an outlet and exposure vehicle for Foxx, Rudy Ray Moore and others, but it was far from perfect. Owner Dootsie Williams is remembered by Moore:

> "Dootsie Williams never give me a dime with the exception of the $100 he paid me when I recorded the album, but I have two albums on the label and I have never received a penny from them. He just didn't pay."

Ventriloquist Richard Stanfield of Richard & Willie also recalls Dootsie as "a heavy set, light-skinned, Creole-looking guy; very good businessman. He was into gold and real estate. He was the first black millionaire I ever met and he gave me some good advice. He said, 'Richard, nothing lasts forever. Save your money.' and he was right."

Richard & Willie recorded on the label, an arrangement that Stanfield said was tainted when he finally read the contract he'd neglected to look over when he originally signed it.

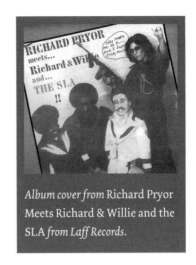

Album cover from Richard Pryor Meets Richard & Willie and the SLA *from Laff Records.*

> "At the time I signed that I was in my 20s. I should have never signed it. It's the most horrible contract. You read that contract you say you must have been an idiot. No, I was a young man who was excited about being in show business six months and I knew I'd get a record out, because this man had put out records on Redd Foxx and a lot of people, but did I know anything about contracts—no. Did I make a few bucks? Yeah! Very few bucks. For every dollar I got I probably should have gotten ten dollars. I made ten times more money at Laff Records with Louis and David Drozen."

Laff Records was started in the early '60s by Louis Drozen and was where Richard Pryor first made his mark with recordings like *Show Biz, Rev. Durite, Are You Serious???, Richard Pryor Meets Richard & Willie and the SLA, Pryor Goes Foxx Hunting, Craps, Down and Dirty, The Wizard of Comedy, Who Me? I'm Not Him, Black Ben the Blacksmith, Insane, Holy Smoke,* and *Outrageous.*

Many of these were compilations with other artists such as Redd Foxx thrown in to supplement the recording. Laff featured other comedians on their roster: Wildman Steve (*Eatin' Ain't Cheatin'*), Jimmy Lynch (*Nigger Please*), Lawanda Page (known then as simply "LaWanda"—*Watch it Sucker!*), Richard & Willie (*Comedy Roots,* along with Redd Foxx), Redd Foxx, Slappy White (who had recordings with Redd Foxx, but also on his own such as *Slappy White for Vice-President: It's Better to Run With a Black Man Than From One*).

It all began when Drozen bought a jewelry store from Harold Maybelle on Fifth and Broadway in downtown Los Angeles. Somebody went to Drozen about putting record racks near the entrance of the store, inside where people could buy albums on consignment and he'd make a profit. He did it and after attending a Leroy & Skillet performance and subsequently recording their album *Two or Three Times a Day,* Drozen recorded their fire dancer, Lawanda Page.

> **Richard of Richard & Willie:** "Louis was the father and the brains behind the organization. I liked Louis a lot. He might have screwed me, but I liked him. Personality wise, I liked him. He was like a father figure. So was Dootsie Williams, like a father figure, but Louis, he ran a good company. They knew how to sell

records, I can say that. They knew how to run radio ads across the country. They got my records moving."

In 1969 Louis was joined by his son David, who before long had learned all he could on how to make a room with about a dozen or so drunks sound like a room full of them. He moved up to producer and was saddled with most of the work that Louis was getting too old to perform. Then Stax Records paid Pryor an advance of $250 thousand to do his star making album, *That Nigger's Crazy*; he gained an additional one million dollars signing with Warner Bros., who actually released the album when Stax suddenly closed in '74.

> "I still had a lot of Richard Pryor tape and continued to buy tape because while he was working road gigs club owners would record those performances and with his permission for extra money that they gave him to buy white powder they sold me those tapes, which is why in a lot of the early albums you hear unmatched sound, because one ten-minute bit could have been done in Atlanta, Georgia and another one could have been done in Philadelphia."

Drozen had no idea how much the club owners were giving Pryor since he bought the tapes from Richard's drug dealer (who will remain nameless). David would go to the dealer's apartment in Hollywood and listen to the tapes.

> "In the middle of the coffee table was a pile of cocaine and a gun. So we'd listen to the tapes and we would decide on an amount and I would take a check with me before I went because I knew I was going to buy the tapes. If they were good enough for him to call me up and say, 'Got 'em,' they had to be good. After we'd negotiate an amount we would leave for the bank with his gun in a paper bag. That's how many of those albums came to be. The one that comes most to my memory is *Are You Serious?*, which is the one where the train is going through his (Pryor's) head. What I would do is every time Warner Bros. would release a movie or a Richard Pryor album, I would release one and market it on the heels of their release. So that album came out with the release of *Silver Streak*. So that's how that album came to be."

Laff kept plugging away with less hands-on participation from Louis Drozen, who still wanted his recognition and went from producer to executive producer. David carried on in the shadows until working with family became unbearable to him. In 1984 David left Laff and started his own label—Uproar.

Richard of Richard & Willie: "Laff went into receivership. That's what happened. I was notified and I went down because all the records they had manufactured were on the floor in the warehouse. I should've hired an attorney right there and then to put a lien on everything. That's what Richard Pryor did and I didn't do it being naïve. I could've got control. The SLA records, they have a lot of them there and Richard Pryor's lawyers got all of them because I didn't protest."

There was still some unsettled business which put the Drozens at cross hairs and in a legal suit. The son sued the father and Thanksgiving dinner was never the same. Reconciliation took place before the passing of Louis Drozen, but the Laff Records that he'd built was but a memory.

WHAT IS THE DIFFERENCE BETWEEN A BLACK AUDIENCE AND A WHITE AUDIENCE?

Dannon Green: "Color."

A. J. Jamal: "A white audience, they all paid. A black audience was comped, VIP'd, guests, catch-me-on-the-next-one, you-owe-me-one. So I say eight percent of a black audience is paid and the rest you're expecting them to get the drinks, but they ain't gonna get no drinks. You could have a no-drink minimum and they ain't gonna get no drinks."

Cedric the Entertainer: "White people will pay. Their credit cards will go through and they sit up front and it's great. Black people—they want the hook-up. They will wade out from the back as you pull up to go into the venue and they will go, 'Ced, let me get in.' You'll go, 'Is it just you?' He'll go, 'Naw, it's all the way to the dude in the blue shirt.' 'Sixteen of y'all is what you're saying you want to get in.'"

Geoff Brown: "There's a net. You have a net when you work with white people. With niggas there's no net and there's spears and lions and tigers if you fall."

Sherri Shepherd: "They (whites) will listen and give you a chance even if you're not doing well. Black people are like predators, they would jump on you. There you are like a lamb with the blood and the tigers are circling."

Eddie Griffin: "Black audiences are in the show; not just observing the show. They partake in the festivities. White audiences are cerebral."

Comedian/Actor, Darrel Heath: "A white audience makes a comic write. A black audience makes a comic perform."

Thea Vidale: "A black audience does not think. It's not one you take a chance to broaden your scope. White audiences will think about what you said, digest it and bust out laughing; even if it's a delayed reaction. Sometimes black people will write it off rather than listening to what you say."

Talent: "Well, the black audience is more real, more judgmental, shorter attention span. The black audience don't have time to give you twenty minutes to get your shit together on stage. Money is different to us. Twenty dollars is different in a black hand than in a white hand. The majority of white hands— twenty bucks—they can throw that away. I'll get it again. Black hand is holding that f*#kin' twenty tight. Man, what if I go in here and the shit ain't funny?"

Sinbad: "Laughter is laughter. It doesn't make a difference what color is out there, but there's some things I won't say when the audience is major white because they'll laugh at it, but they don't know why they're laughing at it. And I'm not going to have you laugh at us. You can laugh with us, but I'm not going to have you laugh at us."

Leslie: "You don't have to curse as much with white people. You don't have to do as much to get the joke across. Like with black people you damn near have to set yourself on fire on stage."

Jay Phillips: "We come to the club with an attitude as opposed to I'm coming to be entertained. We need to be entertained instead of wanting to be entertained."

Keith Morris: "A black audience—it's hard to make them laugh. A white audience, they'll sit there and watch you and after you get off the stage they'll tell you how great you was. With a black audience, they'll judge you before you open your mouth up."

Mark Prince: "A black audience puts me to the test more. They want me to be well-rounded. They want me to do my best. Black audiences are not going to let me go out there and become famous, not on their account or their accord anyway half-ass. If you see a black comedian who's made it and he's half-ass—that's because he was doing white rooms first."

Tommy Chunn: "Black people love performance. White people love wit."

Shaun Jones: "Black people feel as though we always got something to prove. I don't know this cat so he must not be funny. You've got to prove yourself to me. I've paid my $5.99. You've got to prove to me that you're worthy of my teeth being shown."

Daran Howard: "Black people want to feel you. I think white people are really just used to coming to the club and wanting jokes. Black people just want to feel you and if they feel you you can get away with a lot of stuff that really you wouldn't get away with."

Pierre: "A white audience; they're willing to go longer on the ride of a joke. You can do a long premise with a white audience. They're willing to sit there and listen to it. They want you to still be funny, but you don't have to be as funny as quickly. Black people, it's like, 'okay, nigga. The economics, I really can't afford to be here with my woman and pay this parking and they're too high on these drinks. I want to laugh now.' A black audience gives you a two-joke minimum."

Melanie Comarcho: "After the show the white audience will come up to you and tell you how funny you were, what made them laugh or whatever. The black audience, I don't know. I could have a really good show and they're laughing all the way through it and then after the show they're nodding their head like 'yeah.'"

Marquez the Greatest: "Black people make you funny. White people make you rich."

Git In Where
You Fit In

CHAPTER 12

"There is no comedian in the world
that is for everybody."
— TOM DREESEN

The Tab Hunter '50s saw virtually no blacks on TV, heard few blacks on radio, and participation in films was limited to supporting roles for white stars and near stars. African-Americans were hardly represented at all except by proxy as white comedians were up to their old tricks—stealing black routines and fraying black nerves.

Brad Sanders: "A lot of those old comics were bitter because Milton Berle, Bob Hope, Jackie Gleason, and others would come down to the club, sit there with note pads, write their stuff down and then they go on and do national TV with their stuff."

However, television wasn't ready for some of the rawer, filthy-minded material comedians the likes of Redd Foxx, Slappy White, and Moms Mabley were telling in nightclubs; they were free to do so since the audiences whose minds they were polluting were also black. Constitutionally, the first amendment was upheld for foul-mouthed comics. That was until Lenny Bruce opened his "sick, dirty" trap.

LENNY BRUCE
Leonard Alfred Schneider was a brother of another color and that was his problem—he was

white, and the first white comedian to gain mainstream notoriety doing and saying the same thing black comedians were. That, my friends, was the scariest thing America could possibly imagine.

Rudy Ray Moore: "Lenny Bruce was the comedian that come out in the white market doing the X-rated stuff that I do so I have to take my hat off to him. He didn't back up. He went on and did his thing."

Richard (& Willie): "I put Lenny Bruce and Richard Pryor in the same category."

This new comic voice as seen on TV's *Playboy after Dark* with Hugh Hefner and in magazine interviews, had college kids and hipster wannabes chomping at the bit to check out this fresh, abrasive cat preaching truth and justice and add the decadent experience to their life resumé. Lenny was rolling and became a target for corrupt local law enforcement. His heroin addiction opened him up to extortion—it was a bribery shakedown in '61 that was the beginning of the end for Bruce. He named names.

In all honesty, he didn't make it any easier on himself, either, by being a Jew ridiculing the all-powerful Catholic Church and breaking many long-standing laws with his use of nasty verbiage. Lenny was the first to curse in front of polite company, meaning white folks. He'd talk as profanely as if it was just him and the needle-marked drummer from one of the strip clubs Bruce cut his teeth in, shooting up in the alley. No subject was off limits and once they started arresting him for running his mouth, there was definitely nothing he wouldn't say since they were going to nail him with some obscure, antiquated law anyhow.

Madd Marv: "He continued to fight for what he felt was right. He would say whatever he wanted to say no matter who would be offended, and just talk about how his life was reflected in a humorous way. I think that he's a great comedian because he was purely ahead of his time. The stuff if he did it now, nobody would give two shits about, but back then it was so outlandish. He was no walk in the park."

They took away his cabaret card (killing all employment) and forced him into a corner of never-ceasing court appearances and mounting legal fees. Convicted for obscenity in New York, the end result was a tired, bitter soul who sought relief for the final time in his trusty syringe. Lenny bid farewell to showbiz and the bastards who ran him out of it in 1966. He never legally appealed his conviction, but was posthumously pardoned in 2003 by Governor George Pataki.

Shang: "Trendsetter, man. He took chances. It killed him, but he took chances and a lot of comics didn't."

Black comedians were figuratively plowing their own ground; non-offensive yet innovative; performing in front of white audiences, but not just telling jokes. They were looking dead at the audience and speaking their minds; not angry minds, mind you, but stories and points of view molded not from minstrelsy or cooning, but of their own making. The most popular and enduring of this front line triad—Nipsey Russell, Slappy White, and Timmie Rogers, became fixtures in the most American of institutions—the game show.

NIPSEY RUSSELL

Nipsey Russell was born in Atlanta, Georgia, in 1924 and was six years old when he first started singing, dancing, and serving as MC for the children's shows he'd stage. Known to today's audiences as "that brother who did all the rhyming," Nipsey first discovered his flair for poetry at the University of Cincinnati where he earned his B.A. in English. When he started out on the chitlin' circuit in the '40s he wore business suits and a porkpie hat.

Russell sharpened his skills in clubs throughout the Midwest and East Coast in the late 1940s and the early 1950s and often appeared at the Baby Grand in New York. He played the normally white-only bastion—the Catskills, challenging his audience's intelligence with his casual use of an extensive vocabulary—as well as the Apollo Theater. But Nipsey never wanted to be known as a "black comic" (no matter how much his skin color kept giving him away). He felt his material was too universal to be squeezed into such a limited category.

His 1959 appearance on Jack Paar's *Tonight Show* led Nipsey to a supporting role on the 1961 sitcom *Car 54, Where Are You?* and this exposure got him regular guest spots on talk shows and, of all things, game shows. As a guest panelist on *To Tell the Truth*, his quick wit, snappy repartee, and impromptu limericks earned him the title of "The Poet Laureate of Comedy," and regular work on *Hollywood Squares* and *Match Game*. Nipsey Russell passed away in October 2005 at the age of 80.

> **Record executive, David Drozen:** "A great comedian and a great person."

> **Rudy Ray Moore:** "A fine comic."

> **Mark Curry:** "I liked Nipsey Russell. Every time I was in New York I would see Nipsey Russell. He was a veteran. I loved him. I'd always talk to him. He's talked to me on the streets of New York City about comedy. He was a veteran. I always ask veterans if there's anything I should do."

The next forerunner had long been misperceived due to his association with Redd Foxx, as a comedian of the hardcore blue comic variety, which he was, but he was also so much more.

SLAPPY WHITE

Born on September 20, 1921, Slappy White began in show business as part of a comedy act, the Two Zephyrs, teaming first with Willie Lewis and later with Redd Foxx from 1951–1955. They were raw, hard-hitting, and not exactly the favorites of white audiences. So Slappy made some adjustments and got a job on Dinah Washington's traveling variety show.

Timmie Rogers

Working in Las Vegas, he was one of the first black comedians to use topical humor in front of a mainstream crowd, bridging the gap of old school black comedy routines with his own material and social commentary.

Rudy Ray Moore: "Slappy White detested raw comedy, not X-rated but comedy that had the lilt of being sort of raw. He did clean comedy and he used to work the Playboy. So he did have that going until the years passed and he started working with Redd Foxx and Redd Foxx kept him going until he passed."

Several writers of his day referred to Slappy White as "the father of the integrated joke." Such a reputation positioned him to become one of the first comics of black descent to be booked into the white sanctuary—the Catskills. He later partnered with white comedian Steve Rossi, did numerous television guest-starring appearances, and toured extensively. Slappy White died November 7, 1995.

The final member of the triad showed America that a black comic didn't have to dress the part of the buffoon to make non-blacks laugh.

TIMMIE ROGERS

Timmie Rogers was a child performer who went on to vaudeville success in the 1930s, but never cared much for blackface. Primarily a singer and dancer, he made a good portion of his income as a songwriter, but gained his reputation for breaking the racial barrier by refusing to wear blackface and being the first black comedian in prime time television in 1949 on *Sugarhill Times*. Rogers' use of satire and social observations branded him "outspoken," but it didn't matter. Rogers stuck to his guns, and armed with the catchphrase "oh...yeah" uttered after about every punchline, it wasn't long before he changed the stereotypical image of the way black comedians traditionally performed. In 1957 he became the first comedian to headline the Apollo Theater and was active for years.

TIMMIE: "I just had a birthday last week, man—July the 4th."

DARRYL: "How old are you right now?"

TIMMIE: "90 f*#kin' years old. Older than pu*%y."

DARRYL: "Damn, that's old. That's real old."

Richard of Richard & Willie: "I remember Timmie Rogers being on the *Jackie Gleason Show* and his thing was 'oh yeah.' He was a forerunner; a groundbreaker."

The triad was complete. Three talented comedians with distinctly different styles changing the way America viewed black stand-ups. That was until a multitalented bundle of voices and characters hit the scene.

GEORGE KIRBY

Master impressionist George Kirby was born June 8, 1924 in Chicago, Illinois. When his boss at South Side Chicago's Club DeLisa caught him doing voices, George went from being the bartender/janitor to a one-year engagement. Following his Army stint in World War II, Kirby toured with Sophie Tucker, appeared on Ed Sullivan's *Toast of the Town*, and got booked in top notch spots around the country. Because he was an impressionist, going from black to white audiences was easier than if he were a stand-up. He used no foul language, sexual references, or overt social or racial commentary.

> **Rudy Ray Moore:** "He was an impressionist to end all impressionists and when he came on the stage it was all over."

It was all laid out for George Kirby until he was arrested in 1958 in a drug raid. He spent the next two years in the United States Public Service Hospital in Lexington, Kentucky for his addiction. Upon his release in1960, Kirby re-established himself in front of the same black audiences that gave him his initial taste of success. It wasn't long before he was back on the air with Ed Sullivan; making movies (Sammy Davis Jr.'s *A Man Called Adam*); and a regular on ABC's *The Copycats*, with fellow impressionists Rich Little, Marilyn Michaels, Frank Gorshin, Fred Travalena, and Charlie Callas.

His subsequent CBS sitcom, *Rosenthal and Jones*, only survived for several episodes. After that disaster, club dates dried up, guest spots on TV shows became nonexistent, and since he couldn't make ends meet by performing, Kirby turned to a more surefire way of pulling in a buck: drug dealing. He should've stuck to funny voices. In 1977 Kirby was arrested in Las Vegas for selling over a pound of heroin for twenty-six thousand dollars to an undercover officer. The times were so bad that even though he was out on bond and able to perform, his drawing power was a thing of the past and he would often only put fifty butts in the seats.

Within a year of his arrest, George Kirby, the wonder king who once pulled down thirty-eight thousand dollars a week headlining, was given a ten-year prison term. He was paroled three-and-a half years later and once again began his comeback: TV guests spots, club dates, charities, and schools so he could warn young people about the true dangers of drugs. He spoke beyond the health risks and pointed out how drugs could hold your life hostage.

In the early '90s he was diagnosed with Parkinson's disease and died on September 30, 1995 in Las Vegas, Nevada at the age of 71.

Like the Three Musketeers, the triad became the Four Horsemen as they rode steeds of unconventionality across the countryside. Still, they were black and their musings on the state of the state remained lighthearted and more along the surface. Society hadn't abandoned prejudice overnight. A black man still had to stay in his place, and there was little slack on the invisible rope around the Negro comic's neck.

White hecklers ran amok. How do you tell a white man or worse, his woman, to calm their butts down so you can continue your show? This matter was also a new wrinkle in the black comedian's presentation. Before, when white hecklers yelled out racial slurs, the comic could ignore it since they weren't looking out into the audience anyway. Because their very act was one of representation versus presentation, they were predisposed not to address any comments. Such an action would have destroyed the illusion of being there only to give a show, not share an experience.

What the country needed (whether it knew it or not) was a black comic that was completely removed from the old-time circuit: one who hadn't absorbed any of the traditional ways and thus had virtually no adjustments or alterations to concern themselves with. There was nothing wrong with the four horsemen, but their mounts had been seen in these parts before. True, they had different racing colors, but it was essentially the same old event with a few new twists and turns. Once you got used to it it was business as usual. That was until Dick Gregory stepped up to the mic.

DICK GREGORY

Roger Rodd: "There, is really the edgiest black comic who ever lived. What I like about Dick Gregory is when you listen to him he did very little comedy. He did a lot of social commentary and satire, but as a comic with balls nobody bigger, because of the time he was saying it we were on the tail end of segregation."

Sandy Brown: "I love what he did with the mind."

Comedian/Actor, Royale Watkins: "You're talking about somebody that can create the new world order within a word. Y'know, that's timeless right there."

In 1932 Dick Gregory was born in St. Louis, Missouri and raised in poverty by his mother. His father, whoever he was, was nowhere around. Gregory went to Southern Illinois University thanks to an athletic scholarship, and once he decided to become a comedian he also made the decision that he wasn't going to struggle on the chitlin' circuit until somebody "discovered" him by chance. So he worked his share of "real jobs."

"I worked at the post office, but I was working to keep from working. My wife was at University of Chicago so I never had bad times because she had a good job."

His goal was to play the top white clubs and make some real money. He sharpened his technique in the black clubs in Chicago in the late '50s, and in 1959 opened his own club called the Apex in Robbins, Illinois, for the sole purpose of working on the social satire he was discouraged from performing in black establishments. By 1960 he was performing at

Dick Gregory, comedienne Edwonda White, and Paul Mooney backstage in 1997.

the Roberts Show Club and had his share of hecklers as could be expected in his era. According to comedian Tom Dreesen, Gregory was prepared for them as well. Not just content to have heckler-handling lines in his arsenal, he prepared himself mentally by having his wife hurl insults at him while he was at home ('Shut up, nigger!' 'Get off the stage you no good muthaf*#ka') and each insult had to be met with a comeback. His wife thought he was crazy, but there was a method to his madness. Whenever a heckler was bold enough to speak up during a Dick Gregory performance, Dick was battle-ready and loaded for bear.

His big break came in 1961 when he replaced Professor Irwin Corey at the Playboy Club for one night. They had canceled the date when they discovered that the room had been sold out to a bunch of white Southern food conventioneers, but Gregory didn't get the memo. At 8 o'clock sharp he hit the stage of the Carousel Room and talked for more than four hours. He talked so long that Hugh Hefner booked him for two weeks at two hundred fifty dollars per week, and in effect integrated black comedy and made Gregory an overnight star. None too soon.

"Eighteen months before I hit it big I was making like sixteen hundred dollars for the whole year with a wife and family. Like thirty dollars a week. Then after I hit in the next eighteen months I made three-and-a-half million."

Time magazine wrote an article that Jack Paar read. He asked Gregory to come on in and was met with a rapid "no." Gregory initially passed on Paar's offer because vocalist Billy Eckstine had told him that Paar was no good: "They ain't never let a Negro sit down." In other words you could come on and do your little jokes, but there'd be no having a seat and chatting with Jack. Paar called back and insisted on a reason why not, Gregory told him, and Paar said he'd let Gregory sit down.

That was the first time in history a black man sat down on the couch...on a TV talk show. NBC got calls and Gregory got letters by the thousands from white people wanting to know more about black people. His salary jumped from two hundred fifty dollars per week to five thousand dollars a night and he made more than a few enemies with the older comedians questioning his rapid ascension and his methods of getting there. They accused him of theft and joke procurement.

> "I'm sure the ones in New York probably had some hang-ups and rightfully so. They out there, they been in there for a hundred years and some little punk ain't nobody ever heard of pops through and breaks and I'm sure they had some attitudes. I saw press where they was mad and all that kind of stuff; claim I stole their material."

His candid approach to race and social issues was unflinching and his non-judgmental style allowed him the freedom to straddle the middle of any issue; for even though he himself was black, he took the stance of the observer as opposed to the observed. White America was so enamored they simply had to have more.

> "My managers, called Broadcast Management, only had two acts. They had Philadelphia Philharmonic and Dick Gregory. So I do this book deal for a one million dollar advance. I was the hottest thing in the country and they wanted a book of humor. So I give them this biography and they were just blown away. They wanted me to name it something funny so when white folks came out to buy it they thought they were getting a joke book."

So in 1962 he released his book entitled *Nigger*. Reaction was mixed.

> "I had the right to name it what I wanted to name it so I decided that I was going to take this nigger snake and defang it and put it out there in everybody's face and I didn't realize it at the time until the homosexuals came out the closet; the whole thing would change. As long as you're hiding they got something on you. Let's bring this thing out of the closet—put it down front. Now, the reaction—it was horrible. Black folks would walk into the bookstore and say, 'I'd like one of them Dick Gregory whatchamacallits.' That's good, because up until then nobody ever conveyed about they didn't want to say the word, they didn't want to hear the word and when I look around today, white dudes waking up in the morning hi-fiving, 'You my nigga, baby,' I say—brilliant—that's what it was about. That fear will go away."

As the Civil Rights Movement advanced, so did Gregory's humor. He took "outspoken" to a new level for black performers—his tone got more cutting as the years wore on.

> **Brad Sanders:** "He took the politics of the day and talked about it in such a way where he really affected the mindset of the people of that era. And he was able to talk about things that were very, very painful and very real and put that twist on it that would make you laugh at it instead of cry about it or be angry about it all the time and it was very observational."

Dick Gregory also took on the role of real-life activist and gradually put comedy on the back burner, canceling concerts and acknowledging that he was more of a social commentator who used comedy as a tool to purvey his message instead of a comedian who utilized social commentary to get a laugh. In 1968 he was a write-in candidate for president of the United States in the hotly contested Nixon-Humphrey battle.

> "Humphrey was running against Nixon. Humphrey lost by 500 thousand so if I hadn't have been in the race...so to think a little poor black boy [could have] determined who the president was going to be in the most powerful nation in the world. Now I never got into the race to take votes away from nobody. I got into the race because I felt a lot of people might feel like me. I think the greatest right you have in America is the right to vote, but when they reduce the vote to less than three then that's not right and I just thought that maybe a lot of people out there that would like to vote for something other than the lesser of two evils and I was going to give them that."

This was historic also because it made Gregory (Freedom and Peace Party) and Eldridge Cleaver (Peace and Freedom Party) among the first black candidates for president to appear on the ballot. Others, such as Jesse Jackson, Al Sharpton, and Alan Keyes, never made the ballot, being stopped cold in the major parties' primary process.

His social activism took on another form in later years when Dick Gregory became consumed in nutrition, popularizing what became known as the Bahamian diet. But understand, Dick Gregory never fully abandoned the art form that made him popular and continues to travel throughout the world, performing an average of two hundred forty shows a year.

> **Tom Dreesen:** "He gave me the best advice that I pass on to this day. He told me that if you want to be a comedian you have to be passionate about it. You can't be mediocre about it. You gotta want it more than life itself, because it's gonna kick your ass. He was right—my wife left me three or four times, I ended up sleeping in an abandoned car, I hitchhiked to the Comedy Store, I'd beg to work for free. Another thing he told me was if you want to be a comedian then study the masters. Go to where those who are on the stages you want to be on are. Watch them perform, not to take their material. Watch the way they operate. If you were preparing to become a brain surgeon would you just study brain surgery? You'd go watch the brain surgeon operate."

Rodney Perry: "He's such an awesome presence. You feel like you're around more than a comic. He's like beyond a comedian. I think Dick Gregory's an awesome human."

DARRYL: "What's your connection between humor and the black church?"

GREGORY: "Well, the fact that that was the only humor I heard. TV wasn't invented when I was born. If you listened to the radio you heard Bob Hope and that white mentality. Black people laughed at him because that's the only thing they had, but it really didn't connect with me. There were no nightclubs in America except where you went to dance or drink and hear a blues singer. And I was too young to get in, but at church every Sunday you heard the preacher with brilliant humor and brilliant satire. He didn't walk up there to be funny, but there was nobody in the community who spoke as much as he did. Every Sunday they had two or three services, but all through the week people called on them to do things. They were informed with the news and back then the news wasn't as vast as it is now. But the preacher always knew because of the porters. The black folks that worked in the railroad would bring news back from California, Chicago, New York, or wherever. So when I look back now I always thought the strongest two forces in the history of America has always been the black woman and the black church. Always been that source of good, healthy, clean humor. And I'm not aware of it when I'm there it's when people ask me who was my idols, I have to say I don't have no idols in comedy. I mean the Nipsey Russells and them. I didn't know them. I never heard of them. They was in New York. Like I said, there were no black nightclubs in Chicago where I lived except the ones that had dancing and blues and what-have-you. So my wealth of feelings for humor is more than a comic, being a comedian and just telling jokes. The greatest laugh anyone's ever heard don't come from professional comedians. It comes from family and friends. And if you look back that wasn't the biggest thing we produced in the black community entertainment-wise. We produced musicians because of the church and singers because of the church. And at that time I never realized that white America didn't permit black folks to stand flat-footed and talk so black comedians were never used in a white nightclub. You could sing and dance and stop in between a dance and tell a funny joke like Sammy Davis or Pearl Bailey, but you couldn't walk out there flat-footed as a man, and that's why I appreciate Hugh Hefner. He's the first one who ever dared to bring a black person in to do comedy and that was me. And he didn't bring me in on no conditions. He wasn't even there that night when I came in. I got up on the stage at 8 o'clock and at 12 o'clock I was still talking and somebody went by the mansion and woke him up and said you need to come over and hear this. And I don't take pride in that. I think it's disgraceful that a white racist system would not let a black person stand flat-footed and talk. Because there have always been blacks that had that type of talent there just wasn't no place for them in America."

DARRYL: "So how did you get started in comedy?"

GREGORY: "You know where I really started comedy was in the Army and that was a threat. The guy said, 'You're either crazy or you're the funniest guy on the planet and if you're crazy we're gonna put you in jail. If you're the funniest guy I'll know tonight because you're going down to the PX and you're going to entertain.' That was the first time I ever walked up on a stage. And I got down there and did little silly, stupid stuff. I said, 'I got arrested today. The MPs caught me impersonating an officer. I slept until 12 noon' and all that kind of stuff. Soldiers went crazy. So after that I won the *All Army* competition and I was supposed to go to the *All Service* and the winner of that went on the *Ed Sullivan Show* and thank God I didn't...I won it, but I think they cheated because of my politics and they picked somebody else, but if they'd picked me and I did that Sullivan show I would have never made it because couldn't nobody told me that I wasn't ready for primetime. What I learned when I went into a little nightclub in Chicago was I learned timing. And the difference in my grandmother telling a joke, is timing. When you walk up on that stage it's timing. If you don't have that you can get off. People will laugh at you one time. That's what happened to me. When I went up into the nightclub I paid somebody to say this big comic just came to town from New York and he called me up and man was I funny. The guy hired me two weeks later and realized I wasn't funny. It's like you come by my house and hear my grandson playing the piano and say, 'wow man.' Now it's different when you go to a concert and you're paying seventy-five dollars to get in to hear him and so that's what it was. I mean to call you up that's one thing, but when you're working the slot as a comic people look at you different."

DARRYL: "You once showed me a suitcase with newspapers from all over the world. Were you always so well read?"

GREGORY: "In the black nightclub I wanted to use that in my act showing how silly the white press was and at that time I didn't know that the white press lied; didn't tell the truth, covered stuff up and was working for the same money people that control the world. When Siegfried and Roy up in Vegas, got attacked by the tiger, they go with the white press and how sad, how we should send a prayer for him, I see the black press—their headline was 'What took that tiger so long?' After all he is a wild beast. They should've jumped off and ate up the first twelve people in the front row. It's just a matter of looking at the news from a white point of view and then switching it with a black point of view; I mean I did that in black nightclubs. So what made me so good when I went in white nightclubs, in a white nightclub that cost big money to get in the white folks don't have time to sit through three shows. So them white comics they might come to town once or twice a year and they do the same thing over and over and that's why their act is so perfected. They do the same act over and over word for word for twenty, thirty years whereas I do it where a person could sit through all three shows and hear different jokes every show. So right now I can go and stand flat-footed and talk for hours, whereas in the white nightclubs to the people coming through they don't need nothing but like forty minutes and that forty minutes is so perfected it's just incredible."

DARRYL: "What was the turning point for you from being a comedian to an activist?"

GREGORY: "It wasn't. I been doing it all along. I just decided in 1973 I was getting out of show business. Because I thought it was unfair to nightclub owners to book me and advertise me and then something come up and I'm in jail. I didn't think it was fair."

DARRYL: "I know you still go around and do shows and tell jokes..."

GREGORY: "Oh, I never stopped doing jokes. I was doing speaking engagements. That's all together different than joking in a nightclub."

DARRYL: "Could you tell me about some of the camaraderie you had with some of the comedians coming up in the '60s?"

GREGORY: "I didn't really. I mean, I was working every night. I mean, Bill Cosby, Richard Pryor and them, they'd come sit at my feet and we'd laugh and talk. I'd give them pointers, but...I mean, I never hung out with entertainers; never went to parties with entertainers. My comrades were civil rights leaders. So I got more out of hanging out with Andy Young, Walter Young (Andy's brother), and Ralph Abernathy than I did with entertainers."

DARRYL: "Do you have any suggestions for today's comedians?"

GREGORY: "A comedian's got the right to be a comedian. I don't expect him to be a brain surgeon, know anything about the missile race or have read five of the top ten books out in America. I don't expect nothing. All I expect him to do is be funny. If I take a loved one of mine to a brain surgeon I don't expect that brain surgeon to be able to sing and dance. Is he or she a good brain surgeon?"

DARRYL: "What do you see in the future of Dick Gregory?"

GREGORY: "Every day when I wake up in the morning I think oh, what a beautiful morning, oh, what a beautiful day. I got a beautiful feeling that everything's going my way. That ain't even debatable. That old Baptist hymn *One Day at a Time*—story of my life—one day at a time, sweet Jesus."

Thanks to Dick Gregory and the four horsemen before him, the stage was set for more new-breed comedians to step forward and say their piece. One of these new idea merchants would not only make the nation turn a blind eye to his color (paper bag brown), but he'd also become the unthinkable—the symbol of American fatherhood.

BILL COSBY

Robert Townsend: "Bill Cosby was always one to really take his time and tell a story and get every little bit of storytelling out of the chunk and I think that's what I loved about Bill Cosby's work as a comedian."

Bill Cosby (far right) with Doreene Hamilton, executive director of the Guy Hanks/Marvin Miller TV and Screenwriting Program (founded by Bill and Camille Cosby) and writer Michael Ajakwe at USC, Los Angeles, 2000.

Ajai Sanders: "If Bill Cosby was a chemist he'd have all the right formulas to create great comedy."

He was born on July 12, 1937 in Philadelphia, Pennsylvania and met the characters, like Fat Albert, Old Weird Harold, and Mush Mouth, that he would later make fun of to great financial gain, in the Richard Allen projects of Germantown. He discovered that he was a funny storyteller while working as a bartender in Philly. The customers loved him so much that the wily owner put a chair on a table and had Cosby perform nightly. Cosby soon left the bar and headed over to New York, where in 1962 he started playing clubs like Village Underground, Café Wha? and the Gaslight Café in Greenwich Village.

Cosby avoided racial material, concentrating on family humor and biblical parodies. His charming, laidback, non-racial style went down easy with mainstream audiences and he was on his way after appearing on *The Tonight Show* in 1963.

Brad Sanders: "He was able to take just a man's observations of life and be a regular person and just turn the entire attitudes of the world around when it comes to black folks and he wasn't trying to change anybody's opinion. He loves his people. He tried to show black people as just being people as opposed to some category that somebody puts them in according to their own point of view."

Cosby's comedy albums were top ten-sellers and he made television history playing CIA agent Alexander Scott opposite Robert Culp in the series *I-Spy* ('65–'68), becoming the first leading male black actor on a weekly dramatic series. Cosby won two Emmys for his troubles. His animated Saturday morning series, *Fat Albert and the Cosby Kids* ran for twelve years and featured Cosby in live action giving life lessons and commenting on the choices made by the animated characters. He also encouraged children to discuss these same problems with people close to them.

In the mid-'70s Cosby co-starred in three comedy classic films with Sidney Poitier: *Uptown Saturday Night, Let's Do It Again,* and *A Piece of the Action.* He was a pitchman for Jell-O in much parodied commercials, boasting the goodness of pudding pops; and in 1984 Bill created *The Cosby Show,* which revitalized the sagging sitcom genre. The show stayed at the top of the Nielsen charts for the majority of the eight seasons it was on the air and garnered Cosby three Emmy awards. It was deemed the gold standard and litmus test for sitcoms to come due to its mass crossover appeal.

> **Writer, Michael Ajakwe Jr.:** "But Cosby didn't try to not be black. It was about upper middle class blacks, but they were very black. All the kids were black. They went to black colleges. The images in their house; the art was black. The artists that were on their walls were black. When his daughter had twins, what were the babies' names? Suzy and Johnny? No, Nelson and Winnie, as in Mandela. So that show was very black."

After its cancellation, Cosby returned to NBC as a sleuth, then reunited with his *Cosby Show* co-star Phylicia Ayers Rashad in the CBS sitcom *Cosby* with Doug E. Doug, Madeline Kahn, and T'Keyah "Crystal" Keymah. Off the set, Cosby later became an outspoken advocate of black parental responsibility, traveling and speaking in cities around the country.

> **Marc Howard:** "He's the most influential black comic, black actor ever. He has major, major influence. Man can sit there and call up and get a credit loan and put a bid on a damn TV network with the greatest of ease. Drop twenty million dollars on a college he didn't even go to and he sits on the Temple University board and helps pick the college coaches. Y'know and he's a damn comic; goes up on stage and tells jokes."

> **Madd Marv:** "I think he's good for what he did as far as opening up doors and letting you know that the black man has some media power in America."

> **Sinbad:** "I call Bill Yoda. He's that bad, man. He's got so much inside of him. He's the only man that I talk to; every time you talk to him you can walk away with something. It's a shame that some cats when they talk about who their favorite comics are not many cats say Cosby. And I say dude, y'all don't even know who this man is. Y'all slept on this guy. Bill writes a new hour right now to this day. And the funny thing is they try to play Bill like he's soft. Bill is from the other side of the tracks in Philly, man. Bill might knock these young brothers out. Y'all don't know who this man is."

Due to the ease and grace of a Bill Cosby blacks could now discuss topics that had nothing to do with being of African-American descent. The door was swung open and one of the first to emerge with color blind notions was Godfrey Cambridge.

GODFREY CAMBRIDGE

Richard of Richard & Willie: "I met him once at the Apollo. I complained to him about something about my show. I remember him telling me don't worry about it, he had the same complaint. I didn't know him beyond that, but he was a very talented person. I never seen him do stand-up. I just saw him in the movies and things like that."

Cambridge was born in Harlem in 1933, but got his primary schooling in Nova Scotia, Canada, living with his grandparents. He went to high school in Queens, New York in a practically all-white environment; practically because Godfrey was there. Admittedly he grew up sheltered from the fact that he was a black individual in a country where that carried certain rules and guidelines for survival and fundamental peace of mind. In the world he'd seen, there was no overt prejudice against him for the color of his skin and so when he reached the point of joining the larger, less congenial world he was slapped crisply across the face with the cold hard reality of his station and situation.

While a pre-med student at Hofstra College, Godfrey made the decision to go into show business and find out what being a Negro in America really meant. At first he was making headway as an actor, performing small parts in Off-Broadway shows, even winning an Obie Award in 1961 for his performance in *The Blacks*. Nevertheless, Godfrey wanted more freedom: the freedom stand-up offered.

Turns out that his unique upbringing was a comedy plus and his articulate, educated manner made his colorblind observations that much more authentic. They placed Godfrey Cambridge in the mainstream comedy line right behind Cosby. Melvin Van Peebles used his talents as the lead in the highly acclaimed box office success *Watermelon Man*. He followed that up playing police detective Coffin Eddie to Raymond St. Jacque's Gravedigger Jones in Ossie Davis' *Cotton Comes to Harlem* and its sequel *Come Back Charleston Blue*.

The parts came steadily and Cambridge appeared to be in it for the long haul. He'd even been tapped to play deposed dictator Idi Amin, when Cambridge suffered a fatal heart attack and died during the filming of *Victory at Entebbe* in 1976.

These seven comedians represented innovation in black comedy. Promoters are not big fans of innovation, and Civil Rights era or not, these comics were kind of scary in their new approach. Where the hell were the minstrel humorists when you needed them?

WHAT TYPE OF RACISM HAVE YOU EXPERIENCED IN COMEDY?

Katt Williams: "I don't even accept racism. It exists, but it doesn't even come into my realm of thinking. That's probably because I'm from Ohio where everything is different for you because you are in a black/white area always. So I never had any racism because white people liked me and I talked to white people."

Derrick Ellis: "I've been to clubs where I've had to hear the white boy's version of what they think about us. I've experienced that racism at some of the 'A' rooms."

Curtis Arceneaux of Arceneaux & Mitchell: "The clubs that are owned by Caucasians they take one or two of us through the door and the rest of us they treat like shit, but I can't remember ever being called a 'nigger' on stage."

White comedian, Darren Carter: "I was in Oakland and people were giving me love, saying things like, 'hey good job' and words of encouragement. So I'm like, whoa, this is cool. Everybody's going to be like this. Then I walked past this one guy and he said, 'Don't you ever let me see your white face around here again.' I was like, 'no problem' and I just walked away."

Mike Bonner: "I showcased at the Comedy Store and tore the house down. Mitzi tells me to call Duncan tomorrow. You're going to be regular. I call Duncan the next day. Duncan tells me that Mitzi didn't say that to me."

James Hannah: "In the white clubs if you're really funny you've got to go up in front of some white boy that actually tells you what you can and can't talk about, but yet this white boy can't follow you. "

Comedian, Bobby Law: "There's a lot of racism that goes on in comedy from the different types of rooms that you play. There's certain places that feel as though there's a certain type of comedy that they're looking for and they will basically let you know that by the way they mistreat you. I went to a room where the guys running the room didn't even want to shake my hand."

Tony Tone: "I was on stage in Lincoln, Georgia when I heard this dude say the N word. They were trying to get him to be quiet and I think I addressed him and I heard him mumble to his girl, 'Nigger' and enough people heard it where I just addressed it and moved on before he eased himself into a butt whooping."

Comedian/Actor, Affion Crockett: "I did experience racism, but it was so under the carpet you had to go under the carpet to see it. I witnessed a tour where they would have the comics go and do white clubs and black clubs. When you went to the black club they would have the black promoter pay you X amount of dollars. Say four times more than you were getting per night and as you went to the white club the night after and the night after that they had it hooked up so that their white friends in that club didn't have to pay you because they got all the money out of the black clubs. Imagine that."

Dick Gregory: "None. I mean, they didn't bring me in because of a court order; they brought me there because I was the hottest thing in the country. Now what I would do, like when I went to Vegas, before when you went to Vegas if you was black, Sammy Davis, Pearl Bailey, you didn't stay in the hotel. You stayed in a tent that looked like Buckingham Palace. I mean, I refused to so when I went I stayed in the hotel and what I did in every city I would go into I would go into the black community and go to the barbershop and I would introduce myself, tell them who I was, then pay them two hundred dollars apiece and see what I'd like for you to do is come by the club tonight. I'm at the Flamingo and don't act like you know me. Just come as a person and then after it's over kind of hang around and I'll come over and talk to you find out if they sit them in certain places, took them a long time to wait on them, came over with an attitude and then right after that I would go back and talk to the owner. When I came in a club, let's say if you was white and I worked your club, my contract said that if you took an ad in the white paper if there's a Negro paper within a hundred mile radius of the club you had to take out an ad in that too. And if you didn't you couldn't get me. Those were the things I just did on my own."

Al Toomer: "In Columbia, South Carolina, and I took pride in having never been called a nigger by a white man and I haven't and I'm from the South and I normally say that on stage. Well, this time being there for the first time a white boy was sitting on the row and said 'nigger.' The room got quiet as a muthaf*#ka, dude. People were about to start a riot and I had to catch myself because he was right there on the front row and he laughed it off like I was just bullshittin' and I was like, man, you almost got hit with this mic stand, but it really would've been a riot then."

Alex Thomas: "I probably average like thirty-five to forty-two cities a year and being a golfer, I go down and do a show in Mississippi or Little Rock, you still get a lot of, 'Dammit, I remember when you niggers weren't free.' I've been to country clubs in the South where they looked at me like, 'Oh, great the caddies are here.'"

Mystro Clark: "The main racism I've noticed, especially on the TV side— Hollywood still have their little templates they want to follow, like you have so many white people. Chappelle was ready to do a show at FOX based on his life and they told him in the meeting that his best friend had to be white even though he didn't have a white best friend. His comment was white people are narcissistic. They like to look at themselves all day."

John Witherspoon: "Well, Johnny Carson didn't want any black folks on his show. They had Richard Pryor and old square ass Bill Cosby. That was the only two on his show. They might have put on Byron Allen later on."

Talent: "Basically the whole comedy club thing. Until *Def Jam* came and did what it did and changed comedy and made black comedy the number one demand for comedy you experienced all of that negative, 'you can't get on stage. We don't want you here. You're not funny. The shit you're talking about's not funny.' And you'd be like for a second, 'okay—I got to fix my shit because I can't talk about that' and then a white guy go right up and talk about the same shit they told you you can't talk about."

Richard & Willie: "Before I was a celebrity I was born in Memphis, Tennessee in the '30s. One thing about entertainers, it's like being a great ball player, even though you're black they respect your talent. They respect the talent. You can do something the average person can't do and that gets you respect. (Internationally) white people didn't see the color as much as they do here. America's a country if they see a man walk through a door I think people don't say there's a man first they say there's a black man. They see color first and then what the person is second. Over there I think they see the person first and the color secondary."

Ruben Paul: "Absolutely. We all experience racism in stand-up whether you wanna admit it or not. The fact that these clubs have 'black nights.'"

Kool Bubba Ice: "A club owner told me I couldn't work his room because I had too much soul. Now when was the last time you heard anybody use the term 'soul'?"

Daran Howard: "The worse part about this industry is I could name, and including you, I could name off the top of my head, fifteen or twenty comedians who would be on TV shows if they were white. White people get more chances than we get. That's the main thing."

Cedric the Entertainer: "I've seen it all. From performing in some of the Southern states to somebody flat out calling you 'nigger.' 'Get off the stage, nigger!' 'You're pretty funny for a nigger.' You know you have to have a quick comeback or a funny response or in my case—jump off stage and beat their ass. This story is legendary. It was in Little Rock (Arkansas) and Little Rock is one of my favorite cities to go to, but during my earlier days I was doing a club there and this dude just wouldn't let up. I mean he started with one remark and it kind of threw me off guard and I came back with a funny remark to try to keep the audience on my side, but this dude was belligerent and the management wasn't doing anything about it and I requested them to do something about it and they let this dude continue to go on so I was in the middle of a joke and he said something and before he knew it I was offstage—way, way off up in his ass. Now they put me out. To let you know how Southern it is, the management was upset. I mean they apologized for the situation, but they told me I was too violent and I couldn't come back. I thought it was fair. I put this dude out. He was yelling racial epitaphs at me. I did it. I handled him in a funny manner. I did a number of different things to continue for the rest of your patrons, but I just feel that that's rude that as far as yawl's establishment, you've got other people in this room. You've got two hundred, three hundred other people paid and you let one guy disrespect your artist. You don't want me back—then f*#k you too. You watch how your ass is gonna get beat."

Willie Brown (& Woody): "With agencies. I hate to say that. It's not just me it's my peers; why we can't get on stage at mainstream clubs because they're afraid we're going to be too funny, or maybe they're afraid we're going to be too black."

Pierre: "I've done comedy shows where if I'm the headliner they (white comedy clubs) don't want three black comics. They'll say if you bring a feature we need a white opener. Now I've seen shows where it's all white, though. Y'know what I'm sayin? Where's the black comic on the white show? So I've seen that racism."

Buddy Lewis: "What I found out is that the level of arrogance white people have towards black comedy is amazing. They don't respect you. They don't respect the level of comedy and so a lot of white folks use black shows as stepping stones to get to the next phase. If a white guy can write black it's a huge commodity. A black guy makes a white anything is just another guy. They categorize you 'Can you write a white show?' What do you mean can I write a white show? That's one thing white folks don't understand—I know about yawl's world. Yawl don't know about mine. I can write about your world. I see it. I've been in it. I grew up watching it."

Director/Writer/Actor/Former stand-up comedian, Rusty Cundieff:
"Yeah, but not in an overt sense. I mean, people wouldn't say, 'Nigga get out the room.' The racial element was more about what you were trying to do."

WHAT DO YOU FEEL ABOUT RACISM WITHIN THE BLACK RACE?

Sinbad: "Well, that's always been there. Now it's magnified. If you're white, all right. If you're brown stay around. If you're black step back. We're put a trick bag so hard."

HOW ABOUT REGARDING CASTING?

Sinbad: "I work less. As a matter of fact when was the last time you seen a yellow leading man? Other than doing our own movies. It doesn't call for a mulatto or light-skinned brother because white society doesn't know us, man. That's why I'm gone more now. I'm going to write my own movies. Do my own thing. I'm not here to make Hollywood open up. They're not going to open up. They can't. It's such a racism regime out here. The media is so racist. And they'll let a couple of brothers get through and give a brother seventy million dollars and say 'See.'"

So This Is What They Mean by "Colored TV"

CHAPTER 13

"They say give to the United Negro College Fund.
Well, you show me some united Negroes and
then you can call me back."
— MADD MARV

The 1970s was a Golden Age for African-Americans in television. Black shows leaped into homes all across America, ranking high in the Nielsen ratings at a time when blacks weren't known for their Nielsen boxes. In the post-'60s era when a non-offensive show like *Julia* was the only snack on the plate, new, hip fare was set before the hungry viewing audience.

Actually *Julia* was quite controversial for its time (1968–1971); it was the first sitcom since *Beulah* in the 1950s to star an African-American woman (the beautiful Diahann Carroll). *Julia* was a gorgeous widowed mom/nurse, who dressed well and made lots of money while raising her only son in a swank apartment with a cool white neighbor/friend. She was also frowned upon by blacks, who were too busy marching to gain equality for the masses to endorse a program that represented a miniscule portion of black society. It was deemed unrealistic and met an untimely end not due to cancellation, but to the refusal of the star to continue after receiving numerous death threats and constant harassment from whites as well as blacks. Diahann Carroll decided to devote her energies to less hazardous employment.

That great experiment failed, but by the '70s, comedy, black in particular, was experiencing an unprecedented freedom. The initial wisp of black exposure was on the highly rated NBC sketch comedy hour, *Rowan & Martin's Laugh-In*. From 1968 until 1973 such black performers as Pigmeat Markham, Teresa Graves, Stu Gilliam, Johnny Brown and ventriloquist Willie Tyler were regular cast members. Sammy Davis Jr., Godfrey Cambridge, Harry Belafonte, Dick Gregory, Nipsey Russell, Diana Ross, Slappy White, Isaac Hayes, and Della Reese made guest appearances and black was back with people literally "flipping" over it...every Thursday night on NBC.

CLEROW "FLIP" WILSON

Sinbad: "I loved Flip, man. I loved Flip Wilson. He was funny. He was talented."

Born December 8, 1933 in Jersey City, New Jersey, Clerow Wilson had twenty-three siblings, which might account for the name. With all those children his parents were bound to have to improvise. It's also said he was a troublemaker. Well, with a name like Clerow they're lucky he didn't grow up to be a mass murderer. Instead he was in and out of reform schools; raised mainly in foster homes until he lied about his age and enlisted into the Air Force, where he killed time entertaining his fellow troops with his flippant sense of humor that earned him the nickname "Flip."

He was so good at it that it was arranged for "Flip" to tour other bases to boost morale. When he returned stateside, he had to bite his tongue and got a dreaded day job as a bellhop. But in 1959 a Miami, Florida businessman made a deal with Wilson that if he'd quit all his other jobs and concentrate on perfecting his craft, he'd sponsor Flip to the tune of fifty dollars per week for one year.

Wilson played clubs throughout California, traveled across country and applied his craft in raunchy dives like the East St. Louis Club (a place reputedly so rough that if you didn't have a knife with you, they gave you one at the door).

Rudy Ray Moore: "Flip comes from the chitlin' circuit. The same circuit I was from."

Then he was off to the Big Apple and the Apollo Theater—his home for the next five years, during which time he cut numerous comedy albums; in 1965 Redd Foxx told Johnny Carson about him, which led Flip to over twenty-five appearances on *The Tonight Show*.

On September 17, 1970, *The Flip Wilson Show* debuted on NBC and became an overnight success, running until 1974. The hour-long variety show was the first of its kind to bear the name of a black man in prime time and in its initial two seasons, the Emmy award-winning program was America's second most watched TV program.

Comedian Franklyn Ajaye recalls his five-to-six-minute appearance on the show:

"That's when Monty Kay became my manager. He was Flip's manager and that was a big break for me. All I can remember is I came out and did my thing, Flip was very nice and I think Jack Klugman was on the show. And I remember being nervous."

Flip had signature characters such as Reverend Leroy of the Church of What's Happening Now!! and Geraldine, who popularized the phase, "The Devil made me do it."

Bobby Law: "All the great comedians had alter egos and Flip Wilson had Geraldine."

Spanky Hayes: "He made it safer for guys to wear dresses."

After his show's abrupt departure in '74, Flip went back to television in 1985 and starred in the short-lived sitcom *Charlie & Co.* with Gladys Knight. He was known for living only off of the interest of his invested income and thus walked away from show business a wealthy man. Wilson died of liver cancer on November 25, 1998 in Malibu, California.

Jay Phillips: "I could definitely appreciate what he was doing and knowing all of the hoops he had to jump through and probably all of the budget that he did get and all of the extra help that he didn't get and all of the work he had to do himself in order to get something funny out on television at that time, in an era where it was really not allowed for us to be on TV and be superstars at the time. He made it possible, man. So I've got to appreciate him for his hustle."

According to Reynaldo Rey, *The Flip Wilson Show* ended when Wilson himself flipped out and painted his manager's (Monty Kay) office completely white (including the desk, the erasers, the pencils, Picasso reproductions, etc.). He then went down the street wearing his Geraldine costume and flirted with the white boys on Sunset.

"So they came and picked him up and locked him up. He was in the nut house for two years."

Comedian Franklyn Ajaye couldn't confirm the account, but had this to say:

"I hadn't heard that, but I do know this—Flip gave his heart and soul to that show and I vaguely remember something along those lines. Flip worked so hard on that show. Just the way he gave everything he had: mentally and spiritually and psychologically, it wouldn't surprise me if it took its toll at some point. I ran into him a few years later and he was just the mellowest cat around. In fact the last time I ran into him he was living in Palm Springs, he had slimmed down; looked free, had a blue Rolls Royce, lived out by the beach. One time I ran into him at Roscoe's Chicken & Waffles right there on Pico. He came in and paid for everybody's breakfast and he had a motorcycle. He was in love with his motorcycle. He said he was through with show business; had been through for a while. He'd done his thing and that was it."

Meanwhile, producer Norman Lear took things to the next level by importing a British comedy, *Steptoe and Son*, and revamping the premise for the ghetto. *Sanford and Son* was born in 1972 and after decades on the circuit Redd Foxx was an overnight hit.

Talent: "So this was not a show where this funny comedian is twenty-five or thirty years old. This muthaf*#ka is an elderly man and like doing it. The shit is reality based. You're thinking it's in a house, but you look outside that door and it's in the back of a junk yard and this muthaf*#ka still finds life humorous."

The show was based on a cantankerous old junk man, Fred G. Sanford, trying to make his way through his Watts lifestyle with his "dummy" of a son along for the ride.

Thea Vidale: "Fred Sanford said everything he felt and thought and he had a valid reason for why he thought those things."

Eddie Griffin: "He was running his own business. Even though it was a junk yard it was his. Y'know what I'm sayin'? And always had pretty good advice for his son."

Deon Cole: "The brother could make a face and it was better than any punchline that anyone could f*#kin' write."

However, the writing staff was incredible: Paul Mooney and Richard Pryor occasionally wrote for the show on top of a core staff consisting of "Bootsie," J. Stafford Parker, Curt Taylor and Foxx's opening act, Reynaldo Rey. And Foxx always cast buddies from the circuit, like Slappy White, Leroy & Skillet, and Bubba Bexley.

As comedian and fellow altar boy, Tom Dreesen tells it:

"Redd would look all over, if he saw anybody that didn't have any money and they couldn't pay their SAG or their AFTRA insurance he would take them to the show and tell the writers, write 'em in, put them on the show. Let 'em get one line. He'd make sure it was a speaking line that way he had to pay different money. Redd did that time and time and time again."

Because of Foxx's generosity, Lawanda Page went from a never-heard-of to one of the funniest characters on TV with her portrayal of the sanctimonious Aunt Esther.

LAWANDA PAGE

Thea Vidale: "A trailblazer who was never given the respect she deserved."

Laff Records album cover Watch It, Sucker! *from LaWanda Page in her "Aunt Esther" garb.*

LaWanda Page was born in Cleveland, Ohio on October 19, 1920 and started dancing at the age of fifteen. As part of her comedy and dancing act, Page swallowed fire and was called "The Bronze Goddess of Fire." She worked the Midwestern chitlin' circuit for years playing in places she later referred to as "dumps," where you put your life in your hands when you walked through the door.

Page went to Los Angeles in the '60s and joined Leroy, Skillet & Co., starting off as a poor man's Moms Mabley then honing her craft and carving out her own niche of raw, rough-edged humor. Her big break on *Sanford and Son* was in jeopardy when her acting wasn't up to par. The producers were ready to fire her; then Foxx got involved and demanded that she receive tutoring until she got the part down. He even worked with her himself and told her to simply "stop acting and start acting like yourself."

She caught on as did her catch phrase, "Watch it, sucker." After the show's 1977 cancellation, Page appeared in the short-lived spin-offs *Sanford* and *Sanford Arms*, films, and TV guest spots during the '70s and '80s. Page died of complications of diabetes at the age of 81 in Los Angeles, California on September 14, 2002.

Tony Spires: "She was underrated. A warm woman, nice and endearing with a lot of history from back in the day. Very cool and down to earth."

Luenell: "I did attend her funeral out of homage and respect. And I went to her casket and it was open and said a little prayer and said, 'Thank you, thank you, for the work that you have done. Had it not been for you there would be no opportunity for me.' I did that."

The next show to make a splash was the saga of the Evans Family on the CBS hit *Good Times*. Created by Eric Monte (writer of *Cooley High* and creator of *What's Happening!!*), the show was a spin-off of *Maude*, which was a spin-off of *All in the Family*. It hit the air in February 1974 and each week told the story of a maid, Florida Evans (Esther Rolle), her chronically unemployed husband, James (John Amos)...

Eddie Griffin: "They would never let the father have a job for more than half the show."

...and their three children: militant Michael (Ralph Carter), super fine Thelma (Bernadette Stanis), and artistic but goofy JJ (Jimmie Walker), and their life in the projects. In other words, the comedy was derived from abject poverty.

Thea Vidale: "*Good Times* showed that if ever there was a race of people that was the MacGyvers of being poor and still having a good time it was black people. We can disguise poor better than any race on the earth and have a good time being poor."

Talent: "They didn't have a pot to piss in, but everyday was funny."

Mark Prince: "Temporary lay-off—how the f*#k is that a good time?"

Set in the Cabrini Green Projects in Chicago, the socially minded sitcom went from mentioning things like Nixon and inflation to being a minstrel show starring Jimmie Walker.

Mark Prince: "He got too ridiculous with it. He felt like the more coon the more better. We're a lot more cool than that. There are a lot of us who are silly and funny, but we don't go over the top. We don't really have coons in the projects."

In 1976 John Amos and co-star Esther Rolle appeared in an article in *Ebony* magazine quoting Amos as expressing discontent with the direction of the show. Once Norman Lear read it (he read *Ebony*?), Amos was released from his contract and his character was killed in a car accident while looking for work in Mississippi. In 1977, Esther Rolle boycotted the show behind the negative, coon image JJ had become, but returned in '78 after producers said they'd tone down JJ's buffoonery.

Tension was so thick during Walker's tenure as the star that he refused to talk to anyone. The only time he would speak was in rehearsal and nothing beyond what was in the script. Guest star David Damas recalls the week he worked on the show:

"He actually started having conversations with me three days after I had been rehearsing with him on the set. Esther Rolle had departed fully. I don't remember the scenario as far as the script, but the press put out that she had health problems; high blood pressure, blah, blah, blah, etc., etc. The real reason was negotiations for money. They did not want to pay her the money that she wanted. Eventually they did bring her back. So I guess they must have straightened out the financial situation."

The experience with Walker was not Damas' initial encounter with the star.

"When I came out here in June of 1978 (from New York) I was standing on a bus stop and I was waiting on a bus and Jimmie Walker drove by in a Rolls Royce with an open top and I waved to him and I said, 'How you doin', Jimmie?' and he looked at me like I was a piece of shit, a piece of dirt; didn't speak and he just drove off. I was so angry and incensed I said that day at the bus stop...I said you know what, I'm a nobody now in this town and you're a big star, but one day you're going to have to deal with me. Y'know what I mean? And I'm never going to forget this. So needless to say three months later when I got the part on *Good Times* (of a gangster) where I got to grab him and push him down and snatch him around I took special delight in doing that."

When *Good Times* taped its last episode in 1979 it had made its mark. The show spawned one of the most memorable theme songs in TV history, a national catchphrase in JJ's "Dyn-o-mite" and made its cast ghetto-fabulous icons and Jimmie Walker a star.

JIMMIE WALKER

Born in New York's South Bronx on June 25, 1947, Walker went from high school dropout to radio engineer to professional comedian. Thanks to fellow comic David Brenner getting Walker a spot on *The Jack Paar Show* in1973, he was cast as the Evans family's older son, JJ on *Good Times*. His comedy album and catchphrase, "Dyn-o-mite," were hits; he was named "Comedian of the Decade" by *Time* magazine; he appeared alongside Sidney Poitier and Bill Cosby in *Let's Do It Again*; and his clout allowed him to hire two unknown standups named Jay Leno and David Letterman that he knew to write for *Good Times*.

Good Times ended in 1979 and his other shows (*B.A.D.Cats* and *At Ease*) were short-lived. People wanted JJ, and that's not what Walker wanted to give them. For a while he was so bitter about being identified only for his former incarnation that if you called him JJ, he'd ignore you, curse you out, or want to fight. That is until a pizza chain paid him handsomely to make fun of it. Wisely accepting his lot he capitalized on the former image in commercial ads then returned to radio and performing stand-up.

The Jeffersons was also a spin-off of *All in the Family*, and originally George Jefferson (Sherman Hemsley) was referred to but never seen; the role was eventually cast as the recurring character of the neighbor of the bigoted Archie Bunker. The twist was that George was racist too and hated "honkies" (as he loved to call them). His wife Louise (affectionately known as "Weezie"), was an earth mother played with pure aplomb by Isabel Sanford. Their college-aged son, Lionel (Mike Evans [1975, 1979–1981], Damon Evans [1975–1978]—no relation), surreptitiously loved to make Archie look like a fool every chance he got.

The formula was surefire. So on January 18, 1975 producers Norman Lear and Bud Yorkin (*Sanford and Son, Good Times, All in the Family.* and *Maude*) unveiled their latest offering of a black man who gets rich through his dry cleaning business and moves his family out of Queens to Manhattan's Upper East Side and a deluxe apartment in the sky.

Thea Vidale: "We had never seen rich black people before who had struggled."

The nouveau riche brood had to adjust to their new lifestyle and people, including an eccentric neighbor (UN translator Harry Bentley, played by Paul Benedict), a tip-happy doorman, Ralph (Ned Wertimer), George's disapproving mother/Louise's nemesis, Mother Jefferson (Zara Cully, who passed away in 1978) and George's new targets for his bigotry—Lionel's fiancée Jenny's parents—the Willises (Roxie Roker [rocker Lenny Kravitz's mother] and Frank Cover). Though Jenny (Belinda Tolbert) was black like the Jeffersons, her parents were mixed: black mama—white daddy. To George, they were "zebras." They even had a white son.

Mark Prince: "I loved *The Jeffersons* because every time it came on they would show that episode of him stepping on the white man's back."

However, the breakout character was their acid-tongued maid, Florence, who was more than a match for her insulting employer; to her he was known as "Shorty."

MARLA GIBBS

Born in Chicago, Illinois, Marla Gibbs was a film lover from the time she was a child; however, acting didn't directly affect her life until she moved to Detroit, Michigan and a chance encounter with an ex-teacher conducting surveys with a tape recorder led to her landing a part on *Juvenile Court*. She nailed the part of the mother, but didn't consider acting any further until a trip out to California, where she studied under the renowned veteran Lillian Randolph. Later, with the assistance of long-time black agent Lil Cumber, Gibbs got into the Performing Arts Society of Los Angeles. She found it exciting to leave her job at United Airlines each day and go to the theater and sweep floors and do whatever she had to do. She'd been employed by the airline for eleven years when she went out on the audition that got her *The Jeffersons*. In a rare Hollywood move, she stayed at her "day" job for another two years until the producers asked her if she would take a leave from her position. They paid for her to take a ninety-day leave from United and at the end of those ninety days she decided to give acting a real chance.

Armed with an increased income and an entrepreneurial spirit forged by her self-taught auto mechanic father, who later ran his own ice business, and her haberdashery- then theater-running mother, Gibbs opened a supper and jazz club, Marla's Memory Lane (formerly Sam Houston's, where a number of comedians performed), and founded the Vision Theater in the Crenshaw district of Los Angeles in 1981.

Once *The Jeffersons* was canceled, Gibbs produced and starred in NBC's sitcom *227* featuring Jackee Harry and Hal Williams; did stage productions like *Me and Mr. B* where she played legendary songstress Billie Holiday; dipped her toes into the soap opera pond with her portrayal of the evil Aunt Irma on *Passions*, and appeared in feature films (*The Brothers* with Bill Bellamy and D. L. Hughley). With all that, celebrity was still hard for Gibbs to grasp. Her attitude was that she was given opportunities so she could in turn make opportunities available to those in the community. She wasn't just some ego-tripping star slumming. As a matter of fact she was so detached from her notoriety that she once mistook an autograph-seeking gentleman for a stalker following her to her car. Unlike most, Gibbs constantly had to remind herself she was a TV star.

Eddie Griffin: "That's my baby, y'know what I'm sayin? The woman is all love. We've done a couple of benefit shows down at Marla's Memory Lane together over the years. The lady is just all heart."

The caring and sharing, Marla Gibbs.

DARRYL: "Did you get any flack for playing a maid in the '70s?"

GIBBS: "No. I thought I was going to get flack from young people. Instead they were trying to find somebody in their family who had been a maid so that they could identify."

DARRYL: "That's interesting."

GIBBS: "I thought that was very interesting because white people and black people would say the character (George) reminded them so much of someone they knew and say, 'When you get him you get him for us.'"

DARRYL: "What advice would you give African-American female performers?"

GIBBS: "What I would say to a person is recognize that they and their source are one and recognize that they can do anything they want to do and they take responsibility for it and they can go wherever it is they're supposed to go. All of us are here on a journey and on your journey sometimes where you think you want to go is not necessarily what you came to do, but you'll discover it when you step out and start your journey. I had an actor say, 'I'm giving this two years and that's it.' You can't put a time on it. You do something because you love it and because you want to do it. Even if you have to work some place else to be able to do it. This job is something that you want to do. A lot of people get into this business to make big money. That's what it's all about for them and they will not last because their heart isn't in it. So prepare yourself—number one. Don't just step out here. You prepare yourself."

Though the program enjoyed an 11-season run (in the top ten for most of it and in '81–'82 it ranked as the number three show on TV right behind *60 Minutes* and *Dallas*), it was not without its critics. A rich black man on TV was of course going to raise some white eyebrows, but it also angered more than a few blacks who questioned if we were laughing with George as he railed against a racist society or at him as he constantly made himself look like a fool with his racist ways and preconceived notions.

> **Talent:** "Here go a brotha that's f*#kin' quote, unquote making it; he doing the damn thing, but this nigga still got his niggerism at the top. He was what white people at that level were so used to them being towards us at a lower level; he was that, but black."

True, *The Jeffersons* utilized standard black humor and occasionally pulled out a stereotype or two (Louise started out as a maid, George strutted about like he just got off a minstrel stage), but overall it showed blacks in a new light on television. Jefferson hadn't scammed to get his money—he earned it. Regardless, the show's audience fell off and by 1985 it was time to pack up the boxes and move to the land of syndication. On July 23, 1985, after 253 episodes, *The Jeffersons* moved on out.

The sitcom *What's Happening!!* was set at the opposite end of the nation and economic ladder—Watts, California. Inspired by Eric Montes' feature film hit *Cooley High*, the show debuted in 1976 and the episodes centered on budding screenwriter Raj (Ernest Thomas), his mama (Mabel King), sister Dee (Danielle Spencer), and two buddies, the always-ready-for-food Rerun (Fred Berry) and catchphrase spouting ("Hey, hey, hey, hey") Dwayne (Heywood Nelson). The friends seemed to have an inexhaustible supply of troubles: school, money, family, and of course girls.

The fun show also featured a Henry Mancini theme song; dated humor; the dance craze pop-locking slipped in almost every show, performed by a pioneer, Rerun himself (a founding member of the original "Lockers" dance troupe); and visits to the local soda shop where the comedy would kick into high gear courtesy of one of the era's top comediennes— Shirley Hemphill. She played a waitress named, appropriately enough, Shirley, who served up a weekly dose of common sense with a snappy delivery.

> **Thea Vidale:** "Shirley Hemphill was not only a funny and dynamic black woman, she was kind. She was a kind black woman to a lot of comedians that are famous."

The show lasted until 1979 and returned as *What's Happening Now!!* for a short run. What distinguished this sitcom from many of the other black comedies (besides future star Martin Lawrence in the latter version) was its level of mischief. It was seen through the eyes of young, optimistic characters. There was innocence to *What's Happening!!* The show could be likened to a *Little Rascals* with teenagers.

That's My Mama showcased a fantastic cast of black actors from 1974–1975: Clifton Davis, Teddy Wilson, Lynne Moody, Teresa Merritt, and Ted Lange. Davis played free-wheeling bachelor Clifton Curtis, owner of his own barbershop (through inheritance), and his problems pretty much centered on his love life. With the help of his mail-carrying buddy Earl (Wilson), the local gossip, Junior (Lange), and his oh so fine sister, Tracy (Moody), there was scarcely a dull moment on this mismanaged show. If only ABC had left it alone to continue its solid ratings this sitcom would be remembered more fondly, but a change in key cast members and a new production staff altered the once funny half-hour to something people decided they could live without. The show lasted only two seasons, but funny ones they were.

Another seldom mentioned, and one of the least remembered, black sitcoms of the '70s was ABC's *Love Thy Neighbor*. Produced in 1973, it was the ongoing story of black and white neighbors living in a community known as Sherwood Forest Estates on North Robin Hood Road. This lightweight entertainment starred Harrison Page and Janet MacLachlan (the blacks) and Ron Masak and Joyce Bulifant (the whites).

The show was a disastrous summer replacement, complete with a twelfth episode with the self-explanatory title *The Minstrel Show*, where the black neighbor comes to the festivities in whiteface and of course the white neighbor shows up with his face blackened. The thirteenth episode never aired. It was the end of that run, and for some odd reason, no reruns. You'll find this gem right next to the pilot script for *Birth of a Nation*.

Whatever the legacy of these shows at the time of their inception, being in the black was good for the balance sheet and ratings. After Fred, JJ, Weezie and the rest, the public was broken in for more blacks on TV. For a full decade they'd been exposed to tubby building superintendents, sassy neighbors, super cool buddies, and big-bosomed mamas. And once that formula got stale, Hollywood turned to little black kids (*Different Strokes*, *Webster*) being adopted by white parents (because the reverse would've been viewed as abduction).

The True "King" of Comedy

CHAPTER 14

"Sisters hate to see brothers with white women.
Why should you be happy?"
— RICHARD PRYOR

In the 1970s a film trend kicked off with blacks being the heroes. No more pushing a broom. They were pushing a foot up whitey's ass. Big bad bold brothers and sisters were lighting up the screen in one low budget epic after another. There were cool black detectives, pimps, coke dealers, avenging hot mamas, international female spies, even brothers coming back from the dead to take revenge. The era reached its pinnacle when Isaac Hayes received an Academy Award for scoring *Shaft* starring Richard Roundtree. Now the whole world knew what a bad mutha the new black brother was.

The list of instant black classics is illustrious: *Aaron Loves Angela* (1975), *Abby* (1974), *Across 110th Street* (1972), *Adios Amigo* (1975), *Amazing Grace* (1974), *The Arena* (a.k.a. *Naked Warriors*) (1973), *Bare Knuckles* (1977), *Big Doll House* (1971), *Black Belt Jones* (1974), *Black Caesar* (1973), *Black Gunn* (1972), *Black Mama, White Mama* (1972), *Blacula* (1972), *Buck and the Preacher* (1972), *Car Wash* (1976), *Cleopatra Jones* (1973), *Cleopatra Jones and the Casino of Gold* (1975), *Coffy* (1973), *Come Back, Charleston Blue* (1972), *Cool Breeze* (1972), *Cooley High* (1976), *Cotton Comes to Harlem* (1970), *Dolemite* (1975), *Dr. Black, Mr. Hyde* (1976), *Drum* (1976), *Five on the Black Hand Side* (1973), *For Love of Ivy* (1968), *Foxy Brown* (1974), *Friday Foster* (1975), *The Great-*

est (1977), *Hell Up from Harlem* (1973), *A Hero Ain't Nothin' But a Sandwich* (1978), *Hit!* (1973), *Hit Man* (1972), *Hot Potato* (1976), *I Escaped from Devil's Island* (1973), *If He Hollers, Let Him Go* (1968), *J.D.'s Revenge* (1976), *Legend of Nigger Charley* (1972), *Let's Do It Again* (1975), *The Liberation of L.B. Jones* (1970), *Live and Let Die* (1973), *The Mack* (1973), *Mandingo* (1973), *Man Friday* (1976), *Mean Johnny Barrows* (1976), *Melinda* (1972), *Norman...Is That You?* (1976), *A Piece of the Action* (1977), *Scream, Blacula, Scream* (1973), *Shaft* (1971), *Shaft in Africa* (1973), *Shaft's Big Score* (1972), *The Slams* (1973), *Slaughter* (1972), *Slaughter's Big Ripoff* (1973), *The Soul of the Nigger Charley* (1973), *The Spook Who Sat By The Door* (1973), *Superfly* (1972), *Superfly T.N.T.* (1973), *Sweet Sweetback's Baadasssss Song* (1971), *Take a Hard Ride* (1975), *That Man Bolt* (1973), *Three The Hard Way* (1975), *Three Tough Guys* (1974), *...tick...tick...tick* (1970), *TNT Jackson* (1974), *Trouble Man* (1972), *Truck Turner* (1974), *Uptown Saturday Night* (1974), *Watermelon Man* (1970), *Wattstax* (1973).

Most of these movies were made for black people, about black people, by whites. Yet the era was known as "Blaxploitation" and even though black stars were being created and black technicians were gaining employment, the product itself was still in the control of whites. Many took issue with this, such as comedian Sinbad.

"I don't call them blaxploitation. You know why? That was a term that white cats came up with. People need to be hip to that. The reason they called it blaxploitation, those movies grossed more money, I mean per capita as far as what you spend to make them, than any movie that was happening. And they didn't mind as long as they were making them. but what happened towards the end of that era, black filmmaking, we decided we wanted to direct and produce our own movies and Hollywood said I'll be damned if that's going to happen. So they started calling them blaxploitation so we picked up on it. 'Oh, these movies are bad for us.' The thing is the movies would've gotten better, man."

Rudy Ray Moore: "I am totally against that term, blaxploitation. There is no such a thing as that. When we came out with our movies they called it blaxploitation because we had the upper hand at kicking whitey in the ass. Then they called it that, but we weren't exploiting anything. We were doing movies at that time that would please our people so that they wouldn't see and have to go through seeing the horrible things that we saw ourselves doing in the white movies at that time from *Gone with the Wind* on down."

WHAT WAS YOUR FAVORITE BLAXPLOITATION FLICK?

Eddie Griffin: *"Superfly. Superfly* said it best. I'm not joining your shit. I'm a revolutionary. When you're ready to walk down the street shooting white folks I'm with you. I'll be the first in line."

Spanky Hayes: *"Which Way is Up?* It's kind of like the shit that I was going through it in real life. That was a time in my life I had double lives with three different women in L.A. and it all caught up with me and I ended up with nothing."

Sinbad: *"The Mack, Superfly, Across 110th Street, Cotton Comes to Harlem,* but my favorite movie...two movies, man were *Cooley High* and *Cornbread, Earl & Me"*

Jay Lamont: *"*It's a tie between *Super Fly* and *Coffy* with Pam Grier. *Coffy* because it was the first movie my older brother took me to. That brings back memories."

A. J. Jamal: "I didn't see *Super Fly* 'til like last week. That's sad, man. I did not really see *The Mack* or *Super Fly* 'til like last week, man"

Deon Cole: *The Education of Sonny Carson, Foxy Brown, Superfly, The Mack.* I loved these 'cause it was all about coming back on the man. Loved the classics."

Rudy Ray Moore without his Dolemite attitude.

Comics were getting in on the filmmaking bonanza. From the do-it-yourself committee came the man some call the first rapper.

RUDY RAY MOORE A.K.A. "DOLEMITE"

Reginald Ballard: "He used to rhyme with his jokes and we used to imitate him."

His brand of films was low budget, cheap looking and full of braggadocio. They were macho fantasies for the man in the hood on the go. The women were all sexy and willing and the star was a sexual dynamo ready to take advantage of that fact, but first he had to call them bitches and bust a rhyme or two in the process. Rudy Ray Moore invented his persona of "Dolemite"—a man's man and a woman's blessing.

Rudy Ray Moore was the eldest of seven children so he moved to Cleveland, Ohio when he was 15 and peeled potatoes to make a living. After watching a local talent show he decided he wanted to be an entertainer. He'd taken modern dancing and had secured work on the Milwaukee club scene as the turban wearing, singing, dancing, "Prince Dumarr" and worked frequently with stage performer Caldonia Young.

Rudy Ray Moore: "She used to take us out to do shows; cabaret parties we called them on Friday and Saturday night in the theater for eight dollars a night and we'd sometimes get a double gig so we'd come home with sixteen dollars."

While in the Army he chose comedy and also found "his" voice.

"I had worked with Caldonia and learned her act and when I put on my shows in the service club sometimes I'd have an act that was late or they wouldn't come out and somebody at the show got disgusted, 'Well, do a joke or something.' So I come out and did Caldonia's act and the rest is history. I've been doing comedy ever since."

Once discharged in '59, Moore moved to L.A. and began emceeing at the California Club.

His first comedy album was *Below the Belt*, followed up by *Let's All Come Together* and *The Beatnik Scene*. Recording an album was one thing; getting paid was another so Moore supplemented his income with a day job. He chose to work at Dolphin Records where a wino named Rico would stop by daily and bum money from Moore on the condition he'd perform his Dolemite routine. That bit became Moore's act/namesake.

Rudy Ray Moore: "Dolemite come up from vitamins in stores that you get to give you energy. So I said I already have energy—I'm going to make myself Dolemite."

And to separate himself even further from contemporaries such as Redd Foxx, Moore decided to not only suggest sex as Redd and others did, he'd flat out say it. Forget the innuendo, Rudy let the expletives fly and became the world's first X-rated comedian.

His breakthrough came in 1970 with the comedy LP *Eat Out More Often*, with The Signifying Monkey and the Great Titanic bits. It spent four consecutive weeks atop the Billboard magazine soul chart and as it began its descent, Rudy released another album entitled *This Pussy Belongs to Me*. The combination made him the first soul artist to ever have two LPs on the charts simultaneously. Another sixteen quickie albums came right behind them with titles such as *The Streaker*, *I Can't Believe I Ate the Whole Thing*, and *Dolemite is Another Crazy Nigger*.

Moore also knew how to sell a record. Besides nasty titles, his album covers were nasty, with him and semi-naked women in suggestive poses. They also felt intimate when you heard them. That's probably because Rudy Ray Moore recorded his albums at his home. He'd invite over friends, serve drinks, and let the engineer capture the raunch.

In 1974 he bankrolled *Dolemite*, the movie—a cheap, action-packed flick.

DARRYL: "On the first film what kind of budget were you dealing with?"

MOORE: "Ninety thousand dollars—just chump change that they would've spent in one day by one of them big film companies. That was my budget and I did the film and I run out of money. Well, I was strong as a comedian at that time so I went on the road and worked for 13 months to get enough money to finally finish *Dolemite* with."

It was awful by all film school standards, but it was a fun movie. So bad it was good.

Speedy: "The creator of the straight-to-DVD movie."

Alex Thomas: "That nigga's movies were so terrible that you laughed. It was the absolute worst thing I've ever seen in my life in film history, but I have the whole collection of Dolemite films. Rudy Ray Moore looked like he did his movies for one hundred thirty-eight dollars. I've seen Rudy Ray Moore movies where it be the same character at the beginning of the movie and at the end it's a different nigga, but in the same outfit."

He made more movies, recorded more albums and continued to tour for his fans.

Keith Morris: "He was the first. Now everybody's stealing his material."

DARRYL: "You're one of the surviving members of your era who is still on the road. How do you like it?"

MOORE: "Let me explain the reason I'm still out here. There are a lot of comedians out here who do not have the power to draw when they go in person. You can't remember anything they did. You remember me from *Dolemite, the Signifying Monkey*...that gives me power. Now it's not like it used to be, but I still have a lot of impact with the one-niters and that is the reason—because my character was so strong."

DARRYL: "Now you sell a lot of merchandise on the road. Sometimes you make more selling merchandise than you do for the actual show. Could you run down some of the things you have besides your movies and CDs?"

MOORE: "I'm lining the back scratcher with rhinestones to make them beautiful; the Dolemite back scratchers. I also get the incense burners and call them the Dolemite incense burners. Then I go to the Players Ball and we make the players walking canes and the player's glass, filled with rhinestones. So my staff sets up a souvenir table and sells all that plus posters and so forth and so on."

DARRYL: "I want to ask you about a couple of comedians."

MOORE: "Ask me about Andrew 'Dice' Clay."

DARRYL: "Okay, Andrew 'Dice' Clay."

MOORE: "Andrew 'Dice' Clay...see, I'm the world's first comedian to go on stage and use the four-letter words like MF and all of the hard four-letter words."

DARRYL: "And what was the first year you did that?"

MOORE: "1969. There were no comedians doing that because it just wasn't acceptable to do it. I did the album and when I did the album I did that just for record sales, but people began to call me and want me to come in person. When I got there in person I had to do it. Now to get back to Andrew 'Dice' Clay. As a white boy he can stand on stages all over the United States and make a fortune and on the Las Vegas circuit I can't even get a job."

DARRYL: "Let me ask you about Richard Pryor."

MOORE: "Richard Pryor was one of the greatest comedians. I say this and I have not liked at all that some people have given Richard Pryor credit for the comedians being as they are today with the type of lingo that they're using which I should not want to claim it, but I am the first one and I don't like them saying that he was the one who did it because Richard did not use the language that I'm using until four years later. He was on Warner Bros. and his albums were clean, not suggestive. 1974, he switched and went into the X-rated groove, but I was doing it from '69. So how could he be the one to start it?"

DARRYL: "Who are some of the newer comics that you admire?"

MOORE: "I liked Joe Torry in the early days. The late Robin Harris was one of my favorites. He would have been a monster today. I think Martin Lawrence is most fabulous. Chris Rock's greatness is there. Eddie Griffin worked with me on my latest DVD and I feel that his talent is very worthy of being among the greats today. Did I mention George Wallace? George Wallace and I became friends when he had his radio show back in Washington, D.C. He is a fine comic and a clean, well-cut comic. So I have to take my hat off to him."

Mainstream Hollywood had also opened its doors. Icon Sidney Poitier took time out from teaching British school kids, building chapels, and being called Mr. Tibbs to get into the black film game as well. He and partner Bill Cosby set the gold standard for movie comedy in the '70s and beyond with a powerhouse trilogy starting with *Uptown Saturday Night* and its bottomless pit of black superstars: the wives, Denise Nicholas and Tracy Reed; their nemeses were Harry Belafonte and Calvin Lockhart; Flip Wilson played his preacher from the Church of *What's Happening Now!!*; and dance virtuoso Harold Nicholas made the scene; as did an underground comic who was making a lot of noise at the time named Richard Pryor, but we'll get back to him later.

The duo followed it up with the perfectly titled *Let's Do It Again* (co-starring Jimmie Walker) and then *A Piece of the Action* with James Earl Jones. These three films defined black humor with style and class, using black talent to its best affect and introducing unforgettable characters in hilarious, non-demeaning situations.

It was a golden decade for stand-up; multiracial, groundbreaking, thought provoking comedy. Ask most comedians who were their favorites from the '70s and the names Pryor, Ajaye, and Carlin are invariably stated. And Carlin wasn't even black, but had the counterculture mind of a talent who spoke anything but America white.

An average-looking white man with above average skills was George Carlin. He began as a straight-laced comedian a generation before, and like Pryor had a moment of truth and readjusted his entire stage persona. Carlin became the cool white boy the brothas could relate to. Along with the Latin comedy team of Cheech & Chong it was Carlin getting the record play at the black households.

Jay Phillips: "When it comes to writing a joke and getting ideas in front of people on stage in a stand-up manner his way of thinking is just so far outside of the box, but it's really not. He attacked issues in jokes from an angle that still I haven't really seen nobody being able to do for as long as he did. He is really the true stand-up comic. I could see him telling jokes as long as Bob Hope, but better. He's a comedian."

To discuss counter-culture comedy Cheech & Chong have to be mentioned. Cheech Marin (the Mexican) and Tommy Chong (the Asian/Irishman) were a team of vinyl. Their comedy albums glorifying marijuana smoking were underground hits with not only stoners, but anybody who got the joke and knew these dudes were hilarious. The duo became their generation's mascots. Their skits, theater-of-the-mind classics, and movies were literally a gas: *Up in Smoke*, *Still Smokin*, *Cheech & Chong's Next Movie*, and *Nice Dreams*.

As the drug culture went from harmless marijuana toking to desperate crack smoking Cheech and Chong made a failed effort, *The Corsican Brothers*, and moved on to separate careers; Cheech appeared in films and TV's *Nash Bridges* with Don Johnson and Chong played guitar, had a recurring role on *That '70s Show*, and got busted for peddling pot paraphernalia online during an election season.

Now back to that Pryor kid.

RICHARD PRYOR

> **Tony Rock:** "...the King forever. He's our Elvis. There will never be another Richard Pryor. Nobody will be better. People are hot and people make the comparison, but no."

> **Tom Dreesen:** "He made comedy look easy."

> **Jay Phillips:** "He finished what Lenny Bruce started."

> **Darren Fields:** "Richard Pryor said things that we were thinking. He really brought it out, things that we want to say, but wouldn't say and he was delirious, just off the chain. Anything that we wanted to do in our minds Richard Pryor was doing it and saying it."

Richard Pryor was born in Peoria, Illinois on December 1, 1940 and raised in his grandmother Marie's brothel. Her son Leroy was also in the business with mom, along with his wife Gertrude Thomas, a prostitute who had been knocked up by Leroy and thus became his wife. The family profession was one thing, but Pryor's mother and grandmother attempted to instill strong moral values in the boy when they spoke to him in between tricks. Yet despite their efforts, the Catholic school system they had enrolled young Richard into didn't share their idealistic view and expelled him upon obtaining the knowledge of the Pryor clan income.

Another valuable lesson he learned around that time from the outside world was that he would commonly be referred to as "a nigger." Understanding that he was different in a number of ways, he became the class clown to keep the bigger kids from beating him up and was so good at getting laughs that in sixth grade his teacher permitted him to entertain his

Richard Pryor with the Luscious Dancers (from left to right) Stephanie Parks (Nweke), Alicia Parks (Littleton), Lupe Ladino, Lema, and Lua.

classmates for ten minutes once a week. This kept him from being a disruptive element the rest of the time and gave the overworked instructor a few good chuckles as well. Plus this weekly "spot" encouraged him to write material and practice.

The following year he joined Juliette Whitaker's drama group at the Carver Community Center. He only stayed there for a year, but the experience helped him develop as a performer. Still, formal schooling didn't agree with him and he dropped out after the ninth grade. Before long he had a child, got married and spent two years in the Army.

After leaving the service he began working the comedy circuit. His inspiration was Bill Cosby and by emulating his style Pryor was getting gigs. He made his way to New York in 1963 where he played clubs in Greenwich Village. This was the early '60s, a time when only clean comedians were getting any real work and it was either be colorless or get into the unemployment line. Despite his lean frame, Pryor liked to eat.

His made the TV rounds: Rudy Vallee's *On Broadway Night*, *The Tonight Show* with Johnny Carson, *The Ed Sullivan Show*, and *The Merv Griffin Show*. He branched out to Las Vegas, then began working out at the Improvisation Comedy Club in midtown Manhattan and playing with a blacker comedic voice and a more character-based style.

Daran Howard: "He put the theater in stand-up."

His penchant for street life started to reflect in his material in 1966–67 and in 1969 Pryor recorded his first album, *Richard Pryor* in which he laid down some ethnic and "ghetto" routines despite advice to the contrary from his reps. But he was frustrated. He was tired of being Bill Cosby lite, and had what he termed "a nervous breakdown" where he said, "What the fuck am I doing here?" and walked off the stage in Vegas.

Comedian/Writer, Franklyn Ajaye: "Well, the one I heard and I really read it in the *Rolling Stone*, he was out there and he realized that he was just not doing the type of comedy he wanted to do and he said, 'what the f*#k am I doing here?' while he was on stage and he just walked off and he ended up trying to squeeze out the side and getting stuck. And that kind of blackballed him in Vegas at that time, because he was known as, y'know—crazy; which he was."

Others claim he stripped butt naked, ran into the casino, jumped up on the table and yelled, "Black Jack!" Ajaye recalls this story as well:

"I think that happened previously. I mean, I had heard that secondhand. Y'know, he was wild. Richard was wild. I don't know if it happened on the time that he walked out. It happened to Carlin too. Carlin did the same thing. He got fired at some place in Vegas where he was changing from George Carlin to the long-haired George Carlin. Very similar to Pryor. Vegas was just not conducive or receptive to counter-culture."

Comedian Daryl Mooney has yet another version:

"When he was in Vegas and he just wasn't getting...see, there's only one Cosby. You cannot duplicate him. That's the Cosby rule. You'll always be second best when you're copying somebody else. You'll never find your own voice. And what happened was he was in Vegas doing his thing and the audience wasn't laughing and then he pulled out his dick and was pissing on stage and said, 'y'all laugh at this, muthaf*#kas.' And then never came back to Vegas and went to Berkeley and that's when he found himself with the path to that whole radical movement."

This was all supposed to have occurred around 1969, but whatever the dates or the actual circumstance, Richard Pryor was going through a metamorphosis. The transformation was taking a toll on his sanity, but he was fed up. Cosby hated it too—the taking of his mannerisms, voice inflection, etc. Pryor had been doing this so long that even when he adopted his own persona lingering traces of Cosby were still embedded. But the grit was all Rich: the pimps, hos, dopers, and his casual use of the taboo stage word *nigger*.

Brad Sanders: "Richard Pryor opened it up for a black man to be a regular ghetto ass, hood rat nigga on stage."

Perhaps, but this new approach was a strange departure for mainstream audiences. Many patrons, including blacks, didn't care for it and simply requested refunds and left the premises, but Pryor stayed the course. He intentionally missed a taping of *The Ed Sullivan Show* to send out a signal that he no longer cared about the mainstream.

He moved to Los Angeles to work on his stage act, but they didn't get him there either so he went totally underground to Berkeley. The city was one big protest movement, with college kids marching on different topics every day. A tortured soul like Pryor was right at home and the rebel comedian boot camp began. He befriended poets, intellectuals, and writers who shared his distrust for all that was America.

It was during this period that he became enamored with the writings of Malcolm X and scripted a story called *The Black Stranger* which would later be developed into *Blazing Saddles* with Mel Brooks and others. More importantly Richard Pryor studied people, and recorded his thoughts on what he saw and made it all the focus of his new stage persona. That new face would emerge when he returned to Los Angeles in '71 to debut the new Rich.

That was the year he released *Craps*, which he'd recorded at the Redd Foxx Club in Hollywood and where he'd unleashed his plethora of street characters. He had a new brand of storytelling. Pryor was setting up scenarios and then launching into one character after the next without benefit of traditional punchline humor. The laughs were coming out of the familiarity of the character portrayed or the circumstance being played out. Jokes were for other comedians. Pryor was onto something different.

> **Robert Townsend:** "Richard Pryor has always been really funny, but then again Richard has always had social commentary tied to his work. He would make you laugh, but he would also make you think. And Richard is a comedian who I think has a lot of gears, what I call gears, where he does impressions, he does physical comedy, he does thought provoking...so he's got an arsenal as it relates to being a comedian."

In September of '71 he taped *Live and Smokin'* before a mainstream crowd at the Improv in New York. Audiences didn't know what to make of this new style. It was so raw, so real, and so brutally honest, and it was inside stuff. Pryor was speaking the language of the streets and these people weren't all from that environment or even familiar with it, for that matter. Lesson learned. From then on Richard Pryor did most of his work in black clubs, black theaters, black places—because black people knew what the hell he was talking about. He couldn't go out and give a course on Negro 101 before every performance and issuing pamphlets wasn't a realistic option either.

He'd have to catch on with his people first then broaden his appeal. It was with the militant faction of blacks that he initially gained a strong following and built his confidence. Pryor sharpened his writing chops penning for *The Flip Wilson Show* and *Sanford and Son* and earned an Emmy as part of the writing staff on Lily Tomlin's award winning special *Lily*, having co-written and co-starred in each of her 1973 outings.

It was all coming together, and even though his out-of-control antics denied him the role he was born to play, Pryor still received writing honors for co-writing *Blazing Saddles* in 1974. In *Lady Sings the Blues* with Diana Ross, his role as Piano Man was so vivid, poignant and well-received that many felt he was robbed by not being nominated for a Best Supporting Actor Oscar. His movie *Which Way Is Up?*, where he played multiple parts, was an underrated tour de force, followed up by dramatic pathos in *Blue Collar* and versatility in *Greased Lightning*, *California Suite*, and (as the title character) in *The Wiz*. He sported a Mohawk in *The Bingo*

Long Traveling All-Stars & Motor Kings with Billy Dee Williams and James Earl Jones, appeared in *The Mack* with Max Julian and made a hilarious cameo in *Uptown Saturday Night*.

His talent spoke for itself and his personal life did as well. By the time Pryor did a cameo in *Car Wash* he was known as the most gifted junkie in Hollywood.

> **Franklyn Ajaye:** "We knew Richard Pryor was going to work two days. And we knew Richard had a reputation for being kind of volatile. Leading up to the time of the work the set was, for whatever reason, tense. And then Richard came in and he worked his two days beautifully. Didn't have any...he just worked his days. I remember he made thirty-eight thousand dollars for those two days, which was big money back then. And he came in and he was happy go lucky and he did his two days. And I remember that all you could feel when he was finished, and this is the whole set, relaxed."

Pryor even tried to direct a film himself. Franklyn Ajaye was a participant.

> "I ran into Richard when I was in college and he was doing some kind of movie. He wrote a movie. Some kind of strange ass f*#kin' movie that never got done. He was shooting it himself. This was something he was financing himself. A strange movie where some white man was on trial before all these black people and I had to do this thing where I washing him like in a car wash or something. And I worked seventeen hours for two dollars an hour and Richard gave me a check for thirty-four dollars and it bounced."

While he waited for his DGA card to arrive, people outside of the radical Panther circuit were starting to catch on to what Pryor was doing. Whites were flocking in to see what all the fuss was about. This translated into a Grammy Award for his 1974 album *That Nigger's Crazy* and another one in 1975 for *Is it Something I Said?* Both went gold.

> **Alex Thomas:** "The guy painted a picture. When I was a kid sneaking, listening to his albums I felt like I was looking at him. It felt like I saw him. He just painted a picture. It was just so amazing. I loved how the world loved him. It wasn't just a black thing even though he was black and he was a great guy—he made the world laugh."

Street brother Pryor primarily collaborated with two writers: Paul Mooney (the sophisticated radical) and David Banks (the country boy). Their method of gathering material included turning on a tape recorder and just talking; allowing Pryor to feed off of each until one, two, or twenty funny things came up. Then came the refining process.

> **Franklyn Ajaye:** "I saw Richard Pryor at the Comedy Store once. I think he was playing a week in 1973 and I went and watched him every night. Sometimes he'd start routines and they'd peter off. The next night you'd see what you'd seen, but he'd have something he added on to it. Until I saw him that week I thought he was just a guy that walked up on stage and was brilliant and I realized, wow—he's working on his thing during the day. He's listening to his tapes, doing his thinking

and that's why each night a routine that started out in the rudimentary phase was able to get longer because he was thinking about it. That made me realize he is more technical than I had thought. That's why his routines are great routines; they're very refined."

Though they worked as a writing team they all knew their roles. Daryl Mooney (Paul's son) explains:

"Pryor as far as writing, always remember, because people get this confused about the writing part, Pryor was the center. He did most of his own writing and his creativity. Pryor wrote his own stuff, man. My father gave him concepts, but Pryor would do the writing. He would go up on stage and just create."

And Pryor, known to have an erratic temper, hated changes. During his days writing for *Sanford & Son* it was an uninformed director who requested changes in person. Daryl Mooney recalls how messing with a Richard Pryor/Paul Mooney creation was risky:

"They used to write so well together, man. The Redd Foxx shows they wrote together were so funny, man that they were Emmy level shows, but Richard would always knock out the director. They come and might want to change some stuff that they had written and Richard would get mad and knock 'em out. That messed up Emmy nominations."

Their writing method for the show was also unorthodox.

"Richard and our father used to sit up at the house. Pryor had his Courvoisier and cocaine. Me and Dwayne (Paul's other son) would be sitting on the couch; they'd be at the table. Our father would be on the opposite end with a secretary in the middle. Pryor, coke, Courvoisier and our father would be like, 'okay, Sanford says so & so &so and Lamont...' and Richard be like, 'Okay, we have Lamont, right? F*#k you, muthaf*#kas. F*#k you and...' My father would be like, 'Richard, TV bro—we can't do that. Richard this is TV.' Our father would have to temper him and make it clean. And they'd go on and on and now Pryor's still half high, right? Coke, Courvoisier so they go on to '...and we'll have Redd say to Aunt Esther, "Bitch, shut the f*#k up. Eat your own pu*#y."' My father would be like, 'TV, man. TV.' By the time they were finished it would be some funny stuff just had to take out the cussing."

Pryor attempted the same approach when he co-penned *Blazing Saddles.*

"Richard would come to the writers' meeting with all these white folks with his Courvoisier, cocaine and Mel Brooks would say, 'Richard, you can't do that.' And Richard Pryor would say, 'Well, f*#k you and f*#k all y'all.' And they fired him."

In 1975 Pryor made a guest host appearance on the hot comedy sketch show *Saturday Night Live*, where he performed a now-classic skit on racial hiring practices along with resident funnyman Chevy Chase. In the sketch Chase runs Pryor through a word association test with a racial slant. The volley gets more heated, starting out innocently with words like "black—white" and escalating to "Nigger—dead Honky."

In 1976 Richard Pryor released his album *Bicentennial Nigger* and co-starred in the box office smash *Silver Streak* along with Gene Wilder. It was in this film that Pryor reversed the blackface routine and smeared shoe polish on white actor Wilder's face to provide him with a disguise to fool their adversaries, and to Wilder's credit he really played it up (Al Jolson would have been proud).

NBC made a smart move in 1977 when they gave Pryor his own show, then showed they weren't that smart two months later when they canceled it. In 1979 he filmed *Richard Pryor in Concert* and firmly established himself as one of America's foremost funnymen. He was voted that decade's number 1 black comedian, actor, and sex symbol (you heard me) in *Ebony* magazine.

In 1981, he reteamed with Gene Wilder for the Sidney Poitier-directed *Stir Crazy* and was seen in two other well-received concert films, *Live on the Sunset Strip* in 1982 and *Here and Now* in 1983. And upon returning from a trip to Africa, Pryor made a speech at the Comedy Store renouncing the word *nigger* and stated that he would never say that word again because he noticed that when he was in Africa he didn't see any "niggers." He never again said it on stage, but did use the word in private.

In the '80s Pryor's film output declined in quality (*The Toy, Brewster's Millions, Some Kind of Hero*) and his cocaine habit was winning the long-fought battle.

Record exec, David Drozen has the following memories:

> "When we signed Richard Pryor we gave him an advance of five thousand dollars. He had to have it or otherwise he was going to get killed. He said if I don't get this I'm going to die. He owed his drug people. Well, two or three days later he was back for five more and that was the end of the checks until he had them coming."

Then there was that time at the club in the hood.

> "I remember watching him do a show at Maverick's Flat on Crenshaw crouched underneath the piano and everybody thought that was a gag and that it was really funny, but what they didn't know is that his coke dealer didn't show up and he was so paranoid and that's why he did the show crouched underneath the piano."

However, business was business.

> "We worked together for many years, but we were never friends because I wouldn't share his cocaine. The vial was passed back and forth in front of me 17 zillion times and I always said, 'No, thank you' and he had a problem with that because maybe he felt I was being judgmental, but the truth of the matter was I could care less what he did. I don't want to do it."

His drug use and violent temper kept him in the news. Who could forget the time he shot his own car? If you did he recreated it for you on stage. In Pryor's version he shoots the tires and they come alive as they do a slow death scene complete with pained faces. It was brilliant, but like any artist's rendition, how much was heightened or exaggerated or fabricated for the sake of the art?

> "The story goes that he shot up his wife's new Mercedes that he bought her. She was the only black woman he was ever married to that I know of."

After a few more public misadventures, a press that wouldn't let him screw up in private, and a new drug wave called freebasing taking over, Richard Pryor quietly locked himself away with his non-criticizing crack pipe and one day took a searing sprint down the avenue. He had set himself on fire after a binge and went running up the street in agony.

The world held its breath as the reports of his condition were updated constantly on the televised news and the street news. Longtime friend/football great/balcony appreciator Jim Brown was filtering out information to the press claiming fluke, but other versions were floating around. Whether it was an accident or intentional depended on who you asked. Even Pryor changed the story from the time he first faintly stated that it was a mishap to the time he filmed a deliberate act in his biopic *Jo Jo Dancer, Your Life Is Calling*. Whatever the case, the reality and truth were that Richard Pryor was never quite the same after that life-threatening incident.

Pryor recovered and made other films, most notably *Harlem Nights* with fellow legends Redd Foxx and Della Reese under the direction of new-reigning comedy superstar Eddie Murphy and a real-small-part-having Robin Harris. He even made fun of the burning sprint in his concert film, but all the skin grafts and attacks to his immune system had taken a toll, along with his rampant drug use over the years. Richard Pryor was not in good health. Then things went from bad to worse when he was stricken with multiple sclerosis. He remained a trooper, though confined to a wheelchair.

> **Madd Marv:** "I liked him because even though he had M. S. he'd still get on stage and tell jokes; the most untouchable comic I met in my life."

Those inspirational yet painful-to-watch stage appearances became less frequent as the disease and age confined him to his home and the care of those close to him.

> **Mystro Clark:** "I met him at his house once. It was a ball; Sunset in the hills; the Beverly Hills, so that was cool. He was just getting in the wheelchair but he was still talking and cracking jokes and stuff. He was having a birthday party and a friend of my manager's invited us. It was pretty low key actually, it wasn't even that late it was like late evening like 7 o'clock, and I remember singing 'Happy Birthday' and I looked over; I'm standing next to Dustin Hoffman. Elayne Boosler was there and she was sexy and I was surprised, I would've never thought. She has some nice legs."

Pryor's condition continued to worsen until he finally succumbed and died of a heart attack on December 10, 2005, leaving the world better for having been here. His one-time writing partner, the Rev. David Banks, in his infinite wisdom, astuteness, and perceptiveness probably put it best:

> "He dead. It might come as quite a surprise to your ass, but that's what he is. He's dead and they ain't paid me enough money to start crying because the nigga's dead so I think you should do like Richard and in all your endeavors take the Lord with you."

Richard Pryor was the ultimate showbiz paradox, for though he was ahead of his time creatively, he was right on time in opportunity. He readjusted comedy in execution and perception and the genre flourished under his reign. Thanks to him people would gather in groups to hear the musings from comedy albums. They were attending comedy concerts; Steve Martin was selling out ball parks. George Carlin had crowds wrapped around the block at some of the top clubs in the country; Robin Williams was being skyrocketed to fame and King Rich made it all possible.

Saturday Night Live took advantage of the climate, made its splash onto the scene in 1975 and was an instant smash. People couldn't believe the things they were getting away with and the subjects they refused to shy away from. The show was making stars weeks after its debut. Chevy Chase was the first breakout with his slapstick antics, pratfalls galore, and a sharp wit aptly displayed on the parody news segment *Weekend Update*. Next came John Belushi (who shared Pryor's love of truth and coke) and his accidental sidekick Dan Ackroyd (later The Blues Brothers). There were the ladies Jane Curtin, Gilda Radner, and Lorraine Newman. And then there was the black guy.

GARRETT MORRIS

Garrett Morris was born on January 25, 1937 in New Orleans, Louisiana. His Baptist minister grandfather first got young Garrett started in show business by placing him atop a chair in church and letting him do his thing. This led to him singing in the choir, attending the Julliard School of Music, soloing with the Harry Belafonte Singers; appearing in *Car Wash* with fellow funnymen Richard Pryor and Franklyn Ajaye; playing the pot-smoking principal in *Cooley High*, and becoming an original cast member on *Saturday Night Live*. He was so multitalented he was called upon to sing an aria or two during his stint there, to overwhelming response. Garrett Morris wasn't just a joke getter, but like a number of *SNL* cast members, Morris also succumbed to easy drugs and a freebasing habit.

It was so bad he became delusional and claimed that he was being controlled by an invisible robot. He almost died on February 1, 1994 when he was shot in the chest and arm by robbers. Morris survived and went on to become a regular on the WB sitcom *The Jamie Foxx Show*, and appeared in *How High* with rappers Method Man and Redman.

Ventriloquist Richard Stanfield (center) with his white black dummy, Mr. Charlie and his black dummy, Willie.

RICHARD AND WILLIE

Stand-up during this time was not without its rising stars either. Even with King Richard lauding over all he surveyed there were other voices making their presence known. Ventriloquist Richard Stanfield and his dummy Willie were becoming recording hit makers with an eventual success of twelve albums, not to mention touring with acts ranging from Nancy Wilson to Sammy Davis Jr. and all the major black acts of the '70s. This all led to lots of money and early retirement for the man with his hand up a piece of wood's "back."

Willie Brown (& Woody): "He was the Richard Pryor of ventriloquists."

Richard Stanfield got involved in comedy because the club owner where he worked needed somebody reliable to fill in for the habitually tardy acts. Why not? The former mailman and policeman was in it for the money anyway. So he got himself a twelve-dollar Paul Winchell doll, painted him black, became skilled and began working. His first year was at the York Club on Western and Florence in Los Angeles under the tutelage of Leroy and Skillet.

> "Those guys were doing it before I was and they did more of a type of vaudeville act. They didn't come out in blackface, but Leroy used to wear greasepaint; a grease that made him sweat, y'know to make him look funny. I got an insight into old vaudeville comedy working with them and the old comic style."

All that learning and hard work culminated in the hit comedy album with Richard Pryor entitled *Richard Pryor Meets Richard & Willie and the SLA.* The latter was an underground band of homegrown terrorists who came above ground when they kidnapped newspaper heiress Patty Hearst. That incident ended in claims of forced sex, brainwashing, a series of bank robberies, and a violent shoot-out/massacre, where the heiress survived and went back to her pampered life and a short-lived career in low-budget movies (usually playing herself), whereas Richard and Willie just made money and stopped at the sex part. According to Stanfield the album sold over five hundred thousand copies.

DARRYL: "Was the life of a comic, or ventriloquist what you expected?"

RICHARD: "That and more. The success was better than I thought it would be; came quicker. It was more fun. I was a single then; lotta women, lotta perks. You go places people treat you different than if you're just an ordinary person, they come at you as being a celebrity."

DARRYL: "How much resistance did you face when you started going blue with a dummy?"

RICHARD: "I got a feeling I was one of the first ventriloquists to go blue and be successful at it. I'm sure somebody may have done it, but they never recorded it. I sold more records than any ventriloquist ever lived—period, point blank."

FRANKLIN AJAYE

Another emerging talent during that era was a young man who Keenan Ivory Wayans would later call the Miles Davis of Comedy, the jazz comedian. His style was intelligent and laid back and influenced by jazz greats, just as were Bill Cosby and Lenny Bruce before him. *Variety* magazine even dubbed him "the black Lenny Bruce" in his early, angrier years. The reference to jazz came because he was always searching and changing up his act, looking for new ways to approach his craft. He strived to be more than a comedian. This cat wanted to be an artist. His influences spanned the creative mediums: Marlon Brando, Miles Davis, Woody Allen, Robert Klein, Joni Mitchell, Gil Scott-Heron, and Picasso. His goal was to incorporate their approach into his comedy; the restless searching of a true creative individual. He was a juxtaposed alternative to the manic wild man known as Pryor. Franklyn Ajaye was not only inventive like Richard, but you never saw him sweat.

> **Robert Townsend:** "Franklyn Ajaye is brilliant. When you talk about somebody who makes me laugh really, really hard—it's Franklyn Ajaye because Franklyn is a smart comedian. A lot of comedians go for the easy joke and it's rare when you see a comedian that is so funny, has their own rhythm, has a unique voice, and I think Franklyn Ajaye is that comedian. I mean he has his own rhythm, but how he writes and how he creates is just brilliant."

Franklyn Ajaye was born in Brooklyn, New York, in 1949 but grew up in Los Angeles. The running joke for him was how he was truly African-American. Dad was from Africa, Mom from America. After dropping out of law school for comedy, Ajaye cut his teeth at the Comedy Store. Being a reluctant performer, his original goal was to be a stand-up comedian for five years and make enough money to quit. The reality was that he dreaded even getting up on stage for those first five years; nerves, thinking about the show all day that he had to do that night, then he'd get on stage and kill. So success made it hard to stick to the original plan. Gaining notoriety and respect altered things as well.

> **Gerard:** "The bit that he did on Carson about coming in last in the marathon in the Olympics was something that I remember from the first time it ran on Carson. It was just a real big thing for me. Also he's real important to me because when I first started doing comedy I was at Morehouse College and I looked and acted and talked just like somebody who'd been in college and so Franklyn always had a...he was basically a mainstream comic as everybody was at that point. Franklyn was not very ethnic. You knew who he was as the fly and some of the other things that he did. He had a very smart and intelligent brand of wit which he still has and I'm still a big fan. Yeah, man. He showed me that you could get this smart, witty, good, strong material off in front of some of these urban...he had that fro. He was a very hip guy."

> **Geoff Brown:** "Incredibly underrated. Probably one of the best writers ever. If all you know about Franklyn Ajaye is the fly in *Car Wash*, you need to know, you need to find out, get somewhere and check out his archives. Fantastic. One of the cats that I watch who will make me write."

Once he got past his first half decade in the business, Ajaye took on a workingman attitude about his profession. He wrote for television shows, recorded three best-selling comedy albums and performed all over the world. In the process he became a comic's comic and an audience favorite, but with the advent of the *Def Jam* era and a more in-your-face comedic style, plus his disdain for the control Hollywood imposed on scripts, Franklyn Ajaye took an extended leave and moved to Melbourne, Australia in 1997.

Occasionally he'd hop over to the States for a show; that is, when he could get one. Comedian Tom Rhodes saw him perform in Australia at a comedy festival and told Ajaye what a fan he was and how Franklyn was so much better than he was when living in the States. Ajaye decided to reconnect with the country of his birth, but all television was looking for were young, new faces. So the living legend wound up taping an hour-long BET comedy special in March 2004 after doing *Comic View* at the behest of longtime friend and host of the moment, J. Anthony Brown.

> "I thought, well, I can't get on any other show. I probably would've never thought about doing *Comic View* at that time, but I thought well y'know that would be an interesting test. Y'know, I thought to myself you've got a book on stand-up comedy out and you've been doing it, y'know, thirty years and at that time I thought the audience is going to be very young and used to the *Comic View* comics; kind of wild and louder and y'know, over the top and very young. I thought it would be interesting to see if I can do my style and entertain them. It was like a test to me at the time. I thought this is a test of my professionalism and my experience.

I've been in another country. I've made a whole other country that doesn't have any of the cultural references that's known to make me laugh. So that was an invaluable experience going into another country and making them laugh, y'know what I mean? So I called them up and they said, 'Yes, please. We'd be honored to have you' and the people at BET, which was quite heartwarming, they treated me amazingly. It was amazing. It was the first time I was welcomed by the country, so to speak. They were like, 'We're really honored to have someone of your caliber.' And then I walked out to do it thinking, well this is going to be...and I had those young people laughing to the point where I did a little nine-minute spot and they gave me a standing ovation at the end. And all the

"The Jazz Comedian," Franklyn Ajaye.

young comics came up to me afterwards. And all the young comics were very familiar with me, which surprised me because I always thought that Pryor and Eddie Murphy, and I guess Martin Lawrence and all of them were really the comedians that the young black comedians had decided to follow and be influenced by and paid attention to and I'd always felt well, they're not paying any attention to me because I'm very low key. In fact it was just the opposite. Every last one of them said, 'Man, I've always been a fan of yours.' I was like, wow!—but then I realized that without changing my style, keeping it conversational and making it low key I was able to take this young black audience and entertain them. That's when BET said would you like to do an hour special for us and I was like, 'Okay, absolutely.'"

The surprise was in the fact Ajaye had written a book to make comics better and felt they were worse. The variance of styles tilted all to one end and as far as he was concerned, his way of doing comedy (laid-back) was from a bygone era.

"I was the laid-back black comic and being laid-back had hurt me over a time, particularly after Eddie hit and the *Def Comedy Jam* because black comedy then became synonymous with, in my opinion, high decibel, very heavily sexually oriented material and a laid-back black comic, they just don't exist. And I was one of them and people would say, 'Ah, your style is too slow for today's attention span. Your style is too slow for today's audience.' And yet I can go out and do a show for a bunch of young kids, I did it in Scottsdale last year, and the young kids are easier to make laugh now for me than they were when I was young. It's easier because they just want to see something...they are so impressed with the fact they're seeing something good; a level above, but yet still accessible. Because that's the whole thing you still want to be accessible even though you're intelligent."

Ajaye felt black comedy and life in general got turned around when we narrowed our perspective. When youth was the only way to go something was lost.

"It's all raw. I mean, in life, you need a mixture of youth and experience. You need youth for the energy. You need experience, veterans, for the refinement, the shaping and if you have a team and you have young people and old people who want to share you really will get the best because they'll shape the younger person. They'll take that energy and teach them the tricks and any young person who's worth their salt; who's halfway intelligent, will want to learn from an older person."

Ajaye was looked upon as unknowingly teaching many within his craft.

Sinbad: "They talk about Steven Wright being a thinking man's comic. Well, that's what Franklyn was, man. Franklyn was just a bad cat. He's still a bad cat, y'know. And I don't think they knew where to place him."

"Right now I'm acting in *Deadwood* and I like that. I like acting on something really good. I'm on a very, very high caliber, very ,very intellectually oriented show that also has the freedom to say anything, freedom to approach any subject, freedom to deal with any type of issue and it's striving for excellence and at this point in my life that's basically all I'm interested in. I've always been interested in the pursuit of excellence in my endeavors. I like the simplicity. All I'm required to do is try to address this role and make it good."

The HBO no-holds-barred western was being produced by David Milch and he wanted the newly returned Ajaye for the role, but a black man in a primetime, uncensored western? One had to wonder how many times he'd be called the N word, but the part turned out to reignite Ajaye's creative juices. And he put future projects in the works.

Royale Watkins: "He laid the foundation for a lot of what we're able to get away with on stage today; such a timeless, classic original act with something to say on stage."

Mystro Clark: "Clever. The first time I saw him I thought he was doing clever stuff. I really didn't know anything about his background. I remember seeing *Car Wash*. He's probably underrated as far somebody you don't really see a lot, but he's a smart, clever dude; very talented guy."

A. J. Jamal: "The most brilliant. I don't know if you realize this, the reason I am a comedian is because of Franklyn Ajaye. I was at Kent State man and I looked at him. I was working as a DJ on like the late shift. I mean it was so late one time I gave away a car and nobody called. That's how many people were listening to my radio show. I took the fifth caller, the third caller then I just said if anybody calls, they win a car. I didn't get one call. So I pulled out a paper, I said forget it. I'm not going to play no more music. I'm going to play what I want to play. I put on a Franklyn Ajaye tape *Don't Smoke Dope Fry Your Hair* and I laughed so hard. I didn't even know who the brotha was, but I said, I want to be like that brotha. I want to do comedy. So if it wasn't for Franklyn Ajaye I wouldn't have even known about getting into the comedy game. I will always credit Franklyn Ajaye as getting me started in comedy."

However, the inspirational force was an enigma to his colleagues and known as one who kept his distance.

AJAYE: "I didn't really hang out with anybody. I was very much a loner, always stayed that way. I was at the Comedy Store at the time, but I never really hung out with any comics, except maybe at the Comedy Store I would talk to guys. Y'know, I would talk to Jay Leno. He and I were kindred spirits in a lot of ways. There was a great comedian, Kelly Monteith. We gravitated to each other because we both had the same style. We'd smoke a joint sometimes behind the Comedy Store together. Then I would go on the road a lot and I was never one of those cats that came back and hung out and formed a lot of stand-up friends. I was respected by them, but I didn't really hang out with them."

DARRYL: "When people meet comedians they expect you to be funny."

AJAYE: "Well, which came first, the chicken or the egg? A lot of cats are 'on' and as a result a lot of people expect them to be on and people expect me to be on. I've had a lot of people when they meet me and they say, 'Well, when are you going to tell me a joke?' I realize we are stereotyped that way and we do help court it. We really do court that. A lot of them are that way; naturally they are 'on.' I think sometimes it's insecurity at being serious and not taking a risk at being dull. I don't mind being dull. I don't mind being boring. I'm not interested in trying to impress no...and then when I am feeling in an interesting mood when I may get into something in the conversation, then people will say, 'Well, man—you don't have to be a comedian now.' So it's kind of a...I say I'm just being natural right now."

DARRYL : "And some people don't understand certain wit at certain times."

AJAYE: "Yeah, right. I'm just being witty; like when you're in school."

DARRYL : "When people talk about Franklyn Ajaye fifty or one hundred years from now, what do you want them to say?"

AJAYE: "I want them to say, 'God, he's still alive. That muthaf*#ka hasn't died. He's 200 years old. How does he do it? How?'"

The Golden era of comedy also introduced the public to something else it hadn't seen before—a black/white comedy team. Jack Benny and Rochester worked together, but they technically weren't a team. Where was Eddie Anderson when Jack had his face pressed up against Carole Lombard's in the World War II comedy *To Be or Not to Be?*

No, these guys were a real, you-don't-see-one-without-the-other team and they did it during a time of racial straddling. Part of America wanted to abandon the stereotypes and attempt to live as brothers and sisters in harmony. The other part of America wanted to drown the first part.

TIM & TOM

The "Happy Days" image of the '50s (which became popular again in the '70s) wasn't every-body's existence. Not all Brill Cream wearers were rocking around the clock or even dancing the Tennessee Waltz. A lot of folks were having hard times and they weren't just black peo-ple, but that's always been the one thing you could say about poverty—it is colorblind.

Tom Dreesen was a poor white kid with eight brothers and sisters growing up near the south side of Chicago in Harvey, Illinois. Living in a shack with no bathtub, no shower, and no hot water made for literally funky times. So Tom did what any little six-year-old white kid would do—he shined shoes. Popping his rag and humming tunes, he moonlighted as a caddy, a pinsetter in bowling alleys, and a paper boy. Then at age seventeen he went into the Navy for four years. There he met an old black man named Washington who guided him toward a diet of self-improvement books to expand his mind. This type of analytical and result-based liter-ature consumption was invaluable years later when Dreesen was doing volunteer work for the Jaycees (a community-based organization) helping out disadvantaged youth. He con-cluded that 70–80% of all teenage crimes were either drug- or alcohol-related. So he wrote a drug education program, teaching grade school kids the ills of drug abuse with humor.

Tim Reid was a black graduate from Norfolk State College and a recruit of E. I. DuPont. He went to Chicago and read in the local paper that the Jaycees were looking for young men. That night he heard about a drug prevention program and approached the originator offer-ing to assist. He was politely turned down flat and told the position for helper was filled, only to get a call the next day from the rejecter saying his previously scheduled buddy had bowed out and did Reid still want to get down. Sure.

From there Reid and Dreesen convinced the school board they could do it and did so for a couple of years, becoming a number 1 program in fifty states and twenty-two foreign countries. They'd simply go into the schools, make the kids laugh and educate them on the sly, but it took an eighth grader to tell them what was really going on. "You guys are so funny you ought to become a comedy team." At first the thought of an integrated comedy team overwhelmed them because no one had ever done it before, but why not, they thought. They played at integrated schools and it had worked.

So in 1969 Tim & Tom became the first black/white comedy team and soon discovered that racism and prejudice never cared much for logic, always hated to see it coming. When they'd perform in a white club, the redneck mentality of the whites who hated the black

The first interracial comedy team of Tim (Reid) and Tom (Dreesen) leisurely clowning around at Mr. Kelly's in Chicago in 1972.

man with a deep, abiding passion weren't mad at black Tim Reid. They reserved their disdain for Dreesen for being a nigger lover. Whereas the brothers at the black clubs who despised and plotted the death of whitey on a daily basis gave Dreesen a pass because they were too busy twisting their faces up at the Uncle Tom that brought the cracker in there in the first place.

Despite the fact that most people who saw them loved the act, there was that element that felt it was their duty to control the amusement of others. The fourth time the team hit the stage was at the Golden Horseshoe in Chicago Heights, Illinois and some big corn-fed galoot put out a lit cigarette in Reid's face. They went flying over tables and chairs to get the son of a bitch, who happened to have played for the taxi squad of the Chicago Bears. Regardless—it was on!

Pioneers have never had it easy, but these guys had to be resilient and ready for anything. Since there was no precedent for their act they played everything from the Playboy circuit to the chitlin' circuit, the black-owned/black-operated chitlin' circuit: The High Chaparral in Chicago, The Burning Spear, The Dating Club Lounge, The 20 Grand in Detroit (owned by known tough guy Bill Kabush, and it's where the Motown performers would break in their acts before they went on the road), The Sugar Shack in Boston, and then the big time—Club Harlem in Atlantic City, which was the apex of the chitlin' circuit.

The odd thing about Club Harlem was that you opened on Saturday (as opposed to closing like most clubs) and you worked until the following Friday. The first show was at 10 o'clock at night. Second show was 2 o'clock in the morning. Third show was 6 o'clock in the morning. That was the breakfast show. The waiters, waitresses, bartenders, and all the night people would come out. The pimps took the hos there regularly to celebrate a job well done for the week. At Club Harlem this meant 1350 black people packed to the rafters and one Tom Dreesen.

On these occasions, the Master of Ceremonies would introduce the comedy *team* of Tim & Tom. Reid would enter, take the microphone and say things like, "We'd like to thank you for coming out, ladies and gentlemen. We're looking forward to giving you a great show, etc., etc." and "we" this and "we" that, yet he was the only one on stage. This would go on until the audience started to mumble about there only being one person out there, yet he kept saying "we." At around that time Dreesen would materialize from the back and look about hesitantly as he slowly made his way to the stage. Once there he'd point out to Reid how there were none of his people in the crowd. "No, it doesn't look like any of them showed up."

"Then I guess we better be funny."

"What do you mean 'we,' white man?"

Working so many different venues they had to know what each other would do in any situation. While working on heckler material Dreesen told Reid that if Tim ever got racist flack in a white club Tom should step forward and say, "Hey, leave him alone. He's mine. Go out and get your own. After all you know how hard they are to train." Reid quickly pointed out to his well-meaning partner that it would be totally racist to say such a thing and that it was ill advised. Dreesen apologized profusely. *"That's okay, Tom. I know you didn't mean any harm. You have to throw out whatever comes to mind when we're writing. We're creating. You just can't say that, that's all,"* Reid said.

That same night around 1 a.m. some drunken brother at the 20 Grand yelled out, "Hey, honky, hey, white boy—what the f*#k you doing here?" Reid wasted no time and said, "Hold on brother—leave him alone. He's mine. Go get your own. You know how hard they are to train." The crowd roared.

The lessons and rules of black comedy were not lost on Dreesen, who'd grown up around blacks. He'd always marveled at black humor when he'd hang around black bars where they knew him simply as "white boy." Dreesen even claims that he was thirteen years old when he found out his real name wasn't "white boy."

"I would listen to black folks talk. There were times I think they had no idea how funny the shit was that they were doing 'cause they have a way of, as you know, cutting through the fat. Brevity is the essence of comedy. Anybody who knows how to write a joke knows the two things about comedy—comedy is number one nine-tenths surprise. So the set-up line has to hide the punchline. And the other rule is there are no victimless jokes. Someone's got to be the victim of the joke; the wife,

Tom Dreesen and Sammy Davis, Jr. when the latter hosted The Tonight Show in 1978. The marquee inset is from the first time Dreesen opened for Davis at Caesar's Palace in Las Vegas and Davis demanded his act's name appear large to give Dreesen future credibility.

the bus driver—or yourself, but somebody. The first time I saw Richard Pryor I was like oh man, he speaks to where I come from. And years later when he saw me working, the first thing he said to me, he was in the back of the Comedy Store and I didn't know he was there and I was doing all this stuff about being raised in a black neighborhood, he came up afterwards. 'Man, don't get off that subject. There ain't a white boy in the world can get away with what you're doing. You lived that. You can tell you grew up there.'"

Dreesen was so into the black experience and so genuine and authentic that he'd often be asked by whites if black people actually laughed at his material. So he recorded his comedy album in front of an all-black crowd and when that question was ever brought up again by white folks, he'd hand them a record and request $10.99.

Though they worked *The David Frost Show* and *The Merv Griffin Show* and put out an album, Dreesen and Reid never considered Tim & Tom as having "made it." They struggled and they attribute that struggle to the reason that drove them apart. After six years together, Reid wanted to go out on his own and went on to play disc jockey Venus Flytrap on the CBS hit *WKRP in Cincinnati*, ABC and the WB's *Sister, Sister, Frank's Place* on CBS, and many other shows, whereas Dreesen toured with the likes of Smokey Robinson, Sammy Davis Jr., and Frank Sinatra (for thirteen years) and made over 500 appearances on national television as a stand-up comedian, including sixty-one of those on *The Tonight Show*. The team that had broken racial ground presenting smart, non-cooning, no jive-talking or pandering material ended in 1975. There has not been another such black/white team since.

The only other one of any note was when Slappy White teamed with Steve Rossi. What they actually did was Slappy's act and Steve's act and combined it. So it wasn't anything new and original. Besides, they lacked the team spontaneity of Tim & Tom. With White &

Rossi, clever took a back seat to watermelon jokes. That act lasted for about a year.

The West Coast club scene for black comedians consisted of hosting for jazz bands or performing in between those bands. One of the established clubs in Los Angeles, or South Central as it was known, was the Parisian Room on the southwest corner of Washington Blvd. and LaBrea Ave. Reynaldo Rey was a regular act there:

> "I was out here two weeks before I went to work at the Parisian Room. I went up to talent night and I went up, I did my thing and they hired me. I was there for eight years. Red Holloway was the bandleader. Played saxophone. He was bad. We had a ball. All the great jazz musicians, Dizzy Gillespie, Ramsey Lewis, Carmen McCrae, George Shearing, Milt Jackson Quartet, biggies came through there, man. Biggies. And I worked with them all. Nina Simone, Esther Phillips. I got paid to work with those people."

> **DARRYL:** "Now I heard that Stu Gilliam once came to the Parisian Room and tried to sabotage your act." [Gilliam was an actor/comedian known for his appearances on *Rowan & Martin's Laugh-In* and his own network sitcom *Harris & Company.*]

> **REY:** "Some big-name female vocalist was booked. Stu Gilliam called the club and put it in the paper that rather than have her with an unprofessional, unfunny, and a few more modifiers, he would work for free on her show. So the owner said, 'Come on. Reynaldo, we're going to let you sit this one out.' I said I've got to see this pro. I've got to go see how a pro works since I'm unprofessional. They ran him off stage the first night. He went across the street to Tommy Tucker's Playroom and got drunk and couldn't go back on and the owner asked me if I'd go up and finish out the night. I said, 'Yeah.' Before they ran him off stage, he'd told the audience, 'You don't have to laugh at me, but I refuse to stoop to your level.' He's an idiot. I wonder whatever happened to him. He just disappeared. He might've dug a hole, crawled in and pulled the dirt over on himself."

The Heir
to the Throne

CHAPTER 15

"For every hundred men that can handle adversity only one can handle success. Because along with success comes the responsibility to remain successful."
— Tom Dreesen

In 1979, the Comedy Store comedians behaved like an organized union. For the longest time they'd performed at the spot that was once Ciro's and had done so for no pay. Well, economic times had changed, the club was on its feet, and those grassroots comics who put it there wanted some show of gratitude. No, they didn't want a percentage of the door or a cut from the bar receipts. They wanted gas money and respect, and when they didn't get it they went on strike. It lasted for eight weeks. In the end management gave in to the tune of $7.50 a show. Gas was cheap back then.

As President Ronald Reagan came into power in the early '80s, the anointed King Richard went into a stupor...for several years. Pryor, like all smokers of rock cocaine, intensified his high to the point of wanting to do nothing more than sustain it. With his almost annuity-like income from films, writing, albums, and other various resources, he was an addict with more of a problem than most. He could afford to get high. He could call his connection and have them bring him his drugs in such a mass quantity that leaving his own home on the compound became a non-issue. He could send out for food and never have to go anywhere. For awhile there, he didn't.

The King was in asthenia and his only trusted advisor was a glass pipe. Black comedy needed a new monarch to rule over the land and the names of Stu Gilliam, Scoey Mitchell, and Dap Sugar Willy didn't exactly send the crowds rushing to buy tickets. Though Scoey Mitchell was one of the first big blacks in the business—producer, writer, director—talent of a renaissance nature meant little to the new decade folks. So a quiet search was being made for the next audience slayer.

Word was there was a funny kid on the East coast named Charlie Barnett. He was hilarious, they said. The only comic who could fill Pryor's vacated shoes.

CHARLIE BARNETT

Q: "Why did Eddie Murphy get *Saturday Night Live?*"

A: "Because Charlie Barnett couldn't read."

Barnett could possibly have been the best stand-up of his generation, but failed to make it to the big time, so instead he's regulated to being a trivia question. This is extremely unfortunate because Barnett was one of those performers you couldn't stop watching. Born in Bluefield, West Virginia on September 23, 1954, he worked on TV (*Miami Vice*), film (*DC Cab*), and headlined comedy clubs. However, his greatest gift was as a brilliant street performer in Washington Square Park in New York City. One of those impressed was a young Dave Chappelle, who Barnett later mentored. A promising career was cut short on March 16, 1996 when Charlie Barnett died of AIDS, presumably from drug abuse.

> **Bob Sumner:** "Charlie Barnett was one of my inspirations in starting a comedy club. He used to spend the night at my house to make sure that he'd get to the gig on time."

> **Ian Edwards:** "The greatest comic I ever saw perform. Here's a good Charlie Barnett story, it was one of those clubs that if you had it on your schedule it would ruin your whole week. Your heart would start beating above an average rate when they booked you on Monday. And your heart would just get louder until after you bomb or do good on Wednesday. You just want to get it over with. As soon as you cross the bridge it was like you were going to your execution. You went to a paid execution. I don't remember how much they were paying, 50 bucks or more, something like that. It wasn't worth it no matter how much they were paying. Even if they were paying a G; even then it wasn't worth the way you felt. So we go to Terminal D. I was booked on the show, and everybody gets in. This is how bad it was—a bunch of state troopers showed up on their night off. There was a bell in the middle of the room and it's a long dark room and somebody would just stand up and ring the bell when they had enough of you. That's how bad it was.

> So that night, everybody got destroyed, and Charlie was last. He was the headliner; Charlie did not go on stage. He did not. He did not hold the mic. He ran

into the middle of the room, stood on somebody's table, told them to turn the lights on, and just performed right in the middle of the room, and proceeded to rip. Charlie can figure out what to do in any situation on top of him being a phenomenal performer. He does it with extreme confidence. He was just smart, he was like, why be in this long ass room on stage—be in the middle of the room. Everybody's gonna be able to see me, everybody gonna have to deal with me. I'm watching these comics get annihilated. This is not going down. He ripped the tablecloth off. He jumped up and just started yelling and doing his routine.

He just gets them. Like Charlie Barnett did not have the best written material. And that doesn't mean it was bad either, but you just never seen anybody perform like this. I've never seen Charlie perform and not get standing ovations. And I remember nobody was faster than him. One time Charlie was in the middle of the room and a heckler started messing with him. So the heckler stepped up to Charlie, he was trying to intimidate Charlie because Charlie was messing him up. So he was all in Charlie's face, 'what did you say muthaf*#ka?' And then the guy unbuttoned his shirt. And then Charlie took off his shirt, and then the crowd laughed at that and the guy took off his shirt. And then Charlie dropped down his pants and mooned the dude. Charlie was willing to go further than the guy. The dude got back in Charlie's face and Charlie moved away and did something else. And then later on, he told me lack of space breeds tension. 'When I was in the dude's face it was a lot of tension like anything can happen at that moment so you relieve the tension. So he also knew psychology, I was like this made me focus more and let me know this is a bigger thing. It's just not going up on stage and telling some jokes and people that know that, those are the good comedians.'"

Charlie Murphy: "Charlie Barnett was like a comet: burned bright, but for a short period of time."

Bob Sumner: "Charlie knew how to make money. Charlie knew how to spend money. Charlie would get on Washington Square Park, man—he's the one that created that whole scene of...y'know they say Michael Colyar did it, but Charlie Barnett started it. In terms of being in the park, making money on the side with the hat out there, telling jokes and making a couple of hundred dollars just by doing that. Great guy. Had a lot of wisdom. Charlie Barnett has a lot to do with Dave Chappelle."

Of course the show must go on and fortunately the demons which possessed Charlie Barnett were ignored when they meandered by Eddie Murphy's door. This young firebrand had made up his mind at an early age of which career path suited him best and was simply waiting to get in close proximity to puberty to fulfill his destiny.

Charlie Murphy: "My brother was always aware of what he wanted to do with his life. From a very young age; almost from the time he could talk he said he wanted to be on TV, which seemed unreal to us because back then there was only one black TV show, *Julia*."

Thus behind every dead or smoked-out comic there's a live, sober one ready to take their place. Soon after *Saturday Night Live* producer Lorne Michaels installed second-choice Murphy in Charlie Barnett's slot as a featured member on NBC's late night sketch comedy phenomenon, Eddie Murphy put on a James Brown wig, got into a hot tub and America found its new black clown.

> **Katt Williams:** "It took four Kings of Comedy to rival what Eddie Murphy did himself at 19. There was a point when Eddie Murphy was comedy and was the comedy voice for young, urban muthaf*#kas. THE Voice and there was not a peer with Eddie Murphy. You have to remember that. He was without peer at that particular juncture of his career. It was not 'Eddie Murphy and...' It was only Eddie Murphy."

> **Chris Spencer:** "Probably the best comedic actor living today. One of the greatest comedic actors ever. One of the best stand-ups ever. One of the most genuine people that I've ever met in terms of giving you insights. He's just a hell of a storyteller."

EDDIE MURPHY

Eddie Murphy was born on April 3, 1961 in Brooklyn, New York and began his doing stand-up at an early age. He performed on *SNL* from 1981–1984, introducing characters such as Tyrone Green, an author with a racist streak; Velvet Jones, whose main mission was to recruit "hos" and Mr. Robinson, his ghetto parody of Mister Rogers' Neighborhood. He gave America a hot tub-loving James Brown, Gumby with an attitude, and a crooning Jesse Jackson singing about "Hymie Town." Life had changed.

> **Charlie Murphy:** "He was doing his thing all his life and when we grew up I went into the service and he started doing *Saturday Night Live*. When I came out of the service he was a star."

Murphy became the breakout talent on the show and like *SNL* cast members before him, Hollywood beckoned and Eddie Murphy answered the call with a smash comedy film trifecta: *48 Hrs.* with Nick Nolte in 1982, *Trading Places* with Dan Ackroyd in 1983, and his next victory *Beverly Hills Cop* in 1984. Oddly enough *Beverly Hills Cop* was written for Sylvester Stallone and reworked for Murphy. It's believed that Stallone dropped out to do the cinematic classic *Rhinestone* with Dolly Parton.

Murphy was box office gold. The laugh, the grin, the wiseguy demeanor and always-in-control attitude catapulted him into being one of the most sought-after actors in Hollywood. Even after lambasting the very community that had made him a more than wealthy man when he proclaimed at the Academy Awards ceremony that he'd probably never receive an Oscar because of his pigment, Murphy continued to pack 'em in where it mattered—the theaters.

Curtis Arceneaux: "They had given him that green light; the keys to the city. One of his jokes on stage was, 'Man, at this point I don't even have to be funny. I can just come on stage and say "bananas" and people will laugh.' And so he said 'bananas' and people started laughing."

Katt Williams: "The movies he did changed movies. There was a *Beverly Hills Cop*. There was a *Beverly Hills Cop II*. There was also a *III* if I'm correct. That was unheard of. That was unheard of at that particular time in history; to do a movie, a sequel and then another one. To do it as a nigga was absolutely unheard of—period. Richard did not achieve in movies what Eddie Murphy achieved and so if Richard is a comedy god and the fact that you don't mention Eddie Murphy as a comedy god automatically means he's underrated because he's achieved the same things as Richard Pryor if not greater. Eddie Murphy did more than Richard Pryor from a financial standpoint as it relates to stand-up comedy and movies and produced and then wrote and then cast other niggas and brought them all together. One man did all that."

Eddie Murphy on top of the world. Courtesy of Comedy Magazine.

In any case, Eddie Murphy was now a star. Murphy did two concert films: *Delirious* and the theatrical release *Raw*, which he co-wrote with friend and fellow Black Packer, Keenan Ivory Wayans. Other box office hits followed, most notably *The Golden Child* in 1986 and *Coming to America* with Arsenio Hall in 1987 and then he pulled a comedy casting coup with *Harlem Nights* starring himself, Richard Pryor, Redd Foxx, Della Reese, Arsenio Hall, Robin Harris, Reynaldo Rey, and Charlie Murphy.

Charlie Murphy: "The ultimate experience. I got to chill with legends. They'd sit back and talk about the old days and this muthaf*#ka Redd Foxx told one of my friends he needs to get his teeth fixed. He f*#ked my friend up, man. My friend had a chipped tooth, a bad tooth. That tooth gave Redd Foxx two hours right there. He destroyed him. He spent two hours on his teeth. Redd Foxx is hands down the funniest nigga I've ever been around in my life."

Actress/Comedienne, Kym Whitley: "Reynaldo Rey said, 'hey, lady as long as I've got a face you've got a place to sit.' I said, 'well, as long as you got a face like that I guess I'm going to keep standing.' Richard Pryor fell out of his seat; spilled coffee everywhere."

Eddie Murphy was so hot he reached the pinnacle of pop culture stardom—he was lampooned in a porno flick entitled *Beaverly Hills Cop*.

By the early '90s Murphy was the Sidney Poitier of black comedies. If you needed a funny black guy—call Eddie's people (And when they couldn't afford him they'd say, "We want an Eddie Murphy type"). Even his own brother Charlie would get massive doses of "EddieMurphymania" when he'd go out on auditions.

Charlie Murphy: "I'd go into these auditions and automatically as soon as I walk in, 'Oh, you're his brother. Can you laugh like Eddie? Can you be like a fake Eddie Murphy?'

No, I can't.

There was a guy I know, I forgot his name, but he gonna come over and tell us he wanted to offer me a contract to sign to be Eddie's lookalike. I told him to 'Get the f*#k outta my face, man. I'm nobody's f*#kin' lookalike.'"

Eddie didn't need a lookalike, he needed a clone: one to work and one to play. Murphy loved the night life. In between flicks he was often seen on the town with his massive and growing entourage.

Comedian, Ricky Harris: "Eddie Murphy had his crew: Robert Townsend, his brother Charlie, and a couple of his security—that was his crew."

Murphy was young and living the life. He was the one who made it possible for young blacks to imagine following in his footsteps. His success seemed more feasible than that of a Pryor. To the newer generation Richard Pryor was from another era, but more importantly, from another mindset. This was a genius, an Einstein, an unattainable goal. Though Murphy was also brilliant, he was a young man talking about things of his generation. Not everybody had come from the streets, much less a brothel.

Edwonda White: "I think he just completely changed the game. Most comedians that came after him, they can lie if they want to, but they idolized him and they emulated him. A lot of them have his mannerisms, his style and all of that stuff. They think that they're being original, but they're really doing Eddie Murphy."

Eddie Murphy: "Before I came out you had Richard and Bill Cosby and Flip Wilson and Redd Foxx and a handful of people. And after I came out it was just a f*#kin' explosion of comics. So because I was so young it made the art form accessible to a lot of people, a lot of young people was like, 'Hey, yo—I can do that shit. That nigga's the same as me.' That's why you see all these millions of niggas telling jokes now."

Rodney Perry: "I knew that I wanted to be a stand-up when I saw Eddie Murphy on *SNL* and I had listened to his albums. It was attainable through Eddie Murphy to me."

Mystro Clark: "When he got on *Saturday Night Live* that's when I first realized that maybe I can do that. Now that's something I can visualize. He was like nineteen. I was like about fourteen and I was like okay, I can relate to that. I used to watch *Saturday Night Live* every week. So that made a big impact on me as far as a young brother doing that type of stuff and looking like he was having fun."

Cedric the Entertainer: "He's just one of those guys that inspire you to believe that you can do it all."

Murphy was so high up he had only one place to go. In the mid-'90s he produced the animated *The P.J.'s* for FOX until the network got nervous over sponsorship concerns and canceled it. *The P.J.'s* was then picked up by the WB, who in turn also canceled it after one season.

Charlie Murphy: "The P.J.'s was watered down. It wasn't real. Too many people got involved who had no concept of what it was like to live in the projects. Muthaf*#kas that ain't got a clue, but they got a job."

Suddenly the town whose streets he helped pave with gold couldn't wait to write him off. Every movie that didn't live up to his heyday work was seen as a death knell for his career. To Eddie it was the business of being in show business. He'd been a stand-up. He knew that you can't get a standing ovation every night. Sometimes people smile, other times snicker, but that's show business, do your best and enjoy the ride.

Ajai Sanders: "Eddie Murphy taught me how to really fall in love with the art form of comedy. One night Eddie Griffin, Suzanne Suter, and some other folks were like, 'We're going up to Eddie's house.' So we go up to Eddie's house and it's a big party. Some people are playing pool, other people are all in different parts of the house, but there was this one part of the house—it had these different parlors and he had this white room where there were like these white chiffon curtains that separated that room from every other part and I remember looking up at the ceiling and I actually saw outside. He had a convertible roof. He had pulled the roof back. I was like, Okay. This is what money does. I was real fascinated, but I was trying not to be impressed. So he invited me to come sit on the couch in the white room and we were watching *Amos 'n Andy* all night. I was like, wow! This is heaven. This is comedy heaven. It was funny because there were so many other things going on in the house. The house was huge, but it was him and I sitting there. He was just like feeding me all this information, the history. It was like a kid. Like he was five years old seeing Christmas for the first time. He taught me how to really appreciate real comedy and never settle for less."

Murphy practiced what he preached. Like a phoenix he never stopped rising to the occasion. In 1996's *The Nutty Professor* (his recognized comeback film) he played eight characters. Upon its release many comics indicated he'd been greedy by opting to play every member of his family and that he should have employed other black actors. When asked whom did they suggest, the answer was always the same: *"Me."* What Eddie did was show a broad range of talent and shore up his legacy as the foremost comedic actor (of any race) to stand before a camera.

Madd Marv: "It's almost seems as though there's nothing he can't do. I think he's the best comedy actor we've produced so far, but I'd like to see him play some drama; should blow it up. Show them he could do like Robin Williams did. You know, just play some off-the-wall characters that's totally different than what he's ever done before."

Murphy was the first hip-hop comic and dominated and dictated what other comedians would try to do for decades. His brash nature was a perfect follow up to the groundbreaking style and impact of the Ruler. Pryor had overturned so much soil the only thing left to do was plant and Murphy had all the tools. He could tell a joke, write a joke, sing, do impressions, mimic, and he also had an intangible; a quality reminiscent of a live-action Bugs Bunny. He always had a scheme up his sleeve, never at a loss for words and he always seemed to know what he was doing even when it blew up in his face. But most importantly, Eddie Murphy always connected to his audience to the point of pulling off a stunt like looking directly into the camera. The moviegoers loved Murphy and like his fuzzy-tailed counterpart Bugs he milked it.

DARRYL: "What's the most gratifying thing you ever did on stage?"

EDDIE: "I guess when I played Madison Square Garden because I sold the Garden out in like fifteen minutes for two shows. I'm from New York so that was a big deal."

DARRYL: "You are without peer when it comes to black comedians or comedy actors. Does it ever frustrate you to be compared to other black talent?"

EDDIE: "Not at all. Not at all. It's flattering and it keeps you contemporary. They call your name whenever there's a new muthaf*#ka come out they be like, 'He's the next so & so' or 'He reminds me of Eddie.' So it keeps you contemporary."

DARRYL: "Who are your influences and why?"

EDDIE: "Richard Pryor because he's the best that ever did it. Bill Cosby was an influence as well because he's a brilliant comedian. Y'know it's interesting a lot of my influences weren't comedians. I like Muhammad Ali and Elvis Presley and Bruce Lee. These guys had as much of an influence on me as anybody else."

DARRYL: "How do you want to be remembered?"

EDDIE: "How do I want to be remembered? I don't know. That's a hard one. I don't know how to answer that. It seems like it's an easy question. How do I want to be remembered?"

Of course the question demands thought because Eddie Murphy, like all brilliant artists, made his brand of comedy look easy. He was more than just a comedian/actor/producer/writer/director/voice-over artist—he was an inspiration. It was his crossover appeal that signaled that maybe white America was willing to allow more of this type of comedy into the fold. Young aspiring comedians dreaming of the day and contemporaries realizing the iron was hot reached out and grabbed their own brass ring.

WHOOPI GOLDBERG

One of the talents to walk through the door Eddie left open was a black woman with problems. On paper she stood little more of a chance than maybe getting on stage a few times a week, settling down with some guy and trying to provide her kids a life with some stability. Whoopi Goldberg was never good at sticking to the cookie-cutter script.

> **Sommore:** "She played their game. She walked their walk."

Whoopi Goldberg was born Caryn Johnson in New York City, New York on November 13, 1949. Her television special, *Fontaine...Why Am I Straight?*, garnered the one-time welfare mother national attention. Goldberg demonstrated a talent for not only comedic characters, but ones with depth and pathos. Much like Pryor, her comedy was derived from the character traits and situations. She thought in multi-layered context and combined political satire, monstrous acting chops, and a flair for what is funny. Whoopi became the new female inspiration. She gained world acclaim and critical accolades for playing Miss Celie in Steven Spielberg's *The Color Purple* in 1985, after starring on Broadway in a one-woman show that opened in October 1984. She won an Academy Award for Best Supporting Actress for her role as the fake psychic medium in 1990's *Ghost*. (Making her the first African-American stand-up comedian to receive the award). At the time only three other black Americans had won the honor in the acting categories (Hattie McDaniel, Sidney Poitier, and Lou Gossett Jr.).

Along with fellow comedians Billy Crystal and Robin Williams, Whoopi started Comic Relief to provide food and shelter to the homeless. She's known for auditioning for any and everything, including the lead in *The Princess Bride*, which eventually went to a blond-haired, blue-eyed actress.

Goldberg starred in *Sister Act* and *Sister Act 2*, produced the game show *The Hollywood Squares* from 1998–2002, and in 2002 she picked up a Tony Award for her work as a producer for Broadway's *Thoroughly Modern Millie*. She was the executive producer and the star of her own self-titled sitcom on NBC from 2003–2004.

> **Loni Love:** "I really like her tenacity. I like her drive. I like what she stands for."

> **Leslie:** "Y'know when comedy was coming out everybody was like, Eddie Murphy and Whoop, Whoop, Whoop, and me I was glad about Eddie and all of them, but I was really glad about Whoopi because I was like damn, she's a regular looking black girl too. She ain't all pretty and everything. Shit, I could do this shit. It made me feel like I could really go and do it."

A number of stand-up comedians retire or semi-retire from the stage once film and/or television obligations become too pressing to carve out time to rant. Regular employees look forward to the golden day in the sun and the company trinket or certificate affirming a job...done. Comedians think differently on just about every other subject than normal society. Their thoughts on kicking back in Bermudas:

DO YOU EVER PLAN ON RETIRING?

Mike Bonner: "At this point Ced retires. Martin Lawrence can retire. Muthaf*#ka's will look up and just quit. I won't get any money from this shit if I quit."

Bernie Mac: "There's no such thing. I have too much life to think about retiring. I'm thinking about directing, bringing forth new talent. No Hell No."

Robert Townsend: "No. When you love what you do you're not really working. So it's not anything to retire from because y'know, what I do is fun. It's not like, 'Ah man, I got to get in there and make a TV show. I've got to make a movie, ahhh, man. I got to show up on the set.' I love it so I think I'll be doing this until I die."

Marc Howard: "When my life retires, that's when I'll stop doing stand-up."

Brad Sanders: "Retire from what? I don't plan on it. I might have to, but I'm not planning to. No."

Pierre: "I don't know. Whenever I see Reynaldo Rey I say no. He's hanging in there and he's still funny. That's actually a good question. I don't know. I do get tired at times of comedy. Well, I don't get tired of comedy. I get tired of the bullshit, y'know that we have to go through as comics. Y'know, the negotiating or the conditions. See nowadays you have so many people that open up so many kinds of clubs. A lot of them are failing because of the treatment they do to comedians. Now if it's at a level where you're taking a limo and there's five thousand people sitting in the seats and it's packed every night, then who wants to retire from that? It's so easy. Look at John Witherspoon. Y'know, now at his age let John go up to a place where he ain't getting paid or paid the money he wants or the turnout's horrible or he's got to go through the kitchen or he's got to ride over in a beat-up truck then he would get to retiring, maybe. But if my conditions don't turn out better I could see myself retiring, probably when I'm about...I don't know. I don't know when. I love it still. I think I have a lot to prove still. My fans who come see me love my act. People who come see me love it. They always ask me why I'm not larger than what I am and I kind of owe it to them to keep it up because they've been in my corner for so long."

Tony Tone: "Naw man, I really don't. I think as long as I function and live I'll always enjoy stand up because that's my high. That's my crack. Comedy is my crack."

Roger Rodd: "Retiring usually requires that you made some money. So that's not even an option."

Ruben Paul: "Never. To be honest with you I kind of thought that when you start doing stand-up and then you blow up and you start doing movies that you just won't have the time to do stand-up. And there really truly isn't any example of any comedian that's really, really, really successful in movies that do stand-up regularly."

Sinbad: "I don't know what retirement is for a comic. I mean think about it is retirement like never working again or is retirement like I can do a couple of movies? We don't know what retirement is for an entertainer. Is it when they quit calling you? Then you get retired."

Reynaldo Rey: "No. I like these paid vacations. If I want to go somewhere I just book myself."

Sommore: "Of course I do. I think when other things strike my interest. When I feel comfortable enough and satisfied with what I've accomplished with stand-up—then I'll probably move on."

Adele Givens: "Oh yeah, definitely. I don't think I'll ever stop being who I am on stage, because 98% of that is me anyway, but that getting on the airplane and swelling up like a bag of potato chips, that's going to have to give."

WHAT ARE YOU GOING TO DO IF YOU RETIRE?

Shang: "Just drink Pina Coladas on an island with naked bitches."

BUT YOU'LL BE OLD.

"I'll be sixty-nine. That's what I'll be."

Darren Carter: "Here's the thing: I'd love to be able to not have to do stand-up, but still want to do it."

Honest John: "Just saying to hell with it? Oh, that thought crosses your mind for about five minutes or so when things are going bad or when you've dealt with some bullshit, but no."

Evan Lionel: "When I do think about that I think about other things in life because I'm only thinking about my child and my family. That's when I'm not thinking about myself. If it was just me I would do this for the rest of my life. Because if I'm on my own I can deal with the ups and downs that go with it, but when you take a family through that, that's a different thing. When your child cannot eat properly because daddy is trying to be committed to comedy that's a whole other ball of wax. That's something that any man who is a man really, really considers and thinks, 'I've got to do better or either I've got to leave this alone to take care of my family.'"

Richard of Richard & Willie: "That's why I can sit here today and don't have to work; about ninety percent of the money I made, fifty percent of it I invested it in real estate and other things and I saved it so I don't have to work until the day I die. I don't have to be a ventriloquist struggling at night at sixty years old trying to make people laugh. I don't have to do that. So thank God."

Edwonda White: "No. I think I will always do stand-up and I think that most people who do stand-up well will always be comedians because they will always have an audience that will listen to them."

Alex Thomas: "I think when stand-up is over I'll be just a straight actor. I will never stop being funny. I'll always have something funny to say. I just want it to be more of a hobby later on in my career versus mandatory to eat. Y'know what I mean? I want to do stand-up when I want to do stand-up. I don't wanna have to do it for a job for the rest of my life. I mean, stand-up comedy was just my stepping stone. It was just my way to get in this entertainment business; a way to get in the door. And once I got in the door it opened up all the doors: stand-up comedy led to movies, movies led to TV and y'know what I mean? I pretty much do it all."

Cedric the Entertainer: "Yeah. I plan on opening up two Taco Bells in Des Moines, Iowa and just sell big beefy burritos and taquitos. Farmers love Mexican food. Y'know, it's some shit they can't grow. I don't really ever see myself as having an official retirement like the rappers do where I'll just do a retirement then come back out of retirement and then retire again. I don't think I'll ever do that. I love to perform."

Jay Phillips: "No. I'm trying to go until the wheels fall off, man. I'm trying to pattern my career after Bill Cosby, George Carlin, folks of that nature who not only started in the game at twenty, twenty-one years old, but now these guys are...I can't begin to know how old these folks are, but well into their upper 50s, mid-60s and they're still doing stand-up; still doing cameos in movies, still doing acting, things like that, man and that's really my goal."

Cocoa Brown: "All the time. I'm actually in school now getting my Masters in Education as a back-up plan because I'm not gonna be a coon. I'm not gonna be a Mammy. I'm not going to use my body and f*#k my way to the top."

Smokey Deese: "Hell naw—from what? Talking! How can I get tired of talking, holding an object that weighs one pound, so it's not much of a workout and if I get tired I just put it in the mic stand and I never get tired?"

Leslie: "Man, that's a good question. I'd like to think that I'll become famous and I'm forced into retirement."

Damon Williams: "No, I want to end my career in Vegas, where old comics go to die."

Eddie Griffin: "We did that when we started doing comedy. I thought I was successful when I could make enough money telling jokes to pay rent."

Vince D: "Oh, yes. Move to Louisiana, buy me a big house and live on a couple of acres."

WHAT ARE YOU GOING TO DO—FISH?

"Fish and lay up."

AND GET OLD AND DIE.

"Exactly."

Down Home Blues

CHAPTER 16

"I wear my wedding ring on the wrong hand
because I married the wrong goddamn woman."
— ROBIN HARRIS

A new breed of hungry, serious-minded black comedians were eager to expand their craft. Admitted disciples of Richard Pryor, they called themselves the Black Pack and like the famed Rat Pack before them these were talented guys who liked hanging out together for their mutual benefit. The group consisted of Robert Townsend, Keenan Ivory Wayans, Arsenio Hall, Paul Mooney, and Eddie Murphy. They supported each other, but were also all driven to succeed.

Working the Hollywood circuit of the Improv and the Comedy Store, they changed the face of black comedy with multiple collaborations, from Murphy's *Raw* to *In Living Color* to *Townsend Television* to Arsenio Hall's show. Then in 1985 a man named Michael Williams came along with a dream—a black comedy club called the Comedy Act Theater—and intrigued Damon Wayans and Townsend. This nirvana was initially on Crenshaw and Vernon, but moved to the Regency West building on 43rd two weeks later due to a financial disagreement with the previous owner.

Michael Williams: "The inspiration came from me not feeling my career
(concert promoter) was going anywhere like I had intended and I was somewhat

depressed so I decided to go to the Comedy Store and that's when I realized, wow, this would be great if it was all black because I saw where there was an opportunity."

Now all he needed was a host to help bring the dream to life. Enter Robin Harris.

"I met Robin Harris five years prior to opening the Act at the Hacienda Hotel on Century where a friend of mine had invited me to come hear her sing and Robin opened the show for her and that's where we first met and that's when I first realized that he was something special."

It didn't take long for things to pick up.

"The second week that I was actually open Robert Townsend and Damon Wayans showed up. I had never seen them and it kind of brought the Comedy Act to prominence in the fact that Damon did not like the way Robin had brought him on and the first thing he said was, 'Doesn't that guy look like a black, ugly Eddie Murphy?' and Robin heard what he said and ran back into the room and he said something back to Damon and Damon said, 'Ah, I got a movie' and Robin said, 'Well, I'm moving on your ass.' They played the dozens in which Robin Harris completely destroyed Damon. And that's how the rest of them found out because those two were so-called Hollywood comedians; black Hollywood comedians and they're the ones that took Robin's name and the Comedy Act's name to Hollywood."

Black comedians from all over made the pilgrimage.

Sinbad: "When Michael called me about doing the Comedy Act Theater they were in a different building, man. They didn't have a spotlight. They had a florescent light above the stage. I said man you got to get a spotlight, man and some lights. And Robin man—I loved him. See, Robin and I used to do this thing on a stage where we would just go at one another. It was fun. It was old school."

Word spread like legs on prom night.

Ricky Harris: "I heard about the black comedy club. I went there and the host was Robin Harris and my friend had said, 'Yeah man, this dude is the funniest dude in the world and I'm like, 'Shit, I'm the funniest dude in the world.' So I walk in there with a f*#kin' attitude and shit, thinking I'm funny and Robin's on stage doing his thing so I blurted out something to the effect of, 'Little black muthaf*#ka.' That nigga tore a hole in my ass. That nigga said, 'Shine the light on that muthaf*#ka' and I think that's the first time he said 'test tube baby' (a famous Harris putdown). They went bananas. And then he bagged on my curl because I had a Jeri curl and he bagged on that. I had helluva acne and he talked about my acne. That was it! He just killed me. That nigga said my face was a cheese pizza with extra cheese.' You better never do a crime because if you do a crime all they have to do is follow the drip.'"

After a month and a half the place was selling out every week. A black comedy club catering to a black audience, and not homogenized blackness, either. None of that Byron Allen, squeaky clean, "apple-pie-at-mother's-on-Sunday" crap. Instead it was raw uncensored black comedians talking about being black and all its variations. Victim turned comedian Ricky Harris remembers this new high and the regular comedians:

"...Sinbad, John Henton, Don Reed, and there was a lot of teams back in the day: Dr. Purvey and the Free Clinic Players, of course Robert Townsend. He was like one of the hot niggas on the set. The hottest nigga was of course Eddie Murphy. Damon, Keenan. Female-wise it was Myra J., but the first lady of it was homegirl that was on *Night Court*, Marsha Warfield. She used to always be at the Comedy Act Theater. The Comedy Act Theater, dawg—the vibe at that time was incredible. It was almost like being in Harlem back when Harlem was really cracking, the Apollo and that whole era. That era used to be cracking because everybody who was somebody in the entertainment industry came to the Comedy Act Theater."

But not everybody dug the black approach. In 1980 Mitzi Shore, the owner of the Comedy Store, had told Robin his comedy was "too black" for her establishment. That was until the industry types, such as Bill Gross of Triad and his cronies, started slumming in the hood to see what all the talk was about. They wanted to know why all the black celebrities from Magic Johnson to Denzel Washington, Mike Tyson to Wesley Snipes, were ranting and raving about this chubby bug-eyed black comedian. Everybody wanted to know what the buzz was all about: agents, managers, athletes, pimps, singers, porno stars, rappers, drug dealers, actors, politicians, directors, gangsters, and all the folks in between. Robin's name was on everybody's lips, and by the time Mitzi Shore got around to putting on the full-press butt kissing, it was too late. Robin didn't need to go to her club in Hollywood—Hollywood had come to him.

There were also new innovations to go with this new club. For instance, in the mainstream setting, when a comedian was introduced he or she entered to silence or the piano player would tinkle some silly, little goofy cartoon ditty to give the appearance of jolliness and merriment before the act opened its mouth. The Comedy Act Theater did things a little differently, thanks to comedian/DJ Ricky Harris.

> "I melded those two entities together; the comedy and the DJing because no other club was doing that shit. Nobody was playing music. Them niggas used to just walk on stage and do their shit."

It was Ricky who introduced Robin's favorite song, ZZ Hill's *Down Home Blues*.

> "Robin was like always on that blues shit. So one day I played that blues shit because I knew that nigga was gonna go bananas. 'Ricky, goddammit that's my shit' and that nigga started singing, 'Down home blues, down home' and he did that shit and he came back to me and he had the biggest smile on his face and said, 'That's it. Do that shit whenever I go on stage.'"

Yeah, the music might have been cool, but whatever you do—don't go to the bathroom. The facilities at the Comedy Act Theater were upstairs and the only way to get there was to make the climb on the right hand side of the stage, going right past Robin and in plain sight. This is when he's utilized another little Comedy Act Theater favorite. Ajai Sanders made the big mistake before she was a comedienne:

> "I didn't know what the rules were. I was wearing a green leather dress and a slit down the back and I remember having to go to the bathroom so bad and my girlfriend was like, 'Girl, do not get up yet.' I was like, 'I got to go pee-pee girl I gotta go.' So I got up and I go all the way around the back and I hear Robin go, 'Uh uh—put the light on her' and I was like, 'Oh, my God!' He said 'Look at her. She got one of them Alpha Beta booties. I get some I'm damn sure gonna tell a friend.' I just kept walking because I didn't know what else to do, so I was like 'Hey' and I just walked away."

And the infamous light followed her the entire time. The very same spotlight used to illuminate the performers was now turned on an innocent paying customer and the audience loved it as Robin would "light 'em up" going both ways. Sometimes he'd wait for the already embarrassed patron to return so they wouldn't slip past him and get their second dose of verbal reprimand for moving during the show. Try to hold it in if you want to: if not Harris would talk about your shoes, hair, pants, jacket, dress, or booty. It was always best to wait until he introduced another act or pay the price.

Robin not only knew how to work an audience, but he had something you can't buy or develop—likeability. The minute he stepped out onto that stage, you felt not only that you liked him, but that you knew him; a long lost relative.

> **Brad Sanders:** "Robin was the guy who bridged the humor of the '30s, '40s and '50s into the era that he was in—into the '80s and '90s. What made him so great is that he found a way to be himself on stage, giving him the rapport with the audience that he had because they were seeing a regular guy. They were seeing

Robin Harris and comedian Andre Lavelle backstage in Chicago after Harris taped his first HBO special, 1989 (courtesy of Andre Lavelle).

somebody who was real talking about real stuff that mattered to them in their lives."

J. B. Smoove: "I thought Robin Harris was well on his way to breaking down a lot of walls with that style of comedy that he had and would have made our style of comedy more accessible. He was the one who was doing something a little different than other black comics. He was a character, which means his style was a little different. The best comics who can tell jokes are people who are characters and he was a true character; the character behind his act. If you saw him on the street that was the same dude no matter what and being the same dude you are on stage as you are off stage you'll find material coming out of the woodwork."

The business was booming and Williams was making plans to open up Comedy Act Theaters in Atlanta and Chicago; people were being turned away at the door and Robin Harris had acquired a legion of faithful disciples: Martin Lawrence, Ricky Harris, Lewis Dix, T. J. McGee, William Wilson, Chris Charles, Joe Torry, Buddy Lewis, Rory Flynn, Jamie Foxx, Lamont Bonman & Brandonn Mosley, D'Militant, Simply Marvelous, Lester Barrie, the female team of Smith and Watson, Myra J, Dave Parker, Jeff Arnold, Ajai Sanders, Keith Morris, Monica Floyd, Vince D, Yvette Wilson, Speedy, Stacy McClain, and Darryl Blacksheare.

Brandonn Moseley: "The biggest joy was introducing comedy to a lot of new people that never had live comedy. Mr. Harris actually introduced me to comedy and brought me on there; working with my buddy, Lamont, and doing some of the sketches. Actually I was involved in one of the major black sketch comedy groups. It was a crazy name that I can't say, but I really enjoyed it."

Robin's signature piece, "Be-Be's Kids,"—about Harris' first date with a woman who brings along her friend and Be-Be's bad, unruly children to Disneyland with them, and who only sent twenty dollars to help get them in—never failed to put audiences in stitches. Ajai Sanders tells how intimidating it was following Harris after a typically hilarious set:

"I remember one time he had just got through doing 'Be-Be's Kids' and then you knew when he was about to bring the next person up 'cause he'd always say, 'Awright!' It was almost like an earthquake had happened because you could kind of feel the room move with laughter, y'know. I remember there was like this thunderous laughter and applause when he said, 'Shit, them's Be-Be's Kids.' I mean it was just so deafening and I was just like okay and he said 'Awright!,' my heart fell straight to the floor. How do you follow that?"

It was that solid showmanship that put Robin Harris where every comedian wanted to be—on the verge of blowing up. The year was 1990 and all of his hard work was finally about to pay off. He had done movies ('*Mo Better Blues, House Party, Do the Right Thing*), there was a TV pilot at CBS, a comedy record about to hit, and rapidly increasing personal appearance fees. Legend has it that Robin was set to host HBO's *Def Comedy Jam* before tragedy struck. Without warning Robin Harris died of heart failure at the age of thirty-six on March 18, 1990, after playing to a sold-out show at Chicago's Regal Theater.

ROBIN HARRIS

Robin was born on August 30, 1953 in Chicago, Illinois to a welder father and a factory seamstress mother named Mattie B. They moved to Los Angeles in 1961 and Robin went to Manual Arts High School where he became a track star, then attended Ottawa University in Kansas under a scholarship. Later he held down a laundry list of jobs, including positions at Hughes Aircraft, Security Pacific Bank, and using his elbow grease at a car rental agency, where he had the job title of "Washer of Vehicles." It was while soaping up an auto that he met ventriloquist Richard Stanfield of Richard &Willie.

"Robin Harris was a person I got started in comedy. He was working at Allstate rent-a-car on Westwood and Wilshire as a lot boy when I met Robin. I came in one day and I was driving in my Rolls Royce which I'd had for years and he asked me what I did. I told him I was a comedian and I told him he should try it and he did. I took him on stage and he opened up with me with two or three jokes. He was going to quit after six months and I told him that's the roughest period. Just hang in there."

Reynaldo Rey: "Robin used to come through the club and I saw him doing a show. He did some of my best stuff. I cornered him and threatened his life. He was like, 'Man, I think you're great. You're funny, man.' I said, 'Yeah, I'm funny because I got material I wrote. Why don't you write yours?' He said, 'I can't write.' So I sat him down and showed him how to write about himself. Y'know, like in 'Be-Be's Kids' how they slap him upside his head, 'Hey, blackie!' And once he started writing stuff about himself he became funny, man. He wasn't funny at first. He became one of the funniest guys on Earth. And he became a friend."

Rudy Ray Moore: "He watched me for twelve years. Me and Leroy & Skillet. Whenever we did shows at Dootsie Williams' Dooto Music Center Robin Harris would be the first one in the row sitting there watching us and watching our movements."

This early guidance inspired a strong devotion to the craft in Harris and that landed him at the Comedy Act Theater, in films, on television (Robert Townsend's *Partners in Crime*), and at a warm place in the heart of a grateful public.

Rudy Ray Moore: "When he did *House Party*, he put a clip of my Signifying Monkey in there. Robin Harris did that for me and I appreciated that; got one thousand dollars for it. He sampled into that movie and I didn't get a chance to spend the money until after he was dead. So I often thought about him."

Norman Mitchell of Arceneaux & Mitchell: "He did for Arceneaux & Mitchell moreso than anybody else. He opened the door for us. He got us in Vegas. He said, 'Come on down, you can open for me. I'm going to introduce you to this guy and this guy's going to take care of you for the rest of your life.'"

Then he was gone, his lifeless body discovered by his mother in his hotel room. His masterpiece, but not forgotten as his signature piece, *Be-Be's Kids*, was made into an animated feature film after his death, with Robin's voice provided by comedian Faizon Love.
Harris' passing left a void even in those who had never met him.

Angela Means: "I started at the Comedy Act Theater when it first opened in Atlanta and on the second week Robin was on his way and I could not wait to perform for Robin. That would've been like going to another grade. I felt like I was in pre-school and once I performed in front of Robin and gotten his critique it would have put me in second or third grade. When he was in Chicago and did his show, he was scheduled to come to Atlanta the next morning and we got the call that night and I, because I was so into the thick of things at the Comedy Act Theater, I was answering phones, serving drinks, telling jokes—I was Miss Comedy Act Theater and the phone just lit up and I felt a huge responsibility. I was like how do I have the right to tell the general public that Robin Harris had passed away and would not be at the club that week. I just felt that I'm not worthy to tell people that he's gone. And so I missed out. I missed out on meeting him that day. I missed out on enjoying him firsthand, but I feel like I know him because he was the Comedy Act Theater."

And of course the suddenness reverberated with pain and shock to those who knew him well, for at the time of his passing Michael Williams had just opened up his second CAT in Atlanta. The christening comedians were Chris Charles, Ajai Sanders, and Joe Torry. Ajai Sanders remembers Harris' last words at the L.A. CAT on March 17th:

"The last thing he said was, 'Well! I'm goin' to Chicago. Guess I'll see y'all later. I'll be back' and that was the last thing he said. I remember speaking to him on the phone really, really late because I remember wanting to talk to him and tell him how my show went because he was still like my dad pretty much and I wanted to call and let him know and he was telling me how cool it was in Chicago. 'Yeah, it's cool. It's cool.' Y'know...and he was, 'All right I'm going to...' because you know Robin Harris had narcolepsy. He could fall asleep at the drop of a hat in the middle of a big dinner. So he was like, 'All right. I'm gonna go get some sleep. See you at the airport tomorrow.' The next day I fly back into L.A. and wait in baggage claim. This young girl walks up to me and she was like, 'Ain't your name Ajai?' I was like, 'yeah.' She was like, 'Umm...Robin Harris dead.' I just walked outside and grabbed a pay phone. The first person I knew to call was Lewis Dix. I called him and then his answering machine comes on and he has 'Down Home Blues' playing on his answering machine and he says, 'I miss you Robin.'"

Joe Torry: "He wanted me to come open up for him in Chicago, but I was headlining the Comedy Act Theater in Atlanta, my first really big road trip. I remember I got off the plane, turned the radio on and I was like, 'Oh, my God.'"

Brandonn Moseley: "Stacy McClain called me at my apartment. She was like, 'You're not going to believe this.' I thought she was joking. There's only been a few times in my life when my actual heart has hurt and that was one of those times. He will never be forgotten."

Ricky Harris: "Robi Reed called me like about 3 a.m. and she was crying and I'm thinking because Robin used to always play on the phone. He used to play, have people call me, 'Robin, he was in an accident.' He would always do shit like that, y'know what I'm sayin? I'm on the other line like, 'Robi, put Robin on the phone. You're a good actress. Put Robin on the phone.' She was like, 'No, Ricky, he's gone.' 'No, he isn't. Put him on the phone.' She said, 'Turn on the radio they're getting ready to make an announcement, but I just wanted to tell you first.' So then I turned on the radio and sure enough on KJLH they announced it that early in the morning."

Michael Williams: "I was at the Black Expo in Atlanta after the first week of my grand opening at my second location and my brother called me about 10 o'clock that morning to let me know Robin Harris had passed. It was not so much a shock it was really more...I knew really from day one; from the first night that I opened that our relationship wasn't going to last long. Somehow he was going to leave and I had no idea death would part us, but it didn't surprise me because it was just something that for me was really overwhelming to see somebody like Robin Harris and to see how dominant he was as a talented individual and I just couldn't sense where that was going to last a long time because, y'know, it was just something I felt in my gut."

Sinbad: "With Robin I think it was the pressure. Remember he was the hottest thing. I remember they had all these executives bragging on flying to Chicago to see Robin Harris. I said I hope he's ready for what's about to come, because brothers want fame, but that trick bag they put you in, man when they decide you're the one. We like what you do, would you quit doing it. We want you to do this other thing. That's the part that can make you go crazy, man. That's the part that can stress you out, man."

Reality—Robin was gone and the week after his funeral the Comedy Act Theater presented a show for a grand total of fifteen paid customers; apparently, no Robin—no crowd. Mike had to do something, and that was find himself another Robin. The club needed somebody to fill his shoes and keep the wave going. Nobody at that time was up to the task. Nobody they asked, anyway. Lewis Dix gave it a shot, but Robin had left some big shoes to fill.

Ricky Harris: "Nobody really wanted to do it, homie."

Nobody that is, but a guy who had nothing to lose, a guy who needed some type of break to merely justify staying out in L.A. and try to keep the career fire burning. To Joe Torry, this was an opportunity, not a chopping block to place your neck upon.

"All I knew was I was this young St. Louis cat out here trying to make a career in this comedy game. I left the girl I love, no money in my pocket, I living out of my car, my brother put me out and Michael Williams is paying me twenty dollars a day so when he gave me a shot I was like, 'Hell yeah.'"

JOE TORRY

Joe Torry began his comedy career talking about people in his native St. Louis and came to Los Angeles in March of 1989. It was his military brother's fiancée's brother who turned him onto the Comedy Act Theater, unfortunately without warning. Torry made the mistake of sitting in the front row and getting up to go to the bathroom during Robin Harris' set and found out what it felt like to be on the other end of a comedian's abusive tongue. Robin ripped him to shreds and no matter how Torry tried to come back the audience couldn't hear it. Joe Torry couldn't wait to get on that stage. When he finally did he was given two minutes. He abandoned his act and talked about everybody within eyeshot. He was funny, but no comedian.

Norman Mitchell: "The first time I saw Joe Torry perform, there were about thirty people who had just come back from this funeral and they were at the Comedy Act Theater. Robin had opened and they finally let Joe go on—Joe cleared the room. The lady started crying and ran out. They were trying to forget and this nigga...."

Robin Harris pulled his coattails and told him he could be hilarious, but needed to study the fundamentals of comedy: how to structure a joke and tell a funny story. Next thing he knew he was part of the newly established improv group that was opening the show for Robin.

"That was the greatest thing because it gave you a chance to get up on stage and get used to the light in my eyes, the mic, getting comfortable with being up on that stage."

Torry moved up quickly on the respect level at the club and when Robin passed and the vacancy was open for a new host the only serious considerations were Lewis Dix, Ricky Harris, and Joe, the comic Harris had groomed by having Torry open for him at local clubs around town like The Pied Piper and Maverick's Flat, both on Crenshaw Blvd. After Robin's passing Torry took over as host with his cowboy hat and boots.

Mystro Clark: "He was in the black cowboy hat and all that; not typical. He was more like aggressive; kind of mean funny."

And had catch phrases like, "F*#k 'em, f*#k 'em, f*#k 'em."

Jemmerio: "Hard core, outlaw, and to the point."

Guy Torry: "Straight to the point. No feelings. No conscience."

He also had a strained relationship with Michael Williams.

"Sometimes I'd get hired out and I'd be like, 'I'm going on the road' and he'd have other people host, but he brought in D. L. [Hughley] behind my back because D. L. would never come down to the club before."

(It was no secret that Harris didn't care for Hughley because of a similarity in style and a natural dislike some people unexplainably have for another person—bad vibes.)

Torry formed a relationship with John Singleton after the director caught his act a few times at the CAT thanks to a heads up by Robi Reed, black Hollywood's top casting agent, who at the time was dating Lonnie, who had been Robin's valet and was now Torry's handshake manager. Torry made *Poetic Justice* (where he would help the actors Regina King and Tupac with their comedy chops and vice versa) and became a major road attraction. He became the warmup for *Def Comedy Jam*.

"When *Def Jam* came out it was an experiment so I didn't mind warming up the crowd and getting used to New York. And I did help book the West Coast comedians."

He went on to host the *Def Jam* tour and when Martin Lawrence moved on Torry's management slid him into yet another vacant slot. He figured that if he could go behind Robin Harris, who he felt was funnier than Martin (taking nothing away from Lawrence, but acknowledging that they were both Harris protégés), he should take advantage of this new opportunity.

Joe Torry left to pursue his personal appearance and film career, offending many on his road. As time progressed, and styles changed and high profile projects fell through, Torry found himself no longer on Hollywood's up and coming list. It was more the been-there-done-that ledger. However, he kept plugging away and like all true talents never gave up on the notion of regaining his former status.

D'Militant: "In show business it's never over until you're dead."

Once Joe left the CAT, D.L. Hughley took over, bringing with him an arsenal of new bag lines. The crowd wanted to get talked about and up until then no group had left disappointed. Joe had carried on the Robin tradition and now D. L. was in place to do the same. He was more than up to the task as comedian Ruben Paul recalls:

"When mama jokes were really popular he taught me a valuable lesson. I was f*#king with him on stage, you know how comics do. I'm in the back of the room and I'm messing with him back and forth and I'm killing him, at this time. And D. L.'s like, 'Give it up to Ruben Paul, a very funny comedian. Ruben, you want to come up and do some time?' I'm like, 'Yeah, I'll come up and do some time.' So he brought me up on stage not knowing I was falling into the biggest trap in the world. I had only been doing comedy three or four months, I go up on stage and D. L. sits in the front row and heckles me off stage and humiliated me."

It wasn't long before Hughley too reaped the benefits of industry exposure and also moved on, leaving another void, one filled by the encroachment of rival clubs. One was right around the corner: Maverick's Flat was the new kid in town on Saturday nights and all the comics who couldn't nab a spot at the CAT were lined up on the couch on Crenshaw. Radio DJ Rico Reed was the Michael Williams of the club and he had his own clientele drop in. His were the young, semi-cool listeners of KJLH 102.3—owned by musical legend Stevie Wonder.

Maverick's touted two shows: 8:00 and 10:30. The strange thing was that even though the promoter had access to the airwaves in one of the largest markets in the country he could never manage to fill the small club on the first show. It became a weekly running joke with host J. Anthony Brown, who sometimes would miss out on entertaining seven people altogether (Lewis Dix had been the first host for a brief period). The rest of the hungry-for-stage-time comedians never took that route. If there was one butt in a seat, the pretzels were put out and the non-alcoholic menu handed to that lucky soul. Showtime!

Comedy was at a fever pitch in those days. The two rival spots were never at a loss for patrons when the 10:30 show rolled around. The CAT still drew in the buppies of the hood while Maverick's got the hip-hoppers. The latter were often comedy club first timers and first timers to any type of nightlife outside of the after prom or a house party (no liquor license meant an under-twenty-one crowd). They'd start forming a line for the 10:30 show as early as 9:15. Nobody was going to miss the crazy old man J. Anthony. He was the new Robin Harris in town and this seasoned vet was "their" discovery.

The other alternative in town was the Townhouse in Inglewood on Tuesday nights. All the up and comers appeared there, from Jamie Foxx to D. L. Hughley, Joe Torry, and Chris Tucker. It was taken over by comics Hope Flood, Wan Dexter, and their partner, U. S. Moore, who formed BASH (Blacks About Social Happenings) Unlimited in 1989, and after Robin's death and a drop in attendance at the CAT it became a place to be and to be seen. Deals were made there. Talent was discovered and the air was intoxicating, with the potential of budding stars launching. Hope said:

> "I think the main thing to our success was one, we were comics so we knew how to treat people because we knew how we wanted to be treated as comedians."

The CAT was still looking for its new BMOC before it lost all of its luster and appeal. Michael Williams had been fighting cancer and management duties were delegated. The search for a new host was seemingly neverending, with a number of comedians attempting to fill the slot. Before things started rolling again, Mike was gone. All that money spent on medical bills had pretty much wiped him out. So he lost his lease.

DARRYL: "What do you want people to say about you?"

WILLIAMS: "More than anything as just somebody who saw an opportunity; that dedicated himself to providing a platform for that generation of individuals who probably would not have existed, y'know, anytime soon, but just helped pave the way for a generation of people who now have an opportunity to see that they can have a career in the entertainment industry; some who have gone on to fame and fortune I hope will recognize that, y'know where they are talented individuals and really did most of the work themselves, but sometimes to look back and say, 'Wow, if it wasn't for Michael, y'know, who just opened the doors and said go for it, and stepped back and allowed those people to just go for it, y'know. I may just one day say, wow, y'know let me just simply call Michael one day and say thank you.'"

Various promoters stepped in to try to recreate the magic at the club, but no such luck. The Robin Harris era ended with Robin Harris.

Rodney Winfield, Hope Flood, J. Anthony Brown
and Wan Dexter at the Townhouse in Inglewood,
California, circa 1990.

Robert Townsend: "Y'know, it's funny with Robin Harris. I worked at the Comedy Act Theater with Robin Harris, Sinbad, Damon, y'know all these comedians and Robin had his own style and I think because we all had different styles no one ever wanted to say, 'hey man, I really appreciate you. I think that your style of comedy...I can't do what you do' and y'know he say, 'I can't do what you do.' So we never really had a conversation and then y'know when I started doing *Partners in Crime* y'know, I really loved his style. I mean it was honest. It was real. It was different and he knew how to handle a room like nobody else and so I asked him to be a part of *Partners in Crime*. I thought Robin's brain was really genius. I mean he was y'know—everyman. The whole "Be-Be's Kids" and just his delivery and timing. And at the time of his death I was working with him on a television series for CBS and I thought he was one of our comedy geniuses."

Harris had come along during a period of black movement within Hollywood. Old friend Robert Townsend had revitalized black cinema in 1987 with the release of a low-budget sleeper called *Hollywood Shuffle*. This gritty film parody skewered everything from casting calls where white execs were instructing black actors how to have more soul, to slave epics where the runaway slave gets all the women including the Massa's lady, to poorly conceived black horror flicks. Townsend had an eye for all that was ridiculous and a deft touch behind the camera.

Red Grant: "Brother started it for comedians being actual filmmakers."

ROBERT TOWNSEND

Robert Townsend was raised by a single mother on Chicago's Westside. He cut his entertaining chops performing for her all the impressions he'd come up with from watching movies on TV; from Bogart to Hitchcock to Cosby with some Shakespeare thrown in for good measure. By age sixteen his talent took him to the Experimental Black Actors Guild in Chicago. He did stand-up at Second City and New York's Improvisation.

Rusty Cundieff: "Robert was one of those guys who came out here (Hollywood) and was fairly polished before he got out here."

Townsend's film career began as an extra in the classic *Cooley High*, and his first credit was in another monster—*A Soldier's Story*, from the award-winning play. Then he made history when he filmed 1987's *Hollywood Shuffle*, a movie about being a black actor in modern day Tinseltown on his own money. The man knew how to cut corners with a little help from his friends. Franklyn Ajaye remembers the pitch:

"I only worked a day and I did it as a favor to Robert. I ran into Robert and Robert was saying, 'I'm trying to do this movie. I'm just financing it.' I was really impressed with the point he was trying to make because at that time the black roles in Hollywood were very limited and the idea of someone saying 'be blacker' or 'that's not black enough,' and that was really happening. I told him, 'you know what—I'll do something in your film for you.' He says, 'I just need you to come play this guy. There's no pay or nothing.' I said, 'sure, why not.' I just thought it was worthwhile. It was worthwhile what he was trying to say, y'know. I would've loved to have done more. And he ended up selling it and he actually ended up paying me."

The film came out with a small print ad and became a word-of-mouth hit. Robert Townsend secured himself a place in the Hollywood machine with his audacious debut as director; introducing talents such as John Witherspoon, Keenan Ivory Wayans, and Dom Irrera, and along with Spike Lee (*She's Gotta Have It*), opened the door for other talented black directors to follow: John Singleton, F. Gary Gray, Matty Rich (okay, not Matty), Bill Duke, Vondie Curtis Hall, the Hughes Brothers, the Hudlin Brothers, and Rusty Cundieff.

Rusty Cundieff: "He, and working with Spike, are what kind of opened my eyes to, 'Hey, I don't have to just keep auditioning for muthaf*#kas. I can go out and write something myself; try to get it done. And he and Spike absolutely are the two people that kind of made me realize that that was something that was doable."

Townsend went on to direct *The Five Heartbeats*, *Meteor Man*, and *B.A.P.S.* On the television front he set the standard for black stand-up filmed comedy with his *Partners in Crime* on HBO, introducing Don Reed, Robin Harris, Damon Wayans, and others.

Royale Watkins: "Robert Townsend was a genius, y'know. I was talking to someone recently about how he was able to come up with that *Partners in Crime* format and how that format exposed so many comics today. I mean that's where I first was exposed to Damon Wayans and was blown away, y'know, when he did the joke about having to talk to his son like Michael Jackson in order to get him to do something. That's pure genius to me."

The multitalented Robert Townsend.

Robert hosted his variety hour, *Townsend Television*, for FOX and starred and executive-produced *The Parent 'Hood* for the WB. He added CEO of the cable television network MBC to his resumé and continued writing, directing, producing, acting, administrating, and doing stand-up comedy whenever he wasn't sleeping.

Marla Gibbs: "The first time I met Robert Townsend we were doing a thing up in Oakland...Robert had tenacity about him. He knew what he wanted and he knew what he wanted to do and he's still doing it to this day so I admire Robert a lot."

Eddie Griffin: "A visionary. I think Hollywood got a little nervous about him. He was doing a little too much I think for their taste. So they slowly, but surely tried to shut the brotha down. He's an independent thinker. He gave me my first movie, *Meteor Man*, so he definitely reaches back, y'know?"

Pierre: "Underappreciated and you have no idea who you're f*#kin' with when you're f*#kin' with Robert Townsend. I got a lot of love for that brotha. He gave me a shot before anyone else would give me a shot. He's a good man. He's a good person. He has integrity. He cares about people and he's just all about show business. He wants to get his hustle on and he wants people around him to be all about show business. No other bullshit, but show business."

DARRYL: "What was the inspiration for *Hollywood Shuffle*?"

TOWNSEND: "The inspiration for *Hollywood Shuffle* was really wanting to do something in Hollywood to make a difference; being frustrated by the roles in auditions that we were getting. The roles that I was auditioning for, the roles that Keenan was auditioning for and pretty much what half the actors of color all across America were going through. And I think, y'know, it really started with, y'know—I did *Soldier's Story* with Denzel and Adolph Caesar and Howard Rollins and after that movie I had a really great feeling and said, 'hey I want to do more stuff like this' and my agent said 'They don't do black movies. That was the one and you may never have an experience like that again.' So what happened was I had saved some money in the bank and I told Keenan we need to make our own movies and just, y'know, bump Hollywood. Let's just create and then if we make it funny enough people will want to see it and that's kind of what happened."

DARRYL: "How much did it cost out of your own pocket?"

TOWNSEND : "It cost one-hundred thousand dollars out of my own pocket; sixty thousand in cash, forty thousand in credit cards, and then eventually Samuel Goldwyn put more money in to make the film look better."

DARRYL : "Tell me about *The Five Heartbeats*."

TOWNSEND : "When I was a kid I loved the Temptations so much that when they broke up it kinda hurt me. It was like a personal thing. I wanted to call David Ruffin myself and say, 'hey man, can't y'all work it out?' And that always stayed in my head as a little kid. So when I became an adult, after I did *Hollywood Shuffle* the next movie I said I wanted to make was about a singing group and what happens inside a singing group. They sing about love, but do they have love in their real lives and that's kind of where *Five Heartbeats* came from and initially it was going to be a short comedy, but then as I starting talking with the O'Jays and the Dells I discovered that it wasn't all fun and games and that's when the story kind of changed a little bit."

DARRYL : "With *Partners in Crime* everybody has used the model and format. How did you come up with that?"

TOWNSEND : "I grew up on all of the comedy shows as a kid and part of the thing for me was watching *The Dean Martin Show* and watching shows like *Flip Wilson*. I always wanted to do a variety show and get to do stand-up and get to do little movie scenes, what have you. And that's kind of how *Partners in Crime*...and then there were all these wonderful comedians that may never have gotten a chance to be seen on television and their first time to be seen was *Partners in Crime*."

Robert Townsend and Robin Harris shared the gift of multiple talents; the ability to go multi-media—stage, screen, or television—and shine in each medium. Most performers attempt the hat trick with varying degrees of success, but even the best have their preference.

WHAT MEDIUM DO YOU PREFER?

Adele Givens: "I would have to say stage because I like the immediate feedback."

Kevin Hart: "I'd have to say stage, man. Film and TV are great. They're amazing, but film and TV do nothing but boost your opportunities on stage. They bring your quote up."

Robert Townsend: "Y'know what—I really love them all. I mean I think there's a side of me that comes alive when I'm doing my stand-up. I think as a director I love creating a universe and working with actors like Beyoncé or Bow Wow or Alfre Woodard, y'know. I think if there was one preference...well I can't even say that. My role model is Steven Spielberg. One day I want to have an empire like that. Just trying to build towards something, where he does movies, television, everything."

Franklyn Ajaye: "I kind of gave up television writing for a while and moved to Australia because I just felt like I just didn't like the network interference and the fact that the network front office people just won't let you do intelligent sitcoms. I felt I was working on sitcoms that were pedestrian and y'know, subject to a lot of network interference and playing to the lowest common denominator."

Alex Thomas: "Movies because you can touch so many more people. I'd rather do a movie and fifty million check me out versus stand up one night and five thousand people or three hundred people in a comedy club see me."

Smokey Deese: "Stage, stage, and stage. And TV when I'm on the stage."

Sommore: "Whichever one is paying me. I like working. I love the freedom of stand-up. You can't beat the freedom. But it's kind of frustrating when you're supposed to go in and deliver a line and you know as a writer in your heart that that shit ain't funny. Y'know what I'm sayin? And you're like 'damn.' And you're looking at them like this just ain't funny and they're like 'stick to the script' and you're like wow. Where do I draw my energy from on this? So I think I like whatever's paying me, but the freedom of stand-up—you just can't beat it."

Eddie Griffin: "I'd have to say I like film more or stand-up more. Film because it's bigger than what you wrote. It's potentially a piece of art if you can keep the suits from going in and tearing up your project. Television, we're just what comes on between the soap commercials. Y'know, you're selling Pepsi."

Bernie Mac: "I prefer to work! But I'm good at whatever I do because of my long journey. I wanted to be able to be onstage for two hours, attack the camera front and beyond, host; me—I'm an entertainer."

Pierre: "Comedy I like because it's instant gratification; right then and there. As an actor I like the response you receive after it comes out; the accolades you receive after it comes out. I love that. Who doesn't like getting accolades for their job? That's why when I deal with people in social settings, regular jobs, grocery stores, whatever, I thank everybody. Because I know how it feels for me to get that kind of accolades so I want to give that back to people; appreciation of what they do."

Darrel Heath: "I prefer film. It's like a fine wine. Television is like a mixed drink. In television there's so many people to impress whereas with film I only have to impress the director."

Thea Vidale: "I like live audiences because I can be close to them. When I sit down in a chair and talk to them, they feel like I'm talking to them and that's what I want to create; an atmosphere where I am talking to you. We are friends. You could tell me anything. I still love television, don't get me wrong. The money is bangin'. I still love that money, but I still love stand-up. I still love getting out in the clubs and being with the people. On television they make you say what they want you to say. When you're on stage I say what I want to say...and it's some silly shit too."

Cedric the Entertainer: "I prefer stand-up in the sense that it is your own personal commentary. It's the one that you have the most control over. You can edit or not edit and be as raw and controversial as you choose to because it's your own commentary and at the same time I really enjoy the world of movies in the sense that you get to develop a character and hash it out and you have a bit more time to do that, but as a performer, just me as a performer—I like it all because my TV show that I had on FOX where I got to do the sketches was also one of my most favorite things to do was to be able to jump in and out of characters on a week-to-week basis and develop them and try to come up with some funny things; kind of write on the fly and a lot of times it allowed for some improvisation so it just kind of lent to the best of both worlds. But I guess stand-up is the place where you are the freest and therefore it's something I enjoy the most."

Marla Gibbs: "The one I'm working in at the time."

Miss Laura Hayes: "I like TV. I love film and I am impassioned about the stage because that's where I started and that's where the real acting occurs. There is no 'cut,' baby. You roll from the time the curtain goes up until the time the curtain goes down, and it's challenging and it's exciting and I always loved the ensembleness of the actors in the theater."

WHEN I SAID STAGE I MEANT THE STAND-UP STAGE.

Miss Laura Hayes: "Y'know, I'm not really into stand-up. I admire you guys who are truly stand-up comedians. I'm really an actor acting like a stand-up."

The African-Americans Are Coming!! The African-Americans Are Coming!!

CHAPTER 17

"I don't know the meaning of success,
but I do know the meaning of failure.
It's when I try to make everybody love me."
— A SIGN HANGING UP IN
SAMMY DAVIS JR.'S DRESSING ROOM

In the late '80s to mid-'90s everybody and his grandmother tried to be stand-up comedians, and the era came to be known as the "Black Comedy Boom." This of course followed the "White Comedy Boom," which produced stars such as Rosie O'Donnell, Jerry Seinfeld, Drew Carey, Tim Allen, Jeff Foxworthy, and Paul Reiser, then quietly left. The black incarnation would be anything but noise-free. It was the post-Iran-Contra Reagan age and like during the post-Watergate-Nixon era, the public was looking for something to take their minds off the bullshit. And in times of crisis comics have always been called to service.

However, this new appetite was much more ferocious than the one that sprung the careers of Richard Pryor, Robin Williams, Franklyn Ajaye, Lily Tomlin, John Belushi, and Freddie Prinze. Black comedy clubs the likes of the Comedy Act Theater (L.A., Atlanta, Chicago), All Jokes Aside (Chicago and Detroit), Jus Jokin' (Houston) and the Uptown Comedy Corner (Atlanta) sprung up. And if you didn't have a club, a bar, hotel lounge, or bowling alley could suffice. Anywhere people could come and the comedy dollar could be made.

The club scene was brisk and fast-paced; especially in New York. The East coast offered comedians the opportunity to get good—fast. Getting strong in any field was never about the number of years, but the minutes, the moments devoted to one's craft. So stage time was the key and New York put the talkers to the test.

> **Ian Edwards:** "The New York scene was real competitive. People are getting on stage one to three times a night and that's during the week. On the weekend you can escalate that up to like seven times in one night because everything is in close proximity."

That's why the East Coast got the reputation as the place to be if you wanted to get funny. The West Coast was the place to be if you wanted to cash a check. There were clubs on the East Coast everywhere. Ian Edwards continues:

> "The Boston Comedy Club. Standup New York. Caroline's. The Comedy Cellar. Gotham's; in the Bronx, you had BBQ's. The Sugar Shack. Bennigan's, down on Wall Street. Manhattan Proper. Nagasaki's in Long Island. In New Jersey, had the Peppermint Lounge and there was another spot called the Terminal D."

Terminal D was in Newark, New Jersey. Former *Def Jam* talent coordinator Bob Sumner got his first experience promoting comedy shows there and admits the atmosphere was not necessarily the best for comedy:

> "First of all at that time ('87) in the Metropolitan area that was the only room that really showcased black comedians. Terminal D it was like pretty rough because a lot of comedians were just starting out and you know people love to heckle and we had a bell up there and they would get up and ring the bell. Almost like how Sandman does."

Another such spot was the Peppermint Lounge in East Orange, New Jersey. It was known for two things: it was always packed (the place held one thousand) and the customers were kinda rough. White comedian Roger Rodd tells about a typical night:

> "They booed Chris Rock and I went on stage and they threw chicken wings at me."

The area itself gave a slight indication of what was in store inside.

> **Roger Rodd:** "The Peppermint Lounge was in an area in East Orange, New Jersey, and when I got off the freeway I got lost. And I was driving around in the neighborhood looking to try to find my way around and try to find where the Lounge was and two white police officers pulled me over and said, quote 'You have got to be lost' unquote, and I said, 'You're absolutely right,' and they said, 'Where are you trying to go?' and I said, 'The Peppermint Lounge,' and they just started cackling and they said, 'What are you going to do there?' and I said, 'I'm a comedian and I'm have a show there tonight.' And they almost fell out of the car

and not only did I get a, 'Good luck to you buddy,' they gave me a police escort to the Peppermint Lounge. They were like, 'We'll show you where it is.' And they informed me when I got there, under no circumstances do you cross the street and walk into that park. If you do you have less than a 50% chance of coming out again. It was like that."

Like New York, Chicago had a bustling comedy club scene. There was Sawyers, Uptown Comedy, the Cotton Club, and their premiere spot—All Jokes Aside, run by Ray Lambert and Mary Lindsey and hosted by George Wilborn. It was an event club. The Comedy Central show *Comic Justice* hosted by A. J. Jamal was shot there. You had to dress up, there were long lines, and people clamored to get into this place where the energy was palpable and the entertainment was top notch.

> **Deon Cole:** "It was booming, man. We had like great comics at the time, like Carl Wright, Bernie Mac, Adele Givens, George Wilborn, Kenny Howell. We had great comics at the time."

> **Damon Williams:** "I hosted the open mic night on Wednesdays and if there was a comic in town you might look up and there was George Wallace on stage, Chris Rock, Dave Chappelle, Bill Bellamy—when they came to town they came to All Jokes Aside. It was run so successfully; from the hosting to the seating to the ambiance to the set up in the club, that they branched out and opened another version in Detroit."

Local celebrities such as Les Brown, TV newscasters and city councilmen gave the Motor City location the must-do quality. Like its Chicago cousin, the Detroit All Jokes Aside was run with courtesy and precision. Unfortunately that wasn't enough.

> **Mike Bonner:** "They didn't want to see a black business thrive in downtown Detroit so they closed the bar down and seized the property through eminent domain to build a boarding facility."

Club closure put a crimp in the aspirations of many a promising comic, but unlike a number of regions where there are practically no places to work on the art of comedy, Detroit had other options.

> **Joe Blount:** "(Comedian) Tony Roney had a night every night of the week so starting comedians could go up. So we got a lot of chances to do time early. Usually you have to build up to that. We had a lot of access to the stage. I remember Club 246, 1515 Broadway, Mambies, Club Med, Strawberry Fields..."

The mainstay in Detroit was Bea's Kitchen and Downtown Tony Brown. The man was a pint-sized, lean sliver of comedic genius. Brown could rival any wordsmith with a filibuster than could go on for day after hilarious day.

Joe Blount: "Downtown Tony Brown is one of the greatest comedians ever. He would headline every week, every show and like the whole weekend he might do like one joke that was the same. I'm not joking."

Visiting comedians playing larger, better-paying clubs or theatres never failed to drop in and watch Brown bestow his brilliance on the room without missing a beat. He was a legend in the Motor City and never left it long enough to be an icon for the masses.

Washington, D.C. had clubs like the Comedy Spot, Bay Street, and Club Elite.

Jay Phillips: "It was alive, man. There was an energy down there: Comedy Café, you could leave there and go over to this small club called Headliners Comedy Club, only seats like about fifteen people, but it didn't matter. From there I'd go to one of the most classic underground spots in D.C. called Mr. Henry's. Everybody was down with Mr. Henry's, from Martin, Chappelle, Tommy Davidson, all of the big boys came out—Earthquake; all of them have graced Mr. Henry's. It's a classic spot."

Another classic to come out of D.C. was a practitioner of the lost art of craft mentoring; the wiser schooling the eager yet inexperienced. D.C. had a sage known as the Fat Doctor, a reputed comedy scientist. He taught comedy classes at comedy clubs with cats coming from as far as New York to take it. He was known reverentially as "The Godfather" and personally mentored Martin, Tommy Davidson, and Donnell Rawlins.

Atlanta was Earthquake country and the Uptown Comedy Corner ruled. There were other clubs over the years: Club 112, the Comedy Act Theater, and the infamous 559 (populated by noisy thugs, quasipimps, crackheads and hos), but Uptown was doing real stand-up comedy. The city of Atlanta gave us Chris Tucker, Earthquake, Don "DC" Curry, Bruce Bruce, and Sommore, to name a few.

The Great State of Texas had clubs in just about every city; most notably, Steve Harvey's Comedy Club in Dallas and Houston was home to Jus Jokin and the Rushion McDonald/David Raibon spot, The Hip-Hop Comedy Stopp. Texas was also a breeding ground for hard-working comedians and special acts like the rare two-man black comedy team of Arceneaux & Mitchell.

Norman Mitchell of Arceneaux & Mitchell: "Most comedy teams were straight man—funny man. Arceneaux &Mitchell was funny man—funny man."

Curtis Arceneaux of Arceneaux & Mitchell: "The audience hadn't seen two brothers do comedy before in such a long time and in some cases they hadn't seen it period."

In St. Louis Joe Torry, Guy Torry, Lavell Crawford, and Cedric the Entertainer got their starts. They also got a cautionary lesson by watching the life of one of their native sons, Rodney Winfield. Who? St. Louis's version of Downtown Tony Brown except he got out.

Bill Graham Productions' Comedy Explosion Flyer for the 1992 New Year's Eve show starring Martin Lawrence, Jamie Foxx, Chris Thomas, and Yvette Wilson.

In the early '70s Winfield was a regular on "The CBS Newcomers" hosted by Dave Garroway. He was young, light-skinned, and funny. He was also a big fan of liquor, drugs and white women. He once said that there are only eleven ugly white women in the whole world. Anyway, bloodshot eyes lose their appeal in the blinding glare of a television camera and before long Rodney was out of TV and back to performing in nightclubs, where he was nothing less than a comedy genius in his sheer boldness, humor and audacity. Rodney never used the comic device of letting time pass on a national or world tragedy before making a joke about it; he'd joke about it while it was happening and do it with insight and perspective.

The man should've been a known quantity, but due to bad habits and poor judgment, he struggled for years on the chitlin' circuit. Bad judgment example: one evening he was playing a casino and had been informed by the management that the owners would be there that night and advised him not to do his Jewish jokes, since they themselves were Jews. Never one to do as he was told, Rodney opened his show that evening with a remark about how the problem with Hitler was that he didn't go far enough. Naturally the owners were insulted and immediately walked out of the showroom. Rodney Winfield, cordless mic in hand, followed them all through the casino's gaming area, hurling more anti-Semitic rhetoric at the hapless couple. Needless to say, he was fired, blackballed, given a one-way ticket to obscurity and was last seen in Texas—being funny, getting high, and hanging out with one of the eleven ugly white women.

Over in neighboring Kansas City, favorite son and comedian/actor Eddie Griffin was simply trying to find a stage to get funny on.

> "There was little or none there. Coming up it was little or none. It was just two comedy clubs. It was the Funnybone and Stanford & Sons and it was your usual club owner bullshit. You had the manager of the club who had never told a joke

Steve Harvey, J. Anthony Brown, and Rushion McDonald on a flyer advertising McDonald's Houston club, the Hip-Hop Comedy Stopp, circa 1990.

trying to tell young comedians how to be funny just so he can ego trip. So I just went down on 18th and Pine to a couple of spots and asked them what their slow night was and started my own night."

On the West Coast on a beach known as Venice was a man and his jokes. No microphone, stage, or spotlight—just a loud, bold, fearless, and funny man named Michael Colyar. What Charlie Barnett was to the East, Colyar was to the West. He'd gather a crowd from scratch and assault them with gentle barbs and one old joke after another with the flare of a vaudevillian; crowds of tourists were held in rapt awe as they stood in the blazing sun captivated by this single black man. Nobody left, nobody moved when Colyar was 'on' and when it was over—the hat, a multiple four figure weekend, and something slightly unexpected—success.

Performing at Venice Beach gave Michael Colyar a following (out-of-towners would have their friends take them to Venice to see him) and more (he won the grand prize of one-hundred thousand dollars on *Star Search* and gave half to the homeless, a state he'd once been in himself). He was working the road right at home, but the over-the-state-line road opportunities were fraught with bad promoters and even worse conditions. It was a new landscape thanks to a swelling interest in black comedy and some of it was good. Some decidedly was not.

WHAT'S YOUR WORST EXPERIENCE ON THE ROAD?

Shang: "I was doing a club in Philly and the lady threw up on stage while I was on stage and kept throwing up. It got to a point where it wasn't funny and I made a joke about it and the crowd turned on me. I said, 'Y'know what—there's only a certain amount of semen you can swallow, boo. Then there's a cutoff point.' She kept throwing up. The crowd hated it, they hated me, and a dude stepped to me."

Mystro Clark: "I did a show in prison one time. My brother was a chaplain. So he called me and they were having a talent show and he wanted me to be the professional MC for the comedy part. It was a maximum-security prison in Ohio and after about thirty minutes of prisoners rapping it's time for me to do comedy. So they had it in the gym in the prison. The speaker system was cheesy, so the people in the back really couldn't hear what I was saying because it was all muffled. So the cats in the back started booing, but the cats in the front were like they could hear so they wanted me to keep going, keep going. So in the back, they were making all this noise, so I said, 'Shut up—it ain't like y'all got somewhere to go.' So the dudes in the front were laughing their asses off at the dudes in the back. Man, so they started raisin' up and the guards started reaching for the rifles."

SO YOU WERE A RIOT STARTER?

Mystro Clark: "Yeah, it started to be a little tense. So I did about another five minutes and then I rolled out. They escorted me out to my car and my brother called me the next day and he said, the warden said you can't come back here. I was trying to make sure they put it in writing that I'm not allowed back in prison."

Al Toomer: "That's easy—I've only been booed once in my life and that happened at a drunken club called Uptown in Atlanta. It was a Sunday night where booing was encouraged. I've done those types of places before, but that has to be my worst experience and even then I tried to go out hard by going off stage threatening people. I almost started a fight walking off the stage and they were still booing."

Mike Bonner: "Toledo, Ohio, in a tittie bar. '91. Bunch of drunks. I was drunk. Plus the tittie bar was after hours so it was a bunch of beat-down pimps going thru déjà vu about what they once had."

Lend a Def Ear

CHAPTER 18

"I called the Comedy Store and one of the first things
they asked me was am I a blue comic. I was like, naw—
I'm black. They hung up in my face."
— SMOKEY DEESE

Prior to *Def Comedy Jam* and *Comic View* the only game in town if you wanted a TV credit was
Showtime at the Apollo on NBC. Bill Cosby was the first host, followed by the late Rick Aviles,
Sinbad, Mark Curry, Steve Harvey, Rudy Rush, Mo'Nique, and Damon Williams. But this
was not the landmark showplace of Pryor, Russell, and Mabley. No, this was the Apollo of an
old lady standing up in the front and leading the crowd in an arm-waving mass gesture to
get the recipient off the stage, accompanied by Sandman's literally sweeping the victim
away and a nasal sound of a droning horn from the audience. Most comedians hated doing
the show, because most comics bombed on it: D.L. Hughley, Jamie Foxx, Ricky Harris, and
so on and so on.

Shang: "They started booing me because I had on white-on-white Nikes, not
because of my act because I hadn't said a word yet. I walked out. 'That nigga got
on white-on-white Nikes.' BOOOO!!! So I thought I said they won't air this and
started calling people names and killing. I killed, but couldn't air it. I did a pu*#y

joke. The lady that always jumps up in the front, she jumped up and tried to give me the wave and I did like the old Richard Pryor joke. 'Bitch, I will slap you with my dick.' It was straight up Richard Pryor, but it got me out of trouble. They stopped booing and started going crazy. So I just kept going and I killed and they didn't invite me back for a long time."

J. B. Smoove: "When I did *Showtime at the Apollo* I got booed like a mug. I ain't gonna lie. I was on the show with Keith Washington. He was the big ballad singer back then. As a matter of fact Cab Calloway was hosting. Cab Calloway. I remember my intro, 'All right, ladies and gentlemen—I know y'all waiting for Keith Washington, but we got another guy coming up before that. Put your hands together for J...B...Slick!' I lasted maybe five seconds before BOOOOOO!!!!"

Still, the Apollo was so revered the Houston comedy team of Arceneaux & Mitchell couldn't wait to play the heralded shrine.

Curtis Arceneaux: "Our first day in New York we didn't know where the f*#k we were so we ended up in the back of the Apollo and we saw Paul Mooney who we had met in L.A. And we were like, 'cool, Paul can get us in.' 'Paul, what's up?' And we had been on the road for like four days, man, so we were kind of dirty. Paul looks at us, 'do I know you niggas?' and they threw us out."

And one thing the Apollo always was—impartial. Didn't matter if you were man or woman—you got the same disadvantages.

Edwonda White: "When I went the first time Mark Curry was hosting and he gave me an intro that was like the set-up for the kiss of death. I had no credits. Nobody knew who I was. I was just a hot comedian on the circuit. His introduction was like, 'This girl says she's funnier than Marsha Warfield and Whoopi Goldberg put together. Here she is from Los Angeles...' (the Apollo hated West Coast comics) I didn't even get my first joke out and they started booing. I had heard about other comedians getting booed, but I didn't expect it to happen to me. It was the worst."

DARRYL: "What did hosting *Showtime at the Apollo* mean for you?"

CURRY: "That was probably the biggest stepping stone that I had. *Showtime at the Apollo* let the world know that I was funny, y'know? If you can be funny in New York at the Apollo Theater, you can be funny anywhere in the world. That's what it taught me. It taught me I could be funny anywhere in the world."

Now when the phrase *Def Comedy Jam* first entered the atmosphere people had no idea another dose of black televised stand-up comedy would change not only comedy as a whole, but the landscape of television, film, and the non-musical concert industry. So how'd they do it? Or better yet how did Def Comedy, the underground comedy, the raw—ever get into people's living rooms with grandmas of all races checking it out?

Talent coordinator, Bob Sumner: "Basically (rap impresario) Russell Simmons and (award-winning director) Stan Lathan were developing a television component to Russell's whole RUSH Communications company and at the time when they were thinking about different types of programming. Russell always had a love of comedy and he would frequent comedy clubs, and when it was mentioned that an African-American comedy series might be cool everybody was in agreement to do it. Stan and Russell had enough confidence in me, especially with the success of my comedy rooms, to go on and make something happen. I took some executives from HBO around to some comedy clubs and they could see black comedy was really popping. Then they allowed us to do a pilot. That pilot turned into eighty-two shows."

So with the show set to go there was only one problem—a host. They selected Robin Harris. Problem solved until another challenge arose—Robin died, forcing Simmons to find a replacement for his newly negotiated HBO program.

Bob Sumner: "We did a show, a tribute to Robin at the Apollo Theater. You had David Alan Grier on the show, you had Paul Mooney on the show and a few other people, but then there was this comedian that was towards the top of this list who ripped a hole in Harlem and his name was Martin Lawrence. And I said this to Stan and Russell and they reached out to Eddie (Murphy) and Arsenio and those guys and they was like, 'Yeah man, this young boy is smoking.'"

MARTIN LAWRENCE

Martin Lawrence was born in Frankfurt, Germany on April 16, 1965 and grew up in Washington, D.C., honing his craft in that city's comedy clubs. He was literally kicking ass and taking names.

Buddy Lewis: "The first time I went on stage Martin was standing in front of the club and some drunk white boy comic said something off the cuff to him and Martin just started socking him. I was like, 'Martin, man, if the police come they're not going to take him. They're going to take you, dude.' Martin was like, POP! POP! POP! POPPOP!"

When he got his fill of that scene, Lawrence made his way to Los Angeles to try his luck at easier-said-than-done stardom.

Ajai Sanders: "I met Martin right when he got the TV show *What's Happening Now!!* He was wearing red shoes, a pair of green pants, and a red silk shirt, and he did 'Shanaynay.' I fell in love with him instantly. You know comedy is very attractive. The person doing it ain't got to be cute. Martin used to drive a Ford Escort and he didn't have a lot of money and I'd hang out at his house and that's how I met his friend, Tommy Davidson, because Tommy lived in the same building, I believe, back in the day. I worked at a restaurant and I'd always bring food over because Martin really couldn't afford a whole lot. He was always really

Martin Lawrence flanked by bodyguards (courtesy of Comedy 2000).

humble and just driven. Just straight up driven. He knew. I remember one day his car broke down I took him to the audition to *House Party* and I'm waiting for him outside the studio gate and he got in the car and looked at it and he said, 'You know what? I got this' and I knew from that point he was going to be a star because he had a whole different light in his eyes."

After his stint on the ABC sitcom and a featured role in *House Party*, he got *Do the Right Thing* in 1989, hosted *Def Comedy Jam* on HBO in 1991 then starred in *Martin* on FOX.

The show, about a Detroit DJ and his girlfriend, was a hit with all age groups, particularly kids who were drawn to Martin's wild and wide variety of over-the-top characters; especially the female neighbor Shanaynay. Life was more than child's play though, when in 1996 the media relentlessly reported Lawrence's alleged drug problems and charges of sexual harassment on the set. If he was phased it didn't show as he went on to write, produce, direct, and star in *A Thin Line Between Love and Hate* with Lynn Whitfield.

Melanie Comarcho: "He's one of the few entertainers I know who has the whole family working with him. When Martin does a film, everybody works. So you don't have that brotha, 'hey, can I borrow twenty dollars?' He brings them in;

they're executive producing and there's not a lot of people who do that. I praise him for that."

Lawrence spit them out from there: *Bad Boys* and *Bad Boys II* with Will Smith, *Life* with Eddie Murphy, and his smash hit *Big Momma's House* with Nia Long, followed by *Big Momma's House 2* in 2006, amongst others. Martin was also a favorite of his peers.

> **Alex Thomas:** "One of the funniest niggas ever. He's crazy, y'know. Martin is super talented. I look up to him. He basically was a guy that really was the man in my era, when I first got started, back in the *Def Comedy Jam* days."

Def Comedy Jam was what any show would want to be—powerful. For sheer influence it was unmatched. It introduced hip-hop black comedy to America every Friday night and nobody went out until the closing credits rolled. It had that rare quality of being a cultural barometer bleeding into every fabric of our existence: the clothes, the language, attitudes, all of it. *Seinfeld* even paid homage to the show when Kramer suggested that Jerry's career was over because he wasn't *Def Jam* enough.

The comedians were cursing, calling their sexual counterparts names, and basically giving the finger to everything in sight. No smirk or knowing looks to indicate apology—just straight-up being angry black folks with issues and gripes. *Def* was watched by everybody regardless of race and they couldn't get enough.

> **Bob Sumner:** "Not many pitfalls with the exception of the show having such shock value, y'know what I mean? You had like *The Sunday Comics*, *Evening at the Improv*, *Caroline's Comedy Hour*. They were all basically whitebread and a black comedian would be sprinkled in, what have you. Now with us, you had four African-American comedians along with a host. So then it being HBO, you'll have the opportunity to not to be censored and present a nightclub act for television."

Not only was the host at his naughtiest and the comedians black, but the half-hour changed the way comedy was presented to a television audience.

> **Bob Summer:** "I was the DJ at Terminal D, y'know what I mean? You had those white mainstream rooms that had the little piano player. Well, I decided that I was going to bring the music to *Def Comedy Jam*. And there was this show. Remember *Budweiser Superfest*? Babyface and LL Cool J was headlining the Superfest at Madison Square Garden and following the show there was an after party and at the after party there was a DJ that was like slammin' and then I looked up at the DJ booth; not only was he DJing he also was talking, y'know. And we was like, wow instead of finding a DJ and an announcer let's incorporate the two and thus, Kid Capri was born."

Def Jam wielded its tremendous influence based on timing. It taped in October of '91, the first show aired in March of '92, and they were on the road touring by the end of that month.

It was so popular it had two touring groups out simultaneously, and on New Year's Eve they did four shows in four different cites. The average touring schedule included forty cities per year with two legs. That way they could go back to those same cities within that calendar year with another set of comedians. This tour went on three years after the show itself left the airwaves and there was even a Broadway run in 2002. Yet the program still had its share of critics.

Bob Sumner: "We got stereotyped; people saying it was so broad. Everybody was just cussing and fussing whereas the truth of the matter is it just seemed like that because you had four comedians at one time. If just one comedian had had that on their album or their special and they're up there cussing the whole time you don't really notice it as much because it's the one person. Take four people and do it..."

Bill Cosby not only labeled it, he wasn't amused by it to the point of dissing the program publicly for the direction it took comedy. Tony Spires was working as a consultant for *Def Jam* at the time of Cosby's remarks:

"I didn't like it. I thought it was unfortunate, I thought it was insensitive, and I thought that he didn't look deep enough into the merit of those things. People can get mad at Mantan Moreland, people can get mad at Williams and Walker and all that type of stuff, but you have to look at the merit of it. You just can't say how come Sidney Poitier always plays those roles where they were calling him names and why'd he have to take it? Because he was a pioneer who did what had to be done. So, I think that for there to be the *Bernie Mac Show* in the case of the comedy, and a Steve Harvey's *Big Time*, for good or for bad, or that you get a show on Comedy Central like Dave Chappelle or a *Martin*, that the *Def Jams* of the world had to happen. That era had to happen and that it had to come and go. So it came and it went."

Bob Sumner: "I mean that's Bill Cosby. He has a right to his own opinion, but we have a right to do our thing too. When you're making watermelon Jell-O commercials and you got cartoon characters talking in Ebonics that speaks for itself. Stop being a hypocrite."

TELL ME ABOUT YOUR *DEF JAM* EXPERIENCE

Mystro Clark: "*Def Jam* was great, man; first time that you got treated like you were important on TV; like a TV star. They got you a plane ticket. They picked you up in a limo. So I felt like okay now I'm in show business. It was a class act the way they did it and I was thankful to Russell for doing that. So okay finally, you're not dealing with the raggedy promoter who's out there to try to take advantage of you or doesn't understand you or your craft and try to act like you're supposed to be happy with what you get, but they put you up in a little dinky hotel. A lot of times people think funny guys can just do comedy by luck. Like they hire a singer

Def Jam group photo with (top row) Russell Simmons (far left), T. J. McGee (next to Steve), Steve Harvey (far right), (second row) Stan Lathan (far left), Doo-Doo Brown, Edwonda White, Miss Laura Hayes, Sheryl Underwood, (bottom row) Bob Sumner (second from the left), Teddy Carpenter, Arnez J, and Andrew Ford in New York in 1993.

and pay them ten thousand dollars and put them in the suites; they try to get you for $500 and put you in the Motel 6 somewhere. So I think a lot of times comedy gets overlooked as being easier than other crafts just because people think. 'Oh, I'm funny.' You may be funny at home, which is not professional funny. Just like everybody can shoot free throws, but not everybody can be professional in the NBA."

Evan Lionel: "It was kind of scary for me when I went out in front of the audience and the audience roared. That scared me. They really liked one of my jokes. There was stomping and roaring and that just scared me. It made me feel really small and I had never felt small before because I'm 6'2" and weigh 200 so I felt small. I was like looking at this audience roaring and stuff and if they rush the stage I gotta go."

Hope Flood: "The first time I went I was so excited about being there that I lost my voice. So when I went on stage it was so horrible, you could barely hear me so they cut me and it hurt me when I got the letter in the mail."

Edwonda White: "It was one of the best experiences early on in my career because everything was Class A. I don't remember what hotel they put us up in (The Macklowe Hotel), but oh, it was bad. It was bangin'. I got spoiled right there. When I got a taste of it for the first time. I loved the lobby. I was like, oh—I have made it big time. They sent a limousine to pick you up and back then I hadn't been a comedian that long so that was my first taste of it. Per diem, people hovering over me to make sure things were okay, chocolates on my pillow, and the shower...I was just standing in the shower like—'wow.' Oh, it was just a class act and then Martin came and talked to us and he was real cool and everything. It was my first time meeting him and he was really cool back then. He was like, 'Y'all ready for this or what? Just go out and do your thing. They're going to love yawl. It's going to be all good.' And then he left and from that day on I thought I was going to be a superstar. That was one of the best experiences I ever had in my career because they treated us as so royal."

Def Jam participants from 1993: (left to right) Edwonda White, Corey "Zooman" Miller, Madd Marv, Teddy Carpenter (seated), Adele Givens, unidentified comedian, Doug Starks, Kid Capri, and Darryl ("D'Militant") Littleton.

Once Martin Lawrence left *Def Jam* to devote his full attention to *Martin*, Joe Torry took over amongst some controversy. Bernie Mac had also lobbied for the job and he had been down with Russell and the show from day one and was a crowd favorite. Whereas Joe was the warm-up act during Martin's tenure and he was managed by the show's producers. He was also Martin's friend and fellow Robin Harris protégé. The scale was allegedly tipped when Lawrence put in the good word for Torry.

Turns out though that Joe wasn't Martin Lawrence, but he wasn't Joe Torry either. He had to dump his trademark black cowboy hat and leather pants for the more traditional hip-hop gear at the request of his new employer, Russell Simmons.

> **Joe Torry:** "He's like, 'You're not that guy no more. You're *Def Jam* now. If you're hosting the Halloween party you've got to dress the part. You can come up with the muscles and the vest; the style is cool, but work it in so you're the host of the show. You want people to remember you. You want them to welcome you into their home. White people are going to be watching and who do you think they'd let babysit, you or Will Smith? You're talking about f*#k 'em, f*#k 'em, f*#k 'em.' So I began to experiment without the hat, my crutch, and I went from country to hip-hop."

He struggled initially to connect to his audience, and eventually made headway, but the following season saw two additions—Adele Givens and Ricky Harris were also brought in as hosts. Each of the three reigned over their own shows separately.

> **Former host, Ricky Harris:** "I was being managed by Russell (Simmons), Stan Lathan, Brillstein and Grey. So I was in Brillstein and Grey's office and Stan

Lathan and Russell, they let me hear a meeting with HBO and HBO was canceling *Def Jam* and I knew that I needed that because I saw what it did for Martin and I saw what it was doing for Joe and I knew I needed just to be on the *Def Jam*. So I'm in this meeting and I'm hearing them talk about they're going to cancel, I'm like, 'No, no, no, no' and Russell and Stan they was good friends and fans of mine because they saw me doing my own shit. I was directing music videos, writing shit for other people, etc. So Russell was like, 'If you can figure out a way to save it— save it!' So nigga, I came up with the idea of multiple hosts. I said, 'Let more than one nigga host.' I came up with that shit. They came back; 'Okay yeah, but we're only going to have three, you, Joe and we're going to have a female' and they picked Adele because Adele was being managed by them. So what they did was shot all twelve episodes, right? Four for Joe, four for me, four for Adele. We all got paid equal wages and it was like a helluva bump. So Chris Albrecht, he was the head of HBO and he comes back to Russell and Stan and goes, 'Hey, if the three comedians worked, why don't you guys do twelve?'"

Joe Torry recalls things somewhat differently as to why he shared his limelight:

"I started blowing up and they didn't want another host running off like Martin and they didn't know what to do so I kind of suggested that (multiple hosts). Then they went that route then they went the all-star route."

Whatever the case, the following year had almost every comic who wasn't performing, hosting. Chris Rock, J. Anthony Brown, and many others made MC appearances over the next two seasons, but by '97 the party was over, not to return until HBO announced comedian Mike Epps as the new host in 2006. Sumner concluded:

"When people realized *Def Comedy Jam* wasn't on the air any longer people started to miss it, but I'll tell you who really missed it and you can tell by when you look at network television now, these sitcoms and what have you. There was a time when UPN, FOX and the WB was giving all of those *Def Jam* comics opportunities for sitcoms and what have you. You never saw that happen with *Comic View* comedians."

A View from Behind

CHAPTER 19

"A nigga is a black man's worst enemy."
— REYNALDO REY

Speaking of the poor cousin to *Def Jam*, over at Black Entertainment Television, a former Detroit late-night variety show host named Curtis Gadson (the Bogeyman), was doing *Comic View*. It became the longest running comedy showcase show in television history, yet the burning question remains—Why? The comedians were paid chicken feed to do a show where they had to fly themselves to the location (California), put themselves up (in a hotel at a BET discount), and if they got hungry there was a vending machine in the hotel lobby because there sure as hell wasn't a per diem.

The tradeoff was that you'd be exposed forever for a flat rate, no residuals. In return *Comic View* would not only air the show you shot, but then cut it up for clip shows, theme shows, promo commercials, still shots for posters, etc. etc. etc. Comics griped, but this exploitation also led to many of the exploited taking advantage of their overexposure and making good livings touring throughout the United States and abroad.

Nevertheless, BET's compensation policy led to an AFTRA (American Federation of Radio and Television Artists)-backed strike. Since BET was not signed to a union contract and thus their only violation was of a humanitarian aspect, AFTRA instructed its members not to appear on the network until a wage increase could be obtained. AFTRA Television/Film Representative Lauren Bailey, who also serves as the Comedian Caucus liaison, relates what happened:

"We had a seminar one day and during one of the Q & A sessions one of the comedians (future *Comic View* host Lester Barrie) stood up and asked what were we specifically going to do about BET. We didn't even know this was a problem until this person brought it to our attention. Because of that we had a long, long battle with BET and many, many meetings later they agreed to give us a contract for the performers and they went from making this $150 to union scale which I believe at the time was $1,060."

Now, to fully understand the ramifications of this move a bit of history is in order: when the idea of *Comic View* was first hatched, comedian/actor Darryl Sivad was the network's first choice to host the show, but was advised by his management to pass because doing BET would ruin his career. D. L. Hughley's manager, Tony Spires, saw things differently. He offered up Hughley and another client, Edwonda White, to shoot the pilot along with comedian T. P. Hearn. The raucous, irreverent Hughley didn't disappoint. The response was overwhelming and *Comic View* was picked up.

Marla Gibbs: "He makes me laugh."

D. L. HUGHLEY

Darryl Hughley was born on March 6, 1963, the third of four children. After he was kicked out of high school he joined the Bloods for a career in the lucrative gangbanging industry. That lasted until his cousin got shot. At that point he ditched his rag, got his GED and found a job at the *Los Angeles Times* during the day, then hopped in his car and cut his teeth at comedy clubs at night, with varying results.

Ruben Paul: "That dude would get up on stage and just joke after joke after joke after joke after joke after joke after joke after joke after joke and didn't let the audience breathe. This is one of the first comedians that never had a closer to me. Like you never knew how D. L. was gonna end. He would just rapid fire and say good night and the audience would be out of breath. D. L. was one of the first comedians I saw kill, but not end on a good note, just simply because the audience was tired. He'd rattle off so many jokes he'd put the audience to exhaustion."

Eddie Griffin: "One of the quickest tongues in the business."

Ajai Sanders: "D. L. became known for stealing other people's material and I found that to be true at one time and I approached him about it and I said, 'you know that's Darryl Blacksheare's joke?' 'Yeah, but I do it better.' That was the last time I ever addressed that issue with him."

Hughley hosted the Comedy Act Theater, the club Ms. Whiz, and Donna Gooch's spot, Birdland West in Long Beach, then a late night talk show on L.A.'s K-CAL Channel 9 in 1990, which aired opposite Arsenio Hall's show. It was canceled after nine weeks, and Hughley got the job as the first host of BET's *Comic View* and made that show must-see TV for two seasons for everybody from prisoners behind bars to uptight conservatives who felt the need to call in and complain about his raw style of humor. Following his departure after a contract snafu, Hughley taped two HBO specials; the second received a Cable ACE award nomination and became one of the highest rated specials in HBO's history.

D. L. Hughley, Ajai Sanders, Christopher "Kid" Reid, Tisha Campbell at the Universal Amphitheater, 1993.

Chris Spencer: "It's weird to see the growth of a comedian. You know him from *Comic View* he just used to bag and snap and now he's become this political satirist in the last ten to fifteen years. That's just kind of interesting to see how a comedian can start out as one thing and mature and become something totally different."

Hughley got his own sitcom, *The Hughleys*, in 1998, based on his real life experiences of moving his family from the city to the suburbs. It did two seasons on ABC, got canceled, was picked up by UPN for two seasons then was axed again. He replaced Guy Torry on the Kings of Comedy Tour, which also featured the talents of Steve Harvey, Cedric the Entertainer, and Bernie Mac, then set out to explore his options.

Marc Howard: "He knows what he can do, but I know he's also very conscious of his own limitations. That helps. If you can do something and do it well and you don't try to bite off more than you can chew and if what you got can work for you, amen. He's a millionaire for it. He's working it, as they say. He's a very good stand-up."

If Hughley was aware of any limitations, he sure didn't show it as he dabbled in voiceovers, co-starred in movies, made guest appearances on sitcoms, sat in on talk-show panels, got his own late night talk show for Comedy Central, and was even a long-distance phone carrier spokesperson.

Adele Givens: "D. L. should run for some political office. I think he should. Anybody that absorbed into politics needs to get into office somewhere. He probably could make a good politician."

Kevin Hart: "A hard worker. Never holds his head down regardless of the situation. Always comes back."

Al Toomer: "Next question."

Comic View executives detested Hughley's blatant disobedience (cursing on camera, long delays, etc.) and placed restraints on him, but since he had no plans to return anyway, D. L. took advantage of a contract error that stated he would make $700 per "segment," not per "episode," as was intended, and because technically a segment is anything that falls between commercials, this mistake quadrupled his normal pay. D. L. sued them and won, leaving a sour taste in Curtis Gadson's mouth and he vowed to never have another host repeat seasons.

Many an employee entangled in the web of BET-style office politics learned that loyalty never was one of their strong points. As a matter of fact, after D. L. announced he wouldn't be returning, Speedy, who had been the warm-up act, was promised the vacant hosting spot. No competition. They were just going to give it to him. Then somebody came up with the idea that the best comic of the season should get the gig and Speedy had to compete like everybody else and lose to Cedric the Entertainer.

> **DARRYL:** "What's the real story behind that?"

> **SPEEDY:** Somebody, one of the head people, I'm not going to name them, that guy had a meeting with me and said, 'Yeah Speedy, we think you'd make a great host. We want to bring you in as the next host of *Comic View*.' He told me I was going to be the next host. I took it and ran with it and I offered him some tickets to a Clippers game. A friend of mine had given me some tickets and I didn't want to go see the Clippers, but I asked him if he wanted to go and the story got out that I tried to bribe my way into becoming the host of *Comic View*, but I think that was just his way of backing out of the situation. That's how it is in this business. People will say things sometimes just to keep you moving, sometimes to feed you and sometimes just to be mean."

Well, whether it was the insult of being offered sporting event passes to view the one-time NBA laughing stocks or an upper level change of mind, the Bay Area Black Comedy Competition played prominently in the end result. Founded by Tony Spires in 1986, the first official competition was in February of '87, and Spires brought in partners Marcus King, Lionel Bea, and Erroll Jackson the following year; King stayed involved for three years; Bea and Jackson for six. This comedy competition brings out industry people who in the past have been introduced to previous winners (Mark Curry, Jamie Foxx, yours truly) and finalists (D. L. Hughley, Mike Epps, Nick Cannon) and is instrumental in putting careers on the right track.

> **Mark Curry:** "It meant great exposure; basically letting me know that I was a pretty good comic. And y'know, you won against a lot of good guys and then exposure and not only the exposure, but the confidence that I could move on in this business."

And once BET got a gander at the format they thought it best to copy it and have the winner of their competition be rewarded with a job for a season.

In any case, the Entertainer man not only filled Hughley's vacant shoes, but brought down-home humor to a big city-tinged program and lived up to his name.

Cedric the Entertainer rightfully grinning as he strolls the red carpet (courtesy of Comedy 2000).

CEDRIC THE ENTERTAINER

Rodney Perry: "A stand up guy and a great person"

Cedric Kyles was born in St. Louis, Missouri and got his first recognition in comedy competing in the Johnny Walker National Comedy Contest in Chicago. Soon afterwards he won the Miller Genuine Draft Comedy Search and hit the road as a headlining performer. He made television appearances on *Showtime at the Apollo*, *Uptown Comedy Club*, *Def Comedy Jam*, and hosted BET's *Comic View* in 1994.

"My *Comic View* run was actually so great for me. It was a very strategic move. I'd done a lot of the shows at that time that were making stars and I'd got a little name recognition around doing the comedy circuit and was able to make a decent living doing stand-up and I wrote all this material and a lot of my contemporaries were telling me not to do BET. They were telling me that doing *Comic View* for me would have been a step in the wrong direction [Haven't we heard this one before?—DL]. They wanted me to wait and do my material on the next season of *Def Comedy Jam*. Don't give it away on BET and so I kind of went against the grain in the sense that I had all this great material and it was relevant and it was current and I had an opportunity to go on the show and perform and it just so happened that they were starting to look for a new host and so it was perfect timing. It was also a strategic choice. I knew that if I could get to host this show I could make myself a household name. That I would definitely change the game for myself and my squad and so that's what we did. We went on *Comic View*, competed, and then became the host and with the host I was able to become a household name; especially among African-Americans and go into their house every night. *Comic View* was a nightly show back then. It came on five nights a week, so I knew it would give a lot of boost to my career. It was a great run. It put me on the map as far as one of the top comedians in the country and I was able to book myself that way and it just gave me a lot of recognition. It didn't give me a lot of recognition in the Hollywood community, though. So I was surprised by that because I was so hood famous. I was surprised that 'Joe Rothenberg' didn't know who I was."

Cedric went on to co-star on *The Steve Harvey Show* for the WB network and scored several NAACP Image Awards as top Male Supporting Actor. He was hired as a national spokesperson for Budweiser and increased his goodwill when he released *The Starting Line Up*, a DVD series featuring seasoned, yet relatively unknown comedians Cedric handpicked to showcase. One such act, Tony Tone, remembers the man who remembered the promise so many comics have made in their early years:

"Cedric is one of the few to actually reach back, help out and grab people. He doesn't forget and I appreciate that. Ced's a good brother; down to earth. What you see is what you get. Pretty much how he is on stage is how he is off stage, just fun."

Part of the reason for Cedric's success landed squarely in the lap of his longtime friend and manager, Eric Rhone. A relationship that began in college in 1983 had blossomed based first and foremost on each man's ability to take care of business.

Manager/Producer, Eric Rhone: "If you do what you say, you're going to instill in people that you're reliable, accountable, and professional."

The partnership joined forces with the FOX network when they produced the variety/sketch show *Cedric the Entertainer Presents*. It lasted one season despite good ratings and a growing fan base. Eric Rhone gives the reason for the cancellation:

"They wanted a different style of show than the show that we initially sold them. They wanted something edgier, a little more condescending. A little more focus on downgrading, the degradation of people, and the images that are out there, particularly African-American images and that wasn't and is not Ced's brand. It's not what he's about. What's for other people we don't have a problem with that. They got to do what they got to do. So they came to us to tell us if we didn't change the show to make it more edgier, make it more condescending towards individuals and different events that was going on in the news, make it more topical, that they were going to cancel the show. We was like, hey we're not going to change our brand for nobody. Cancel it if you want to."

The Entertainer Man and his partner decided to concentrate on film, with his role as Eddie the opinionated elder shearsman in the Ice Cube blockbuster *Barbershop* making the most noise. The character's cutting barbs regarding Martin Luther King Jr.'s sexual life and Rosa Parks' laziness raised many an urban eyebrow. There was flack.

Cedric the Entertainer: "I think that historically these were two great individuals that were the catalyst and the leader of the growth of the overall existence of African-Americans, the way we are today. The way we see ourselves and are able to identify with ourselves. It was perpetuated by the act of Miss Rosa Parks and then communicated, preached, and doors knocked down by the actions of Dr. Martin Luther King, and that leadership is necessary for the lifestyles that most of us get to live today. And so from my point of view those are two very important people historically that led to life as we know it. You definitely take flack for that, but the thing that we were trying to express and that we felt got out of proportion is that inside the barbershop there is a certain degree of...where people are going to cross the line. Where people are not going to always say what is so politically correct and we were trying to get that open and start dialogue and when I had to defend myself or discuss those actions that were taken in that movie that's what I expressed. Here I am sitting on CNN and we're discussing the relevance of Rosa Parks and Martin Luther King and I'm sure that for this current generation they probably hadn't discussed these two people except for in February. And we're sitting up here in March and September and I think that it's important and the reason why you have to do certain things out of the box sometimes is to get people to start thinking and talking and discussing and getting that dialogue going and now we've got kids with an opinion about these two people and that's more important than what you think of me right now."

Eric Rhone: "It was controversial. We never meant it to be controversial. We don't want to harp on it, but every human is human with all the frailties that come with each one of us, but we were able to get past it and we apologize to everybody that felt offended by it. To all the fans of Reverend King and Reverend Sharpton and whoever else. It was a barbershop conversation and in that environment you hear all kinds of shit in a barbershop. Cats in there talking all kinds of craziness about religion and what they do when they're laid and how many of this and that. That's a barbershop for you. That's the essence of a barbershop. We were just trying to bring the real environment to light to the screen."

From that notoriety Ced and Rhone took a meeting with MGM/Sony and ironed out a two-year motion picture deal to bring however many projects they wanted. The Entertainer was lovable to everyone who liked the bottom line. Likeability = money.

Doug Williams: "A brilliant entertainer. I think he brings an array of things to the table. He's a multi-faceted entertainer. Fun to watch and a great guy. I like him."

And fortunately not all nice guys finish last. Cedric was hell-bent on success right out of the box.

CEDRIC: "I went to college and approached life from aggression so I probably would've been an entrepreneur of some sort. I was in the insurance game for a while. I went to school to study law. So who knows exactly what I would've went to? But it would've been some heights, for sure. I definitely was the kind of person who wanted to be an achiever and strive to achieve."

DARRYL: "Who were your influences?"

CEDRIC: "Comedically, probably my greatest influence was the late Robin Harris. He was a person that I identified with the most in the sense that his comic sensibility was one that he was so accessible. He came across and performed as this uncle or cousin or guy you already know and he made it seem so effortless. He didn't really have the typical Hollywood good looks or those kind of things. He just performed in a regular manner, but was the funniest guy on stage. So it made me identify in the sense that I didn't necessarily have to be anything in particular, but funny on stage. So then of course there were the influences of Richard Pryor, Eddie Murphy. All the early Eddie Murphy stuff was amazing to me; as a stand-up and then as a performer on *Saturday Night Live* and also his early movies. Robin Williams, Billy Crystal; all of these cats were influences to me. I thought they were quite funny."

DARRYL : "What was your goal when you got into comedy?"

CEDRIC: "Comedically you just want to get on the stand-up circuit and then you want to become a headliner. I mean you kind of keep it really simple. Then you want to go on and possibly get a TV show and then do movies. It always kind of stayed that simple. You want to perform and perform to the highest of your ability, but I think that one of the goals, I wanted to strive to be like in the old days like Redd Foxx, to be a big Las Vegas act where people come to see you and you have this huge stage show and so that's probably one of the final things I want to fulfill, that was on my initial list that I need to check that box off."

DARRYL : "Tell me about the Cedric the Entertainer 'brand.'"

CEDRIC: Ideally I try to do comedy I feel is broad, but specific. I try to hit those buttons where you can identify with it, where people feel like they know me. You feel like I'm accessible to you whether you are a corporate executive or a brotha selling weed. I try to have that kind of comedy that is identifiable to us all without it being intentionally designed to be that much of a crossover appeal. I don't really intentionally design it to do that. I definitely try to stay specific to who I am and what I'm talking about."

During his single season tenure on *Comic View* Cedric's co-host was Laura Hayes, a.k.a. "Miss Laura." She made a splash on *Showtime at the Apollo* with a showstopper where she whipped off her wig in the middle of a story to the crowd's complete shock and disbelief.

"MISS LAURA" HAYES

A native of Oakland, Laura Hayes enjoyed the street life and its people. At one point she was a booster living with a pimp. This choice led to jail time and time to reflect. Upon her release she joined a theater group and found acting to be her calling. She developed an array of characters and was soon appearing as a fixture on BET's *Comic View* as Miss Laura from 1994–1996, with hosts Cedric the Entertainer, Sommore, and Don "DC" Curry. After that stint she worked on *Martin*, then on the Queens of Comedy Tour.

The problem for Laura in '94 was that BET hadn't said anything to Cedric about him sharing his limelight with an older woman. He had no idea he was going to have a co-host and she wasn't aware she had the job until the last minute when they informed her she'd have to break that news to Cedric.

His reaction surprised her. Expecting an ego attack, he was cool with it because he knew how BET operated, so they figured out a character relationship and went to work.

> "Once we established who we were to each other, y'know that we were like cool. I was an older lady that flirted with him or whatever—we were always able to bounce off each other. And I'm telling you, those are the best gigs to me when you have that common bond."

The following year the seasoned female comic Sommore replaced the outgoing Cedric and the executive board kept a close watch for any signs of overt sexuality from their new host. She'd appeared on *Def Jam* and talked about servicing Denzel Washington. This made the board quite nervous even though every other comedian appearing on their show was either talking about sex, oral sex, or group sex.

DARRYL: "You were the first female host. What was your feeling about this?"

SOMMORE: "Well, it brought me into homes on a nightly basis, into black homes and it was overwhelming. I never knew the impact that it would have. And one television show—one season. I think the high lasted five years. It made every black person in America feel like I was their cousin."

DARRYL : "Any particular stories?"

SOMMORE: "See female comedians are different than male comedians. We come to work. They come to play and other things. First of all they have groupies. They have women who wait backstage for them. We get no groupies. We get old women with sweet potato pies."

In 1996 *Comic View* was hosted by comedian Don "DC" Curry and saw the addition of *The Blackberry Inn*, an intended-to-be-funny soap opera starring Laura Hayes, that turned into an outrageous, over-the-top, live-action cartoon. Laura didn't like the change.

> "I realized that a live action cartoon, if not done in the right way, is buffoonery."

Actors were encouraged by director Gadson to "buck your eyes" and characters consisted of white racists, flaming gay cross-dressers, blacks in whiteface, chicks with cone-shaped bras (the lone white actress was paid union scale, the black performers were not), characters going in fast forward and reverse motion, ranting militants and midgets. I mean dwarfs. Or is it little people?

The overt sexual tone of the episodes was not in line with what Laura Hayes felt comfortable with, but the writers kept churning out T & A scripts. So she delivered an ultimatum and told them that if the show was going to be all about women running around with their tits bouncing up and down, she wasn't going to return for another season. They wished her well and immediately started looking for a replacement.

In 1997 (hosted by Montanna Taylor) *The Blackberry Inn* was canceled. To regain a disenchanted public, *Comic View* threw on every comic that submitted a tape in '98. If it turned out that they weren't funny, the production staff dubbed in cricket sounds and showed an impassive audience staring at the performer in a state of disgust with a nasty phrase encased in a comic strip bubble inserted above the comedian's head.

> **AFTRA executive, Lauren Bailey:** "When I watched it I didn't like it. To me, the move to go that route creatively just wasn't necessary and I thought it did more harm than good even to the credibility of the actual show. I didn't find it funny. I thought it was actually very juvenile."

This was the season that white comedian Gary Owen hosted. He'd captured the heart of the African-American studio audience during the competition semi-finals when he said the word *nigga* during his routine, got a standing ovation, then landed the job over black comedians George Wilborn, Al Toomer, and Mike Bonner.

> **Mike Bonner:** "To give it to a white dude, and I'm not saying this from a racist standpoint; I'm saying it from a standpoint of racially conscious; *Comic View* and BET were institutions. You don't give institutions away. When they made a new host for *The Tonight Show* when Johnny Carson retired they didn't say Eddie Murphy, Arsenio Hall, Whoopi Goldberg—they went to a white boy because that's a white institution."

> **Hope Flood:** "The day that Gary Owen got the host spot, I felt like the president had died. It was just a sad day in black comedy for me."

In hindsight it wasn't the happiest for Owen either, as he soon discovered that it's not that easy to work for black people. After securing the coveted position, Owen was offered a small role in the Jamie Foxx film *Held Up*. He took it, even though it conflicted with his *Comic View* schedule and he missed the first round of tapings. In his absence, co-host Reynaldo Rey handled Gary's duties, but Gadson was not happy. Part of the reason Owen was selected was Gadson's desire for controversy to draw curious viewers to his show, but this new host was making him look like a fool and there was nothing he could do about it. He

1998 Comic View *host Gary Owen and co-host Reynaldo Rey at the Normandie Casino in Gardena, California during a break from taping, 1998.*

would have looked even more foolish if he publicly dumped his great white hope after such a grand unveiling and widespread protest.

So when Owen returned, Gadson wanted nothing less than 100% from him. When he didn't get it, he went off. The first day back there was a wardrobe problem, and when the new host wouldn't take the stage because his clothes had not arrived, it was more than Mr. Gadson could stand. The tape shoot was running behind schedule, which meant paying the venue and crew for overtime. So Curtis Gadson rushed into Gary's trailer and made his obvious displeasure forcefully known.

Gary went onstage with the clothes he was wearing. Co-host Reynaldo Rey said he didn't actually see it, but he heard all the noise when it went down.

> "I heard quite a few explicatives and go on and get his ass on out there, yeah, I heard that."

WHAT DO YOU THINK ABOUT WHITE COMICS DOING BLACK COMEDY?

Joey "J-Dub" Wells: "If they just do comedy I'm okay with it, but if they come in and try to use the vernacular and try to walk a certain way like, 'yeah, nigga' and 'hos' and then I got to go why the f*#k is he doing it like that? Because now it's getting degrading. You're insulting us by going, 'yeah.' Just be funny. If you walk on that stage, just be funny. And in your eyes this is how you see black people; this is how you see white people—then just say that. That's your perception of them, then okay that's funny, but if you come with the whole, 'play that music! Play that music!' Now if you do that in a white club then I'm down with that."

Norman Mitchell: "If they've experienced what they say they've experienced then it's okay for them to talk about it, but if they're just doing it just to take money out of the African-American community then we need to shut 'em down. And prove you're real. If you can hang one night in the hood with no money and not get your ass kicked—you're cool. I say we gather 'em up, drop 'em off, and go back the next day and pick 'em up and if they're all right; if they ain't crying; if they ain't jumping on their cell phones and calling their managers and whatnot—then they're cool. Then they can stay."

Mike Bonner: "It's bullshit a lot of them because it's condescending. 'I got a boo. I want a boo.' Or the black thing. 'My auntie drinks Colt 45—that's black.' Don't monkeyshine me. Don't try to trick me into laughing at that bullshit. Just do the f*#kin' jokes, man. If you're good we'll embrace you for being good."

T. Faye Griffin: "Hated it! Don't like it, don't like it, don't like it. Unless it's really organic to your experience. Ray Lapowski, white guy, married to a sister. He does material about being married to a black woman and his whole experience with that, but he never forgets he's a white man. He doesn't do his voice to try to sound black. He never forgets who he is. Whereas some white comics are crip walking on stage."

Hope Flood: "I hate to see it. I have nothing against those guys, but I think it's a sad shame where our mentality is that a black comedian can get up there and say the same thing and you look at him. A white comedian can say a couple of black references and he's an idol. And I don't get that. I don't understand that at all. That ain't funny to me."

Spanky Hayes: "I just think it's wrong, man—because if we act white we're f*#kin' Uncle Tom sellouts."

Tony Tone: "If it's really them I'll go along with it for a while. You got a couple of Eminems in the comedy game."

Tom Dreesen: "There's only one rule in comedy—be funny. That's the only rule. There's a distinct difference between ethnic humor and racist humor."

Evan Lionel: "It's way easier for them than it is for us. Black audience looks at me when I come up like, 'This nigga better be funny. He ain't gonna be funny.' Whereas if a white guy comes out there they're already laughing because he's white and then all he's got to do is say, 'What's up, homies?' then they falling out."

Leslie: "Now in this era it's so exaggerated and f*#ked up it's not even really brilliantly done. It's almost like they're minstrel. It's like they're imitating black people."

Ruben Paul: "Can't stand it. Absolutely can't stand it."

"Miss Laura" Hayes: "Sometimes I'm with it. Sometimes I'm not. But what can I do about it?"

Marc Howard: "I think the same as for anybody because there are black comics doing white comedy. I think that any time you subject yourself to one style to conform to one particular type of audience then you limit yourself. I don't think there should be a problem with a white person coming to a black room or being on a show with black people. If they're funny, they're funny."

J. B. Smoove: "If that's how you grew up and that's your experience by all means talk about it. If you're a white guy raised in a trailer park around black people—go for it. But I don't like it when people try to jump onto the bandwagon and they're doing black jokes because black comedy is hot right now. I rather they be totally honest in the experience they're talking about. It's like me being on stage trying to tell a political joke and know damn well I never voted."

Mystro Clark: "I really don't mind it. It's not a big deal as long as it's majority black comedians doing supposedly black shows, but what they need to do is let more black people do white shows."

Reynaldo Rey: "Doesn't bother me. I got my start…my first influence was a white comedian, several white comedians; Lord Buckley, long before I heard about Redd Foxx; Lord Buckley and a redneck down South, white boy—Brother Dave Gardner, funny as hell, little bigot, but funny."

Ricky Harris: "At first I used to f*#kin' hate it, y'know what I'm sayin? Because those white muthaf*#kin' owners would never let me get down at their club."

Keith Morris: "Hate it, because the black audiences cater to them more than they cater to their own people. And then the club owners cater to them more than they cater to the black comedians."

Rudy Ray Moore: "The only one I went to see was the one who talks about people in person…Don Rickles. I guess I can accept him because he's not one-sided. He did a joke on us. Says, 'All right waiters, hide the watermelon—the coons is coming.' But he talked about everybody so it wasn't one-sided."

Mark Prince: "I think they need to have more of them come and sit down and watch our black comedy. I think that that's a good f*#king school and a good start for them because their comedy is corny. But these white comics have to learn one major thing—don't come in front of a black audience trying to be us; thinking you can talk some jive to us and get over. Bet you won't pull that same act in a white club, because you know you're not going to get a TV show trying to act like a black man."

Tommy Chunn: "It's a double-edged sword. On the one hand that black consciousness is getting out there, but on the flip side you've got white kids doing black moves and if that keeps happening new kids will be born and they won't know where that art form comes from. They'll believe that Jimmy and Chad and Todd made it up."

Willie Brown (& Woody): "I'm not impressed. A white comic who does black comedy can be white later on in a board room meeting. He'll be black on stage, but when he goes home he's a white cat."

James Hannah: "I hate 'em. I hate 'em because they patronize the audience. The average black male and black female is programmed to listen to what the white man says. So all a white comic has to do is say a few jokes that end in a black slang and they're a hit."

Edwonda White: "I have a problem with that—I do. If you're a comedian like Roger Rodd—Roger Rodd is a guy who does comedy that can cross over to whites or blacks, but he's not out there trying to be black. So that's different. He talks. He keeps it real and he might every now and then make a reference and say something like, 'I'll holla' or something. That's not trying to be black, but if you have another comedian which I won't name who it is, that's trying to be like, 'whoop, whoop!' Y'know what I mean? You're not black so to me it's really offensive to do that. It's really disrespectful and those people don't go far because it's a fad. It's something ignorant people say to you, 'oh, that white boy is funny' and then five minutes later it's not funny anymore because the novelty wears off."

Curtis Arceneaux: "I think it's excellent because comedy needs a new something. I mean, white comedians really coming out of the box using black slang—at least it's new. It hasn't been done before, y'know? It's something I don't see every time I go to a f*#kin' club."

White comedian, Darren Carter: "If they're good at it I like it. To me, if it seems like they're putting on an act, trying to be down—it turns me off completely."

Melanie Comarcho: "Well, y'know you've got the whites that are just in black rooms doing comedy, y'know. Some people just grew up in a black area or around black people and that's where they're comfortable. And then you've got the ones that 'act' black and see, I don't like that. When they come up, 'Yo, yo, yo, yo, yo—Whassup?' Naw! Excuse me. I dare you to go do that in a white room."

Over the years *Comic View* saw a variety of hosts: D. L. Hughley, Cedric the Entertainer, Sommore, Don "DC" Curry, Montanna Taylor, Gary Owen, Lester Barrie, Ricky Smiley, Bruce Bruce, Arnez J., J. Anthony Brown, and Sheryl Underwood. Each gained some level of notoriety, but a face that became synonymous with the show was the face of a ghetto-fabulous comedy legend.

Eddie Griffin: "Everybody's grand-uncle. That's the one that will come over and take the last piece of chicken and then ask you why you didn't have no more muthaf*#kas."

REYNALDO REY

Born in Sequoyah County, Oklahoma, his parents were African-American and American Indian. Reynaldo got bitten by the performance bug while teaching in Wichita and dabbling in experimental theatre there at the University. This was after receiving his Bachelor of Science in Education from the Kansas State Teacher's College and as he was working toward his Masters. He moved to Cleveland, Ohio where he spent the next seven years teaching and working out his craft in the prestigious Karamu House Theatre. From there he got noticed and began touring with musical stars the O'Jays.

He bypassed the chitlin' circuit route when his first agent surmised that Rey wasn't somebody who had dropped out of high school and jumped on stage telling jokes. He booked his educated client in all-white clubs from Maine to the Florida Keys with Rey specializing in political satire, science fiction jokes, and generally elevated material to go along with his expansive vocabulary, which he had no qualms about displaying.

After moving to Los Angeles he signed a recording contract with Laff Records where he did several albums. He worked not only as a stand-up comedian, but as an actor, director, producer, and writer.

Derrick Ellis: "He's a songwriter too. He wrote stuff for Johnny 'Guitar' Watson."

Rey was the opening act for Redd Foxx for fifteen years and was managed by his mentor for twelve of those years. He played the wisecracking mailman on NBC's *227* starring Marla Gibbs, a skittish father in the movie *Friday* with Chris Tucker and Ice Cube, and a loud-mouthed, low-level gambler in *Harlem Nights* with Redd Foxx, Eddie Murphy, and Richard Pryor. His other films include *Sprung*, *House Party 3*, *Be-Be's Kids*, *White Men Can't Jump*, and *A Rage in Harlem*. He was a judge and later co-host for *Comic View*.

Rudy Ray Moore: "Reynaldo Rey is one of the finest comedians out today. He has delivering ability with high energy."

Marla Gibbs: "I love him. He's probably one of the funniest men on stage today. You have to take Reynaldo off the stage. He loves it, he's immersed in it and he can tell a story."

DARRYL: "How did you meet Redd Foxx?"

REY: "I was in a club on Hollywood Blvd. called Grits 'N Biscuits. After the club closed they'd serve grits and biscuits early in the morning. And the waitress comes up to me after my show and says Redd Foxx would like me to join his table. And I'm like, 'Ain't no Redd Foxx in this greasy ass joint.' She said, 'Okay, I told you.' I went to the bar. I was drinking my liquor. Redd slapped me upside the head and said, 'Oh you won't have a drink with me, huh, you red sonofabitch?'

I said, 'Redd, man—I thought the broad was jivin'. Man, I had no idea you was off up in here.' He said, 'I heard about you, nigga. Came to see you.' I said, 'Ah man, look I apologize. I'll be happy to join you.' He said, 'I don't want you to join me now' and he walked off and I ran after him, begging, 'C'mon Redd, please, please. I love you' and he said, 'Get away from me. Get away from me.' I sat down and he told his bodyguard, Big Barry—weighed about 900 pounds, all muscle—and Redd told Barry, 'Kill him.' Barry said, 'Uhh aahhh.' I feared for my life. Redd said 'all right, spare him. Sit down, fool.' No. It was 'punk.' That was Redd's pet name for me—'punk.' If I wasn't sure of my masculinity I would've developed a complex because Redd called me punk all the time, man. When he'd offer me those narcotics and I'd say no thank you, he'd say, 'You old, punk.'"

DARRYL: "Tell me a Redd Foxx story."

REY: "We were playing the Hacienda. Redd Foxx's Carnival of Comedy. Slappy White, Bernie Allen, Redd Foxx, and me. Slappy borrowed $500 from Redd. Said, 'I'll pay you next week when we get paid.' Next week Slappy sneaked off. He didn't pay Redd. Next week Redd said, 'Man, pay me my money.' And Slappy said, 'Ah man, five hundred punk dollars. Man, don't be approaching me in public talking about that little pu*#y piece of money. Goddamn' and walked off. So he didn't pay Redd that week. The next week we're in the green room and Redd pulls out his derringer. He takes one bullet out the gun and he pops Slappy upside the forehead with that bullet. Slappy said, 'Man, what the hell was that all about?' Redd said, 'If you don't pay me my money the next one will be coming much faster.'"

DARRYL: "You were a judge on *Comic View* during the competition years. What was it like judging some of those comics?"

REY: "It was rough because half the time I heard my material. Comedians get up with me sitting there as a judge and tell my jokes. Of course none of those comedians ever made it past the first round because originality was one of our criterias and how the hell do you display originality when you go up and tell a judge's joke? If you hear me and somebody else tell the same joke they got it from me. Except for one joke; I fess up I stole a joke."

DARRYL : "From who?"

REY: "I can't remember from who. I want to give him some money because it's a hit every time I do his joke."

DARRYL : "Well, how long have you been doing it?"

REY: "Ten years."

DARRYL : "It might be one of mine."

The reign of Curtis Gadson and his cronies expired in 2002 when BET decided to go in another direction "creatively." The new regime at *Comic View* had a bit more compassion than the outgoing crew, but comedians didn't care who was in charge; they just wanted to get on TV, blow it up, hit the road, and get plenty of money and sex. They knew nothing of business.

In one pathetic example, a comedian discovered while filling out his paperwork that a portion of his money would be going to the union, AFTRA. The comic snapped. Talent producer Joyce Coleman remembers:

"He said, 'I'm not going to do the show because I don't even know who AFTRA or what AFTRA is.' And this young man had been on TV a lot and I kept thinking that's impossible. And so when I sat down and talked with him because I wanted to talk him into doing the show, I said it's hard for me to believe you have no idea what AFTRA is. He said, 'I don't know what AFTRA is, I just know they want to take my money.'"

Coleman advocates some type of class so young performers grasp the complexities of their business. They need guidance and realistic goals instead of hoping someone someday will see them and sweep them off their feet and they live in Kentucky.

T. Faye Griffin: "*Comic View* has done a disservice by editing the shows in such a way that it looks easy. People at home don't see all the crap that ends up on the floor; how these sets are tightened, edited, pulled up to try to make these guys look funny. And there's this whole generation of comics that go, 'Shoot, I can do that.'"

The chaos and (often) embarrassment of *Comic View* met its inevitable demise with a whimper when, due to sagging ratings and a schedule that was scaled down from six days per week to a measly two, it was quietly canceled in April 2006. BET, under the leadership of Reginald Hudlin, was looking to go in a new direction, apparently opposite from the one Gadson and friends had taken it.

The comedy landscape was massive and this new cottage industry was overwhelming to those ill-equipped and ignorant of the opportunities available. From 1992–1997 exposure was the least of their problems. You couldn't turn on the TV without seeing a bunch of stand-ups being exposed. Besides *Def* and *Comic View* there was *Showtime at the Apollo*, *The Apollo Comedy Hour*, *Comic Strip Live*, *Comedy on the Road*, *Comic Justice*, *Comedy Compadres*, *Evening at the Improv*, and *The Uptown Comedy Club*. The latter featured stand-up and the sketch talents of Tracy Morgan, Flex, Debra Wilson, Jim Breuer, Arceneaux & Mitchell, Rob Magnotti, Horatio, and Angela Means.

Comic Justice was hosted by veteran comedian A. J. Jamal on Comedy Central before it was Comedy Central. The network had a name but no identity, no flagship show to set it off and attract viewers. *Comic Justice* was determined to be that show. It booked great comedians and the host was a wrecking machine, but no viewers came.

Too bad. Jamal was a seasoned pro who got his share of ink, as he and Mario Joyner were the golden blacks of mid-'80s comedy. A glance at the weekly *TV Guide* kept their names in your face. Each week they were shown on cable's *Evening at the Improv*. Then *Def Jam* hit and their brand of smart, clever, thought-provoking comedy gave way to a louder, more confrontational approach to making people laugh. People liked the noise, and clever ended up on Comedy Central, but that didn't stop the host from retaining fond memories.

AJ: "I loved *Comic Justice*. One, it put me in the homes of a lot of TV people, even though it was Comedy Central. At that time Comedy Central wasn't featuring a lot of black talent; but now...they gave Dave like fifty million and they gave me like five thousand. So that's the difference of the times. And I think Dave Chappelle used the N word a little more than me. You'll never hear me use the N word. If somebody offers me fifty million I'll say, 'N-word, please.'"

DARRYL: "How did *Def Jam* affect your career?"

AJ: "It did a lot for me because you have to buy volume one to get the other volumes. I'm on volume one. My residual check was so fat, oh Lawd, I love *Def Jam*."

A Different Shade
of Black

CHAPTER 20

"Went over to this guy's house,
d*#k was so small, went down to give him head
it was like smoking a joint."
— Hope Flood

Much has been said about white comics doing urban comedy. Once again, it's a trend that you can't stop. No more than they could stop Jerry Lee Lewis or Elvis from doing Rock & Roll. However, comedy is not music. A gimmick or catchy tune cannot get you through for long. No laughs—no career. And if you're a white boy trying to do the black *thang* it better be genuine. You're not going to crack 'em up with dry, antiseptic humor. Or even worse—trying to be cool, when it's obvious you're not. Bottom line—if you are going to talk the talk, you should walk the walk.

Shang: "If it's pure, if they really are from there, good, fine. But the ones that pander and are culture vultures, that take our shit and run with it—I ain't feeling that."

Bob Sumner: "I mean if they've lived the life and they're not trying to be themselves black it's cool. If they actually grew up like Eminem, because with Eminem you can tell he lived the life. But these guys just trying to mimic, these guys just trying to Vanilla Ice it, y'know, that's just what it is. You can tell the difference and the cream rises to the top. The cats that are sincere about it are the ones that will be successful with that brand of comedy. The ones that are out here trying to bullshit us—we know it."

Some of these guys are actually the real deal—most are not. When I say that I mean that most are true white boys at heart and only cater to the black audience for financial gain.

Roger Rodd: "White comics doing black comedy usually falls into three categories: one of them is the white comic, he legitimately grew up in a black neighborhood and they never run around saying it because they don't have to because all they have to do is open their mouth people know that's the real deal. Then you got the whole generation of wannabe young white kids who really don't have a clue what's going on and they grew up in a black neighborhood called Bel-Air, and they bought a Hummer and they've gotten gold chains, and they all of a sudden watch a bunch of rap videos and they think they're black. And they're in that category, and they usually don't fare too well; even though one of them ended up hosting *Comic View*. And then there's the type who basically get over by kind of being white minstrels. They do funny dances and they're goofy white guys who look like they do a caricature of a black guy."

WHERE DO YOU FIT IN?

"I don't fit into that crowd. I just try to be a comedian."

YOU DON'T COME IN PANDERING?

"Well pandering is death in front of a black audience. The dancing, unfortunately that works very well, but after you finish dancing you have to have some jokes and that's where there's very few who pull it off."

But then you have Jim Carrey; crazy, madcap, imaginative, and the undisputed champion of urban white comedy. The man who walked on stage at the Comedy Store's Twentieth Anniversary wearing nothing but a three-foot-long sock on his penis got over on *In Living Color*. It was on that ultra-popular half-hour sketch comedy show that Carrey regularly dazzled the nation with his rubberlike antics and diverse characterizations.

Actress, T'Keyah "Crystal" Keymah: "Jim Carrey scared me at first because I didn't know anyone that physically agile. I remember saying to someone, 'The white guy kind of scares me. I don't know what I'll do if they put me in a sketch with him,' but he was just the sweetest guy."

From 1990–1992, *In Living Color* dominated the comedy scene. Working on a show of this magnitude was every performer's dream and every performer showed up to fulfill that dream. Original cast member T'Keyah "Crystal" Keymah wasn't crazy about trying out for Wayans' show since she'd been protesting his movie *I'm Gonna Git You Sucka*.

"Who would do a film with a title that ignorant?"

Regardless, she contacted casting agent Robi Reed and was instructed to bring something from her stand-up routine to the Regal Theater in Chicago for the open call. The problem was that Keymah wasn't a stand-up—she was an impressionist/actress. Still undaunted, she put together 10 minutes from old theater presentations and wrote some new material and went to the audition with friends Lance Caruthers and Ali Leroi. She gained some confidence as she surveyed the competition.

"There were some other actors there who were really horrible. They were doing comedy monologues from staged comedy shows that are not at all appropriate in the same room with stand-up comedians. I thought, God—if I'm going to look like that strike me dead right before I go on and that'll be my sign that I shouldn't go forward."

In Living Color set a new standard for sketch comedy with edgy characters that shoved and choked the envelope every week. From the disgruntled Homie the Clown to the scamming Homeboys Shopping Network to Damon Wayans' homeless derelict walking around with a pocket toilet (a jar filled with his own defecation), the show embraced anything taboo.

No group was immune. Gays were flamboyant and over the top. Preachers were lecherous and money grubbing. Celebrities wore their flaws and misdeeds on their well-paid sleeves and the whole country couldn't stop laughing. True black humor was out of the closet. Keenan Ivory Wayans showed us that all of it was funny.

KEENAN IVORY WAYANS

Alex Thomas: "An icon. I love Keenan Ivory Wayans. He was just the epitome of a guy that said, y'know what? I'm not gonna sit around and wait for Hollywood. I'm gonna create my own shit, and I respect that. And he took it to the next level."

Keenan Ivory Wayans was born in New York City on June 8, 1958 and began his career as a stand-up comedian, working with Robert Townsend, Robin Harris, and others at the Comedy Act Theater. He wrote *I'm Gonna Git You Sucka* in 1988, co-wrote and directed Eddie Murphy's *Raw*, and earned his place in black comedy history when he got the new FOX network to air *In Living Color*, the sketch show where every member of his family earned a check, including brothers Damon and Shawn (as DJ, SW1) and sister Kim. Without complaint, one former cast member likened it to a launching pad for the Wayans Family, and of course they got first dibs on skits.

"It should have been named In Living Wayans."

But since there weren't yet enough Wayans to do all the skits, they also enlisted the talents of Tommy Davidson, Kim Coles, David Alan Grier, T'Keyah "Crystal" Keymah, Kelly Coffield, and the white guy named Jim Carrey. Later on Jamie Foxx, A. J. Jamal, and Chris Rock would pass through on their way to being Jamie Foxx, A. J. Jamal, and Chris Rock.

Keenan kept busy himself working with old partner Robert Townsend on *The Five Heartbeats* in 1991, then penning and starring in *Low Down Dirty Shame* in 1994. He co-starred in *Glimmer Man* with Steven Seagal, had his own late night talk show in the mid-'90s and later directed his brothers Shawn and Marlon in *Scary Movie* (2000) and *Scary Movie 2* (2001).

> **Royale Watkins:** "Genius. Y'know, anytime you're creative enough to put together an *In Living Color* and to use those sketches as a medium to give all of these different acts broad exposure and to launch them into what they've become now, y'know all of them stars in their own right and to allow them to shine, to allow their talents to shine in the best possible format, you can't be anything less than a genius."

> **Ruben Paul:** "What he did with *In Living Color* cemented him a place in black comedy. It was the first time someone said, 'Hey *Saturday Night Live* is cool, but black people have experiences too and black people have point of views too and these are some of the things that black people find funny.'"

> **Vince D:** "I like what he and Damon have done as far as bringing along their family members. You know, some family members shouldn't be famous, but they did it anyway which is cool."

Keenan was the mastermind, but Damon was invaluable in putting it over. He was already a brilliant stand-up comedian and gifted actor, but the show offered him the room to run his gamut of abilities and he wallowed in it.

> **Affion Crockett:** "He's one of my favorite comedians because I've seen him on the grind. I've seen him in the clubs when it's two people or when it's two hundred people. That's a real comedian."

> **Chris Spencer:** "He's the one who really taught me how to be funny."

DAMON WAYANS

Damon Wayans was born on September 4, 1960 in New York City, New York where he grew up with nine brothers and sisters. He found stand-up comedy to be his forté and became a regular at the Comedy Store. He once said, "Stand-up is like the Internet. A lot people are doing it, but not a lot of people know what to do."

Damon was a featured performer on *Saturday Night Live* and writer/performer on the Emmy award-winning *In Living Color*, where he popularized Homie the Clown.

Damon Wayans signaling how many more worlds the family has to conquer before they're satisfied (courtesy of Comedy the Magazine).

T'Keyah "Crystal" Keymah: "I liked doing Homie the Clown because the little girl character could make him laugh and break character. So that became my goal every week. It was like he could look at anyone else and stay in character, but there was this one face I made that he would just break. So he would try not to look at me when we were doing the sketch and I would try to make him look at me."

Wayans wrote and starred in the films *Mo Money* (1992), *Blankman* (1994), *Major Payne* (1994), and was featured in *Celtic Pride* and *The Great White Hype*—both in 1996.

He had his own self-titled sitcom, *Damon*, in 1998, playing a funny detective; and portrayed a sellout TV writer in Spike Lee's biting satire *Bamboozled*, the film that shows what happens when a brother trying to get out of his contract writes a degrading "minstrel show"—and to his dismay network executives love it and it becomes an overnight hit with America.

In 2001 he co-created, wrote, and debuted *My Wife and Kids* on ABC, seeking the universality of the *The Cosby Show*. An old-school disciplinarian himself, Wayans says much of the problem with kids today is not enough parents *"taking that foot to that ass."*

Jemmerio: "Smart man. That whole Wayans family is smart and they got a good strategy. They know how to go in and plot situation and execute it and watch you enjoy it. And plus they've got that universal audience locked down and that's real good."

DARRYL: "What do you feel has been your impact on black comedy and how has it affected your life?"

SHAWN: "Our, I think I speak for the family, our impact on black comedy...I think that we helped broaden black comedy. Still keeping it black, but making it accessible to the masses."

DAMON: "Not Massa."

SHAWN: "Not Massa, masses. And still keeping our edge, but allowing other people to enjoy that great edgy comedy that black people are used to."

The other cast members were also breaking ground and influencing their peers.

Alonzo Bodden: "When Tommy's 'on,' I think he's one of the funniest people in the world."

TOMMY DAVIDSON

Born in 1964, Tommy's life started off rough. He was the son of a Civil Rights activist mother in Mississippi who left him with her friend when she couldn't take care of him herself. That friend, also a civil rights worker, eventually adopted Davidson. Prophecy played a hand in his early school career when his first grade teacher dubbed him "the comedian."

He began his professional career in an impromptu performance at a nightclub and admits his act is still impromptu, feeling the room out and filling that need as opposed to a set routine.

Pierre: "I did a competition; Craig Frazier, Vincent Cooke, T. J. Johnson was in it and I was a young comic. I was eighteen years old. I don't know shit, but everybody was like, 'Pierre, you're hilarious. You're funny, you're funny.' And I went to this big theater and we had singers and comedians and whatever. I forgot what all it was in the competition and Tommy went on before me. He went right before me and he blew the stage up. He tore it up with impressions and singing and shit. The crowd gave him a standing ovation. 'And the next comedian we have is Pierre.' Blah, blah, blah, blah, blah, blah, blah, blah. I was so shell-shocked I couldn't follow him. I didn't know what to say after him. I did my act, but I stumbled over shit, didn't know what to say, and I was blown away. And that was my first introduction to Tommy Davidson."

The D.C. scene was good because Davidson was getting some notice and he was soon opening for acts like Luther Vandross, Patti Labelle, and Kenny G.

Once he moved to Los Angeles, he headed down to the hood to The Comedy Act Theater. There he met two men who would shape his future: Robert Townsend and Keenan Ivory Wayans. His relationships, coupled with a lot of talent, got him *Partners in Crime* and *In Living Color*. On the latter, America discovered multi-faceted Tommy as he nailed every impression: Sammy Davis Jr., Michael Jackson, and Sugar Ray Leonard, plus any character part that came up. He went on to have three Showtime specials and co-star with Halle Berry in *Strictly Business*. Tommy was featured with old friend Jim Carrey in *Ace Ventura: When Nature Calls*. He appeared in *CB4* and was Magic Johnson's co-host on the failed *The Magic Hour* lack-of-talk show.

Davidson acknowledges how hard it is in Hollywood for African-Americans, but points out that despite things getting better blacks are still more than singers, gun-toters, and joke tellers.

> "We are often faced with making decisions that present the question of whether it's our livelihood or integrity. Though family, living, and mortgages help you quickly make those decisions."

Come to think of it, Davidson co-starred in *Booty Call*, the title of which has become synonymous with bad films, whereas it was not so poorly rated when it first premiered. Noted critic Roger Ebert gave the film three out of four stars. Tommy defends the flick as well by pointing out that it was nothing more than a comedy.

> "It's like taking *Animal House* or *American Pie* and analyzing it."

In 2000 Davidson co-starred with famed tap dancer Savion Glover in Spike Lee's biting satire *Bamboozled* and said that working on that film put him and Glover through emotional changes just in putting on the makeup, realizing the struggle black entertainers had to go through just to survive. He praised director Spike Lee for expanding his artistic horizons.

> **Lauren Bailey:** "Can get me every single time. Brilliant with what he does with comedy."

> **T'Keyah "Crystal" Keymah:** "Too much energy in a little bitty bottle and every once in a while the top just pops off because there's so much in there and you see how brilliant he is and he needs to be contained. You need to put the top back on, but there's just all kind of stuff in that bottle."

The men on *In Living Color* were garnering rave reviews and being eyed for other opportunities. The women were living a different reality. T'Keyah "Crystal" Keymah had come from a theatrical background and was the least known of the cast members. In turn, she was treated as if she was the least known.

> "Because I was probably the lowest person on the totem pole on that show, I was rarely given characters to do. It would be, 'Okay Jim, here's the piece where you play such & such a character and Crystal you're the woman that comes in and y'know...yeah! Tommy you're the so & so and Crystal you're the girl who comes in and...yeah!' So week after week I would create characters that were the girl, the woman, the lady who comes in and then Keenan would say, 'Oh wow—who's that girl?' I'd be like, 'Oh, this is so & so.' 'Okay, play her again in this sketch and play

her again in that sketch or we'll give her her own sketch,' but that's how I got work on the show by kind of auditioning in other people's sketches."

She became the resident impressionist on the show. Any time there was a character nobody else wanted to do they called on Keymah, like the time Kim Wayans didn't want to play Whoopi Goldberg in a *Ghost* parody. Keymah was given a video of Goldberg and instructed to study and be ready by the time tape rolled.

But even a show run by a black man still carried a certain amount of racism for the integrated cast.

> **TCK:** I remember this one sketch that Tommy and I were doing and it was funny and it was cute and the producer went, 'Something about it, something about it— let's try it with Jim and Kelly. Ah yeah! That's better.' It was just a general sketch. It didn't have any chicken or watermelon in it and that might've been the test."

The other black female of the cast also experienced the racism/sexism quandary.

KIM COLES

Kim Coles comes from Brooklyn, New York. She couldn't sing, dance or act, but she wanted to be artistic, so she picked the hardest art of them all—comedy. She loves the fact that her comedy is "squeaky clean" and it was her unwavering clean routine on *Showtime at the Apollo* that attracted Sinbad, who swooped her up to be his opening act for his national tour. She was later featured in *In Living Color* and then co-starred in *Living Single* with Queen Latifah, also on FOX. She was a judge on the BET comedy showcase program *Coming to the Stage* and intends to do stand-up until she's eighty. Her philosophy is *"there's nothing wrong with so-called blue humor, as long as there is room for red, purple, and cocoa humor, too. After all, as a race we are a colorful bunch of people!"*

> **T'Keyah "Crystal" Keymah:** "One of the most pleasant performers that I've ever worked with. She's sweet and funny."

Cole lasted one season on the show and mysteriously disappeared. In her place was not another woman, but a man who played the hell out of one.

JAMIE FOXX

> **Bob Sumner:** "The Jim Thorpe of comedy. A great guy. One, who, I can tell you right now, never forgot where he came from."

Eric Bishop was born in Terrell, Texas in 1967 and was raised by his grandmother. She made the reluctant budding athlete practice piano, which he hated. He wanted to be a famous musician, but found getting attention as a solo artist to be harder than expected, so he became a stand-up comedian and moved to California.

It was a week-long stint at the CAT in Atlanta (his first road gig) that turned into a month

Jamie Foxx (right) hanging out with good friend and comedian Speedy and writer Johnny Mack (center) at the bowling alley.

that transformed Foxx and opened his eyes to the potential of his new, stepping-stone craft. After that journey he described it to many as going to the mountain top. Having changed his name to "Jamie Foxx" to get spots after noticing that there was a shortage of female comedians on the sign-up list at clubs, he buckled down on his strengths, chiefly impressions. Many an evening Foxx would entertain his fellow comics with spot-on impersonations of them and anybody else you might call out. His delivery was impeccable and his characterizations flawless.

When he got his gig on *In Living Color*, Foxx sat back and watched the dynamics of his fellow performers. He didn't get into the fray of comic competitiveness, but instead observed and very quietly made a place for himself; at the same time offending no one and competing with no one. From this feature act status the character of Wanda was born. The loud ugly girl with the soul that would melt the audience at the turn of a dime by simply gazing into space, the facial expressions speaking volumes of all the nights spent alone with surely that very same look. Comedy and pathos at the same time. Who did this guy think he was— an actor?

Whatever Foxx thought of his own abilities he was making an impression, as the work kept coming. He landed his own self-titled sitcom on the WB network, during which time he made his foray into films with more standing than his previous hood efforts, such as *Booty Call* and *Players Club*. He did films like *Held Up* and *Bait*, then landed the co-starring role opposite acting legend Al Pacino in Oliver Stone's football epic *Any Given Sunday* along with LL Cool J and Dennis Quaid, and showed what he was really made of.

From that revelation of a performance, Foxx formed a relationship with writer/director Michael Mann and was next seen in the Muhammad Ali biopic *Ali* starring Will Smith in the title role. The three-plus hours might have been dedicated to getting Smith an Oscar nomination, but all anybody could talk about was the raw emotion Foxx purveyed as Bundini Brown, a long-time Ali associate. This maneuvered Foxx to another Mann project, *Collateral* with Tom Cruise. He was nominated for a Best Supporting Actor Academy Award, but he lost that year to Morgan Freeman.

Foxx had made the mistake of overshadowing his own work with the part-of-a-lifetime performance as the incomparable Ray Charles in Taylor Hackford's *Ray*. Foxx became the first African-American male comedian to win an Academy Award for best performance by an actor and the third black male to ever do so behind Sidney Poitier and Denzel Washington. And if that wasn't enough, that same year (2005) he was nominated for an Emmy for his searing work as Tookie Smith in the cable film *Redemption*, playing the reformed co-founder of the notorious L.A. street gang the Crips, and also appeared in the feature film *Jarhead*.

In 2006 Jamie's *Unpredictable* CD went to number one and he was set to star in two more big films: *Miami Vice*, co-starring Colin Farrell and directed by Michael Mann, and *Dreamgirls*.

Dreamgirls, the long-awaited screen adaptation of the Broadway musical, also features Beyoncé Knowles, Jennifer Hudson, Anika Noni Rose, Danny Glover, and Eddie Murphy, and is directed by Bill Condon.

By anybody's standards, 2004–2006 were damn good years, but then again Foxx always managed to have a good time. He'd become notorious for throwing great parties, wild parties, and after becoming a bonafide celeb everybody wanted to say they'd been to one. Chris Spencer remembers the new "friends" Foxx picked up along the way:

> "Like Jamie would have a party and all of a sudden after the party you would see strange people cleaning up. 'It's like, who are you?' Oh man, people would do stuff to try to get in that would blow me away; people doing his dishes, trying to walk the dog, and calling him the wrong name."

The gargantuan acclaim brought out accolades from peers as well.

Speedy: "The master of everything. No matter what he puts his mind to. When he first got in this game he was trying to become a singer and he was thinking of ways—how do I get my record and for people to know that I'm a singer? So he became a comedian and as a comedian he became an actor and as an actor, now he wants to sing and he can, because he was always a singer who could do it all."

J. B. Smoove: "He's always Jamie. He ain't one of them cats that blows up and acts like he don't know you. Jamie's always Jamie; that's the word I got for him—always Jamie."

Chris Spencer: "Jamie Foxx might be one of the most underrated comedians due to the fact his dramatic career launched so prominently."

Rodney Perry: "That *Foxhole* special he did was a beast and then for him to have taken his acting to the level he's taken it has just like knocked down doors for us as stand-ups. So now when they consider a dramatic role they will consider you."

Alex Thomas: "My nigga. I learned so much by being on *The Jamie Foxx Show* for two years. I was there as an amateur comic just sitting in the audience, just watching him the night Keenan Ivory Wayans picked him in a showcase for *In Living Color*. I mean I was there when he pulled up in a 1985 280ZX and to hang out with him now and see him with ten cars and a Bentley and an Oscar—hey man, that's my boy. Y'know what I mean? I'm so happy for him. He's opened up doors and made it possible, y'know. He's the first (male) comedian to ever win an Oscar, I think, right? And that just gives me all the motivation in the world. That just let me know man it's possible. And he's a pimp and I love going to his parties. He's like the black Hugh Hefner. He can't f*#k them all by himself. I'm there to lend a helping dick. I've got a lot of trickle down pu*#y from Jamie Foxx. I've been to his house and there's thirty bad bitches—hey, he can only f*#k ten of them. So I just helped him out."

Well, not everybody needed help. The show that had broken so much ground was ran into it by meddling execs intent on fixing a wheel that showed no signs of being broken.

Charlie Murphy: "The reason the show went off the air is because muthaf*#kas try to come in and when they see shit working right try to come with that 'it can't be right unless I had something to do with it.' Muthaf*#ka just sit back and take a check. Bitch, you ain't creative, muthaf*#ka. As soon as they got involved it went straight down the tubes."

And the Nights Got Darker

CHAPTER 21

> "I knew I'd lost a fight with my wife
> when the cops came to my house and asked me
> if *I* wanted to press charges."
> — KEVIN HART

Television was good for comedians in the late '80s and early '90s. If a show wasn't named after a black performer, black performers were infiltrating other shows. NBC favorite *Night Court* (1984–1992) featured the acerbic Marsha Warfield. She had been a featured player on *The Richard Pryor Show*, but as the court bailiff her common sense remarks cast her as one of the normal people in the quirky, offbeat sitcom.

She took over the part in the fourth season when the previous bailiffs, Selma Diamond and Florence Halop, both elderly showbiz vets and heavy smokers with raspy voices, died of lung cancer almost one year apart. For a while there was thought of eliminating the character altogether to avoid another dead actress, but Warfield was neither old nor a chain smoker. She not only outlived the show's run, but brought in a whole new fleet of black viewers who liked to hear her talk her minimal brand of dry, deadpanned trash.

Thea Vidale: "Marsha Warfield was not talking about her pu*#y. She had thoughts; intense thoughts and she was clever."

Martin Lawrence, Carl Anthony Payne II, and part time actor Michael Ajakwe in a scene from the episode "Cole on Ice" from the hit FOX sitcom Martin, 1995.

There were shows like *Frank's Place* (1987–1988) on CBS; set in New Orleans with funnyman Tim Reid, a stellar ensemble cast, great writing, music, and no laugh track. No wonder it was canceled so quickly. And *Benson* with Robert Guilliame as the governor's wiser-than-his-station butler (a spin-off character from the ABC sitcom *Soap*). It ran from 1979–1986 and even promoted the servant character to the job of Lt. Governor. The show was pulled from the schedule immediately thereafter.

Robert Townsend was over at FOX with his *Townsend Television* variety hour on Sunday nights. He featured everybody from the O'Jays to Tupac Shakur, but low ratings sunk that noble effort after only thirteen weeks. Too bad; he was good for comedians.

> **Paula Jai Parker:** "Robert Townsend loved bringing in young talent, like young comedians. And he would always use younger male comics, but usually he'd get actresses that were funny upfront, except 'LaBoca' (Suzanne Suter). She was one of the few female comedians that he would use and another young lady named Paula (Belle). She was a white girl. I got to work with those two and I have a lot of respect for stand-ups."

The new FOX network was also fond of stand-up comedians and was initially generous when it came to black programming. *Sinbad* was a show they banked on along with *In Living Color*, *Living Single*, *True Colors*, *Roc* starring Charles Dutton, and *Martin*.

Martin was a standout among these shows for the singular personality of its star. Martin Lawrence was Mr. *Def Jam* and had established himself as a force in black comedy. This sitcom was his opportunity for more creative input, and he made sure that if it failed it wouldn't be because he was puppeteered.

> **Charlie Murphy:** "He was in control of every aspect of his show. There was no part of that show where somebody could say, 'I'm responsible for this.' That nigga was in charge of everything, man."

The result of his aggressive manner was a hit show.

"Martin" writer, Michael Ajakwe Jr.: "The show was so real and so authentic. It spoke to black people, to the black experience without knocking white people. When white people tuned into *Martin* back in the day they learned. They watched Martin to learn what we were talking about."

Besides the wide array of eccentric characters Lawrence himself would portray, there were also his friends Cole (Carl Payne) and Tommy (Tommy Ford), girlfriend Gina (Tisha Campbell) and her friend and Martin's verbal sparring partner Pam (Tichina Arnold). One of his most memorable characters was the neighbor who identified himself not only by name, but which floor he lived on each time he'd visit Martin's apartment. And this was no standard sitcom distraction. This guy didn't enter through the front door without knocking or peering over the fence. "Bro Man" came in through the window. He might come in for anything—to make a sandwich, borrow something, or just to kick it and talk. Former construction worker, delivery man, and theater major, Reginald Ballard brought the totally original character to life and made a comedian out of an actor.

BALLARD: "When I got the *Martin* show, J. Anthony Brown got me into comedy. Told me to go to this club in Houston and bring up some comics for him one weekend. From then on somebody saw me in the audience, man, and took me all over world and the country doing comedy, man. That's how I got started."

DARRYL: "When did you realize you were a celebrity?"

BALLARD: "When I was in Houston at that same club just listening. I didn't go there to perform. I went there one day because I'm from Texas. I went in there and when they said I was in the audience everybody was standing up clapping and screaming. That's when I realized, ah, this must be something special."

DARRYL: "How was it working with Martin?"

BALLARD: "Ah, it was cool, man. It was like comedy college, man."

The show guest starred established black artists such as veteran comedienne and *Sanford and Son* co-star LaWanda Page, who'd gladly pass on pointers about the world of television to other actresses such as recurring character Laura Hayes, such as *"first thing you're going to have to learn is not to take rejection personally. These muthaf*#as don't give a damn about you."* Her advice to the younger performer was that *"you know that they'll be treating you like a bitch and a ho so just do your thing and keep your mind focused on what you have to do. It's been like that and it's going to be like that. It's just a little slicker now."*

Though the show itself was fine with its audience the word was out that Lawrence was difficult, unpredictable, and sexually aggressive on the set and the show was canceled after five seasons (enough for syndication).

Syndication is the great reward for successful shows and the starting point of others. It's the nether land of advertisers and Wall Street. A solid viewer magnet can stay on the air forever—game shows, reran classics, and of course talk shows, a medium not normally identified by its black idols, until a brother finally got the chance to attack it with a vengeance. He went by a single name and the morning after his debut that was all he needed.

ARSENIO HALL

> **Red Grant:** "He opened the door for black America to see that we could do shows like that; interviews and be successful at what we do. Be articulate and all that."

Arsenio Hall, son of a Baptist minister, was born on February 12, 1955 and was drawn to magic because he wanted to make more money than the average paper boy. So starting at around six years old, he'd go to a magic shop in Cleveland and watch the owner do tricks. When Hall was older and the man died, Arsenio stepped to the wife and asked for a gig showing the tricks that the business sold. He took his knowledge outside the magic shop and did enough shows to help put him through college.

He attended Ohio State, but soon transferred over to Kent State University where he first became involved in stand-up comedy. He attended The Cleveland Playhouse which gave him a forum to work on his newfound craft. In 1979 he moved from Ohio to Chicago, where he was discovered by Nancy Wilson, the renowned jazz singer. He'd been working the Comedy Cottage, a club where comedians like Bernie Mac would hang out, when Hall auditioned for a guy who ran a club called the Blue Max in the Hyatt Regency and got the gig opening for Wilson while she was in town. That led to a longer gig opening for her on the road, ending in Hollywood.

Packed and ready to return back home after the tour, it was friend/future rival Jay Leno who encouraged Hall to stay out West by asking him if he was out of his mind: back to Chicago—for what? Leno helped him find an apartment. Then in 1987 Hall replaced Joan Rivers on FOX's *The Late Show*, doing such an outstanding job that Paramount Studios signed him onto a picture and TV deal. He used this opportunity to insist that he own the rights to the show. This wise approach extended to the show's theme song, *Hall or Nothing*, that he wrote himself on the suggestion of musical legend Quincy Jones. Arsenio gets paid every time that song is played.

That same year he co-wrote and co-starred in *Coming to America* with pal Eddie Murphy, and on January 3, 1989 *The Arsenio Hall Show* hit the air nationwide. *TV Guide* declared Arsenio Hall the magazine's first "TV Person of the Year" in 1990. Beyond booking non-mainstream guests like a young Bobby Brown, he had groundbreaking events on his show—like shade-wearing presidential candidate Bill Clinton blowing sax.

The inspiration for his famed "dog pound" came from his director, Sandy Fullerton, who advised him to look for a hook; something people could remember Hall for. They decided to work the Cleveland angle, remembering that when Hall had mentioned on another show where he was from that the crowd started barking. It was at a time when the Cleveland dog pound craze was in effect, and fans would sit in the Cleveland stadium and throw milkbones on the field for their football team the Browns.

Kym Whitley: "Arsenio was fun to work with. I really was his assistant like on special occasions like the MTV Awards; when he was hot and he was hosting and I was his assistant and it was kind of cool. He'd have me hold all his jewelry and I'd sit around backstage and he always had to have a glass of wine before he went on, right? We had an expensive bottle of white Zinfandel and we couldn't find a bottle opener. So I ran to a stagehand and got a big screw; it had to be about four or five inches long; then I got some gaffer's tape and screwed it all along the top of the screw then screwed it down into his wine bottle and pulled out the cork."

Arsenio Hall (courtesy of Arsenio Hall).

And he had good reason to drink up—America loved him and his annual check of $14 milion was well earned, for the revolution he ignited by getting all those young kids to go out and buy products in mass quantities and for the viewers he attracted to a genre known for its old fogyism. The problem became the syndication game, where his markets were often fewer than his direct competitors, like David Letterman.

During the time the late show tug-of-war between Letterman and Leno for retiring Johnny Carson's spot on *The Tonight Show* was going on, Hall's show was up for renewal. The tussling going on at NBC had a direct effect on his immediate future. If Letterman went to CBS, Hall would leave late night television. If Letterman didn't go to CBS, he'd stay.

Hall wanted Letterman to get *The Tonight Show* job because it would have strengthened Hall's network market outreach. If Letterman went to CBS many of those owned and operated CBS affiliates would have opted to use Letterman in that prime spot vs. their only late night option—Arsenio. He knew his show would have been aired, but he didn't relish winning a 3 a.m. time slot.

Since Hall received no salary and earned his revenue as part owner with Paramount, his check was based on numbers. The better the numbers were, the more money he made. Once super-agent Mike Ovitz (Hall and Letterman's agent) came to Hall with the news Letterman had taken the CBS offer, Arsenio made up his mind not to die on the vine. Though he could have survived one more year while Letterman and CBS affiliates prepared for his takeover, Hall would've had to sign on for another three to five years (standard agreement in the syndication world). Hall opted to take their offer of producing the show with someone else hosting for that guaranteed year.

Hall wanted Bill Bellamy (who was contracted with another Viacom company, MTV), but the company desired others, including Magic Johnson and John Salley. Eventually it went to Jon Stewart (also under contract with MTV), who was not a compatible fit with the average Arsenio Hall devotee. Before that bump in the road was smacked into, Hall sent his letter of non-intent to Paramount and booked Louis Farrakhan. That one interview, which was booked and conducted after Arsenio Hall had decided to leave late-night television, caused much backlash with Hall's relationship with white America.

The run ended officially in 1994. From there he starred in the ABC sitcom *Arsenio*, a CBS show *Martial Law* with Sammo Hung, and he hosted the revived version of *Star Search* on CBS, but considers that his worst career mistake was turning down the chance to star opposite Martin Lawrence in *Bad Boys*.

> **A. J. Jamal:** "One thing Arsenio was good at was the politics of the game. If you're in this business you should know how to politic because to get to the next level, to stay on the 'A' list it takes a little politicking. Y'know that's why Bush is in office. He politicked his way into office. He didn't win nothing."

> **Ruben Paul:** "Trailblazer as far as his late night show and he left a void that still hasn't been filled on TV to this day."

Hall, like a number of his peers, got bitten by the comedy bug at an early age.

> **ARSENIO:** "I guess there are certain things in life you see someone do and it changes your life, y'know. Whenever I watched a comic work, nothing ever affected me like that does. When you go see Al Green and you're twelve years old and you see a guy come out that no one knows with a stool and a mic...there's just an amazing power about it that every comic understands, but nobody else will ever understand; the amazing power to take you on an emotional roller coaster with words. Even when the word is 'muthaf*#ka' and 'suck my d*#k.' But the bottom line is it was watching guys that do that. The moment when I said I gotta do that I was watching Franklyn Ajaye on the Kent State campus when I was a junior, senior. I think Steve Harvey was a student there at the same time. I, for some reason remember, A.J. Jamal being around so maybe he either played ball with us or he was going there at the time. We were probably juniors because I don't think Steve made it to the senior year. But the bottom line is I got that moment when you say this nigga is smart. What he's doing is some shit to strive to get good at. I remember that and while he was trying to get some pu*#y that night on campus, because you know when you're on the road and you perform someplace you hold court after the show to get local pu#*y. I mean that's part of stand-up. He was holding court and this little knucklehead nigga from Cleveland kept asking him questions and that was me and that's why when I meet young comics I'll talk to them; because guys like Ajaye, Cosby when I knew they were trying to get pu*#y, when I knew after the show it was pu*#y time, very much like Miller time, but it smells worse; when it was pu#*y time I was like, 'So Mr. Cosby can I ask you one more question?' I knew what the deal was, but they talked to me. They gave me their time and they talked to me about stand-up and encouraged this guy who thought he wanted to do it and as a result of that I try to pass that on. As a matter of fact I had a comic say that to me one time. I forget exactly who it was but I remember I said, 'Thanks I could never repay you.' He said, 'Pass it on.' I think it was Richard. 'Pass it on to somebody.'"

DARRYL: "Tell me about your first time on stage."

ARSENIO: "First time on stage was a horrific experience. Ironically my two favorite things in the world are stand-up and pu#*y and if you think about it those are the two things that I f*#ked the worst the first time I did it. The first time I had sex I came in my hand on a ripped condom wrapper. I could see the condom, but that's the closest I got to wearing it. The only other thing I wore was c*# all over my wrist and hand area. I remember messing that up and we went and made some cheese sandwiches, fries, and stuff so I could get myself back together, y'know? I didn't take long. I mean, I was fifteen. You eat a quick cheese sandwich. I was ready to f*#k back then. Now I have to go to Maine, catch a lobster in a net, kill it, steam it, and maybe I can get my d*#k hard again...this month. Anyway, stand-up was the same way. My first stand-up experience was at the Comedy Cottage in Rosemont, Illinois. I went up and I bombed even with other people's material. I did the shit I wrote and that bombed. I was like, I'm not bombing in this muthaf*#ka. Not my first time because I may never do it again. I started bombing in other languages, with other people's shit. I stole from thieves. Y'know, the guys you know that you don't want to perform in front of because you know they steal. I stole from thieves and continued to bomb. I remember saying some Richard shit. I'm like, damn if a Richard Pryor joke can't...but instead of discouraging me and making me not want to do it, it made me realize I had to become a writer. It made me realize I had to try harder. All my life stuff came to me easily. And even though I thought as I left the stage they will never see me in this muthaf*#ka ever again, I was back that next week. I really wanted to succeed at it because I had never had something slay me like that. Unfortunately stand-up is like that, though. You could never conquer it. Richard said that to me one night. Richard said, 'Everybody bombs.' I was naïve and young when I first met him and he talked about bombing and I said, 'You bombed?' and he said, 'Nigga, did I bomb?! You gonna always bomb. You gonna bomb forever.' And that was very weird because I guess as a naïve young guy just getting into it I'm thinking Richard ain't bombed in twenty years. Richard said, 'Oh, yes I have.'"

DARRYL: "Just not on the concert films."

ARSENIO: "Exactly. By the time he gets that camera rolling...as a matter of fact he told me a story about some shit he shot at the Improv and I think it's a classic last line a lot of people...you hear jokes stolen and reworked so many times sometimes you don't know where you know something classic from, but the first time I ever heard somebody say, 'I picked the wrong night to do my *In Concert* film was the night Richard said it on the video that not a lot of people have, but I think it was shot at the Improv in New York and it was a night when he bombed and it's on video. But it's interesting...years later some of the same material shows up on *That Nigger's Crazy* and it won a Grammy for that. So it just shows, he wasn't ready to shoot...like he said I wasn't ready to shoot my shit tonight, baby. You didn't even have to load the muthaf*#kas with film tonight."

DARRYL: "What about the backlash you experienced after the Farrakhan interview?"

ARSENIO: "I took a huge hit (with white America) for doing that one interview. There's a reason you don't see Farrakhan on *Oprah* or *The Entertainers with Byron Allen*. From hate mail, death wishes, to people trying to kill me, you name it, man. I had the crazy death phone calls. I thought I was in Mississippi in '54. It was crazy, but all that happened. Y'know what it is—we have heard it and we hear it. We go to Chicago and hear the tapes and watch it on C-Span, but for a lot of people they were like how could the guy who asked Brooke Shields if she's still a virgin, and we loved him in our living rooms, even talk to Farrakhan? It's very weird because I remember talking to Whoopi Goldberg, ironically about this and Whoopi had interviewed the Grand Wizard of the Ku Klux Klan..."

DARRYL: "...and got no flack for it."

ARSENIO: "Yeah, and I was like, well, I don't know what the difference is, but maybe with us there's an unwritten rule that we're not supposed to talk to black people we're told not to talk to, y'know? And I was this guy who...obviously when I booked him it was like, 'Don't do that.' A lot of people came out against me and all this other stuff. 'Don't do this interview.' But my whole thing is I have a friend; a guy I know—used to hang out at the park; knock niggas out—take shit from 'em. Crazy brotha and I saw him recently wearing a grey suit and a bow tie. And the bottom line is you can't throw the baby out with the bath water. There is a lot good about everybody. But the point is it's not important if you like Louis Farrakhan or whether I like Louis Farrakhan or whether he's a good guy, bad guy, or whether he's a racist or anti-Semite. None of that's important. What's important is that I interview him. I don't like Dabney Coleman or Elton John, but the bottom line is they have projects or involvement in our world and my job was to bring you interesting people who have involvement in our world; who can change your life artistically or politically. President Bill Clinton is not my best friend, but he was the most interesting person I could bring to America that night and I haven't seen him anymore than I've seen Louis Farrakhan since that interview. Bottom line is my job was to bring an interesting show and in that sense I thought I did and if I have to have people lose a love for me so be it. If I had to do it all over again I'd do it again because somebody other than Barbara Walters, has to and you know what I don't like? I don't like being told by the white community, 'let us handle this.' Because in that same year I've seen Ted Koppel, Barbara Walters do their edited pieces on, and I put a heavy emphasis on edited, because I did it straight through live, y'know. Some people have to edit it just in case you don't think of a person what they want you to think of them, they'll bend your perception even further and more effectively. My thing is like; don't say the nigga can't talk to him. You let Barbara Walters do the interview, Ted Koppel do the interview. I'm not a journalist. I'm an infotainment show. See, I was in a pop-culture environment where Minister Farrakhan was ever-present in lyrics. I was watching him take charge of niggas and keep them from robbing white folks and cutting their hair and cleaning themselves up and making an attempt to change their lives. I don't think you want to kill that message. Let's hear what this brotha has to say. That was my job. And my job is also to be hated by people. America's a trip, man. I got a death threat one time for putting on an openly gay comic. Don't forget this was '90-something. It's crazy to even say that. F*#k what year it was...I put an openly gay comic on and got death threats. This woman's first joke was about Hillary Clinton. 'Finally a first lady that we can "schtupp."' She did her thing, little white girl, y'know— dyke, straight up, but bottom line is giving everybody a shot. I didn't go and watch that lesbian woman f*#k her girlfriend after the show and I didn't go and have a bean casserole with Minister Farrakhan. I did what I do and the bottom line is what I don't do is interview everybody BUT Farrakhan. And I really don't do what I'm supposed to do to be loved because I think it's more interesting to bring you good television than to strive to be loved by everybody. I'd love to be loved by everybody, but I have a feeling that if I was I wouldn't be doing anything interesting. So I did what I did, man. I wish I had more on the line because when brothas come up to me I feel kind of guilty when brothas come up to me and say, 'Yo, I know what the white man did to you.' Because everything happened around the same time; I was still on the air and getting the Jon Stewart show ready and a lot of people were like, 'You're a hero, nigga.' I'm not really a hero, but yes I did interview Louis Farrakhan and there are a lot of people who hate me for it or aren't fans of mine for it, but I'm definitely not D'Militant."

Smokey Deese: "Great. Great. I've seen his stand-up a couple of times and he is by far one of the greatest on that stage. He's got punchlines as sharp as razor blades. He's like a boxer with a helluva over-hand right, man. You won't see it coming, but you'll damn always feel it."

What America felt, admittedly or not, was a sense of loss from Arsenio's departure. It was hard to envision a late night without him. With Hall off the air, television attempted to keep late night interesting with a mixed breed of talk show hosts. They tried former NBA and Lakers great Magic Johnson, but they soon discovered that one of the pre-requisites of doing a talk show is the ability to talk. Magic was amiable and likable, but most times not completely understandable. The show lasted about as long as a no-look pass.

Next came the duel debuts of *Vibe* and *Keenan* (as in Wayans). The creator of that behemoth known as *In Living Color* was chatting it up for more of a stretch, but it was missing something. There were those that said the set wasn't right. Others blamed the wardrobe department. There was even the school of rabid viewers who suggested the time slot might have been the problem. The time slot?! It was on late at night when late night talk shows air. Whatever the reason, including the misalignment of the stars, *Keenan* also didn't last long.

One of the problems with Wayans' show might have had more to do with competition. Musical genius and composer/arranger extraordinaire Quincy Jones entered the fray with a confection he called *Vibe*. The show was hosted by a virtual unknown, Chris Spencer, an industry darling, who lacked the broad-based recognition many of his peers enjoyed. This guy hadn't even been on *Comic View*.

DARRYL: "Tell us about *Vibe*."

SPENCER: "Laugh Factory owner Jamie Masada and my manager at the time were approached by Quincy Jones about doing a talk show and we were like, 'No, I don't want to do a talk show. I'm an actor.' Quincy Jones was like, 'Who the f*#k is this guy?' Quincy was like 'I want to meet with him.' And I was like, 'No, I don't want to meet with him because if I meet with him I'm going to do the show.' So they kept looking at people, looking at people. Months went by finally I said, 'Let me go meet him, maybe get a free meal out of it.' I met with Quincy Jones. He did his razzle dazzle, next thing you know I'm in the audition process. I'm thinking, 'Do I want the show? Do I really want the show?' And then I finally got it and it was a great experience in the beginning."

DARRYL: "Where do you think things went wrong?"

SPENCER: "Well, they hired me, Chris Spencer, because I had a certain little *oomph*. I had a certain little stink to me that made me special and it seemed like their whole goal, after me doing the pre-shows to the actual show, was get me to be who they wanted me to be and wash my little stink off so I became a kind of a puppet. They were insecure because Keenan's show was on at the same time. It was a ratings race so they knew the only successful model for this format was *Arsenio* and they tried to gear the show to look too much like *Arsenio*. We had *Arsenio*'s old director. Our stage had *Arsenio*'s old colors."

DARRYL: "Did they want you to have a dog pound and bark?"

SPENCER: "No, no, no triangle haircut, nothing like that. But see Arsenio was a hero of everybody. He was the shit and they were trying to make me like him. And even he looked at the talk show like, 'Don't that show look a little too much like mine?'"

Whether it was too much or not enough, the public wasn't feeling *Vibe*. So after two months of stilted monologues and lackluster interviews, Spencer was replaced by comedy pitch hitter Sinbad. No reason was ever officially given.

DARRYL: "So how did they break that to you?"

SPENCER: "My grandmother called me one morning and said, 'Hey, did you know you were being replaced?' I was like, 'What?' I mean I had done getting this thing right. So I called them and I was like, 'What's going on?'

'Hey, want to go to breakfast?'

"I was like, 'No, why don't you take my lawyer to breakfast?'"

DARRYL: "So what was your feeling about Sinbad taking over? Or did you even watch it after that?"

SPENCER: "I watched it. I just know that as brilliant as Sinbad is those people over there didn't know what they were doing. So it's kind of hard to be great and they're not letting you do what you need to do. They said this, 'You can't do that joke because the white lady in Iowa won't get it.' I'm like, 'What's she doing up at 11:00 at night watching my show anyway?'"

Chris Spencer (courtesy of Chris Spencer).

Sinbad was also reluctant to do the late night *Arsenio* imitation:

SINBAD: "Quincy Jones called me up and said, 'Man, could you help me out with *Vibe*.' I didn't want to do a talk show. A talk show takes your whole life up. You can't do movies or anything. I didn't want to talk about movies, I wanted to make movies. So when I took *Vibe* I was only supposed to do it for like a couple of weeks. And then we made a deal. They gave me a movie deal. They said if I could do *Vibe* for eight months a year I could do this movie. Well, that movie they happened to offer me was a movie called *Blue Streak* that ended up going to a guy, Martin Lawrence."

The show was canceled soon thereafter and the search for the next Arsenio Hall continued. Seemed everybody was trying to replicate the magic that Arsenio had wrought, but what did the originator think?

DARRYL: "You had *The Magic Hour*, you had *Vibe*, you had *Keenan*—what did you think about those shows?"

ARSENIO: "You know what? It's a very hard vehicle to be successful at and I was blessed by God to come along at a time when it was needed versus a time when people were trying to either imitate it or capitalize on the demographic that it was profiting from. I was just lucky, y'know when you're a young black man from any inner city, Detroit, Chicago, St. Louis, and you're watching the *Tonight Show* you're like, 'Damn, I've got to wait a long time between nights where you see a nigga.' And that's the way I grew up. I grew up watching the *Tonight Show* saying, 'Al Green is on tonight and maybe next month I'll see Leslie Uggams.' But the bottom line is you grow up saying that's what I wanted to do. Before I knew I wanted to be a stand-up I knew I wanted to be a talk show host. And mostly it was because there wasn't a show that showed the shit I wanted to see and it was too far and in between. It was like damn I get to see Ray Charles once a muthaf*#kin' year?! Y'know, when I grew up I did a show where I can put Ray Charles on as much as I wanted to and the bottom line is it was timely. The guys who came after me were simply capitalizing on economics that they saw or projected. There's a huge urban audience out there let's just split the pie up a thousand different ways. The big problem when you put *Vibe*, *The Magic Hour*, and *Keenan* up against each other what you do is you pit three niggas against each other splitting the pie in as many pieces as possible and basically not enough pieces to keep any of the shows on air. They actually canceled each other out by all hitting at the same time. It would have been better if one guy who was competent at it did it and everybody just stepped away and wasn't so f*#kin' greedy."

DARRYL: "Who was the best at it?"

ARSENIO: "Out of Sinbad, Magic, and Keenan? I'd have to say Keenan, but you know what—Chris Spencer could have been better if they had left him alone. Chris Spencer was given a show and not given the creative freedom to do what got Chris Spencer to that point. Quincy and everybody, and I love Quincy dearly, but Quincy and everybody got in Chris' way. We never saw Chris emerge. If Chris and his boys were allowed to do what they do, and when I say his boys I know he has a lot of funny guys around him that he depends on, if Chris was allowed to do the show...if you remember there was a point where there was a segment within Chris' show where Quincy interviewed Bill Clinton instead of Chris. That show was never allowed to become a custom-made suit of talk for Chris. My show was allowed to be customized for me. Chris might have been the best of any of those guys. If I had to pick one...if somebody said executive produce one, I'd go with Chris in a second. Chris is better than Magic because first and foremost Magic is a great athlete. Chris is a wordsmith who makes his living talking and making people laugh. So he is inherently more qualified to do it from jump street. Sinbad, I love him dearly, but the most incredible joke ever written was when Damon Wayans said Sinbad thought that a talk show meant he talked all the muthaf*#kin' time. Sinbad has to be one of those guys who is a guest because Sinbad loves to talk and Sinbad will outtalk a guest in a muthaf*#kin' second. You'll have Alan Greenspan on and Sinbad will tell you what *he* thinks about Wall Street. So Damon...that's a classic comic evaluation of Sinbad. And as far as Keenan, Keenan would be second behind Chris Spencer, because he's a stand-up; he has a good barometer inside of him as to when to talk and when to shut up, but Keenan wasn't going to succeed while there were so many people going after the same demographic; an urban audience."

The comedian who enjoyed the talk of the talk show had made his mark on the original *Star Search* with Ed McMahon when the energy and audience were there. And he milked the moment to lay the groundwork for an extremely profitable career.

SINBAD

David Adkins was born on November 10, 1956 in Benton Harbor, Michigan and credits his success to both parents being there for him as a child even though times were hard financially. His first love was basketball. He even won a basketball scholarship to the University of Denver, but dropped the sport to do comedy...belatedly. Sinbad came out to Hollywood at the ripe old age of twenty-eight saying he should've left college his sophomore year, but that he was so hung up on basketball.

Sinbad and comedienne Luenell getting loud at Geoffrey's Inner Circle, Oakland, CA, 1995.

"I should've let that game go and followed my heart and done entertainment."

He decided to go clean because he wanted his father and mother to be able to come to his shows, but times were rough. For a while he stayed at the Hooker Hotel in the sleazier part of Hollywood where a transvestite watched his room when he went on the road on what became known as "The Poverty Tour." He went around the nation on Greyhound buses. It was the number one comedy tour that summer.

He later jumped to prominence when he was a finalist on CBS's hit talent showcase, *Star Search*, and from 1987–1991 he had a steady gig on NBC's *A Different World*.

Ajai Sanders: "He taught me a lot about the red light. Sinbad showed me some tricks of the trade. As a comedian being on a sitcom in an ensemble cast you got to make sure you know how to light your light and let it shine in the right time in the right space."

His expertise before the camera came in handy as the creator, star, and executive producer of his FOX sitcom *The Sinbad Show* (1993–1994) featuring actor/comedian T. K. Carter, and his theatrical releases, *House Guest* with Phil Hartman in 1994 and *First Kid* in 1996. He tussled with Arnold Schwarzenegger as an overworked man out to get his son a last-minute, popular and practically sold-out Christmas toy in *Jingle All the Way* (1996).

For years Sinbad was known for his annual HBO music specials, featuring acts like Chaka Khan, Earth, Wind & Fire, Kool & the Gang, Smokey Robinson, and the Stylistics. The festivals (staged in Jamaica, St. Martin, Aruba, and the Virgin Islands) also highlighted the comedy of Geoff Brown, J. Anthony Brown, and Jonathan Slocomb. Sinbad was inspired to mount these old school shows when he noticed the void in contemporary soul music after attending the Cool Spirit Jazz Festival sponsored by *Jet* magazine. He liked the soul music from the '70s. *"Brothers used to cry about losing their women, now they sing about dissing them."*

DARRYL: "Who were your favorite comedians and why?"

SINBAD: "There were so many. I don't have just one or two. Oh God...I mean Richard Pryor, Bill Cosby, Red Skelton, Pigmeat Markham, Slappy White, Redd Foxx, Alan King—there were so many guys I saw as a kid growing up, man. It's a wide range of people. I always look at Bill and Richard as two phenomenal people. I'm talking about the amount of material they could put out that was excellent. I'm not talking about a laugh here, a laugh there. I'm talking about excellent material. And a lot of people get caught up in what's clean and what's dirty. Y'know it's not about what clean or dirty it's about what's funny. Because to me a guy...like Richard—he could do it clean or he could do it dirty. He's just as funny. Redd Foxx was the same way. If his mother showed up in the audience he wouldn't cuss. And he could do another hour, hour and a half, man."

DARRYL: "What were the differences when you became a celebrity?"

SINBAD: "The only difference was, man you don't get to be a fly on the wall and observe stuff, because people know who you are now. Whereas before you were able to interact more with life. When you're not a celebrity you can hang. That's why I say what was so phenomenal about Cosby and Richard—that they were able to do it whether they were celebrities or whether they weren't celebrities. I mean, they just put that material out, man."

DARRYL: "Let's discuss your FOX show."

SINBAD: "I thought that was going to be my show. Y'know the one that goes for like six or seven years. When we put the show together, I wasn't supposed to be doing TV. I was on the tour and Disney wanted to do something with me. I wanted to make movies because I really didn't know how TV was going to work out for me because although people kept trying to play me up as this crossover comic, my thing was I was on the edge of doing some things that wasn't like...'He's the next Cosby.' I'm like, 'Well, I'm not Cosby.' There's only one Cosby. And I had my own thing I wanted to do. But Disney said they'd give me a movie deal as long as I did a TV deal with them. I'm thinking we'll make this deal, but we'll just never do a TV show. But we happened to pitch that show. I just pitched that off the top of my head and they bought it. I thought, oh, my God I got to do this show. So I was still on the road. I thought when we come back we'll do the show, but when I got back producers and the writers that I'd picked would not talk to me. I was fighting to talk with the writers and the producers of my show. It's almost like they were begging for a job to produce it, but then once they got the job it's like I didn't count. And it was a rude awakening for me about sitcoms. I look at most sitcoms—they're not having fun. It's amazing how many sitcoms are made and it's a fight and a struggle every day on the set. And I said man this is probably one of the most unfun things I've ever done in my life. Although I loved my cast, I loved the crew I had...I missed an opportunity to do what I really wanted to do with that show. I don't have many regrets in my life and that's one of them."

DARRYL: "How about *A Different World*?"

SINBAD: "*A Different World* was a cool show, man. Just because of the crew, the people...I always felt like the outside man on *A Different World* because I wasn't really a cast member that was picked. I ran down there and begged to warm up the audience for the pilot of *A Different World*, figuring in my heart, I'm going to get a part in this show. Cosby ended up putting me on the show, but I was never really in the mix totally as a cast member."

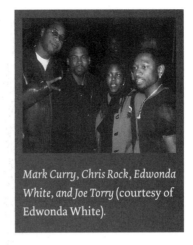

Mark Curry, Chris Rock, Edwonda White, and Joe Torry (courtesy of Edwonda White).

Michael Williams: "Sinbad was one of those rare individuals who was just magical. Every time he came to the club (the Comedy Act Theater) people just lit up, y'know because he was so funny, so energized that it was always a treat and a bonus whenever he came to the club. He was an extreme plus to the black comedy scene."

He was also a plus for the show *A Different World* (a spin-off of *The Cosby Show*). The show, about black college life at Hillman University in Georgia, starred Lisa Bonet, Jasmine Guy, Kadeem Hardison, Cree Summer, Mary Alice, Dawnn Lewis, Lou Myers, Charnele Brown, Darryl M. Bell, Sinbad, and later Glynn Turman. It was executive produced by Dr. William H. Cosby himself and directed by famed dancer and award-winning choreographer Debbie Allen. The show ran from 1987–1993.

Stand-up comedian Mark Curry was doing fine on ABC in his show *Hangin' with Mr. Cooper* (1992–1997) based on his real life exploits as a former basketball player and featuring Holly Robinson and later the ever-present Dawnn Lewis.

DARRYL: "Can you tell us a little about what it's like to have your own show; the responsibilities and the emotional high?"

CURRY: "Well, the emotional high is incredible, of course. Sure, it's a responsibility just to be funny basically and make sure that every time they see you, you do a good job; the people that see you on TV. And I think I did that. I think all my shows were decent. Y'know, they were good. You just want to leave your mark, y'know? Where's your indelible mark?"

That show also benefited from the addition of a new cast member when her show left the air. Nell Carter had been over at NBC filming *Gimme a Break* before she joined Curry and company. The Alabama native who'd made her mark earning a Tony Award for her searing, breakthrough lead performance in *Ain't Misbehavin'* in 1978 was playing Nell Harper, the housekeeper for a retired cop and his daughters. Carter not only sang the title song, she also earned two Emmy nominations during the show's 1981–1987 run. Following *Gimme a Break's* cancellation, Carter bounced to ABC and *Hangin' with Mr. Cooper* (the same season they obtained Raven-Symone). An admitted drug addict who struggled with diabetes for years, Carter was found dead in her Beverly Hills estate on January 23, 2003 at the age of fifty-four.

Another diva making the sitcom rounds was comedienne/actress Thea Vidale and her self-titled sitcom on ABC playing Thea Turrell, a mother of four.

> **Luenell:** "The first black female comedienne to have a television show in her own name."

The show co-starred Yvette Wilson of *The Parkers* and was R&B singer Brandy's first foray into television.

> **DARRYL:** "What are your feelings about *Thea*."

> **THEA:** "I didn't have as much fun as I should have. I didn't have what I believe were the right people around me. And there's just as many wrong white people as there are wrong black people."

Even non-comedic blacks were tackling situation comedies. Will Smith was a rapper and part of the team the Fresh Prince & DJ Jazzy Jeff. They were the sect of safe, non-offensive hip hop for the masses and it paid off with the genre's first Grammy Award.

The duo was riding high; writing the rules as they went along and living large. Too bad Smith never bothered to buy a calculator during one of his shopping excursions or he'd have noticed he was going broke. The wealthy rap star pulled an MC Hammer and found himself embarrassingly in the red, but fortunately for Smith a man named Quincy Jones was born and Q picked Smith for a new sitcom based on the life of record tycoon Benny Medina, and the Fresh Prince was now a TV star with *The Fresh Prince of Bel-Air* about a poor kid from Philly who goes west to live with his rich relatives in California.

It was a mega hit and catapulted Will Smith into a career as one of the top box office draws in the world. After the show's run he buffed up and became an action star in films where a black man was saving the world against aliens in *Independence Day* and *Men in Black*. He teamed with Martin Lawrence for *Bad Boys* and Jamie Foxx when Smith took on the title role of *Ali* and got nominated for an Academy Award for best actor in 2001. A true Renaissance man, Smith continued to record and perform music, produce television programming, and make funny movies. Even in his action mode, Smith always had a sense of humor and his films always made money of the big variety.

NBC was hoping to further capitalize on the black trend when they enlisted young *Def Jam* alumni Royale Watkins to head his own NBC sitcom, 1997's *Built to Last*. The running joke would be that it wasn't, but it opened a door for fledging black talent at a major network. Not since the '70s had a black act been promoted with such gusto and never with a complete unknown. Writer Michael Ajakwe Jr. recalls the situation:

"It was Royale's first time doing this and he and I became friends because I knew he wasn't happy with a lot of what was happening and we would talk. And I encouraged him. Hey man, you only get one shot to do something like this. You need to assert yourself. You're a producer on the show. Tell them what you want. Show up in that writer's room. Talk to these people. And don't feel bad about it because you're the star of the show and if it doesn't work they're going to blame you. They're not going to blame these guys. We're going to go on and do other stuff. And of course they were telling him to wait until the show gets picked up and then we'll make these changes. Of course the show wasn't picked up. It was canceled after six episodes and Royale got blamed for it."

Will Smith during a break from filming Made in America *in Lake Merritt, Oakland, CA 1993.*

DARRYL: "What do you feel about the politics of television, meaning do you feel [*Built to Last*] was given a chance?"

ROYALE: "My experience with *Built to Last* is that I felt we put together a wonderful show, but again if you're not a name brand coming out the gate in television or if you're not an entity the networks feel they will eventually be able to make money off of then y'know you don't get as hard a look as some of the other so-called stars in television, and so me being a new comedian, y'know I felt the odds were stacked against me and it was a ratings issue with my television show so I don't know. I don't feel like there are a whole lot of politics in television. I feel like funny and money wins. Those are the two things. You be funny, you make the network some money and you stay on the air—that's it."

DARRYL: "Do you feel black shows are judged differently than white shows on network television?"

ROYALE: "Well, it depends on who's judging them. On some level the quality of a lot of the black shows isn't as good as white shows on television to be quite frank with you. Y'know, I've watched shows like *Six Feet Under*; show is amazing. You watch an episode of *Six Feet Under* and then you watch half the black shows that are on television and you look at the quality of story telling. Y'know, we have to ask ourselves, what stories are we telling and the level of writing that goes into telling those stories and you be the judge."

Mo Money, Mo Money, Mo Money

CHAPTER 22

"Terrorists say they going to blow up the malls.
Blow 'em up! I ain't got no money anyway, but now
if you blow up that 99-cent store I'll go over
to Afghanistan."
— Loni Love

The mid-'90s saw institutions were being overturned and massive changes in politics (the president stopped Congress from shutting down the government), sports (Jordan retired), law (OJ got off), and naturally entertainment. One of the most enduring shows on television went full circle and had a complete makeover. In 1997 *Soul Train* got a new host.

It was pretty earth shattering when you think about it. Don Cornelius had been the venerable ringmaster since the show's inception in Chicago on October 2, 1971 and through its move to Los Angeles and national prominence, but aging and declining health put things in perspective for Don and he went on a search for a different guy. Why mention this turn of events? Because he replaced himself with a comedian.

For those of you who have ever watched *Soul Train* I'm sure it had nothing to do with the wit and humor of stone-faced Don Cornelius. He was known for being smooth and stoic. Not the kind of guy you look for to bring a smile across your face. So the choice of an established funny man was a bit bizarre, but it went to show how just about everybody was looking for comics during the "Boom."

The comic he selected? Mystro Clark.

DARRYL: "How did you get the gig?"

MYSTRO: "It happened when they first started using the guest host in '94 and '95. I guest-hosted it once, and I guess I did a pretty good job compared to some of the other people that came in for a day and just muddled through. Don Cornelius remembered it and two years later when he decided to go with one single host again they just called my agents and said they wanted to make an offer."

DARRYL: "Why did you leave the show—contract expired or what was the situation?"

MYSTRO: "We started having disagreements after my third year, because he has a big ego. You know, he's been on TV for thirty years. You tend to get a big ego. So he got mad at me if I didn't say things the way he wrote it. See, I paraphrase; as a comedian that's what we do and he'd be mad about that because he wrote all the questions himself."

Not everybody was as concerned about their Shakespearean prose, and comedians were popping up everywhere in non-traditionally comedic roles. Wanda Sykes and white comedian Dennis Miller were later used on sports shows. Arsenio Hall was the host of the talent competition show *Star Search*. Comedians such as Rosie O'Donnell to Jenny Jones were given talk shows. Even serious panel programs such as *Politically Incorrect* and the line-ups on CNN and their rival stations spoke more to comedians than ever before, and not just for comic relief but ofttimes for a fresher perspective. So entertainment overall benefited from this seemingly meaningless move.

Another comedian making noise was almost a trivia question.

CHRIS ROCK

Roger Rodd: "Chris Rock is a brilliant man, who was hitting on all points at all times about every body and what they are about to think. He doesn't pull any punches. He's not a black comic. He's not a white comic. He's not a sellout and a crossover. He's a top notch, cutting edge brilliantly written comic."

Willie Brown (& Woody): "A combination of Pryor and Carlin."

Marc Howard: "Probably gonna go down as one of the top five all time comics, y'know."

Chris Rock was born on February 7, 1966 in Brooklyn, New York. He got into stand-up when he was a teenager in the mid-'80s and was discovered by Eddie Murphy on the New

York club scene and appeared on HBO's *Uptown Comedy Express* in 1987.

Ian Edwards: "This is a thing about Chris back in the day. Chris Rock would get on stage and look at his notes. 'Yeah, okay, I'm done. Was that joke all right?' Then he turned back and looked at his paper. He used to work the room with the same material people are laughing at right now, because if it was Chris Rock people accepted it. Some people would be offended because he used the stages as a classroom. Yet he don't care and that takes balls. He's got a lot of balls. He's not afraid to fail when testing his writing."

That hard work and balls got him a job writing and performing on *Saturday Night Live* from 1990–1993. He co-wrote and produced the gangsta rap parody film, *CB4* and then nothing happened. No show. No-big time movie package—nothing. So Chris Rock, a comedian at heart, hit the road making personal appearances across the country.

Chris Rock with comedienne/actress Ajai Sanders at the Strand in Redondo Beach, CA, July 24, 1992.

Ruben Paul: "...after leaving *Saturday Night Live* he said he was a little down after that experience and he just said forget trying to get a TV deal, forget trying to be famous. Let me go out and be the best comedian that I can be."

During this process, Rock got a good swift kick in the teeth from some of his peers. Martin Lawrence was Chris' feature act and destroyed him in concert, and other comedians seemed to thrive on using his notoriety to their best advantage and his least.

Angela Means: "I love the fact that he did not deviate from who he was. He could've gone down a different road, but he just stayed on course. I remember working with him and the show was myself, Jonathon Slocomb, Jamie Foxx, Joe Torry, and Chris Rock, and Chris was recording his CD at the time, but by the time it got to Chris Rock it was 1 o'clock in the morning. They were like, 'I'm gonna be the funniest nigga on this show and I'm gonna show this audience who's really funny.' By the time it got to Chris Rock there was only half the audience there and they were so tired, but I watched him and he did not alter. He did not say I do not want these niggas on the show. It was his show and the record label was there recording and Chris stayed right with what Chris was doing. What I saw in him was that he had a plan. He had a course of action and I just admired him for that.

And I saw that he had a vision and he was going to go with what he had and he was going to stick to it."

Chris was on a mission. He'd stated that if he couldn't turn things around in his career he'd quit show business. He established his new attitude during the 1996 Republican Convention when Rock played political analyst for Comedy Central and stole the show.

In 1996 his HBO comedy classic *Bring the Pain* earned him two Emmy awards. From his jabs at D.C. Mayor Marion Barry's crack problem to his "I love black people, but I hate niggas" routine, Chris Rock became not a "King" of comedy, but its reigning monarch.

> **Katt Williams:** "He brought intelligence back to stand-up comedy. He would talk about intellectual things and yet he was funny and talk about nigga shit at the same time."

His triumph was followed up with his own late night show aptly titled *The Chris Rock Show* on HBO from 1997–2000; it was a Cable ACE award winner. This led to the 2001 film *Pootie Tang*, a sketch character on the show. As portrayed by comedian/writer Lance Caruthers, Pootie had taken on a life larger than TV and deserved celluloid. Though the critics were not kind, movie goers dug it and Chris Rock was back in the film production business, appearing in the film as well.

> **J. B. Smoove:** "The thing I like about him are the projects like *Pootie Tang* and *The Chris Rock Show*. He had a great mix of people, man and I liked how they worked together. I loved the camaraderie that they had together, how they wrote together, they talked together, going through the paper and laughing at things that's going on in the news. I was amazed."

Rock continued to expand as an artist, co-starring in other people's movies such as *Lethal Weapon 4*, *Dogma*, *Bad Company*, *Nurse Betty*, and *The Longest Yard*. He produced two more of his own, *Down to Earth* and *Head of State*; used his influence to get D. L. Hughley's show, *The Hughleys*, on the air, as well as his own sitcom (doing the narrative) on UPN entitled *Everybody Hates Chris* in 2005. That same year Rock hosted the Academy Awards, overseeing the historic ceremony when black comedian/musician/actor Jamie Foxx won for Best Actor for *Ray* and black acting legend Morgan Freeman took home the Best Supporting Actor for *Million Dollar Baby*.

> **Tom Dreesen:** "I think Chris is brilliant, but I think Chris will fall into a trap like everybody else that after a while you can't make everybody love you. I think a good example is the Academy Awards on which I thought he was hilarious. But y'know you just have to know the venue you're in. What Chris didn't do, Chris didn't conform to them. He brought Chris Rock to the Academy Awards—take it or leave it. That's what I admired about him. You don't like it, f*#k it. That's who I am. Don't chide me for being who I am. To me Chris was just being Chris. When young kids see Chris Rock they're seeing an original."

An original and a yardstick for young comedians for his ability and integrity.

Tony Rock: "I like my brother. I'm a little biased. We came out of the same vagina, so I'm a little biased."

Geoff Brown: "Tells it like it is about everybody, about everything and makes it funny and shit and he's never left stand-up."

Mystro Clark: "Quiet. He doesn't draw too much attention or make too much noise except on stage, but in person he's real mellow; he's real nonchalant."

Bob Sumner: "*Def Comedy Jam* helped Chris Rock. The reason I say that is because Chris Rock was pre-*Def Comedy Jam*. A lot of people didn't understand Chris being under Eddie Murphy's wing and what have you. A lot of people didn't understand Chris Rock's humor until they saw how genius it was after watching some of the *Def Comedy Jam* comedians."

Chris had the gall many of his contemporaries lacked when it came to socially relevant material. He followed the tradition of the great comedians who preceded him. He placed himself at odds with popular sentiment and sold his point of view. Whether it was race, relationships, politics or all that's celebrity—Rock took aim and fired.

In the process of giving '90s comedy a wake up call, Rock introduced a few talents. Mario Joyner, who had been one of the rising young black comedy stars prior to the *Def Jam* explosion, was getting renewed interest. *Pootie Tang*'s Lance Caruthers, and writer/performer/co-creator of Rock's semi-autobiographical sitcom *Everybody Hates Chris*, Ali Leroi, were also getting their phone calls returned. However, when asked about his impact on black comedy Rock doesn't see the big deal.

"I have no impact. I'm just another nigga out here telling jokes."

Yeah, right, and Minnie Riperton was just another chick singing high notes. Like Redd Foxx before him, Rock's presence allowed others to be seen within his limelight. His so-called lack of impact changed one funny lady's life and kept us rolling.

WANDA SYKES

Born March 7, 1964 in Portsmouth, Virginia, the writer/comedienne/producer/actress/multi-media star honed her skills on the East Coast.

Marc Howard: "Came from my hometown of D C. Wanda was fortunate, especially in D.C., because there weren't any female comics so she was soaking up work when they wanted a female, but she was good. She's a good, talented stand-up comic. I'm not misogynist, but there just aren't many women cracking you up like men. Out of all the comics there's only a handful of female comics and out of the female comics there's only a handful that are actually funny. And it's unfortunate. I think it's a little harder for women, but Wanda is solid. What I mean is she ain't never going to be bad. She may not blow you off the stage, but she's good."

Sykes worked all types of gigs under all types of conditions.

Ian Edwards: "Me, Wanda Sykes, and J.B. Smoove had the same management and they used to book us together. We did a college tour. This was in the early '90s and one time we put on a show in Indiana. We flew into an airport, which was like two hours from the school. They picked us up and we're driving and it was a one-lane highway, you know, with one lane on either side. Somebody tried to overtake us. In the other lane they were coming straight towards us and that car was about to come through my door, but the girl driving swerved out of the way and the car ended up on its side in a ditch. They had to come and get us and we were supposed to meet Jim Breuer at the show. And then we got to the show and the crowd still booed our ass. We would have done better staying in the ditch."

Sykes kicked things off in '92 with her first appearance on the *Tonight Show* and then popped up on just about every sitcom involving laughter. She worked on good friend Chris Rock's show as a performer and writer as well as co-starring in *Pootie Tang* and *Down to Earth*. Sykes also had her own show on FOX, *Wanda at Large*.

Her persona was also used to fine affect in *Monster-in-Law*, playing opposite screen legend Jane Fonda. Sykes has hosted awards shows, collected awards for her work, and if that wasn't enough, she did *Inside the NFL* on HBO. How's that for impact?

There were also two new networks trying to make a name for themselves by repeating FOX's strategy of years past by clamoring for black viewers (*True Colors*, *Roc*, *In Living Color*) right off the bat.

Cedric the Entertainer: "When they wanted to build their networks, basically these white-owned networks put on the blackface. They put black shows on and let them build their networks up and then you look up and you don't have a black show on at all. It's for them to save face with themselves, but they've always got a different goal."

The WB got early recognition with programming such as *The Wayans Bros* (siblings Shawn and Marlon) and Robert Townsend's *The Parent 'Hood*; while UPN came up with *Homeboys from Outer Space*, *Moesha*, and *Malcolm & Eddie*.

The latter boasted a former Cosby kid and one cocksure comedian.

EDDIE GRIFFIN

Sherri Shepherd: "I said, 'You're very funny.' He said, 'Yes, I am.'"

Born in Kansas City, Missouri on July 15, 1966, the always-ambitious, young Eddie opened up a dance studio when he was just fifteen years old. Everything was fast with Eddie. He got married at sixteen and joined the Navy at seventeen (which of course had nothing to do with his matrimonial status—because by then he was divorced). He was discharged a year later at age eighteen and at nineteen he spent six months in jail for assault.

He became a comedian on a bet, which required him to perform stand-up at a Kansas City club. Once bitten, Griffin made his way to Hollywood where he became a regular at the Comedy Store.

> **Honest John:** "All comics have a problem with the fact Eddie Griffin does way too much time when he gets up on stage, but really a cool guy. Some guys just can't get off the stage and he's one of them. It would be better off for him if he could, but I do understand that compulsion. So please Eddie if you're reading this—after an hour, get your ass off the stage."

> **Curtis Arceneaux:** "I watched that nigga be homeless to a millionaire. When I first met Eddie, he was working the door at the Comedy Store and of course him not having a home of his own the Comedy Store was his home. So being on stage for three hours at a time per night...he didn't have nowhere to go. He didn't have shit to do so that was his way of dealing with his homelessness and it was f*#kin' genius."

Eddie Griffin at the Lady of Soul Awards (courtesy of *Comedy the Magazine*).

During one of his lengthy performances, Griffin did such a dead-on impression of Andrew "Dice" Clay that the targeted comedian took Griffin on tour with him.

> **Chris Spencer:** "In terms of performance there's nobody more committed. Eddie Griffin can make his performance strong for an audience of three as much as he will for an audience of five thousand. I wish I could do that, but I don't want to talk to three people. I'm sorry. He's an entertainer."

In 1991, Griffin toured with Robert Townsend and the Dells to promote Townsend's feature film *The Five Heartbeats*, and in 1993 he'd work with Townsend on the FOX variety show *Townsend Television*.

> **Paula Jai Parker:** "I worked with him on *Townsend Television* and he told me on the set of Robert's 'Nigel Spider' (recurring detective sketch) that one day he was going to do his thing and he was going to produce movies and star in them and I was going to be his first leading lady. And that was while we were doing *Townsend Television*. Fast forward for blah, blah, blah years and he got his first movie deal.

He co-wrote it with Pope Daniels and he got the deal with Miramax and sure enough he starred me in it and that's my honey. I love me some Eddie Griffin."

'93 was also the year Griffin co-starred in Townsend's *Meteor Man*. In 1994 Griffin's HBO comedy special was so well-received it was nominated for a Cable ACE award and in certain circles he was being referred to as "the king of hip-hop stand-ups."

Daryl Mooney: "Eddie Griffin started off buffooning. Eddie Griffin has come a long way. I love the idea of Eddie Griffin telling his truth. There's a fine line between cocky and confident and I think he goes overboard trying to be super gangster black man, but overall I like Eddie. I like his independence and I like what he's trying to do."

That same year, Griffin showed his dramatic chops as "Rat" in the Jada Pinkett/Allen Payne love story *Jason's Lyric*. Then he and Payne teamed up again as soldiers in 1995's *The Walking Dead* (a gripping Vietnam War drama), on his way to co-starring in his own sitcom opposite former *Cosby* kid Malcolm Jamal-Warner.

Malcolm & Eddie was one of UPN's longest running sitcoms, airing 1996–2000.

Eddie Griffin: "We had a nice four-and-a-half-year run. It was my first shot at television. Y'know, it was an experience. It taught me a whole lot about the business."

Griffin played Eddie Sherman, a happy-go-lucky truck driver who befriends and goes into business with Jamal-Warner's aspiring sports commentator. Griffin co-wrote the show's theme song with Jamal-Warner. He also had a hand in writing, producing, and directing a number of episodes.

In 1997 he did *Voodoo Child*, his highly acclaimed HBO hour-long special. Then he did his semi-autobiographical film *Foolish*, played a pimper of men in *Deuce Bigelow: Male Gigolo*, and brought to life the Internet cult favorite *Undercover Brother* in 2002.

After the release of his concert film *DysFunkTional Family*, Griffin took a lot of flack from the gay press, who felt the film was hatched from the mind of a homophobic individual. He made a joke about having a gay son and how he'd tie the kid to the bed and send a whore through every hour. Well, when the gays came down on him for a joke, the comedian pointed out that if gays want to be treated like everybody else as they claim, they should be able to laugh at themselves the same way other comedic targets do such as the Asians, Mexicans, whites, blacks, fats, and uglies.

Spanky Hayes: "Eddie Griffin is my guy. Eddie Griffin has given me money. I love Eddie Griffin."

Katt Williams: "As a comic you have to respect Eddie Griffin. There's no f*#kin' way around it. There's no type of personality quirks or anything he has can take away from his f*#kin' deal as a comic."

Jay Phillips: "I think he's a genius, man. The first thing I think about when I think of Eddie Griffin is Lenny Bruce. I think he's riding along the same line, man. He's a genius. He's been blessed with talent, that man I swear I wish that I had. I just think that he's a superstar, man. He is. Bottom line he's a superstar. I love his work, but sometimes I don't like his play. I wish he would still take as much time as he did before with his comedy."

DARRYL: "You opened for Andrew 'Dice' Clay. What type of racism did you experience on that tour?"

GRIFFIN: "Twenty thousand white folks—one brotha. Yeah! Let's just say we ran into it."

DARRYL: "Who makes you laugh?"

GRIFFIN: "Richard Pryor, Dave Chappelle, Bernie Mac, George Carlin…"

DARRYL: "Now you're known as a comedian who can talk forever on stage. What's the longest you ever stayed on stage?"

GRIFFIN: "Five hours and like fifteen minutes or some shit."

DARRYL: "Where were you at, man?"

GRIFFIN: "I was in the Belly Room at the Comedy Store."

DARRYL: "What time did you go up?"

GRIFFIN: "I went up at 9 p.m. I got off somewhere around 2:30 a.m."

DARRYL: "Was anybody left?"

GRIFFIN: "I think you was there that night."

DARRYL: "I might've dropped in for like forty-five minutes or so. How long can you go?"

GRIFFIN: "It depends on the situation. Now if I'm locked up in jail and I'm trying to keep a nigga off my ass—I can go."

DARRYL: "Of your movies, what are your favorites?"

GRIFFIN: "I'd have to say *Foolish*, *The Walking Dead*, and *Undercover Brother*."

DARRYL: "Is there any part you want to play?"

GRIFFIN: "Aww, shit—Miles Davis!"

Along with the televised goings on there was another player changing the game over the black airwaves. In 1990, Tom Joyner was making seven figures annually in syndicated radio due in no small part to his incorporation of numerous comedy skits. Besides being a programming genius with an impeccable nose for talent, he truly was the era's "hardest working man in show business." Tom would fly back and forth from Dallas to Chicago daily, thus earning the name "The Fly Jock."

He assembled a great crew of gag writers: Tommy Davidson, Rusty Cundieff, Larry Wilmore, Myra J., Buddy Lewis, Joe Torry, Roxanne Reese, Doug Starks, Mark Wilmore, Greg Eagles, Jedda Jones ("Miss Dupree"), Joey Gaynor, yours truly, and many other gifted artists.

Director/Writer/Actor/Former comedian, Rusty Cundieff: "It was one of those things where you would go in and they would pay like fifty bucks a bit. I'd go up there with about eight of them and try to make my rent. It was a great gig; especially when you're starting out because you're just looking for a lot of ways to make enough money so you can keep doing what you want to do."

Tom's show was number one on CBS radio in its time slot due in no small part to his excellent and inexhaustible head writer, Brad Sanders. Rusty Cundieff remembers:

"Brad kinda ran the whole session for Tom. So you would go in and basically you would pitch the idea to Brad. Brad had good instincts for what Tom's audience was; what they were looking for, because that was a national show. He was great. Brad was definitely like a mentor."

Joyner and Sanders joined forces by hap chance and before long it became evident how fortunate they were it happened.

"We started in about '85 when I was in Dallas, Texas doing my stand-up and he saw me do the 'Clarence Update' of *The Young & the Restless* and that's where I do a synopsis of *The Young & the Restless* as part of my act. I had a whole hunk of material about soap operas. I went on his radio program, the phones lit up and eventually I came to the decision that this could be something for radio that I could use. I didn't know exactly how, but it was revealed to me by God that this was an opportunity. I had no idea that I could take this show from my stand-up act, try it on radio and lock down a radio deal, calling up collect and doing it right over the phone. Anyway, I ended up on ten radio stations doing the show ten times a day, five days a week, making collect phone calls, and then I got approached by a radio syndication company; which now they sold the company, but they sold the company for a little over $200 million and that show is what put them on the map: Premiere Radio Network. And since I didn't know enough about the business to have control of the product, I wouldn't take a salary, I took a percentage. So I made a few dollars and I ended up with my own business, my own production company, Babysitter Productions specializing in producing and syndicating radio programming."

The relationship through Joyner continued into the '90s when Tom decided he wanted to give something back to his loyal female listeners in the way of a daily soap opera, *It's Your*

World, and they loved it. Written by Sanders and Myra J., the show was both over-the-top dramatic with a sly wit and charm as it explored the town of Wellington where all its citizens are doing what else—well.

Film was good for other blacks as well. The timing was perfect as well for one Earvin "Magic" Johnson. After being diagnosed with the HIV virus and reluctantly retiring from the L.A. Lakers basketball team, Johnson devoted his efforts to his health and surprisingly enough, business ventures. He joined forces with several silent partners and using the clout and popularity his name still supplied, his empire came to include real estate; TGI Friday's; and the cornerstone of it all, the Magic Johnson Theaters, where the on-screen image of Johnson smiling and rubbing his huge hands together as he awaited his popcorn and high-fiving with a youngster propped up on his father's shoulders before the show gave the audience a comforting, unified feeling.

And the houses Magic built would have their reels full because hood flicks were coming out at a staggering pace: *Sprung, The Five Heartbeats, Woo, Fear of a Black Hat, CB4, Don't be a Menace to South Central While Drinking Juice in the Hood, The Great White Hype, Meteor Man*, the remainders of the *House Party* trilogy, *Friday, How to Be a Player, The Player's Club*, and many more instant classics bought quick money and introduced an entire new industry to the ghetto—bootleg tapes. In many cases you could buy the bootleg before the movie even hit the big screen, or in these cases (ghetto theaters), the mid-sized screen.

ICE CUBE

A film and talent combination that nobody would've predicted was hard core NWA rapper Ice Cube, not only starring in a comedy, but co-writing one (along with DJ Pooh). Surely, it had to be one of those dark comedies where people getting stabbed in the face is supposed to be funny, right? Had to be. This was the guy who wanted all hos on their knees and to bust a cap in all cops. His film *Friday* turned out to be one of the biggest surprises in Hollywood history. His onscreen girlfriend, Paula Jai Parker, recalls the snarling rhyme master's on-set style:

> "He was a part of the process every single step of the way. Watching him and his wife work together was inspiring to me because she was always right there. It was never about being obtrusive or oppressive. Her presence was always known without necessarily having to be felt. Y'know what I'm sayin'? Very respectful for a woman working on a set and her husband is interacting with other women; sometimes it can be a little intimidating for some women and they can be standing in the corner, gritting at you and rolling their eyes and carrying on. I've had it happen. So it was very wonderful to see her on the set every single day, working—doing her thing. She was there listening and taking care of all the business behind the scenes while Ice Cube was doing his stuff in front of the cameras and still micro-managing everything going on as well. Ice Cube is just a great guy and ever since *Friday* I think he has looked at me as like a little sister. Like, 'I'm looking out for you.' He's a very great guy and I was blessed to have worked with him and I really hope I get to work with him again."

Kym Whitley and Ice Cube in a scene from Next Friday (2000) (courtesy of Kym Whitley).

Geoff Brown: "A prime example of the American dream; to start with little or nothing and then have absolutely everything."

Charlie Murphy: "He's a real brother, man. He showed me a lot of love. He's a tremendous artist and I've got a lot of respect for him."

O'Shea Jackson was born in Los Angeles, California on June 15, 1969. Along with Easy-E, he co-founded the hardcore rap sensations NWA (Niggaz with Attitude). The acclaimed *Straight Outta Compton* in 1989 was followed by his solo effort a year later—*AmeriKKKa's Most Wanted*. That record went gold in ten days (without the benefit of airplay) and in '91 Cube co-starred in John Singleton's *Boyz N the Hood* with Lawrence Fishburne, Morris Chestnut, and Cuba Gooding, Jr. He directed more than a dozen music videos before he and DJ Pooh grabbed a skinny kid named Tucker and a fat kid named Love and made history in 1995 with *Friday*.

Reynaldo Rey: "I was going down the street once and I heard some excerpts from one of my albums (*Simp the Pimp*). The guy turned the corner before I could ask him what it was. So then I was on Sunset and Faizon (Love) approached me and was like, 'Man, I heard you on one of Cube's albums.' I said, 'I haven't been on any Cube album.' He said, 'Yes, you are, man' and he went and got it and he played it for me and it was me. So I went by where they were filming *Friday* and went to his trailer and I said, 'Hey man, you owe me some money. I'm on one of your albums.' So he laughed and invited me in, paid me for it, and put me in the movie. Good dude."

The gangsta rapper was now a comic impresario with mucho crossover appeal.

John Witherspoon: "Mostly white people bought that *Friday*. Black people were there also, but white kids made that thing a success; white kids from the colleges."

He followed it up with *Next Friday* and *Friday After Next*. His work ethic impressed.

Katt Williams: "What I appreciated about dealing with Ice Cube was that he was a professional. It was his shit, but he was there on time. He came to work. He knew what he was going to do. He knew what he was trying to do. He wasn't f*#kin' groupies. He didn't have bitches in and out of his dressing room. He wasn't having a party. The nigga was handling his f*#king business."

Kym Whitley: "Ice Cube thought it would be fun during one of the scenes for me to take out a little bottle of Courvoisier and he thought it would be funny. It was supposed to be ice tea, but it was the real thing. When the cameras rolled it burned like hell. My eyes were watering, but it was my first film and I was like, 'I'm not going to break down.' He thought it was very funny."

Cube directed and starred in these projects as he did in 1998's *Player's Club*.

Alex Thomas: "That nigga was a gangsta thug director. Y'know like most times when you do movies, you mess your lines up, the director is like, 'Oh, you need some time? Go to the back, get your lines straight and then come back.' Cube was like, 'Cut! Nigga better learn they lines. F*#k your line up one more time, nigga I'm gonna bomb on you. Straight up! Nigga f*#k your line up one more time.'"

Whatever his methods they were working as he maneuvered himself into another comedy franchise: *Barbershop* and its sequel *Barbershop 2*; both featuring the normally cuddly Cedric the Entertainer as the acid-tongued, controversy-spewing barber Eddie, who got a bad part in his even worse natural.

Cube went on to star in *All About the Benjamins* with Mike Epps.

Mike Epps: "He gave me a break when nobody else would. I'm always down with him"

In 2005 Cube had the number one film opening with the kiddie flick *Are We There Yet?* and continues to employ deserving black talent on both sides of the camera. Though he's never done stand-up nor had his own sitcom, Ice Cube's contribution to the world of black comedy is indisputable and welcome.

"I met Ice Cube at the Soul Train Awards. He's a quiet dude actually. I liked his music when NWA was out; had my head moving and had me thinking. He made good stories."

WHAT DO YOU THINK ABOUT ICE CUBE'S CONTRIBUTION TO BLACK COMEDY?

Mystro Clark: "It's basically through hiring black comedians for his movies so I think that's a good contribution. So yeah, I've got a give him thumbs up."

John Witherspoon: "Cube is smart. Smart. Used that rap world, came into the movie world and did very well. Now he can float back and forth if he wants to, y'know. He's smart, smart. Got a perfect thing he's got going. Everybody can't do that. He had the wherewithal to get up and move out of that rap world because a lot of them rappers get old. Now he can do what he's doing for a long time."

Alex Thomas: "My nigga. I love how he's the epitome of the type of doors hip-hop can open up for you. He started out as a gangsta rapper with a curl and now he's got f*#kin' twenty-five, thirty movies under his belt. I'm not mad at him."

Angela Means: "Ice Cube loves comedy. And thank you, Ice Cube for *Friday*, y'know. Awesome. He goes down in history. He's a maverick. NWA to being on the PTA. He's had an amazing life and God, I love him."

CHRIS TUCKER

Many of the comics who did *Friday* were alumni of *House Party* and the names of Big Worm (Faizon Love), Ezell (A. J. Johnson), and Deebo (Tiny Lister) became ghetto fixtures. But it was the character of Smokey that not only stole the film, but made an overnight star out of Chris Tucker; though it wasn't exactly a slam dunk. As fellow cast member Angela Means recalls, Tucker's eventual casting was the result of hard work and some midnight oil being burnt:

> "Chris went in and apparently his first audition wasn't so well. He left the audition and called me. At the time I was studying with a well-known coach (New York's Mike Edelstein) and everyone knew it. He was on the top of Stan Lathan's list of acting coaches he sent all of us to from his stable of comics. So I was studying with this guy and Chris calls me like, 'Angela, I need help. I just left the audition. They told me to go work on this. Give me your coach's number.' I said, Chris they don't want you to go to a coach. Ice Cube saw you in a club, he brought you in— they want Chris Tucker. He doesn't want something fabricated. I said, I'll tell you what—just come over here. We're gonna work on it. I made a big ass pot of spaghetti. Me, Chris, and Faizon sat in my apartment for about eight hours and I remember the scene. It was the scene with Yvette Wilson. I said, all right say the line and he said the line and I said now tell me what you're thinking. Keep going. And then he said the line and I said, add a line and he added a line and I said keep going. Don't stop until you just get tired of talking about this subject. We were in my apartment for eight hours screaming with laughter at Chris. We were like dammit—that's what they want. They want you to come in there and give them Chris Tucker. He left my place. The next morning he booked it. I haven't heard from him since, but that's life and I don't have any regrets and I harbor no ill feelings because everyone has their path."

The Atlanta transplant was the last choice most of his fellow comedians or industry types would have selected to be the "next one."

Chris Tucker giving the "I-make-$20,000,000-a-movie" hand gesture (courtesy of Comedy the Magazine).

Tony Spires: "Chris approached me about management many years ago back when he first moved to L.A. He had ten minutes max by the same token D. L. Hughley was threatening leaving my management if I signed him up. The rest is history."

Similar to Dick Gregory generations before him, Tucker was unsung before his ascension. Decked out in leather slacks and a turned-around baseball cap, he was no different than hundreds of other brash young men his age. "Miss Laura" Hayes recalls the time Tucker and a limo driver got into it in Chicago:

"I thought he was going to whoop this muthaf*#a's ass. I mean you ain't seen nothing 'til you've seen Chris Tucker hot. Oh, it was funny. You think the voice is high now?"

That's what made him so immediately distinctive. It was when he opened his mouth that the difference became apparent. Tucker was a live-action cartoon. He had a voice meant for comedy: high, sharp, and biting. That along with his wild-eyed stare made him a definitive personality.

Ruben Paul: "The first time I saw him I knew he was going to be a star and it had nothing to do with his material, but it was his persona. He was funny and he was unique because he had this high-pitched voice and this attitude that was undeniable and he had this confidence and this swagger. A lot of people hated him when he first started and a lot of people hated on him, but he came to L.A. to stake his claim. Like he didn't come to fit in or make friends. His whole attitude when he came to L.A. was, 'Yo, there's a new sheriff in town.' And that was his attitude and a lot of people resented him for that, but he always had a plan, man."

There was literally nobody else like Chris Tucker in show business. Those didn't come along until later. Comedienne/actress Angela Means recalls her first glimpse:

"I was hosting the Comedy Act Theater in Atlanta...and I come back in—everybody in the club is on their feet; a standing ovation. Not his first time on stage. He had been doing comedy at his high school assemblies and he's just a funny guy. I walk in there and I'm going through people trying to get back to the stage and I said to myself, 'What the f*#k did I just miss?' And I got on stage, 'What the f*#k did I just miss?' Nobody heard me because they were still applauding him. He'd done like a tight, maybe ten minutes and I came thinking let me get this dude off stage and I walk in and it's just (roar) was just unleashed and I knew at that moment he was someone special and he was a force to be reckoned with and nobody could touch him and then he came back a couple of days later and I saw his set and I realized that I just wasn't funny."

Chris Tucker was born on August 31, 1972 in Atlanta, Georgia. He left Atlanta for Los Angeles soon after graduating high school and a brief apprenticeship at Atlanta's Comedy Act Theater.

Ajai Sanders: "The first time I ever met Chris Tucker is when we were opening up the Comedy Act Theater in Atlanta and everybody was talking about this new young cat. And I was hosting the show and I brought him up on stage. I introduced him and people knew who he was there. I just stood in the back of the room and watched this young little boy do his thing and when that little nigga got off the stage I was like, 'Come here. You need to get to L.A. immediately.'"

It didn't take long for Tucker to become a regular at Hollywood's Comedy Store and start making a name for himself. He won some competitions (*Soul Train* Comedy, Olde English) and then traveled north to Oakland, California on an excursion to meet his fate.

Bob Sumner: "Had an angel by his side. The Bay Area Comedy Competition 1992, I come into Oakland; they asked me to come in to judge. There's sixty comedians over three nights. I'm trying to line up like *Def Comedy Jam* line-ups for the new season. Even though I'm just supposed to be there Saturday night to judge I want to see all sixty comedians. So I come in on Friday night. So I got in late, but I got there in time for the show. Show's going on, Chris Tucker's on the show, right? I didn't know the guy from a can of paint. At the end of the show they picked the top seven out of twenty to move into the semi-finals. This guy isn't one of the seven. I thought he was by far the funniest of the twenty. So when they all come out on the stage I see him drop his head and I'm like I understand. I got up immediately, ran back stage, told him who I was, y'know what I mean? 'Bro, let me tell you something, this is just a competition. There's only going to be one winner in this competition anyway in terms of what the competition's about. In my eyes there's a bigger reward in life. My name is Bob Sumner. I'm from *Def Comedy Jam* and you have my word that I will be putting you on the show next season' and on top of that I put him on as the first comedian because I thought he was that hot. That's what I think about Chris Tucker. I think he had an angel on his side and it just went from one thing to another. I mean we all know about *Friday*. He did it and got into another league. For the sequel he got offered a million dollars a day and he turned it down. The boy's doing it like that."

After shooting *House Party 3* and his star making part in *Friday*, where he played an irresponsible carefree pothead, Tucker got mainstream Hollywood's attention with the Bruce Willis vehicle *The Fifth Element*, in the role of a 23rd century talk-show host, which got him rave reviews and put him in another tax bracket. It was said that Tucker could make caffeine nervous.

He hit it out of the park again with *Money Talks*, co-starring Charlie Sheen, and *Rush Hour* with Jackie Chan. Tucker received an unprecedented payday for a co-star (his name had yet to be placed over a film title alone)—twenty million dollars (*Rush Hour 2*). While most actors would have cranked out as many films as possible while the demand existed, Tucker chose to mysteriously lay low. He involved himself in humanitarian causes and spent a good period of time with former president Bill Clinton. Fun times for Tucker, but his audience waited for his next film and other comedians wondered what was up.

Vince D: "He owes me some money."

Kym Whitley: "Chris still owes me six dollars for some chicken wings at the Comedy Act."

Spanky Hayes: "The first person to blow up off of one phrase, 'Come on, man.'"

Guy Torry: "Unfinished business."

Geoff Brown: "Electrifying personality"

Marc Howard: "Stand-up wise if you look at it Chris has never been known as someone who could actually sit there and go through the pain of paying of the dues and the going out, do clubs and actually headline shows when you're supposed to do at least forty-five minutes to an hour worth of material, things of that nature. But when he's had to perform and shine in different situations Chris could come up with what he needed to come up with. If he only had ten minutes, he did it on one show. If he needed another ten minutes, hey—he'd come up with a new ten minutes. I've seen him do that."

Shang: "One note. Funny, but one note. Never really did nothing groundbreaking materialwise. Great character; half-awake, bug eyes. Strong, rich, done well, but when he first came out, 'Watch out, man. What's up, man? Hello, man. Whatchu gonna do, man?'"

Honest John: "A lot of people player hate on Chris because he was only doing comedy like four years before he got on *Def Jam* and blew the hell up. Hey, I understand people who've paid dues and haven't gotten as far as Chris player hating, but hey—he's got the talent to back him up. More power to him."

Black films were still turning a nice profit. Eddie Murphy was back in old form and returned to the top ranks with hit remakes *The Nutty Professor* (1996), *Dr. Doolittle* (1998), and a buddy film, *Life* (1999). Paired with Martin Lawrence, they played Depression-era unfortunates who find themselves at the wrong place at the wrong time and are sentenced to life in prison. Other inmates include Bernie Mac, Miguel Nunez, and Guy Torry, who cherished the experience.

"That was a dream come true, man because it was almost like me being a young Kobe Bryant playing with Shaq and Jordan. Like a young cat who has so much to bring to the game, but at the same time you're in awe. But at the same time I was on the Kings of Comedy tour with Bernie so we would do the set and leave and go do that and so, I mean it was just dope man because I learned so much from Eddie and Martin just from being around them, man and they weren't shy about giving up knowledge about the game. Y'know what I'm saying? You got two of some of the greatest comedians around, three actually and you'd be stupid not to pimp them for information."

Another breakout player was a vet from the old school. Back in the day a lot of brothers worked the mainstream circuit and were either never seen or ignored by the average fan of black comedy. When the new era came in some of the guys who were paying attention acknowledged such talents and thank God they didn't overlook Spoon.

JOHN WITHERSPOON

John Witherspoon was born on January 27, 1942 in Detroit, Michigan. He was a male model then ventured into comedy and got his first big break on the short-lived *Richard Pryor Show* in '77, then roles in *What's Happening!!* and *Good Times*.

Witherspoon made his film debut as a nightclub MC in the Neil Diamond version of *The Jazz Singer* and got his recognition in Robert Townsend's *Hollywood Shuffle*, playing the owner of a rinky dink Winky Dinky Dog hot dog stand. This was followed up by *Boomerang* and the *Friday* trilogy.

DARRYL: "You started off as a male model, didn't you?"

SPOON: "No nigga, I didn't start off as a male model, but I dabbled in male modeling when I saw those people in the magazines and I looked better than they did. I did some work in magazines and newspapers."

DARRYL: "I saw you in *Jet* magazine. Weren't you one of the Mr. Dukes?"

SPOON: "What was that Mr. Duke—the hair?"

DARRYL: "Yeah, the process they used to do."

John Witherspoon (courtesy of John Witherspoon).

SPOON: "Naw, I wore clothes. I think I did a Winston cigarette ad, when they used to put ads in the paper with people smoking and stuff."

DARRYL: "When you mention John Witherspoon everybody says, 'Bang, bang, bang!'"

SPOON: "I create lines everywhere I go. I created my own lines. Every line I create people repeat them and they become the lines of the signature of the movie."

DARRYL: "What do you want your impact to be on black comedy?"

SPOON: "I don't give a f*#k about my impact, nigga. I made my money. I made money. Ain't got nothing to do with impact no more. I like my standing ovations when I walk into the Bank of America. I don't give a f*#k about an impact. That don't mean shit to me. When I'm gone, shit, I don't give a f*#k about that shit. People gonna say what they're gonna say. I lived a good f*#kin' life, because before I wasn't living no good life, but now I'm living a good one. I ain't worried about what they gonna say after I'm gone."

When We Were Kings and Queens

CHAPTER 23

"The trouble with unemployment is that the minute you wake up in the morning, you're on the job."
— SLAPPY WHITE

Those not fortunate enough to make their living on a sound stage hit the road. Comedians were all over the country filling the insatiable need and getting screwed in the process. Bad promoters and black comedy were synonymous. The backbiters were abusing traveling jesters with faulty airline passes, shabby hotel accommodations (sometimes motel), risky transportation with questionable transporters, and worse, not issuing full payment for full work.

Not only did the comedians suffer back then; the audience wasn't doing much better. Solid, no-nonsense name performers were making these crooks jump through hoops before they'd even consider driving to the airport. Prices went up dramatically in part to discourage the non-serious or money-strapped. A number of promoters could come up with the good faith deposit, but some were running off when the door didn't supply the balance with profit.

The tragedy was that most of these promoters were black. The white club owners of the 1990s had no interest in booking black comedians. Black booking agents were pulling teeth to get a black in a white club back in the day. Tony Spires explains:

"The black comedians they booked would be guys who were famous. The white comics they booked, you'd never heard of, they'd never been on TV in their life and they were headlining. To me there was nothing else to call it but racism. The white acts worked these 'mainstream' rooms for forty weeks out of the year. The black acts had to, and in many cases are regulated to, doing holidays and the first and fifteenth and that's if you're famous. And if you're black and not packing the room out they're sending a wire to all their cohorts. They don't do that to the white act. There was and still is a double standard on how they want a black act to perform at the box office."

Everybody had a run, but it was the road laid out by *Def Jam* and *Comic View*. The road where a comic who might have killed for seven minutes on TV (their entire act) was getting slaughtered when they had to do a forty-five-minute set in front of live people with no 'wrap it up' card. Some comics made the adjustments. Others met the end of their careers on these runs, discovering they didn't have the heart to be a black comic or the understanding to become an African-American comedian; a professional.

T. Faye Griffin: "There are people that are on stage for every other reason, but for the people and these people have worked hard; they put their little pennies together to buy their little outfit and their two-drink minimum and the cover charge; you are there to entertain them, but so many people are on stage to get some kind of self-glorification or to get some pu*#y after the show, but very few people are there for the people."

Enter impresario Walter Latham and the *Kings of Comedy Tour*: an all-star road show packaging seasoned veterans Cedric the Entertainer, Steve Harvey, D. L. Hughley (replacing Guy Torry), and Bernie Mac. The tour ran from 1997 through 1999. Each act was putting butts in the seats separately, but combined they became the highest-grossing comedy tour in history.

Cedric the Entertainer: "We could fill up theaters with just black people and the white people didn't even know we existed and we were making money. It was rock star status. Literally we were pulling up and we were performing in front of ten, twenty thousand people and doing stand-up. You, being a stand-up, of course you know that's one of those things you just don't really fathom. When you start doing stand-up you just never really see yourself performing for twenty thousand people at one time. This was like being the Rolling Stones or something, man. City-to-city we'd come in and do two nights in Chicago selling out the United Center. I mean, who heard of anything like that before? It was that type of magic and to be on there with peers, where it's laughing and one-upsmanship on so many levels. I mean everybody's nice dressers so we had fun pulling out the suits and hats. Who's squad is going to look good and do this and then we'd come back with the same thing, with sitting around afterwards and eating a meal; joking about the night and one-upping each other; having these great stories to tell. So it was truly a very magical experience, one that I don't think can ever really be duplicated. The first two years of that tour it was not the big crossover thing that it became once the movie came out."

The Spike Lee-directed concert film, *The Original Kings of Comedy* (2000), is one of the top-grossing comedy concert films of all time. And Bernie Mac (the only one without a TV show during that period) became a household name. Then Latham repeated the formula with *The Queens of Comedy* tour (Mo'Nique, Laura Hayes, Sommore, and Adele Givens, appearing as a film in 2001, and *Latham Entertainment Presents* (D. L. Hughley [again], Bruce Bruce, Sommore, J. Anthony Brown, Earthquake, and Rickey Smiley) in 2003.

Like all good ideas, it was simple. The key was in assembling the right combination of players to pull it off. Every ego had to be in sync and Latham grabbed a handful starting with someone not known for sharing the limelight.

STEVE HARVEY

Bob Sumner: "OG. Been through the chitlin' circuit and back and back again and back again. Deserves everything that he's achieved because he never gave up."

Born November 23, 1956 in Cleveland, Ohio, Steve Harvey began his comedy career in the early 1990s and soon was running a comedy club in Texas and assuming the role of elder statesman.

Mystro Clark: "He always had that air about him that he was already famous. He already had the mentality."

He and his air, along with friend and manager Rushion McDonald, moved to the west coast to make it big. Harvey hosted *Showtime at the Apollo* and toured extensively. He also made it clear that he didn't get into show business to make friends.

Damon Williams: "If he likes you, you've got yourself a great friend. If he don't know you—he don't give a damn about you and he will tell you that because he don't owe you nothing."

Harvey wound up on ABC with his first show, *Me & the Boys*. Despite its strong showing in the ratings for a new program with a virtually unknown artist, the show was canceled. Harvey regrouped and next was seen on the WB with *The Steve Harvey Show*, co-starring Cedric the Entertainer.

The show garnered numerous Image Awards from the African-American community regardless of its practically non-existent bleeping on white America's radar screen, but Harvey and Cedric proved a likeable combination, and so Walter Latham recruited them for the *Kings of Comedy* tour, though Harvey insists the name was a business move and that the true King of Comedy shall always be Mr. Richard Pryor.

Harvey parlayed his black standing and became a face in the community, doing almost every award show BET aired. He got back on the WB once his sitcom was cancelled with *Steve Harvey's Big Time*, a variety show featuring people with unusual talents, such as skeeting milk out of their eye ball into a cup and drinking it. The show received criticism from some corners but characteristically Harvey let it roll off his back and kept his eye on the next project.

Ever-dapper, Steve Harvey showing off another suit (courtesy of Comedy the Magazine*).*

> **Rodney Perry:** "A person that everybody don't like, but who I think is very consistent and just a grown ass man and a great businessman. I think he may be one of the most misunderstood cats in comedy. He said, 'you know how you keep a muthaf*#ka off your back? You never bend over. If you're standing up, nigga can't ride you. If you all hunched over with your head down, yeah, muthaf*#ka's gonna ride you all day.'"

He played minor parts in minor films and then wielded his power to become a national radio personality. He started off in Los Angeles doing the morning stint from 2001–2005 then went national with a deal with Premiere Radio Networks and the Inner City Broadcasting Corporation.

> **Adele Givens:** "Steve needs to own him a damn radio station. You ever hear him on the radio? He tears it up. He needs to buy him a radio station so he can sell Steve Harvey propaganda all over the world."

> **Tommy Chunn:** "I felt he got a little bitter later on by listening to him on the radio and he got a little Hollywood, but overall he's a good dude."

Guy Torry served as MC for the *Kings of Comedy* tour from December of 1997 to December of 1998. He was approached by Walter Latham at his night at the Comedy Store known as "Guy Torry's Phat Tuesdays" which was known to expose deserving talent from the African-American ranks. Besides noticing Guy's hosting ability, Latham observed how Torry was that rare breed of comedian who got along well with his fellow comics.

> **GUY:** "It was a blessing to do it because I was a young cat in the game and being around such veterans, man just really allowed me to see where comedy can go. I mean we were selling out arenas, man. We were doing no less than twelve

Guy Torry (courtesy of Comedy the Magazine).

thousand a show. It was just that energy and it was a great experience. Those cats just took me under their wings, man and taught me a lot and were real cool, but I left the tour for two reasons: 1. Because I got a TV show; 2. I wanted to get back to the clubs and really work my act and get to the status where they were because they were some funny cats. I mean we'd get fifty-two dates and I knew every joke, but I would laugh every time. Those are comedians, not comics. There's a big difference between the two."

DARRYL: "What is your definition of the two?"

GUY: "A comic is basically someone who's close to a clown. No disrespect. That's just some cat's POV. That's their style. That's their energy. It's just bada—ba! Bada—ba! Punchline. Kind of just set-up, punch. Doesn't really take you on a ride. He's just really worried about getting laughs, getting a big laugh and getting off the stage. A comedian takes you on a journey, man. A comedian has his point of view. He has his ups, his downs, his peaks, his valleys and lets you leave with a piece of a comedian with you. Not just like, 'Okay, dude made me laugh.' Yeah okay, but I left with something there. You saw somebody in that comedian. Somebody you know or a piece of you or whatever. You've seen that character before or you've heard that story before just never quite like that."

BERNIE MAC

Bernie Mac was another ripened ego plucked from the vine and a prime example of perseverance. This man was in the business almost twenty-five years before he "got over." And most of the public first became aware of him after his now-famous *Def Jam* appearance where he stated, *"I ain't scared of you muthaf*#kas,"* followed by a cue to resident DJ Kid Capri to "Hit it!" and dancing as the musical interlude segued him to the next bit. This tactic was the work of nothing less than a seasoned pro. Before Bernie had hit the stage another comedian had bombed and the New York crowd was ready for more blood, but Mac wasn't having it and showed the world how to handle a situation wrought with peril and the new jack comics the way an OG gets down.

DARRYL: "What was going through your mind when you said, 'I'm not scared of you muthaf*#kas?'"

BERNIE: "The reason I said that was because the comic before me got booed off the stage. The audience, all the other comics, assistant directors, grips— everybody back stage was laughing. And I was up next. Martin Lawrence tried to calm the audience down but they didn't so when I went out there 'I ain't scared of you...' just came out."

Evan Lionel: "Always a professional. He always treated comedy like a job."

Bernard Jeffery McCullough was born in Chicago, Illinois in 1958 (the year is disputable) and cut his stand-up teeth performing in that city's subways for spare change. In 1990 he won a citywide talent contest, which got him local club work and local parties.

Damon Williams: "There was this party promotion group. They were called 6-0-1, and they used to give the biggest parties in Chicago and they would get a hotel ballroom and it was kind of bougie and they'd dress up and hob knob and one month they were going to do Bernie Mac as the entertainment. So the place is energized, people are mingling and they're dancing and the DJ is pumping, nice little party and they say, 'Okay, we're going to stop the music. We got a comedian for you—Bernie Mac!' I ain't ever heard of Bernie and I wasn't doing comedy at the time. The man sat there and did his time. People were not listening. They were walking around. The ladies were frowning up because they really weren't ready for his style, but Bernie stuck at it. He hosted a lot of rooms around Chicago. He's the person that basically drew HBO to Chicago for *Def Jam*. They came to see Bernie and so Adele Givens, Kenny Howell, George Wilborn, Tony Sculfield got their first *Def Jam* because Bernie was there in Chicago."

Comedian/Photographer, Andre Lavelle: "Bernie became the permanent host at the Cotton Club and basically the Cotton Club had the name. All the celebs rolled through there. That's how he knew about *Def Jam* before everybody else."

And when *Def Comedy Jam* made it on the air, Bernie Mac was a hit, but memories are

The long journey to success is over. No wonder Bernie Mac is grinning ear to ear (courtesy of *Comedy the Magazine*).

short and Bernie Mac, though more popular and making a lot of money on the road and in clubs, was still just a stand-up comedian on the road and in clubs. Then he got his own show, *Midnight Mac* on HBO, a variety show featuring music and comedy that mirrored his road act, but failed to capture the imagination of the home audience and the moon stopped rising for the Midnight man.

He had a recurring role on *Moesha* and stole scenes, if not entire movies, in every hood flick he appeared in. Then came the *Kings of Comedy Tour* in which Bernie challenged Hollywood to give him his own show, claiming they were too scared to put Bernie Mac on TV. That challenge did not go unanswered and Bernie got his wish—a sitcom on FOX, then high-profile feature films: *Ocean's 11* and *Ocean's 12*.

Chris Spencer: "I wouldn't mind emulating Bernie Mac's career right now. Being yourself and letting everybody know he still enjoys eating fried chicken with niggas."

Doug Williams: "When I think of Bernie I think of durability. Besides being a great stand-up comedian he was durable and I think we all need to infuse those qualities in us."

Daran Howard: "Bernie Mac is Bernie Mac because Robin Harris isn't here. You feel like Bernie Mac is part of the family. That's what makes Bernie Mac, Bernie Mac. I love Bernie Mac."

DARRYL: "Did you enjoy the journey to stardom as much as being a star?"

BERNIE: "I'm not a star, stars fall; but I would not trade my journey for nothing in the world."

DARRYL: "If you weren't a comedian what would you have become?"

BERNIE: "I think I am what I am, a jack of all trades. I used to be a coach, pro mover, scrapyard worker, steel mill worker, cook, UPS, Wonderbread worker, beer crew at Soldier Field, physical director, painter, janitor, laborer. Oh yeah, and a pimp. I didn't have any money so my name was Dirty Pimp. All my workers was on welfare. I've done it all. I am what I am."

DARRYL: "Tell us about your experience doing the *Kings of Comedy*."

BERNIE: "It was a beautiful experience because it gave other people the picture to dream. When you see something of that magnitude it just makes you wonder if you can do it. I give it five stars."

There was a school of comedians who insisted that the *Kings of Comedy* tour destroyed urban comedy as it once existed. According to their charter, after producer Walter Latham's recordbreaking moneymaker passed over the country twice, B and C level comics found it nearly impossible to get the same paydays they'd enjoyed in the past. Promoters began the practice of either booking powerhouse names for big cash or as many moderate names as a marquee could hold, lowering the money for each.

Because the public viewed big names as the way to get their laugh fix, many a black comedy club was forced to close its doors. Big names don't do clubs and you soon run out of moderate names that consistently capture the fickle public's imagination.

Tony Spires: "I think it helped in that it was kind of like the Jackie Robinson theory. Jackie Robinson helped black folks because he broke into the major leagues. He hurt black folks, particularly black entrepreneurship, because it signed a death warrant for the Negro leagues. See it's just that I don't want to make it sound in any way that his contribution to history was in a bad way because it was a great thing. It could have been Satchel Paige or Josh Gibson or Roy Campanella. It could've been anybody but whoever was going to be put in the front to be successful, it was going to destroy something on the back in which was the Negro League, right, and so the same thing with this *Kings of Comedy* thing for things to happen it has made millionaires and ghetto superstars if not moreso, out of all the players involved. But for everybody else it made it hard for them to sell a ticket and get booked. To create a bigger show and deal with the feeding frenzy that the public had or at least seemed to then, the promoters demanded more. So now if you don't have a whole gang of comedians on a show your chances of selling out are very remote, and now that raises the price of the ticket. So the average person can't even afford it and if they do go they're going to be disappointed because it's not the *Kings of Comedy*. And if they do go to that show they're not going to do it next week or the week after or the week after or the week after. It takes money out of the marketplace. It makes people be more selective about the shows they go to and it hurts the business. So the *Kings of Comedy* hurt the comedy business and a lot of promoters are gone."

Michael Williams: "Black comedy really boomed and instead of comedians doing clubs they were doing concert halls and the amount of money they can make they realized, y'know was really an opportunity for them to now have a career. It was really that phenomenon that made it worse on black comedy around the country because what a comedian could make in one week he could make in a night."

The tour naturally had imitators; most notably *The Kings of New York*, consisting of Rob Stapleton, Gerald Kelly, Capone, Drew Frazier, and Talent. They brought together their collective following from coast to coast from 2000–2002.

Talent: "A lot of important people was interested in it, but eventually the egos did burst and subside the whole project."

There was the brown version—*The Latin Kings of Comedy*, and of course *The Queens of Comedy*. This grand experiment in female togetherness started with Sommore, Miss Laura Hayes, and Adele Givens doing a little *Queens of Comedy* tour. It worked out well so Sommore took the idea to Walter Latham, who took it to another level. Comedienne Myra J. was the host (Sommore, Adele, and Mo'Nique were the featured acts), but Myra couldn't do all the dates so they kept bringing in different hosts. Since all the girls were familiar and comfortable with Laura, she was recommended.

The camaraderie was apparent as they naturally gravitated to one dressing room to just hang out and kick it even though they all had their separate quarters. They shared limos in large part because they didn't want to be apart. According to Hayes there was no drama, not even behind members of the opposite sex. Half the crew (Laura and Adele) had brought their husbands along for the ride. And as far as egos—they were there to entertain people, they were doing what they loved and making money; not to mention having fun in the process. There was no time for ego tripping.

The Queens of Comedy put a spotlight on female comediennes and showed their viability. So despite comments from comedy icons such as Jerry Lewis that females weren't funny—he said Lucy was okay—lady comics were making headway, but just how far was another question.

A major problem for female comedians has always been one of equity in pay. This mathematical mindset had to be readjusted once the public spoke and the receipts were counted.

Rulers emerged from *Queens* and not since the days of Marsha Warfield and an early Whoopi Goldberg has any one comedienne dominated the genre. That tour might've finally answered the question of who was the female counterpart to Jamie Foxx, Chris Rock, Dave Chappelle, or Chris Tucker.

MO'NIQUE

> **Kevin Hart:** "Another hard worker, doing what she's supposed to do, but at the same time trying to pull herself up and actually has a message that she's trying to put out. Like Mo'Nique is actually doing something positive. She's trying to show big women that they're sexy too and I like what she's going for."

Mo'Nique Imes-Jackson was born on December 11, 1967. The entertaining native of Baltimore, Maryland began her life in show business as a plus-size model at the age of seventeen. Stand-up comedy entered the scene when a dare provoked her to try it, and once she got those first laughs she ventured into the world of humor performing for high school and college students with a positive message and funny bits.

Steady work wasn't far behind; opening up for acts like Keith Sweat and Bobby Brown; performing stand-up on *Def Comedy Jam*, *Showtime at the Apollo*, and *Comic View* and running her own comedy club in the Baltimore area. She gained popularity playing Nikki Parker on the UPN sitcom *The Parkers* then toured in the *Queens of Comedy*. She co-hosted the morning radio show on WHUR in Washington, D.C. In the summer of 2002 she left.

She appeared in the films *Two Can Play That Game*, *Baby Boy*, *Soul Plane*, and *Domino*, and her first starring vehicle *Phat Girlz*. She's won numerous NAACP Image Awards and hosted several BET award shows. Mo'Nique wrote the book *Skinny Women Are Evil* and continues to push her agenda of empowering full-figured ladies of all races.

> **Marc Howard:** "She's taken what she has and she's run with it. She's made the most of being big, being a woman and y'know she uses that to her benefit. She has a style that's working for her and as the girls say, she working it. So she's making the most of her business and she's a good person and I'm happy for her."

> **Tony Spires:** "I think she's a talented comedic actress. Whenever I see her she's funny, and she was in that movie with Whoopi Goldberg and she held her own. It was amazing to see her; she could hold her own with anybody as far as I'm concerned. She's a very talented actress. I've seen her in some other things, less substantial films and TV shows like *The Parkers* and all but she was always a strong on-screen talent."

The Queens of Comedy had a symbolic captain, now all they needed was a line-up. The key to a profitable tour would be recognizable names and *Comic View* had produced two high-profile comediennes. They found one ripping up stages wherever she went, with a fan base comparable to the men.

SOMMORE

Cocoa Brown: "I really digged her class and her style on stage."

Oprah Winfrey: "A force to be reckoned with in the New Millennium."

Sexy comedienne Sommore (courtesy of Sommore).

Born in Trenton, New Jersey, in 1970, Lori Rambo went west to California where she won the Birdland Olde English Comedy Competition in the early '90s, appeared on *Showtime at the Apollo*, *Def Jam*, and *Comic View*. She became that show's first female host and parlayed her good looks and sexy persona into a lucrative personal appearance career. The sisters came out to hear it and see what the fashion diva was wearing and the brothas just came out to see Sommore. Her next stop was the *Queens of Comedy* on her way to earning a listing in the Guinness Book of World Records as the first female comedienne to perform for over forty-four thousand people in Atlanta, Georgia at the Georgia Dome when Latham Entertainment showcased both the *Kings* and *Queens of Comedy*. The *Queens of Comedy* was the highest rated special in the history of the Showtime Entertainment Network, and she later worked on another Latham Entertainment tour dubbed *Latham Entertainment Presents*.

Sommore appeared on *The Hughleys*, *The Parkers*, *Politically Incorrect with Bill Maher*, and several rap videos. Superstar Busta Rhymes even wrote a song for her, *Gimme Sommore*. She made her film debut in Ice Cube's *Friday After Next* and continues to tour and make that money.

Mystro Clark: "I ran into her a couple of weeks ago for the first time after a couple years. She still looks the same, she still looks good. She's still working the road a lot."

The last player on the squad was a wrecking machine and such a lady.

ADELE GIVENS

Angela Means: "One of the greatest comics to ever live. Watching *The Queens of Comedy*...she writes material. She writes set-up, delivery, punch. She writes material. One of the greatest female comics to ever live."

Adele Givens hails from Chicago, Illinois, grew up in the ghetto and her comedy reflects that. Early in her career, the childless Givens pointed out that even though she made her mark as a foul-mouthed comedienne, if she had kids she wouldn't want them to hear her talk like that. But it was her ability to talk trash like a man that got her a slot on HBO's *Def Comedy Jam*; she did the tour and was co-host of that show along with Ricky Harris and Joe Torry in 1995.

Cocoa Brown: "I think Adele has not gotten her just due. She is probably the first female comic I ever saw on *Def Jam* where I was like, 'That bitch is funny' and when I became a comedian I patterned myself after her because she was definitely someone I looked up to. I loved her brashness. I loved her confidence up on stage."

Talent: "Still didn't get a lot of the opportunities and notoriety due her."

DARRYL: "Tell us about the *Queens of Comedy* Tour."

LAURA: "It was the worst and the best all rolled into one. Of course there was the little drama with the money, but I had so much fun. It was the one time in my career where I could say I had fun. I looked so forward to seeing them bitches every week."

ADELE: "Right, because we knew we was going to see each other and so it was a different kind of going-to-work thing. It was a whole 'nother, 'Hey, I'm so glad.'"

SOMMORE: "Well, when we did the *Queens of Comedy* we came together and we knew that we were trying to prove a point. First of all it was stated that all-women shows do not sell. So we wanted to prove them wrong with that and then we wanted to prove that women can be funny."

DARRYL: Name your top three favorite comedians."

SOMMORE: "James Hannah, D. L. Hughley, and Bernie Mac."

ADELE: "Richard Pryor. George Carlin and Nellie."

DARRYL: "Nelly?! The rapper?"

ADELE: "Nope. My mother, Nellie. My mother Nellie Bell, funniest lady you never heard."

DARRYL: When did you realize you were a celebrity?"

LAURA: I guess that would have to be after the first *Apollo* that I did. Actually it was the people that I was around who looked at me different. I mean I saw a different look in them. Y'know some were like too much in awe. Which was kind of like, 'Ugh, c'mon now.' And some were cool because they were happy for where you were and delighted to know you."

SOMMORE: I still struggle with that. I don't see myself as a celebrity. I see myself as a popular person. That's what *Comic View* did for me. *Def Jam* didn't do it. With *Def Jam* people would look and whisper, 'Is that the girl that was on *Def Jam*?' But with *Comic View*, I would like go into a soul food restaurant—all the cooks from the back would come out. That was about three months into it."

ADELE: When people started asking for autographs. It was after *Def Jam*, definitely. It was when we were doing the *Def Jam* tour. So yeah, it was definitely back then when I can remember first experiencing that, yeah."

DARRYL: Was it that somebody just came up and said, 'Ooh, it's Adele Givens let me get your autograph.'"

ADELE: I said, 'What! What! Let me get your damn autograph!' I don't trust this type of shit. You write your name down. I'll write my name down. I made the lady write down her name. I still got it."

DARRYL: "Have you experienced more sexism or racism in your career?"

SOMMORE: "Both. I don't know. I've been black forever and a woman forever so I think they're just equal. I think it's equal. I can remember times when I was on shows and I know I was making more money than everybody on the show, but because of men's egos, they was like, well, I got to headline. And I'm saying if you know you're not making the most money, but yet you want to headline—go ahead!"

LAURA: "Sexism. You will find that women are so looked at as not being able to do this and that. Either they ain't gonna be funny. They ain't gonna do this. They ain't gonna do that. I will not pay her I don't give a damn if she that funny I ain't gonna pay her as much as I'm gonna pay a nigga."

ADELE: "Y'know, I ain't been measuring it. I'm not aware of a lot of either, though I'm sure I have experienced it, but I'm blissfully ignorant of it."

Whether comedic royalty or just a plain hardworking merrymaker, most comedians hold the opinion that a major attraction to the craft was the unbridled freedom it offered. The ability to speak one's mind and deal with the consequences later put the microphone in a lot of hands.

WHAT MADE YOU BECOME A COMEDIAN?

Angela Means: "Fred G. Sanford. It's was just a natural situation, y'know when the odds are against you, you look for what's going to get you through whatever it is you're going through and being an only child with an only parent who used to drink only Scotch, I was just gifted with a resource and that was comedy and then when I saw *Sanford & Son* it just blew my mind; that comedy even existed blew my mind and it's been my savior."

Nick Cannon: "I always had that hyperactive energy as a kid, y'know what I mean? I was on stage since I was like eleven. It was like really a way for my parents to gear my hyperactive energy and all my creativity into like one solid area."

Paula Jai Parker: "Well, I'm just silly. I don't know. When I was in school they said my fate was comedy, but I just never really paid attention to it. I just know I like imitating people and I just like being silly."

Sherri Shepherd: "I took a comedy class with Judy Carter. For me it was good because I didn't know where to start. She taught me the technique of when you go on stage to move the mic stand out of the way. She taught me the technique of when you're talking to the room about how to turn your body. She taught me the writing technique, but she hated all my jokes."

Franklyn Ajaye: "I probably wouldn't have if I'd liked law school. I was going to Columbia Law School in 1971 and I realized that I really hated it. I was bored with the curriculum and I realized, boy this is a mistake and I was in New York City and I'd always been a guy with one of the best senses of humor in high school and stuff like that and I was an aficionado of comedy. Bill Cosby. I was a big fan of Bill Cosby. I'd seen him on *The Tonight Show* in 1964. Big Richard Pryor fan. Pryor at the time was doing the clean material that he started out with and I knew they had started out in the Greenwich Village area. So I was in law school and my student friends all said when I'd talk and hang out with, 'Y'know you're really, really funny. You should become a comedian.' I remember that had an impact on me because I'd just met these people. I remember thinking, they just met me and they think that. All my friends in high school and college had kind of told me that, but these people are new so maybe I should do this and I really didn't have any other options. I remember thinking well I don't want to go back to school to study something else and I don't want to go into the nine-to-five work forces so let me take a shot at this."

Melanie Comarcho: "It was a dare. I went out with a few co-workers to the Comedy Act Theater and I didn't feel the comedians were funny. So I was teasing my girlfriends at the table, 'Shoot, I could do that' and they put fifty dollars on the table and dared me and Sharon (Michael Williams' sister was put in charge while he fought his bout with cancer) gave me five minutes, I did it and she asked me to come back."

Mike Epps: "I needed a job."

Jerry Lewis Never Heard a Sister

CHAPTER 24

"I once dated a handicapped girl. She had
a big old booty, but weak legs."
— RODNEY PERRY

The Queens of Comedy flung open the doors of opportunity to all funny ladies of color. Struggling stand-up Sherri Shepherd was finding multiple opportunities as the cute, bubbly black girl on one show after another, most notably on the Brooke Shields sitcom, *Suddenly Susan*. Comedienne Edwonda White became the go-to girl for heavyweight headliners such as Dick Gregory, George Wallace, and Paul Mooney, while Melanie Comarcho lent support to the young Turks: Martin Lawrence, Chris Tucker, and Katt Williams. Angela Means of *Friday* fame used her good looks (though not in *Friday* as the crackhead Felecia) to land numerous guest starring spots and a regular gig on Nickelodeon's *Cousin Skeeter* (voiced by comedian Bill Bellamy); sexy Paula Jai Parker co-starred in the Gina Gershon vehicle *Snoops* for golden boy producer David E. Kelley; played Monique Lattimore on *The Wayans Bros.*, and later provided the voice for *The Proud Family*'s Trudy Proud.

Even former Comedy Act Theater mainstay and *Different World* co-star Ajai Sanders (Gina) eyed a comeback. She'd been in virtual seclusion since a stalker in the mid-'90s made her re-assess her public activities and her privacy was never quite the same following a series of comedy shows in the Deep South. Once it was ascertained that the location of her home in Los Angeles was known to an overzealous fan whose method of contact was leaving messages like "I told you I would find you" on the answering service of her unlisted phone number, life was spent looking over both shoulders.

DARRYL: "What was your goal when you got into comedy?"

SHERRI: "I wasn't a very confrontational person and I noticed that women on the road had to be very confrontational because there was a problem with getting paid. I met Sheryl Underwood—at the time this was '91 and I noticed she'd have to curse everybody out to get her money and I'm not good at cursing people out and telling people I've got a gun in my purse and that I'll use it. So I didn't want to go on the road and I decided to focus. I saw people doing TV. So I thought let me take some acting classes. I thought that might be fun."

ANGELA: "Actually my goal was to perform on the Apollo stage and at the time that was our graduation. That was a black comic's graduation."

DARRYL: "Have you experienced more sexism or racism?"

MELANIE: "As the black female comedian I can do the black night in any club in the country, but when it comes to a white night where there's a white audience, they're not putting us in those slots."

AJAI: "When Robin Harris passed, of course the Comedy Act Theater was never the same again, but then there was a moment where it started to rebuild itself and the crowd started to come back a little bit. Well, I don't know if they (club manager Michael Williams and his sister Sharon) were jealous or mad at me, I didn't know what was going on, but there was a lot of tension. I'd go and try to work on my new material. I'm on TV so I've got credits. I'm thinking I've got a little juice, but they just kind of turned cold for a while. 'Oh, there's no room.' 'Sorry we're all booked up.' 'Can I do five minutes?'

'No, not tonight.'

"I'm on TV! I'm on an NBC top-ten rated show. Yet I would see Martin pop in from out of town and they'd slide him right on in and people would get excited and it was cool. They never did that for me so I'm thinking maybe this is what sexism is all about. That was my first taste of sexism."

PAULA: "I don't think you can experience one without the other. I don't know. Every time I've experienced sexism I wondered if there was a little racism attached to it. I don't know. It all goes hand in hand to me. I experience them daily."

ANGELA: "Well, being the house nigga that I am I don't get it as much. I have my own black experience and it's a little bit different because I'm not bi-racial I'm by slavemaster. So I get a different type of racism. I'm light skinned. I go places. I

Ladies of comedy (left to right) Miss Laura Hayes, Chocolate, Adele Givens, Edwonda White, Angela Means, and Melanie Comarcho.

get in, but when I get in I'm still black and I've never wanted to be anything else. I like black-eyed peas on New Year's Day. I really don't want pork loin and mashed potatoes for Christmas dinner. Y'know, I like having an attitude. I love my attitude, y'know? I like to roll my neck. I like to talk shit. I like being part of a race that's forgiving. I like being part of a race that I believe was the first man here. I like being part of my race, but I just don't experience the same kind of racism in person. On paper it's different, but in person I get chosen."

EDWONDA: "I don't get into the sexism because I'm a strong woman and I don't try to compete with men because I know my role as a woman. A lot of women don't know their role."

DARRYL: "What do you mean by your role as a woman?"

EDWONDA: "I believe in the secondary role of a woman. A woman is a helpmate to a man. A man is the head of the household and I'm old-fashioned; I'm old school. I don't want to wear the pants. I could wear the pants, but I don't want to. I want the man to take his rightful place as the man of the household and I will be the helpmate. I will be the strong force that helps him to get his goals out there. I'm not trying to be a man. I'm not trying to get out there and compete with the men. I'll be a strong black woman and if that's good enough—cool because I'm a strong woman so being a strong woman is already going to make me stronger than most weak men."

One of the mysteries within the funny female ranks was the wild card, Sherri Shepherd. Once she got the career ball rolling the only time this dynamo took a break was when she'd give birth and then it was right back to the set, prompting her peers to quietly wonder how

Shepherd, a simple stand-up comic, always got virtually every part she tried out for. What was her secret, they all wanted to know? How'd she do it?

SHERRI: "How do I do it? Jesus Christ number one, I have to say Jesus. It really is miraculous. That's the only answer I have."

DARRYL: "Could it be a situation of not only being spiritual and living right, but also being prepared, being professional, being on time, and not causing problems? Would it be a combination of those?"

SHERRI: "Yes. It's a combination. He will bless you, but you have to be prepared when you go into that room. They have to know that you can work and I've seen this on all the shows where we pull comics. When a comic does a show, what we do is very singular. We're onstage and it's all about us. When you come to work on a (TV) show you have to be a team player and you have to be willing to back up and sacrifice your funny for the series regulars. I've been a day player, a recurring player and a series regular and I've done it all and there's a level to each one of those things and when you come in you want to show them you know how to serve that function. When you walk into the audition you make that room your own. You go in there and you own that two minutes. When you get the part they tell you you have to let it go, because it takes away from the series regulars. I've been on shows where they fired people who were comics because the comics say, 'I have to stand out.' But then you're taking away from Sherri and they pay me a lot of money to be funny. So they're not going to let that happen, and so a lot of times comics have a problem transitioning into doing television. You have to show them you're a team player and all these people want to know is, can you do the job. And will you do the job and make me look good."

DARRYL: "What would you say to a young, female performer?"

SHERRI: "Don't sleep with the other actors. It will take you ten years to get your reputation back."

This brings up an age-old question of a person's love of their profession. Some professionals have equated their peak performance in that profession as being comparable, if not better than, intercourse. Let's find out what comedians think.

IS COMEDY BETTER THAN SEX?

Kevin Hart: "I agree. I agree. I f*#kin' agree. If you have sex and it's not good that's just one person you weren't good with, but when you're on stage and you stink that's a f*#kin' thousand people that know that you ain't shit and they think that you need to get your life together."

Rodman: "Amen to that."

Tony Rock: "It depends on who you're f#*kin'. It might actually be more gratifying for me. Like you have sex it's pretty much the same, different girl, different positions, but comedy is different every single time."

Jemmerio: "Hell, ain't nothing better than sex. Sex is sex. Sex is a treat."

Sandy Brown: "Yes, yes!!"

Ruben Paul: "Absolutely. Absolutely, and not to say I don't love and enjoy sex, but comedy has so many different purposes and can do so many different things, man. It heals you."

Al Toomer: "I'll never say that. Nothing's better than a piece of pu*#y. I love going up and getting the great laughs and all that stuff, but let's face it once we get the laughs what are we waiting off stage trying to do? Trying to get some pu*#y."

Derrick Ellis: "I think it's one of the best highs you can get."

Adele Givens: "I don't think so. They are two separate categories. It's like the Olympics—you can't put a swimmer against a bike rider. They both good in their own way."

Shang: "No. Whoever said comedy is better than sex is out of their mind. I think sex is better than comedy. Comedy is better than a grave burial."

Alex Thomas: "I would say it's a close tie. Believe it or not—if you're a real true comedian like yourself and like myself, it's one of the greatest highs there is. I would say a standing ovation in front of two thousand people would be the equivalent of getting the best blow job you ever got in your life."

Smokey Deese: "I love comedy and it's better than masturbation, but is it better than sex with somebody that you like—naw! I would have to say 60/40, dude. Unless you're talking about a standing ovation, in that case comedy is better than sex. The reason I say that is I never had any pu*#y that made me want to stand up and clap."

Sommore: "No. Sex is the bomb. If you find an audience that don't dig you you move on to the next audience. That's the same with sex. No, it's not better than sex."

Eddie Griffin: "Whoever them comedians was ain't doing no f*#kin. I love comedy, but it ain't coming close to no pu*#y."

Doug Williams: "It depends on who you're having sex with. I've been married now for a few years so some nights comedy is better than sex. But with new pu*#y—naw. Can't compare comedy to new pu*#y. Old pu*#y—yeah. Hope my wife doesn't read this."

Rudy Ray Moore: "Yes, I would say so because I enjoy it that much. I enjoy it better than I do sex and at this age I enjoy it ten times more."

Talent: "I've even said that out of my mouth, 'This is better than being with a woman.' There's those elite sets; y'know everybody does good and have good sets, but then there are these sets that are so elite, so Jordanesque that nothing can f*#kin' miss, y'know what I mean?"

Mark Prince: "I can't put anything above sex, not even marijuana. Sex is the best thing ever given."

Speedy: "It's close. If you're real funny you're going to get some pu*#y."

Kool Bubba Ice: "Depending on how you do on stage it can be just as relaxing and fulfilling."

Joe Blount: "I think it's been established throughout humankind that for sheer pleasure nothing beats sex. I know you love your art which I do too, but c'mon."

Curtis Arceneaux of Arceneaux & Mitchell: "Anybody says that must be f*#kin' themselves. Ain't nothing better than sex."

Pierre: "Naw, naw. I've busted a helluva nutt with sex; ain't never busted no nutt with comedy. I never wanted to ask my comedy to get the f*#k out of the room and go home. I've never had to duck from my comedy's husband. Unfortunately some of those comics—their comedy act may last as long as their f*#kin' sex act. They only got a two-minute bit and that's it."

From Hambones
to Hummers

CHAPTER 25

"I want to make enough money to be a black Republican. I want to have so much money that when I say, 'Yo nigga, what's up?'—I'm not asking how you're doing. I'm asking, what are you doing in my neighborhood?"
— ALONZO BODDEN

Once America got over the panic of the Y2K scare and thoughts of the sky falling, old pursuits could be resumed. The system hadn't crumbled and those with bad credit were not spared the persistent nagging of those calling to collect on a debt. Anarchy hadn't overthrown the land with survivalist hillbillies emerging from their caves and holes in the ground to start the new world order. Nor did the Earth open up and swallow us all whole because all the computers would supposedly blow a gasket when they couldn't rotate over to the year 2000 on their clocks. The panic was just that.

John Witherspoon: "White people all of a sudden start getting itchy. Their hemorrhoids start flaring up and their hair starts itching and their dandruff starts falling off their head."

None of the doomsday prophecies came to pass and society should've been embarrassed about running out and purchasing duct tape and grade-C gas masks.

The field of black comedy saw a new consciousness and an awareness. The boom had long since been over and the survivors were looking for more lucrative ways to survive. Dreams of stardom and entourages were giving way to the realities of financial security in a business in which so much time had been devoted. Movers and shakers such as Cedric the Entertainer and manager Eric Rhone were mounting independent projects away from the limelight in a continuing effort to create jobs and control wealth. They also had a mission—to educate.

> **Eric Rhone:** "My advice would be get in where you fit in. You might have to take a position that's not quite in your field, but as close as you can get. The main thing to do is just get in. In the entertainment business there are directors, writers, producers, craftspeople, y'know there's all types of job opportunities and careers that are very rewarding. A lot of people try to get in and they want to be the star, they want to be the main person, but there's a lot of power and money to be made in all forms of entertainment."

The former Monsanto executive and his client had concentrated for years on upping Cedric's visibility and building up his "brand" in the marketplace. Many of their moves made in his career were geared toward increased reconcilability. This led Rhone to offer some insight to young people looking to blow up before their time.

> "The money will come. Young people and people in general have to understand that if you build the right brand then the money will take care of itself. Now you can go chasing dollars and you can chase a dollar right into a dead end. If you build a brand then you know. Take your time; build a brand, the money will come."

One disciple of this philosophy was a struggling playwright/actor/producer known as Tyler Perry. Born in New Orleans on September 13, 1969, Perry was the ripe old age of 36 before his brand became a national phenomenon. A playwright since the age of eighteen, it was his matriarchal character Madea (who Perry portrayed in drag), which slowly built a cult following in the African-American community from his stage plays and video/DVD sales of those performances. By March of 2005 sales had grossed over seventy-five million dollars. However, it was the grosses from his first film, *Diary of a Mad Black Woman*, that exploded with a box office bonanza in 2005. Budgeted at five-and-a-half million dollars, the unexpected success confounded critics (who'd given it poor reviews) and shocked Hollywood bigwigs; few had ever even heard of Tyler Perry. The total gross was 50.6 million.

But his growing fan base knew who he was. He was the man who put up twelve thousand dollars of his own money in 1992 to mount the play *I Know I've Been Changed* in Atlanta, only to watch it flop. He was the often homeless, struggling artist who scratched and starved for the next six years until his play met with a successful run in 1998 at Atlanta's House of Blues and then at the Fox Theater. He was the new kid on the block whose next play, *Woman Thou Art Loose* (from Bishop T. D. Jakes' book) grossed over five million in five months. Then Perry sucker-punched the film industry on February 24, 2006, when the first weekend gross of *Madea's Family Reunion* at thirty million dollars (it took the number one spot and ultimately pulled in over sixty-two million dollars) cemented him as a bonafide hitmaker. He went on to cobble out his brand in the literary world when his first book, *Don't Make a Black Woman Take Off Her Earrings: Madea's Uninhibited Commentaries on Love and Life* debuted atop the *New York Times* nonfiction bestseller list in April of 2006.

One significant brand eliminated from the comedy landscape in the new Millennium was "Guy Torry's Phat Tuesday" at the Comedy Store in Hollywood. His weekly showcase had become an institution of sorts, helping to launch careers in an environment conducive to industry attendance. The audience was young, hip and ambitious, and the atmosphere was hype. Guy had his "black" night for about a decade when he finally shut down on August 23, 2005 and moved onto other career pursuits.

During his era, every Hollywood*esque* nightclub had evenings where they went dark. The Laugh Factory had "Chocolate Sundaes." The Improv had "Mo Better Mondays." The Haha Café had "Wacky Wednesdays" and many spots around the country had their own versions of "Love-a-Nigga" nights. The problem was that these black acts, after being labeled as such by performing on those chosen evenings, found it hard to erase that stigma and get bookings on any other night of the week, meaning on "mainstream" nights.

> **Marc Howard:** "I heard a comic say he started losing spots on the mainstream nights because he worked on the black night. I think it's a comfort level because we use 'nigga' very liberally and that makes white folks uncomfortable. And when we go out and showcase and try to get into these clubs, if we're not somebody already established then it's going to be hard-pressed to get a spot or be listed as a regular for some of these rooms."

> **Gerard:** "We get trapped in that hell. When the industry wants black comics they don't ask them to come down on Wednesdays and Thursdays, they come and find us on Sunday, Monday, and Tuesday where they know we're going to be, which is really not fair because that's not what they want when they finally come and see us. You want me to do something mainstream then you need to have me showcase at the Improv. I know this (black) room and I know I can't showcase material here and I'm not going to. So if I rip doing what I'm supposed to do in the room and then you don't want me for what I'm auditioning for. Damned if you do and damned if you don't."

According to Guy Torry, racist club policies and industry expectations were not the only deterrents of a wider acceptance of black comedians.

> "Comedians are a trip, man. I ain't gonna front. Comedians are muthaf*#as, man. Running a comedy club really gets to see you...I hate comedians! Comics. I take

that back I hate comics. You got the cats that you love working with, you enjoy seeing, but some of these greedy, selfish, self-centered muthaf*#as I can just really care less about. I mean I understand that it's all about them, but when you're running a room, they don't understand about running a business. They don't understand the business and you can't take it personal it's no disrespect, but if you're not funny enough to be on my show—you ain't funny enough to be on my damn show!...and work your way to it. I tried to use this room as a brass ring. I wanted everybody to get to the point where they can perform in this room. This is the Comedy Store. This is the legendary Comedy Store where legends have performed. Everybody from the Rat Pack to Pryor to Chris Rock to Eddie Murphy to you name it. Yakov Smirnoff. Jim Carrey. So for us to be on Sunset on a Tuesday night...you come to this muthaf*#in' stage don't disrespect it. Bring it! I try to teach cats, 'Hey man, this ain't a play toy. If you beg me too much and you bomb this is probably your last muthaf*#in' time on this stage. So just wait your turn. Don't think you're just going to move ahead of the pack, of cats who've been putting it down for years and you just been doing comedy two months and you ain't funny and you're going to get that easy ride, no. With comics, man I notice how they respond to me when I'm running a room and when I'm not running a room. I get totally different treatment. When they want to get on your stage, they're nice to you. When they can't get nothing out of you they're really like, 'F*#k you." Not all of them, but the ones that are, are the ones I don't like putting on the stage. So it's a love/hate relationship with comics. And it's not a bitter thing because I want to see every comic win. Trust me, I'm a fan of comedy. So I want to see every comic who's brave enough, every person who is brave enough to get on that stage and tell some jokes. I want to see us all win. I want to see us all work. I can't tell every joke. You know how many comedy clubs there is around the country? I can't be in Chicago and New York at the same time. Somebody's got to keep the Chicago club open while I'm doing the one in Connecticut. So we all need each other. I just wish there was more camaraderie and less stealing and less hatin', but that's the world. That's the world we live in and you're going to get that in every profession you deal with."

On the television end of the comedy profession, reality TV was the disruptive force. No stars to cater to, no agents, managers or lawyers to haggle with, just plain old folks looking to line their pockets at any cost and get their fifteen minutes of fame to boot. This was fine for the networks and home audience, but for artists, craftspeople and assorted talents it was leading to financial ruin. The few jobs available were harder to squeeze into than a ten-year old prom tux and for a black writer...make it twenty years old.

Writer/Comedian, Lamont Ferrell: "It affected me a great deal because reality shows, they're not scripted; there's no writers. They have what they call story editors, which are actually editors; they kind of edit all the footage together. You can produce the shows really cheaply and you can get higher numbers and because of that a lot of networks will pick it up over a sitcom. And so because of that it has affected the comedy writers and you see a lot of people out of work;

especially with African-American shows. Instead of a network picking up their one or two or pilots at least—they might wind up picking one or none."

Fortunately one network was picking up whatever slack they could. UPN was cranking out a steady stream of black comedies. One was hard to distinguish from the next with sing-song titles like *All of Us*, *One on One*, *Half and Half*, yada-yada-yada, but they were giving work to black talent. Ferrell worked on *Moesha* and discussed the stringent requirements necessary to work in television:

> "One of the comedians I worked with back in Philly was Warren Hutcherson. Warren was one of the head writers on *The Parent 'Hood* when I was there. When it got canceled he got a job as a head writer for *Moesha*. So Warren brought me and my writing partner, Norman Vance, Jr. to do punch-up for the show. So we got hired on staff, but as punch up writers and we ended up getting on staff and becoming regular full-time writers."

Most African-American writers weren't friends with Warren Hutcherson so they had a rougher road to travel. Ferrell was well aware of the traditional route, but was quick to point out that it's not what you know, but who you know that gets you hired. Plus the normal way was confusing.

> "Typically you will write a spec script for a current, funny white show; because most of the industry don't watch our shows. The top show on our ratings is like the one-hundredth show on the Nielsen ratings. The ironic thing about that is you're writing shows that 99% of the time you won't be hired for."

And that's not all.

> "Ageism is a problem; fortunately I haven't gotten to that point yet, but I would say it is a young business. I have experienced ageism slightly in pitching, because you'll go in and pitch and you'll bring up a show that some of these kids don't know about. You'll give an example, 'It's kinda like *Welcome back Kotter*' and they're like, 'What? Oh yeah, comes on Nick at Night.' 'How old are you?' 'Twenty-four.'"

NBC should be commended for having, not one, but two black males on a single network program, but don't fill out your ballots for the Nobel Prize too quickly—the show was *Last Comic Standing* where one of them was going to be kicked off anyway. The three season (2002–2004) reality/comedy show placed stand-up comedians in a house for twenty-six days with a series of challenges and head-to-head competitions for elimination until one comedian fit the description of the program's title. The first winner and relatively new comic Dat Phan got a development deal, money and a few guest shots on TV and film, not to mention touring for even more money (five thousand dollars a week average out the box). The following season the veterans of the comedy field got off their butts and auditioned. When the final field was weeded out the winner was white comedian John Hefron.

For the third season it was decided that the first season's comedians would compete with those from the second. The audience scratched their heads and went to the TV Guide Channel to see what else was on, for none of the contestants had captured the national imagination. Sure, they were fine when you were watching the show, but you'd be Sherlock Holmes' idol if you could ferret out a bootlegged T-shirt of any of them.

Thus the third season was a disaster because nobody remembers who won. Oh, there was a winner, but the finale show was pre-empted by an episode of a computer-animated half-hour that starred a showbiz lion who worked for Vegas showmen Siegfried and Roy entitled *Father of the Pride*. This well-meaning and compassionate concoction debuted only months after animal trainer Roy Horn was severely mauled by a tiger during a live performance. NBC was obviously seeking out the highbrow crowd when they programmed this one. Sister station Comedy Central did air the final episode of *Last Comic Standing*, but by then the public had jumped ship and the hoopla was minimal when the name of Alonzo Bodden, a black man, was announced.

The bald and physically imposing Queens, New York native and former airline mechanic had beaten the odds and destroyed his counterparts, but nobody knew. Bodden took it in stride and counted his blessings. He'd been a late bloomer in comedy, starting at the ripe old age of thirty, but was aggressive in his approach.

> "When I had just four years in I did Montreal (for the annual industry comedy festival). Now I had no idea. I knew it was big and I knew people got deals, but I didn't know enough about it to be scared of it. So I went up there and I did my first set and it went great. And I did this joke where I say I don't like hockey. You say that in Canada and they go berserk, right? They're yelling and I tell the crowd to 'Shut up!' and I said I don't like hockey because the only thing black is the puck. Golf, on the other hand...They just started roaring and my manager told me, he said, 'When you told the audience to shut up all the industry stopped talking, asked who you were and the bidding war began.'"

He got that deal and became a full-time comic; the best solo profession in the universe, but *Last Comic Standing* was a group situation. Backstabbing and broken alliances were reality show staples and the comedians saw their share. The dissing started off with the NBC contract that basically said the comedians were the peacock network's property for a year. You were only being paid AFTRA scale per show (roughly one thousand dollars), you could get a development deal, but it only paid you eight thousand dollars. You weren't allowed to do any other shows. You weren't allowed to appear anywhere else. You weren't allowed to etc., etc., etc.

Like most reality shows where living quarters are involved, the requisite cast of characters were put into place: the all-American white guy, the jock, the girl(s), the gay person, and of course a black guy, but in this case there were two: Bodden was the mainstream black and Corey Holcomb was the brotha from the hood. Holcomb was voted off because to America he was a sizable, dark-skinned black man with a threatening demeanor. Whereas despite Bodden's awesome frame all the audience saw was a gentle giant, not to mention a prolific and inventive comedian.

> **Lauren Bailey:** "I think Alonzo Bodden is brilliant and in a whole category by himself. Alonzo Bodden, Richard Pryor—that's where I am with him. I call him 'the heat.' That's what I call him. If I were a professional comic I would never want to follow behind him."

All was good until they pulled the plug on the show when nobody was looking.

> "The show aired Tuesday. America voted. They called us Wednesday morning and said NBC canceled the show. Then at some point they brought it back and Thursday afternoon they canceled it again. So now Jay (Mohr, the producer) is pissed. So Jay goes on whatever (radio station) was airing (promo ads) at the Tempe (Arizona) Improv that week and says 'Screw NBC. Alonzo Bodden won.'"

Bodden kept a good outlook by joking about it on stage. *"They canceled the show when they found out the brotha won."* The unfortunate aspect of course is that Bodden didn't get the publicity of Dat Phan or John Hefron. No *Good Morning America, Howard Stern,* or *The Tonight Show.* The winning black comedian was written up in *TV Guide* and *USA Today*—that's it. The rest of the entertainment press completely ignored the win, but despite this snub and even though the general public never got a gander at that last episode, Bodden went on to tour, buy a house, watch his previously recorded comedy CD sell off the shelves, and put enough cash away that first year that he never had to worry about money again. Touché, brotha. Ironically the show returned to NBC's line-up in May of 2006.

Meanwhile, CBS had brought back *Star Search* with Arsenio Hall replacing Ed McMahon as its host. In this new, revamped version, comics weren't faring well. Panel judge Naomi Judd was getting a reputation of being a career breaker when it came to comics as week after week she'd crush their spirits with adjectives such as "unoriginal," "amateurish," "unfunny," and "so-so." Even seasoned veterans weren't living up to their previous hype.

There were several who did manage to slip past the bad review board with a fresh take on an old format. One was a black comedienne who'd paid her dues on shows like BET's *Comic View* and doing road gigs and clubs, good and bad. Loni Love had spent most of her adult life working in the "real" world, but comedy offered her a creative outlet and she took it. Getting time off from her day job of ten years at Xerox (project manager), Love (her stage name) took a shot on the new *Star Search* and made it all the way to the finals, where she came in as runner-up to white male comic John Roy. However, as it happened when Clay Aiken lost to Ruben Studdard on *American Idol,* second place is sometimes the winning slot. Love went on to work on the VH1 cable show *Balderdash,* the movie *Soul Plane,* tour extensively, and get a deal with NBC for a role in a sitcom.

DARRYL: "Has the life of a comedian been what you expected?"

LONI: "The life of a comedienne has been very interesting, because what I'm finding out about comedy is there are different positions of stand-up. You have the road comic, which is very hard on women because you travel all around and you're going from club to club, you're doing a lot of shows in a night and that's a different type of lifestyle. Then you have the stand-up who is maybe like a television/weekend comic; get a couple of television gigs here and there and you also do comedy; like you do live performances and that's pretty good for a woman because you can kind of stay in town instead of always in a different town every week or whatever. And then you have the more high-end comics that like do television gigs. They kind of like turn into actors and they do special performances. That's like a Wanda Sykes type of comic or something like that. So to answer your question—you can make stand-up what you want to make of it. So what I'm trying to do is to have like a name so then I'll still be able to do the live shows. I'm trying to get on the high end, which is working out well for me. The plan that I've made has worked out pretty well for me so to answer your question—has stand-up been for me what's it's supposed to be I can say yeah."

DARRYL: "Tell us about your *Star Search* experience."

LONI: "The whole thing about *Star Search* is you have to do a minute and a half. It's not about who's the funniest. Comedy is subjective and you have to be within yourself. In the semi-finals was me, Ty Barnett, and Jeff Garcia. And Jeff had been really good previously and so everybody was like, 'Jeff's gonna win. Jeff's gonna win.' From that you go on to the finals and that's where problems started coming up because then CBS started getting into the material. It's network television. You have to have a certain type of material and I wanted to do something. The producers wanted me to do other things and we were going back and forth literally. The censor guys they have at CBS, I'm in there for an hour with these people going over what I can say and what I can't say and this is for the final. There was this one joke I wanted to do about a particular airline. Now I'm supposed to go shoot the final at 5:00 and at 4:55 they come in and say you can't do that joke. I have to take it out and I had to try to change it with something else. So five minutes before I'm supposed to go up I have to change my whole set. This is the final. This is one-hundred thousand dollars on the line. This is the type pf pressure that you go through when you're dealing with network television and it just taught me that from now on there are certain jokes you have for network, there are certain jokes you can have for cable, things like that. So I dealt with that and then once I got to the final, it was against me and John Roy and we tied. Carol Leiber gave John Roy one point above mine and so he won. Everybody was kind of shocked because I was getting four stars, four stars y'know and then we get to the finals. They gave it to him and Naomi Judd was hilarious. She was like, 'You'll be a good writer, but Loni should be the winner,' something like that. It's interesting. I'm not bitter because I didn't win. Actually because I didn't win *Star Search* I was able to keep doing other things. What was funny was—it was a fight to get out of my contract. The president of CBS (Les Moonves) was so nice to me he let me out of the contract because he wanted me to be able to pursue my career and stuff like that and I really thank him to this day. But it really taught me a lot about don't you sign. Don't just pick up the pen and sign because you're happy because it will come back to bite you. It really will."

Rap impresario and sampler extraordinaire P. Diddy mounted *The Bad Boys of Comedy* on HBO in 2005 and did his own version of contract misunderstandings.

> **Damon Williams:** "We were told it was going to be a straight-to-DVD project. I wouldn't have been so raw if I had known it was going to be an HBO show."

Besides raw it was loud, raucous, profane, and not funny enough to make people forget it was a *Def Jam* clone. There also seemed to be something else missing.

> **Luenell:** "Females were totally excluded. I resent the f*#k out of that."

The entrepreneurial spirit was alive and well as black film also marched on.

Comedian/filmmaker Pierre pulled a Robert Townsend and took seventy thousand dollars of his own money earned from his acting fees in *How to be a Player* and *B.A.P.S.* and made the film comedy *For the Love of Money*. Shot on 35mm, he got picked up quickly at a black film festival. They bought it and put it out for theatrical release, then Sony picked it up and put it out worldwide.

> **Pierre:** "It was everywhere from Brazil to Amsterdam to South Africa in video stores. I couldn't believe it. So a big agency saw it and they were impressed by what I did and brought me on to look at movies to direct on a higher budget. Now they want me to direct like five million dollar movies. From seventy thousand to five million dollars is pretty big."

Veteran urban auteur Ice Cube had developed franchises to keep the ball rolling. He'd not only knocked it out of the park years earlier with the *Friday* films, but *Barbershop* 1 and 2 had also proven to be box office guarantees. In the process of shooting his projects, Cube had made film stars of Chris Tucker, Cedric the Entertainer, and Tucker's *Friday* replacement.

MIKE EPPS

Mike Epps was born in Indianapolis, Indiana and had eight brothers and sisters. To gain attention, Epps entered a stand-up comedy contest at a club while still a teenager. He later moved to Atlanta and became a regular at The Comedy Act Theater.

It was suggested that he go to New York to hone his skills and off to New York he went. From there Mike got on the *Def Jam* tour, appeared at the Laffapolooza comedy fest and worked top clubs like the Comedy Store. He made his film debut in Vin Diesel's *Strays* in 1997, but things exploded for Epps when he was spotted by Ice Cube during a standard funny performance in 1998 and was pegged to replace Chris Tucker in the comedy *Next Fri-*

day in 2000. He reprised his role of Day-Day in the sequel *Friday After Next* and established a solid film career away from his mentor.

> **DARRYL:** "Who are your influences and why?"

> **EPPS:** "My influences are all the brothers out there in the streets that didn't make it. They're my influences because they are in the trenches and they're dealing with real reality and that's what inspires me; people down living reality. Dealing with people that are real that live everyday regular lives."

> **DARRYL:** "When did you realize you'd gotten over?"

> **EPPS:** "After I did *Def Jam*."

Katt Williams (courtesy of Katt Williams).

Ice Cube also introduced another talent to the world. The breakout character in *Friday After Next*, Katt Williams a.k.a. "Money Mike," was also looking to lay claim to the title of new-breed millennium comedian and he made it clear he was a comedian, not a "comic" with a raw energy and unbridled passion for the craft. In a series of television appearances, he demonstrated not only a manic physical capability, but that his medulla oblongata was doing just fine as well; riffing and mixing the visual along with a firm grasp of the world around him and how it was funnier than the tragedy we all were experiencing. Strangely enough it was his own personal dilemma that got him into the profession in the first place.

> **KATT:** I was in a f*#ked up position. I had got my son so I needed some sense of stability. I had no skills for the workplace, nor the desire. I remember I had done comedy once on an open mic and it had worked so I wanted to see if I could make that happen. So that's how I started; out of desperation. I knew I had to make something work."

Another veteran and the undisputed failed-TV-pilot king also got a break; a chance to show what he knew all along—that he was worthy of all the excitement; that his comedy deserved to be recognized if only he could control it himself. Comedy Central went out on a limb and did just that. The result was a bombshell—*Chappelle's Show*.

DAVE CHAPPELLE

David Chappelle was born in Washington, D.C. and began doing stand-up comedy at the age of fourteen with his ordained Unitarian minister mother taking him to his gigs.

> **Ian Edwards:** "I worked with him for about a month and a half in Montreal. We did Scotland in '92. We had the same manager; the Jewish guys. He was with Barry Katz. They saw him in D.C. and asked them if he was willing to move to New York. He was like sixteen at the time. He had to get his grandmother's

permission, because she was the one raising him. Then he came to New York and he was all over TV."

Norman Mitchell: "The first time I met Dave was at a comedy club in New York. This little skinny brother came into the room and was like, 'hey man, you think these people will enjoy my kind of comedy?' Hey man, I don't know—give it a shot."

Dave had the typical career trajectory: HBO comedy special, appearances on the late night shows—*Politically Incorrect, Late Night with Conan O'Brien,* and *The Late Show with David Letterman* and throughout his career he performed at prestigious venues such as Radio City Music Hall and Lincoln Center with heavyweights like Aretha Franklin, Richard Pryor, and Whoopi Goldberg. It was unsung hero and brilliant New York street comic Charlie Barnett who personally taught Chappelle the most—all great comedians have a definitive point of view.

Ian Edwards: "Dave used to hang out with Charlie Barnett, because Dave had a desire to be a great comic. Dave would do street shows with Charlie Barnett. Anywhere he could go he'd go, but he never stole Charlie Barnett's style, because Charlie Barnett was loud. He was all over the place. Dave was just laid-back and he would just get great laughs. The best thing to do as a comic is just to be yourself. The audience can tell when you're putting on an act, when you're faking it."

It's been said that Dave has depth and delivery which is a rare combination, possessed by luminaries the likes of Pryor and Carlin. It is Dave's natural affability that helps render an audience off guard as he sneaks in a sharp, biting point, as well as his fearlessness.

Ian Edwards: "We were at the Montreal Comedy Festival, like back in '93. We went to a warm-up show before the Festival really started and Dave said, 'I'm going to do a street show.' Next thing I know he was like, 'Showtime, Showtime' and just like Charlie Barnett he had a whole bunch of people gathered around. He performed right in the middle of the street. They put money in his hat and we went to a strip club."

Bob Sumner: "Great guy. I know stories about Dave that's a lot deeper than just being a comedian. He's a Good Samaritan. Him and David Edwards saved a little girl from being apprehended on a Washington subway one time. They were hanging out late after a gig one night and they noticed that this guy had this girl on the subway and this girl was giving them like y'know, little things like something wasn't right. They come to find out she was being kidnapped and Dave and Dave actually got the girl to break loose, y'know and then they got the guy."

Madd Marv: "Dave Chappelle to me is a genius. I hung out and smoked weed in New York with him. He's pretty much smoked with every comic in the country. I guess what people don't know about him is he can play the saxophone. He has an extensive saxophone collection. The soprano sax, the tenor, he has all the saxophones sitting in his living room on racks. He took me to some cool jazz places in New York, where people were straight getting down. Dave Chappelle, he will give you the coldest New York City tour you will ever have."

Dave made his film debut in *Robin Hood: Men in Tights* directed by Mel Brooks. He was the black guy. In 1996 Dave played in *The Nutty Professor* as baggin' *Def Jam*-style comedian Reggie Warrington, who taunts Eddie Murphy's Professor Klump and viciously points out to the club audience which part of the professor has more crack than Harlem. Then he appeared in *Con Air* until Nicolas Cage killed him. He was working, but only long enough to taste craft services, and since nobody was beating down his door to star in a movie he cut to the chase and wrote his own, becoming a cult icon of the college kid circuit with the film *Half Baked*. The movie dealt with the joys of smoking marijuana, a subject near and dear to Dave's heart.

> **Ajai Sanders:** "I remember one time he was riding in my Pathfinder and he helped me get my gas and forgot to put my gas cap back on. Let's just say we were both not in our right minds. It was the only time I've ever been that pissed off at Dave. I was like, 'Dude, how could you forget my gas cap?' but after a while we just started giggling and laughing and then we just got hungry and we got something to eat."

He went on to co-star with Tom Hanks, Martin Lawrence, and Eddie Griffin in various films while shooting and being rejected in TV pilot after TV pilot. He was turned down by almost every network that didn't feature cooking until he struck gold with a Comedy Central deal.

The network needed anything to put on the air that was different so they gave Chappelle the latitude he needed to assault his audience with raw, uncut gut laughs. Everybody talked about *Chappelle's Show*. It brought in a whole new audience to Comedy Central; his DVD sales went through the roof and the network awarded Dave with a deal worth fifty million dollars.

> **Daryl Mooney:** "His biggest problem: overnight he had millions of black folks loving him and that's a responsibility in itself for that. Because you know, Dave Chappelle was always liked by white folks. When he got that show all of a sudden black folks were introduced to him. Now he can attack, but he couldn't do it before that show. It be like Dave who?"

> **Katt Williams:** "It's kind of depressing that black people are just now recognizing that he's a f*#king genius, but he was a genius ten, fifteen f*#king years ago and it's kind of sad that nobody got him then."

Dave went into his third season taping period as the hottest comedian in the world with a highly publicized incentive deal (encompassing two years and based on DVD sales as well as salary for performing and executive-producing the show) and a legion of new fans. Episodes were being shot. Billboards and posters blanketed towns across the country announcing the debut. Calendars were marked and the busier fans were TiVo-ready and then all of a sudden, out of nowhere—Dave left without warning, ended up in Africa and made sure to say he wasn't smoking crack. Nobody knew anything and if they did they weren't saying. Comedy Central scrambled to neutralize the fallout; first claiming a delay, then throwing in the towel and announcing a full-fledged retreat. But why? One popular theory was that the network wanted to be more hands-on and Dave felt pressured. Former *Chappelle's Show* director, Rusty Cundieff:

"That's not really the case in terms of what I saw. I'm not in every meeting Dave is in. He's privy to things that I don't know, but from what I saw the last season and even the second season, Comedy Central were far more hands-off than they were the first season. The first season we would have a table read and they would give a bunch of notes. The second season we sat down and read through the script—*The Niggar Family*—they had no notes. So from Year One where they're trying to give you notes on the most mundane of things to a sketch where you say 'nigger' twenty or thirty times and they ain't got no notes; so that doesn't feel like they were getting tighter. What I kind of feel happened; from my observational standpoint—Dave is a brilliant comic who goes all the way to the edge and he's brave enough to really bear his soul in his stand-up. A lot of the shit that he talks about is stuff that other people deal with, y'know, the racism, reverse racism, black people being embarrassed of other black people, self-hatred, that kind of shit; and most people don't want to talk about it and/or deal with it. So a lot of that stuff that Dave did was like really showing that blemish on the underside of your body. It's like, 'here's my ass. Take a look at how crazy this shit is.' And the other thing is he was doing satire and one thing I know about satire is—not everybody gets it. Or a lot of people laugh at it. So some of the stuff that he was doing, like for example, *The Niggar Family*, where his point was the ridiculousness of this word; the kind of holding-up-to-a-light. What does the word mean? Is it the word that does it? Is it the meaning behind it? All of that stuff is kind of being addressed in there or *The White Supremacist* sketch that we did. He's blind, but he's black and it's like if you look at something like that, you're like, this is brilliant and if you're on his wavelength or somewhere around his wavelength— you get it. If you're not around his wavelength, then you're the guy who comes up to Dave in the street and goes, 'Nigger lover!' and is laughing not with Dave, but at Dave. It's the same thing like when you watched *All in the Family*. How many people are laughing because they understand the show is saying Archie Bunker is a bigoted asshole or how many bigoted assholes are laughing at the show because they're like, 'Archie Bunker is our hero and finally somebody's saying what we believe'? And that, in a large, big way, I feel, is the issue Dave found himself facing on *Chappelle's Show*. He's doing this cutting-edge stuff. He's putting it all out there and he doesn't know if people are laughing because they get it or because 'hey, this is a really fun coon nigger.'"

DID YOU EVER SEE ANY SITUATION WHERE SOMEBODY SAID SOMETHING STUPID TO HIM AND YOU COULD SEE WHERE DAVE HAD HAD ENOUGH?

"I don't know if I can think of a specific example, but I can say that we did a sketch the last season, that if it hadn't been something that Dave was doing, I probably wouldn't have directed it because I would've said, this shit is too wild. It's too crazy. People are going to be offended and pissed off, but we did a sketch about a nigger pixie. It's a pixie where if you're a black person and you find yourself in a certain area like, Dave is in first class and this little nigger pixie pops up in front of him like, 'oh, you a first class nigga. Wow—how did you get up here?' And then the stewardess comes and asks Dave if he wants the fish or the chicken and the nigger pixie's like, 'oh, take the chicken. The chicken, nigga!' And he's in blackface. The nigger pixie's in blackface. It's funny, but it's dancing on the graves of a lot of raw emotions and stereotypes, but at the same time—it's real. I mean, maybe not for every black person, but I definitely know black people who go through those things. You question yourself at different times. Do I want to order watermelon in this restaurant? I really like watermelon, but do I want these muthaf*#kas to know I like watermelon? So it's that stuff. Anyhow, we were doing that thing and it was even mentioned I think in a *Time* or *Newsweek* magazine article about this; that as we were doing this sketch, Dave might have heard somebody laughing a little too loud and a little too hard and I could totally see that. And there were other things that we were doing towards the end of the show where, without getting specific, I know Dave felt uncomfortable about."

DO YOU THINK HE GOT PRESSURE FROM THE NAACP OR BLACK PEOPLE LIKE, "MAN, YOU CAN'T REPRESENT US LIKE THAT"?

"I don't know if he got pressured by them. I know he felt that pressure in his head. I know that he had begun to question some of the work that he was doing. Whether he was doing the right thing or the wrong thing in terms of his race."

Thus, the plug on the show everybody was waiting to see got reluctantly pulled and Dave Chappelle momentarily went back to his simple guy life of living on an Ohio farm with wife and child. He returned to the stand-up stage, laying low from the media, while Comedy Central compiled the previously shot footage and with the assistance of Dave's sole writing partner, Neil Brennan, edited the segments, that began to air in July 2006 as *The Lost Episodes*.

Vince D: "The only thing I don't like about Dave is thanks to him they'll never give another nigga fifty million dollars."

One of the stand-out sketches on *Chappelle's Show* and a classic was the Rick James skit, which coined the phrase said throughout the country from all walks of life: "I'm Rick

James, bitch." (A take-off of cast member Donnell Rawlins' patented line, "I'm rich, bitch.") The funkmeister himself appeared in the segments in mock seriousness. It was a fitting tribute to a music innovator who'd fallen prey to too much partying before, during, and after his shows.

The bit itself came from Eddie Murphy's older brother, Charlie, reminiscing on the set. To pass the time Charlie would entertain the crew and other cast members with tales of hanging out with his superstar sibling. After he'd rattled off a good number, somebody came up with the idea of him re-enacting some of these wild yarns on the program and calling them "Charlie Murphy's True Hollywood Stories" in parody of a popular E! Entertainment show, "True Hollywood Stories" where everything ended with the celebrity winding up on drugs or dead.

Murphy's tales weren't much different except for the fact they were absolutely hilarious and a welcome addition to *Chappelle's Show*. It also made Charlie Murphy's name famous. The days of being under his brother's prominent shadow were about over. Interestingly enough, another unsung sibling was receiving attention for his own efforts. His name was also being said with the so & so brother attached. Tony Rock (Chris' brother) was co-starring on UPN's *All of Us* and touring clubs throughout the country. Stand-up was practically a birthright.

"In my blood. My grandfather was a preacher. Three of my uncles were pimps. So Rock men just have a way with words."

All DNA aside, being the sibling of anybody famous comes with a certain amount of baggage, but when they're at the top of their profession and you follow in their footsteps that's another story altogether.

DARRYL: "Has the name helped or hurt you?"

CHARLIE: "When I first started doing stand-up I saw a whole audience lean in and they're looking right in my mouth and they're going, 'I know this nigga getting ready to say something funny' and they didn't know I didn't have nothing funny to say. I was scared as hell. I almost ran off the f*#kin' stage."

TONY: "It's a blessing and a curse. It opens some doors and it makes the expectations unbelievably high for someone starting out. I'm graded on Chris' scale as a new jack. Like when I'm doing open mic shows they want to see Chris' scale of comedy, but you have to acquire that. You have to work for that. It doesn't happen overnight."

Chappelle's Show featured many great sketches including "Negrodamus" featuring long time comedy legend, Paul Mooney.

Spanky Hayes: "The grandmother of comedy."

"Miss Laura" Hayes: "He's the only comedian that's ever made me pee."

Paul Mooney (center) with his sons The Mooney Twins (Dwayne and Daryl) at the Pied Piper in Los Angeles, CA circa 1990.

Luenell: "I kiss his feet. I have wonderful stories of him; even when he cursed me out"

PAUL MOONEY

Born in Louisiana, Paul Mooney grew up in Oakland, California, then ran away to join the circus where he boasts about being the first black ringmaster. He began doing stand-up in high school. Richard Pryor was his mentor, and that's how their relationship began. However, Mooney had his own voice on stage. He was pissed off.

Franklyn Ajaye: "Paul was actually quite interesting. I used to look at him. I used to think the difference between him and Richard is he's not the performer Richard is. At that time Paul was very hit-and-miss with the audience. He was the angry black man and the Comedy Store had predominantly white audiences and some nights they would sit there and laugh and he was very biting and some nights, man—they would just walk out on him. I used to tease Paul. Every time I'd see him in front of the Comedy Store I'd walk up and say, 'Hey, Paul, how many white people you kill today?' He'd come back, 'Hey Homie, I don't like that.'"

Tom Dreesen: "After a show an old white woman walks up to Paul and says, 'Young man, I don't think you're any good for my people or your people.'"

Talent: "I've watched white people sit and just turn red and sit through an hour of Paul Mooney and he's f*#kin' blaming the world on them, but they're not leaving. They'll clap occasionally and look at each other. 'Is it okay to laugh?' and they'll probably wait until they get home and close the garage door, go in the house and say, 'How dare that nigger say that about us?'"

Mooney was a multi-media artist, writing for *The Flip Wilson Show*, *Sanford & Son*, *Good Times*, Pryor's 1974 NBC specials and Pryor's *Live on the Sunset Strip*, and material for *JoJo Dancer, Your Life Is Calling* as well as the Whoopi Goldberg film *Call Me Claus*, which appeared on Super Station TNT. He mentored Sandra Bernhard and also wrote for Redd Foxx, Sam Kinison, Shirley Hemphill, Robin Williams, Tim Reid, and John Witherspoon. Mooney was more than generous with advice.

Bobby Law: "I asked him what I needed to do to be a comedian and he told me, 'you can't teach a ho to be a ho. If you're a comedian you're going to be a comedian.'"

His imagination extended to Arsenio Hall and *In Living Color*, in the creation of Homie the Clown and his famous line, "Homie don't play that."

T'Keyah "Crystal" Keymah: "I love Paul Mooney so much I could be the president of his fan club. When word got out that Paul Mooney was coming to the show (*In Living Color*) there was a panic among the white writers."

It was Mooney who wrote the classic "word association" skit on *SNL* which featured Pryor and cast member Chevy Chase engaged in a racial battle of words and wills. According to his son, comedian Daryl Mooney (of the Mooney Twins), it was Paul who named the most famous of Pryor's albums: "*Bi-Centennial Nigger, That Nigger's Crazy*, anything with 'nigger' in it our father named it."

Mooney acted: *Which Way is Up?* starring Pryor; playing Sam Cooke in *The Buddy Holly Story*; appearing in *Hollywood Shuffle* directed by fellow Black Packer Robert Townsend; and he played the comedian Junebug in Spike Lee's *Bamboozled*, the spot-on satire that offended many blacks with its depiction of blacks in blackface.

Mooney also knew how to offend with a mixture of political and racial material.

Marc Howard: "Idolized him a lot. I love his boldness to be able to sit in front of white folks and to talk so much shit to them and tell them the truth about themselves for the most part. Of course he had to pay the price for that, y'know."

Shang: "He says what's on his mind, but that's not necessarily a good career move."

It was his uncompromising stance on race and his utter lack of restraint when dealing with the subject of the white man and his antics that kept this artist regulated to cult figure status.

Roger Rodd: "If he were anything but a black man he would be branded a very hardcore racist, and I understand where the anger comes from, but at times it's a little too harsh even for me."

The difference between Mooney and most comedians is when Paul doesn't get a laugh from his audience, he'll pause, look at them and chide them for not laughing at funny material. *"Oh, get a sense of humor. This shit is funny. You'll repeat it later and won't give me the credit."*

The stage was his Mount Olympus. Mooney had been part of a select group of comedians the Comedy Store had begun with and was always put on stage late at night around 1 or 2 o'clock. This was the time most people would be leaving a club, but Paul's time became known as "Mooney Time" and there were people who wouldn't show up at the club until 11:30 just to catch a glimpse of the guy and stay there until 2 or 2:30 a.m.

He attempted to record his stuff in the '80s; taping material at the Comedy Store for an album that was to be produced by Richard Pryor and David Banks. Unfortunately somebody dropped the ball and the project ended on that Main Room stage. It was never released. But the *Def Jam* era breathed new life into Mooney's career as a stand-up. He was now viewed as an OG of comedy that connected with the new jacks.

His reputation was well earned. His CD *Race* in 1993 was a financial and critical success. His second CD *Master Piece* released in '97 suffered the same fate. On the stage he regaled audiences with bits like "Blame a Nigger" about a phone service you called when you needed a scapegoat, and "The California Raisins" where the popular ads were accused of being racist for subliminally making the raisins African-American and how he should take marshmallows, put little arms on them and call them the Beach Boys. His frequent appearances at Caroline's Comedy Club in New York had him proclaim he was the only black on Broadway who didn't sing or dance. And he was featured in the comedy segment *"Ask a Black Dude,"* and as "Negrodamus" on *Chappelle's Show*.

Marc Howard: "He's going to be one of the ones that will be greater after he's gone."

Shuckey Duckey: "Should've gotten more recognition for some of the stuff he's come up with and some of the things he says and the imagination he has."

J. B. Smoove: "I think down the line Paul Mooney's going to be on a level like Richard Pryor, man because he's like Lenny Bruce was y'know. He put a mark on what he does and Paul Mooney has that same kind of thing going on. I've been in the streets. I know what going on in the streets. I have my decoys in the streets and I'm working in the streets. He's got all those things going on for him big time."

Honest John: "Paul Mooney is great. I was a little intimidated meeting Paul Mooney because his act is so militant and all that. Here I am; I'm the white guy doing the black clubs. So I was a little intimidated, but he was extremely cool and

I remember one time at the Comedy Store he took me aside and he said, 'You know there's a couple of the comics here who try to do what you do, but none of them can.' And that really blew me away."

Edwonda White: "Paul Mooney has always intimidated me. When I'm in his presence I'm always intimidated. I don't know why. He has never said anything to me bad or anything, but I saw him on stage a lot of times before I actually met him and then when I met him he was like the most intelligent man that I ever met; no lie. The brother is so awesome, like sitting there listening to him was amazing to me."

Seasoned vets were en vogue and blazing a path for the future. In mid-August 2005, HBO unleashed a monster comedy special from Atlanta powerhouse Earthquake. He'd finally arrived and the world needed protection.

Affion Crockett: "Earthquake is one of the funniest comedians to me because of his delivery, his demeanor. He always makes me laugh. He's ridiculous."

Earthquake's down home country style and common sense approach was killing audiences everywhere he played. The former host and known owner of the Uptown Comedy Corner was a *Comic View* favorite and had built a solid reputation as one of the funniest black comedians in the country and demanded five figures. This was for an act that had never starred in a TV show or a motion picture. He was just simply putting butts in the seats. So by the time the industry gave him any consideration, he'd amassed a hoard of fans nationwide. The underground was about to go above ground by way of Earthquake.

DARRYL: "How has black comedy impacted your life?"

QUAKE: "The fact that I was part of the revolution of black comics in Atlanta by owning two clubs in Atlanta and just made a standard that we in the ATL followed: be funny, creative and be original and I was instrumental in that part. That's what I take credit for. And how comedy has impacted me? It put my daughter through school. It allows me to let God be my alarm clock. I get up when I feel like it and that's how it's impacted me because that's all I do is tell jokes."

The new generation was also making noise. Veteran black producer/writer T. Faye Griffin created the competition *Coming to the Stage* for BET to suck in the audience who liked to watch people get defeated and to counteract the sagging ratings *Comic View* was experiencing. It was meant to be adult comedians only, but an anomaly slipped in—a 'tween named Little JJ not only competed with the old guys, he beat them consistently. His jokes fit the knowledge of a person his age. At the same time it displayed a child's common sense approach at viewing life and the emergence of JJ put kids back in the fold. They had a role model now. Eddie Murphy, Dave Chappelle, and Nick Cannon had all started stand-up while in middle school or high school, but their role models were grown men; men of comedy, not boys. Although JJ went on to win the grand prize on *Coming to the Stage*, when he went on the road touring it was another matter as far as audience support. Nightclub and paying theater patrons don't care when your mama's water broke, they just want to laugh. You say you're a professional comedian—come with it! JJ's people used his name to draw in the crowds, but when it came to headlining the show, they'd hire a seasoned veteran for those duties. JJ was good for a performer of his age and experience, but even the seasoned veteran has crumbled before a rowdy gathering of discontented customers. When audiences would heckle and curse, JJ's lack of stage time showed he was not yet a headliner. Besides, few grown folks were going to tolerate a child telling them to shut up for being too loud. However, the seed was planted.

A female seasoned vet was spreading her wings and people were noticing. Raven Symone was not the teen magazine fodder of white peers Lindsey Lohan and Hillary Duff, but Symone was a crossover dream. Her show *That's So Raven*, which debuted on the Disney channel in 2002, was pulling down solid ratings and settled in for a long, profitable run. Symone made a few youth-geared movies for the network of *Kim Possible*, *Even Stevens*, and *Lizzie McGuire*, and her merchandise never could seem to stay on store shelves long.

It seemed like ages since she had been on Bill Cosby's NBC show as she had developed into a buxom young lady, but she still maintained the little girl wonder that had endeared her audience to her and helped her make the nearly historically impossible transition from child star to adult player. It was her charm that convinced her TV mom T'Keyah "Crystal" Keymah to sign onto the show in the first place. Some changes from the original vision of her character had soured Keymah; something she intended to make clear at the first table read:

> "I came to quit. I came to tell them, 'I don't know who you think I am, but yakkity, yakkity, yak...I came there to quit and then heard Raven Symone read and I thought, who is this girl? This girl is who I wish I could be at her age and there was no such animal. There was no such possibility of a black girl having her own show. I wanted to be a part of this and she's why I stayed."

Never before had so many young comics taken control of their careers en masse, overseeing the business end of show business with so much savvy. This was the generation born around the time of Al Pacino's Tony Montana and *Scarface*, where the mantra was "The World is Yours." Well, it's not known if their mothers took them to that film or recited the credo while they were still womb-bound, but they used it with gusto.

One of the top carriers for his tonda (the other artists one comes up through the ranks with or started with) was a kid from San Diego who used to hang outside the club until his manager gave the okay that it was time to go inside, go directly to the stage, tell the jokes and make a beeline back outside. Nick Cannon might not have been old enough to be where he was, but he was smart enough to know what he was doing.

Kevin Hart: "Young. I won't say my competition, but somebody that I look at and he pushes me. Hard worker; whether it's music or acting or writing or producing. He's got his hand in everything at a young age. Definitely he'll be successful."

NICK CANNON

Nick Cannon was born in San Diego, California in 1980 and was a *Soul Train* dancer before deciding to become a stand-up comedian.

Mystro Clark: "I brought him into my management company when I was there. That was Tollin Robbins. My manager was actually at the Improv to see me and we saw Nick Cannon for the first time. He was still in high school; used to hang out a little bit. He would ask a couple of questions every now and then about comedy too. So yeah, we used to rap when he first started out a lot. I gave him a couple of little pointers here and there, but he was always a good kid."

Cannon soon found a home on the youth-oriented Nickelodeon cable channel and got busy: as a cast member on the sketch comedy show *All That*; writer for *Cousin Skeeter* and *Kenan & Kel*; hosted *Saturday Night Nickelodeon*; and created *The Nick Cannon Show* and later *Wild 'N Out* for MTV. He got small parts in the films *Men in Black II* and *Whatever it Takes* until his first starring role as Devon, the cocky percussionist in 2002's *Drumline* followed up by *Love Don't Cost a Thing*, *Shall We Dance?*, and *Roll Bounce*. Nick even had time to write and rap, collaborating on the song *Shorty (Put it on the Floor)* with Busta Rhymes, Chingy and Fat Joe; and in 2003 releasing *Nick Cannon* on Jive Records and went on to work with the infamous R. Kelly on the hit single *Gigolo*, but it all started with comedy and that first rush a comedian gets when they bust their cherry.

NICK: "First time I was on stage was at McDonald's cafeteria in Charlotte, North Carolina. It was a talent show and that talent show led to an Apollo audition. Like the winner of the talent show got to go to the Apollo in New York and I came in second. And that was the first time I was ever on stage, eleven years old telling jokes back in 1992."

DARRYL: "You're one of the top ten moneymakers under thirty in your field. Number one is Ashton Kutcher. You're number ten, but you're the only black on there. How do you feel as far as your responsibility to keep the ball rolling?"

NICK: "It's my responsibility to bring ten more in, y'know what I mean? That's why I try to do stuff like *Wild 'N Out* and produce my own shows and bring in more talent. We're blessed so we can be a blessing. I feel like I got this opportunity so I can open more doors for people just as talented and even more talented than myself."

The youth market had another prominent entry. Not only was he a comedian, he could also write and produce. It was this combination of talents together with the forethought to hang out where the deals were made and not where the backs were stabbed (in the open, anyway) that positioned him for out-of-nowhere notoriety. Kevin Hart burst onto the scene with his own film and television show and nobody saw it coming.

KEVIN HART

Born in 1980 Kevin Hart was working as a shoe salesman in Philadelphia when he decided to give stand-up a try at a local comedy club's amateur night. This initial success led him to perform at the Boston Comedy Club, Caroline's, The Improv, The Laugh Factory, and The Comedy Store in Los Angeles. It was his performance at the Montreal Comedy Festival that got him the notice he was looking for and work in feature films such as *Paper Soldiers* (2002), *Scary Movie 3* (2003), and *Along Came Polly* (2004). From there Hart executive-produced, wrote, and starred in the ABC sitcom *The Big House* and had the lead role in *Soul Plane* (2004), about a man who is awarded one hundred million dollars as a settlement after a freak accident on a commercial airline flight. But even a go-getter like Hart was awed by the number of options comedy offered.

HART: "At first I didn't know how many doors comedy can open up. I don't think when you first start you realize it. You kind of take it for granted, y'know? You don't realize all the opportunities that stand-up can actually give you and that's what I did. All I expected was to basically be funny and travel and tell jokes all day. I didn't know that comedy could get you into acting or radio, etc., etc., etc. It opens up a lot of doors. Fortunately for myself I was able to get through a couple of those doors and 'Shazam!'—it was through comedy which is my first love."

DARRYL: "What's your worst experience doing stand-up?"

HART: "I don't have any really. I know a lot of people probably have horror stories, but my road was a little different than a lot of people's. Because I'm only twenty-six, so my stories, you'd probably listen to them and say, 'Is that it?' My horror story's probably just getting semi-booed at Caroline's. I don't have anything that's bad, man. My worst experience was getting booed, but that's like every comic is booed sooner or later. But I don't have any stories about getting stuck in the city, trapped or not getting paid or stuff like that. I just don't have any."

DARRYL: "But you say you did get booed at Caroline's."

HART: "Yeah had a guy throw a lemon peel at my head. He was so pissed off at my comedy he decided to stand up and throw a lemon peel at me and tell me to shut the f*#k up."

DARRYL: "How long had you been in the game when this happened?"

HART: "About two years. See when I first started out I stayed local for my first year and a half, I didn't want to leave out of Philadelphia. I was getting a lot of laughs at the comedy shows, plus I had a lot of friends and family showing up for support. So when I got out of town I couldn't talk about the local shit I had been talking about anymore. It got a little difficult. Jokes about streets and local stuff don't go over because they don't know what you're talking about. I tried to do it at Caroline's and it didn't go over and I'm getting booed and a guy threw a lemon peel at me and I tried to come back and he stood up and he was taller than me from just where he was standing and I was on the stage. So I just let it go. I didn't want no piece of that ass whooping."

DARRYL: "How long have you been doing comedy?"

HART: "Since I was eighteen, I'm twenty-six now."

DARRYL: "To most people you came out of nowhere. All of a sudden Kevin Hart is starring in his own TV show. Kevin Hart is starring in his own movie. How did that transpire?"

HART: "I'm kind of mainstream. Like I said my road is a little different from other people's. And I would rather not make money doing comedy to be in the right position; the position where you're around industry. Where you're around the same people that a lot of these Caucasian comics are around constantly and they're getting opportunities that a lot of African-Americans don't even realize are out there. But the reason that we don't realize they're out there is because we're not patient. We're not willing to sacrifice as much as a lot of those guys. So when I saw the opportunities that they were getting I put myself in that position and one thing led to another and you wind up with good agents and managers and they put you in the position where you can win. Go to auditions and you kind of learn what Hollywood is about. That's what I did. I learned what Hollywood was about and I stayed true to myself which is being funny being myself, not letting anybody change me, at the same time being accepted as a funny comic. Being accepted as a funny comic can get you into a lot of places and that's what it did for me."

DARRYL: "Do you think your look might have helped, because you're twenty-six; you're 5 feet 4 ? inches, because of your height and you do have a baby face regardless of your age—obviously you feel that's helped you, right?"

HART: "Of course, of course; an innocent smile and an innocent look can definitely help you. If you're not menacing and you don't come off threatening it definitely puts you in the position to win a little more. Like I said it's Hollywood. You never know, man. You never know what their reason was for giving you the opportunity. You never know, but I guarantee that doesn't hurt; the fact that I'm the cute black kid with an adorable smile that can dance. It helps. It helps to be in the right position, that's all."

DARRYL: "You co-wrote and starred in *Soul Plane* and everybody saw the bootleg before the movie came out (in theaters). What's your attitude about bootlegging?"

HART: "It is what it is. That's how some people survive. It's a business. It's not something that I'm ignorant to. I was a person who bootlegged material myself, but what it does is it gives you that street love and that's what I have now. And it gave me that black love regardless if people realize it or not so I don't knock it, y'know. I have a certain community who's in love with *Soul Plane*, who love it and they probably all of them bootlegged it, but I don't knock them for doing it; to each his own. Hopefully the next one...they don't bootleg this one and let it get to the theaters. We'll see."

DARRYL: "*The Big House* was a great opportunity for you and put you on the map as far as a lot of people. Do you have any memories good or bad of working on that show for ABC?"

HART: "Good, of course I would say more good than bad. The only bad thing is that it got canceled. But the reason why it got canceled had nothing to do with my show. At the time the network was in turmoil because they were between presidents. They didn't know which way they wanted to go; which direction they wanted to go in networkwise. But I was twenty-four at the time and I was executive producing, starring and writing in my own television show. That's an opportunity and blessing in itself. Not many people get that opportunity. The fact that I had it is the shit to me and now it just gave me another learning experience; something else that I know. And now the television world can respect me as a producer and not only as a stand-up comic and they can respect me as a writer because I have proof of what I can do, y'know. I've had material that I've produced so now it's just time to keep creating. You don't stop. You don't get comfortable. You keep on rolling."

DARRYL: "Were you surprised by the amount of player-hating that went on?"

HART: "Y'know, not really, because if you focus on that that's time that could be spent doing something else. My time spent worrying about what somebody else is thinking about me is time that I could be writing; time that I could be out doing something productive. So I don't think about none of that shit, man. Nobody's voice has anything to do with another man's plan. That's how I look at it. So I just keep moving, stay low-key, keep moving."

Black comedy keeps doing the same thing—moving. It is as indomitable as the people who make it; from those early days of poking fun to spiritually survive to the lucrative era where a well-received television or film appearance can make a career. African-American humor has not only buoyed the spirits of blacks for centuries, it has enriched the art of comedy for a nation. For despite the verbal abuse, ridicule, and mockery the forefathers kept their heads up and their eyes down as they swallowed their massive pride and imagined a larger prize: future generations. The dream of a better lot in life for those who followed was not just one for entertainment, but for all existence, and so they marched forward and endured.

The question current and future generations of African-Americans have to ask themselves is, are they worthy? Would their ancestors feel their sacrifices were justified; the chain continuing to be forged from the same metal they wrought? Or has arrogance and complacency taken root? Are they just as dedicated? Will future generations have their shoulders to stand on or will the entire effort crumble in the hands of errant caretakers?

For black comedy to continue to be a vibrant force the artists themselves have to set a standard of excellence not only individually, but for those who also claim to carry the banner of the black comedian. Whereas mediocrity had always been discouraged in the past, it should steadfastly be shunned and the malaise that crept into its practitioners exorcised from the ranks. It is only this type of policing of such a solo endeavor that the doors will stay open for business and black comedy will remain a true American art form.

SOURCES

African-American Registry. http://www.aaregistry.com, 2005.

Altman, Susan. *Encyclopedia of African American Heritage.* New York: Facts on File, 1997.

Ankeny, Jason. "The Naked Truth." *All Music Guide,* 1999.

Berger, John. "Wayans' World: Damon Wayans Takes a Break From an ABC Project to do a Hawaii Show." *Honolulu Star Bulletin,* June 29, 2000.

Castellini, Mary Sky. "Outer Limits–Scary." *Sixties Forum,* February 8, 1999.

Celebrity Artists Entertainment, http://www.caentertainment.com/bios/Sommorebio.htm

Comedy Cartel. "Robin Harris was a very funny man!" *African American Registry, African-American Registry.* http://www.aaregistry.com, 2005.

D, Christelle. "An Actor's Diary D. L. Hughley." *BlackFilm.com,* 2002.

Deane, Pam. "The Jeffersons." *Museum of Broadcast Communications,* March 5, 2004.

Epstein, Lawrence J. *The Haunted Smile: The Story of Jewish Comedians in America.* New York: Public Affairs, 2001.

Epstein, Lawrence J. *Mixed Nuts: America's Love Affair With Comedy Teams.* New York: Public Affairs, 2004.

Fact Monster. Boston: Pearson Education, 2000–2006.

Foxx, R. and N. Miller. *The Redd Foxx Encyclopedia of Black Humor.* Los Angeles: Ward Ritchie Press, 1977.

Gates, Dr. Henry Louis Jr. *African-Americans: Voices of Triumph.* New York: TimeLife Inc., 1993.

The Good Times Online Scrapbook. http://www.valdefierro.com

Internet Movie Database Inc. http://www.imdb.com, 1990–2006.

James. *J-Notes.Com,* January 2003.

Jones, Steven Loring. "From 'Under Cork' to Overcoming: Black Images in the Comics." In *Black Ink.* San Francisco: Cartoon Art Museum, 1992.

Judell, Brandon. "Eddie Griffin Gets a Clue?" *Gay City News,* 2004.

Latin Heat Online Magazine, http://www.latinheat.com

Levy, Shawn. *Rat Pack Confidential.* New York: Doubleday, 1998.

Lorenz, Megaera. *Betty Boop Before and After the Hays Act.* Toyko: Heptune, 1998.

Lorenz, M. and B. Lorenz. *Betty Boop in Minnie the Moocher.* Toyko: Heptune, 1999.

Millin, Janette M. "Sinbad: Keeping the Funk Alive." *Black Collegian,* 1999.

Monroe, Irene. "What's in a Name? Plenty, That's What!" *A Globe of Witnesses,* 2002.

Morgan, Thomas L. *Jazz Roots.* http://www.jass.com, 1992, 1997.

Robertson, Regina R. *Africana.com,* February 12, 2004.

Smith, Ronald L. *Cosby.* New York: St. Martin's, 1986.

Tobey, Matthew. "All Movie Guide." *New York Times,* 2004.

TV.com. CNET Networks, Inc., 2006.

Watkins, Mel. "Black Humor: From Slavery to Stepin Fetchit." In *The Redd Foxx Encyclopedia of Black Humor,* by Redd Foxx and Norma Miller. Los Angeles: Ward Ritchie Press, 1977.

Watkins, Mel. *On the Real Side.* New York: Simon & Schuster, 1994.

PHOTO CREDITS

The author graciously acknowledges permission to reprint the following:

Harper's Weekly, 1876, page 5.

Harper's Weekly, 1876, page 6.

From a poster for the London Surrey Theatre, 1836, page 15.

From a poster for Callender's (Georgia) Minstrels, circa 1870, page 20.

Sheet music cover for "James Bland's 3 great Songs," 1879, page 20.

Chas. H. Crosby & Co., Lith., 1880, page 21.

Harper's Weekly, 1876, page 22.

Sheet music cover for "We Are All Loyal Klansmen," 1923, page 24.

Sheet music cover for "All Coons Look Alike to Me," 1896, page 31.

"Hogan," http://health.bytes.com/hogan.htm, circa 1900, page 31.

Yale Collection of American Literature, circa 1896, page 32–33.

http://Waynesweb.ualr.edu, 1921, page 34.

"Silent Ladies & Gents," http://www.silentgents.com/GriffithDW/DW07.jpg, circa 1920, page 40.

"Hattie McDaniel," http://members.aol.com/ttelracs/Hattie.htm, page 41.

"Little Rascalz—Our Gang," http://www.rivalquest.com/ourgang/pic2.html, 1925, page 44.

"All About Amos 'N Andy and their Creators Correll & Godsen," http://www.geocities.com/Hollywood/2587/
    freemangosden, 1930, page 56.

Harper's Weekly, 1876, page 64.

Fuel 2000 Records, page 79.

Alicia Littleton Collection, "Hollywood Palladium," 1982, page 81.

Tom Dreesen Collection, "A Night Under the Stars, Caesar's Palace," 1978, page 85.

Courtesy of David Drozen from *Laff Records*, page 87.

Courtesy of Timmie Rogers, page 96.

Courtesy of Edwonda White, page 99.

Michael Ajakwe Collection, USC, 2000, page 105.

Reynaldo Rey Collection, 1981, page 116.

Courtesy of David Drozen from *Laff Records*, page 117.

Marla Gibbs Collection, 2005, page 121.

Courtesy of Edwonda White, page 127.

Alicia Littleton Collection, "Hollywood Palladium," 1982, page 132.

Courtesy of David Damas, page 140.

Franklyn Ajaye Collection, 2003, page 143.

Tom Dreesen Collection, "Mr. Kelly's," 1972, page 147.

Tom Dreesen Collection, "The Tonight Show," 1978, page 149.

Luenell Collection, 1989, page 168.

Courtesy of *Comedy the Magazine*, 2000, page 209.

Courtesy of *Comedy the Magazine*, 2000, page 215.

Courtesy of *Comedy the Magazine*, 2000, page 229.

Courtesy of *Comedy the Magazine*, 2000, page 233.

Michael Ajakwe Collection, "Cole On Ice," 1995, page 238.

Arsenio Hall Collection, 2005, page 241.

Chris Spencer Collection, 2005, page 247.

Luenell Collection, "Geoffrey's Inner Circle," 1995, page 249.

Courtesy of Edwonda White, page 251.

Luenell Collection, "Lake Merritt," 1993, page 253.

Ajai Sanders Collection, "The Strand in Redondo Beach: July 24, 1992," page 257.

Courtesy of *Comedy the Magazine*, 2000, page 261.

Kym Whitley Collection, 2000, page 266.

Courtesy of *Comedy the Magazine*, 2000, page 269.

John Witherspoon Collection, 2005, page 273.

Courtesy of *Comedy the Magazine*, 2000, page 278.

Courtesy of *Comedy the Magazine*, 2000, page 279.

Courtesy of *Comedy the Magazine*, 2000, page 281.

Sommore Collection, 2005, page 285.

Courtesy of Edwonda White, page 293.

Katt Williams Collection, 2005, page 308.

Courtesy of *Comedy the Magazine*, 2000, page 310.

Courtesy of the Mooney Twins, page 314.

INDEX

Abernathy, Ralph, 104

Ace Ventura: When Nature Calls (film), 231

Ackroyd, Dan, 139, 156

Adderley, Cannonball, 77

African Americans: humor of, 13, 29. *See also* black comedy

Aiken, Clay, 305

Ajakwe, Michael Jr., 239, 253

Ajaye, Franklin, 80, 114, 115, 130, 133, 135, 139, 180, 183, 187, 242, 288, 314; background of, 141, 142; comedy style of, 143, 144; influences of, 141; as loner, 145

Albrecht, Chris, 203

Ali (film), 234, 252

Alice, Mary, 251

Ali, Muhammad, 160

All About the Benjamins (film), 267

Allen, Bernie, 220

Allen, Byron, 169

Allen, Debbie, 251

Allen, Fred, 68

Allen, Tim, 187

Allen, Woody, 141

All in the Family (television series), 86, 117, 119, 311

All of Us (television series), 313

Amazing Grace (film), 43, 45, 79

American Idol (television series), 305

American Pie (film), 231

AmeriKKKa's Most Wanted (recording), 266

Amos, John, 117, 118

Amos & Andy: blacks, reaction to, 56; and Miller & Lyles, 34; as radio program, 51, 52; stereotypes in, 52; as television series, 45, 55

The Amos 'n Andy Music Hall (radio program), 52

Anderson, Cornelius, 52

Anderson, Eddie: background of, 52–53

Andrew Sisters, 76

animation: black characters in, 61, 62, 63, 64

Animal House (film), 231

Any Given Sunday (film), 233

The Apollo Comedy Hour (television series), 221

Apollo Theater, 78; Amateur Night at, as institution, 77

Arceneaux, Curtis, 108, 157, 190, 196, 218, 261, 296

Arceneaux & Mitchell, 190, 196, 221

Are You Serious? (recording), 88

Are We There Yet? (film), 267

Arnez J., 218

Arnold, David, 19

Arnold, Jeff, 171

Arnold, Tichina, 239

Arsenio (television series), 242

The Arsenio Hall Show (talk show), 240

At Ease (television series), 119

Australia: minstrelsy in, 14

Aviles, Rick, 195

Babyface, 199

Bad Boys (film), 199, 242, 252

Bad Boys II (film), 199

The Bad Boys of Comedy (television series), 307

B.A.D. Cats (television series), 119

Bailey, Lauren, 205, 214, 231, 305

Bailey, Pearl, 55

Baker, Josephine, 34

Bakshi, Ralph, 63

Balderbash (television series), 305

Ball, Lucille, 283

Ballard, Regina, 239

Bamboozled (film), 229, 231, 315

Bandana Land, 31, 32

Banks, David, 135, 139, 316

B.A.P.S. (film), 180, 307

Barbershop (film), 267, 307; as controversial, 211

Barbershop 2 (film), 267, 307

Barnett, Charlie, 154, 155, 156, 309

Barnett, Ty, 306

Barrasso, F. A., 75

Barrie, Lester, 171, 206, 218

Barry, Marion, 258

Bay Area Black Comedy Competition, 208

Bea, Lionel, 208

Beard, Matthew "Stymie," 43

Be-Be's Kids (film), 173

Beck, Martin, 77

Belafonte, Harry, 114, 130

Bellamy, Bill, 120, 189, 241, 291

Bell, Darryl M., 251

Belle, Paula, 238

Belushi, John, 139, 187

Benedict, Paul, 119

Benny, Jack, 53, 68, 146

Benson (television series), 238

Berle, Milton, 55, 68, 76, 93

Bernhard, Sandra, 315

Bernie Mac Show (television series), 200

Berry, Fred, 122

Berry, Halle, 231

Best, Willie: background of, 46

Beulah (radio program), 41, 45, 55, 113

Beverly Hills Cop (film), 156

Bexley, Bubba, 116

Bicentennial Nigger (recording), 137

The Big House (television series), 320, 322

Big Momma's House (film), 199

Big Momma's House 2 (film), 199

Big Time (television series), 200

The Bingo Long Traveling All-Stars & Motor Kings (film), 134–35

Birth of a Nation (film), 70; as innovative, 40; reaction to, 39

Birth of a Race (film), 70

Bishop, Joey, 80

black audience: and white audience, difference between, 89, 90

The Blackberry Inn (animated cartoon), 213, 214

black comedians: and political commentary, 69; racism toward, 301; and white audiences, 94

black comedy, 322, 323; bad promoters, as synonymous, 275; and blues recordings, 84; boom of, ix, 187; new consciousness, emergence of, 300; and white comics, 215–18, 225, 226

black comedy clubs, 187; in Atlanta, 190; in Chicago, 189; and craft mentoring, 190; in Kansas City, 191; and Peppermint Lounge, 188; in St. Louis, 190; and Terminal D, 188; in Texas, 190; in Venice Beach, 192; in Washington, D.C., 190

Black Entertainment Television (BET), 57, 205, 206, 214, 220, 221

blackface minstrelsy, 13, 16, 19

black humor, 84; white humor, as different from, 83

Black Pack, 167

black record labels, 84

Blacks About Social Happenings (BASH) Unlimited, 178

Blacksheare, Darryl, 171, 206

Blackson, Michael, 13, 25

The Black Stranger (Pryor), 134. See also *Blazing Saddles*

Black Swan Company, 84

black/white comedy teams, 146, 149

Blake, Eubie, 34

Blake, Robert, 43

Bland, James, 20–21

Blankman (film), 229

blaxploitation films, 125, 126, 127

Blazing Saddles (film), 134, 136

Blount, Joe, 43, 63, 189, 190, 296

Blue Collar (film), 134

The Blues Brothers, 139

Blue Streak (film), 247

Bodden, Alonzo, 230, 299, 305

Bonet, Lisa, 251

Bonman, Lamont, 171

Bonner, Mike, 48, 53, 71, 108, 162, 189, 193, 214, 216

Boomerang (film), 272

Boondocks (television series), 64

Boosler, Elaine, 138

"Bootsie," 116

Booty Call (film), 231, 233

Boyz N the Hood (film), 266

Bow Wow, 183

Brando, Marlon, 141

Brandy, 252

Brennan, Neil, 312

Brenner, David, 119

Breuer, Jim, 221, 260

Bring the Pain (television program), 258

Brooks, Mel, 134, 136, 310

The Brothers (film), 120

Brown, Bobby, 240, 284

Brown, Charnele, 251

Brown, Cocoa, 14, 164, 285, 286

Brown, Downtown Tony, 189, 190

Brown, Geoff, 46, 70, 89, 142, 249, 259, 266, 271

Brown, J. Anthony, 142, 177, 178, 203, 218, 239, 249, 277

Brown, Jim, 138

Brown, Johnny, 114

Brown, Les, 189

Brown, Sandy, 71, 98, 295

Brown, Willie, 34, 47, 63, 71, 110, 217, 256

Bruce Bruce, 190, 218, 277

Bruce, Lenny, 131, 141, 316; notoriety of, 93–94; as trendsetter, 94

Bryant, Willie, 68, 78

Buck & Bubbles, 44, 76

The Buddy Holly Story (film), 315

Built to Last (television series), 252, 253

Bulifant, Joyce, 123

The Burnt Cork Review (radio program), 51

Butler, John "Picayune," 14

Butterbeans and Susie, 78, 84

Buttons, Red, 76

Caesar, Adolph, 181

cakewalk, 29, 31

Caldonia, 127

California Suite (film), 134

Callas, Charlie, 97

Call Me Claus (film), 315

Calloway, Cab, 84, 196

Cambridge, Godfrey, 59, 106, 114; career of, 107

Campanella, Roy, 282

Campbell, Tisha, 239

Cannon, Nick, 35, 208, 287, 317, 318; background of, 319

Cantor, Eddie, 32, 76

Capone, 283

Carey, Drew, 187

Car 54, Where Are You? (television series), 95

Carlin, George, 130, 133, 139, 164, 263, 286, 309

Caroline's Comedy Hour (television series), 199

Carrey, Jim, 226, 231

Carroll, Diahann, 113

Carson, Johnny, 114, 214, 241

Carter, Ben, 45

Carter, Darren, 70, 108, 163, 218

Carter, Judy, 288

Carter, Nell, 251, 252

Carter, T. K., 249

Carter, Ralph, 117

Caruthers, Lance, 227, 258, 259

Car Wash (film), 135, 139, 142, 144

casting: and racism, 111

CB4 (film), 231, 257

Cedric the Entertainer (Cedric Kyles), ix, 16, 59, 89, 110,
159, 164, 184, 190, 207, 208, 213, 218, 260, 267, 276–77,
307; background of, 209, 210, 211, 212; on *Barbershop*,
211; as brand, 212, 300; and *Comic View*, 209;
influences of, 212

Cedric the Entertainer Presents (television series), 210

Chan, Jackie, 271

Chappelle, Dave, 58, 154, 189, 190, 200, 222, 263, 284,
312, 317; affability of, 309; background of, 308, 309,
310; disappearance of, 311

Chappelle's Show (television series), 308, 310, 312, 313,
316; as cutting edge, 311

Charles, Chris, 171, 174

Charlie & Co. (television series), 115

Chase, Chevy, 137, 139, 315

Check, Double Check (film), 56

Cheech & Chong, 130, 131

Chestnut, Morris, 266

Childress, Alvin, 56

Chingy, 319

chitliin' circuit, 57, 75

Chong, Tommy, 131

The Chris Rock Show (television series), 258

Chuck and Chuckles, 76

Chunn, Tommy, 71, 90, 217, 278

The Clansman (Dixon), 39

Clark, Mystro, 25, 57, 61, 63, 71, 77, 109, 138, 144, 158,
176, 193, 200–1, 217, 256, 259, 267, 277, 285, 319

Clay, Andrew "Dice," 129, 261, 263

Cleaver, Eldridge, 101

Clinton, Bill, 240, 244, 248, 271

Cohen, Sidney, 77

Cole, Bob, 33

Cole, Deon, 17, 23, 26, 43, 44, 47–48, 69, 84, 116, 127, 189

Cole & Johnson, 33

Coleman, Joyce, 220–21

Cole, Nat King, 57, 79

Coles, Kim, background of, 232; clean routine of, 232

Collateral (film), 234

The Color Purple (film), 161

Colyar, Michael, 192

Comarcho, Melanie, 25, 48, 58, 69, 90, 198-199, 218,
288, 291, 292

Come Back Charleston Blue (film), 107

comedians: socioeconomic background of, 67

comedy: ageism in, 303; brevity, as essence of, 148; and
reality shows, 302; sexism in, 292

Comedy Act Theater, 167, 168, 169, 170, 173, 177, 178, 292;
success of, 171, 174

Comedy Central, 221, 258, 304, 308, 310, 311, 312

Comedy Compadres (television series), 221

Comedy on the Road (television series), 221

Comedy Store (Hollywood), ix, 153, 301, 302, 314, 316

Comic Justice (television program), 189, 221

Comic Strip Live (television series), 221

Comic View (television program), ix, 142, 205, 207, 209,
213, 214, 219, 220, 276, 286, 317; cancellation of, 221;
hosts of, 218; origins of, 206

Coming to America (film), 157, 240

Coming to the Stage (television program), 232, 317, 318

Condon, Bill, 234

Cooke, Sam, 315

Cooke, Vincent, 230

Cooley High (film), 117, 122, 139, 180

Cooper, John W., 34

Cooper, Ralph, 78

The Copycats (television series), 97

Corey, Professor Irwin, 99

Cornelius, Don, 255, 256

Cornmeali, Signor, 14

Correll, Charles J., 51, 55

Cosby (television series), 106

Cosby, Bill, vii, 43, 59, 104, 107, 119, 130, 132, 141, 158, 160, 164, 195, 242, 250, 251, 288; American fatherhood, as symbol of, 104; and black animation, 64; black parental responsibility, as advocate for, 106; career of, 106; on *Def Comedy Jam*, 200; as influential, 106; as laid-back, 105; material of, 105

Cosby Kids (television series), 64

The Cosby Show (television series), 106, 229, 251

Cotton, Ben, 15

Cotton Comes to Harlem (film), 86, 107

Cousin Skeeter (television series), 291

Cover, Frank, 119

Crackshot and Hunter, 76

Craps (recording), 134

Crawford, Lavell, 190

Crockett, Affion, 108, 317

Cruise, Tom, 234

Crystal, Billy, 161, 212

Cully, Zara, 119

Culp, Robert, 105

Cumber, Lil, 120

Cundieff, Rusty, 111, 180, 264, 311

Curry, Don "DC," ix, 190, 213, 218

Curry, Mark, 17, 72, 95, 195, 196, 208, 251

Curtin, Jane, 139

Dahomey (musical), 31

Damas, David, 118

Damon (television series), 229

Daniels, Pope, 262

Danson, Ted, 26

Dap Sugar Willy, 154

Davidson, Tommy, 190, 197, 264; background of, 230, 231

Davis, Clifton, 123

Davis, Miles, 141

Davis, Ossie, 107

Davis, Sammy, Jr., 55, 76, 79, 97, 114, 140, 149, 187, 231; in Las Vegas, 80

Davis, Sammy Sr., 80

Deadwood (television series), 144

Deese, Smokey, 13, 47, 71, 81, 164, 183, 195, 245, 295

Def Comedy Jam (television program), ix, 143, 172, 176, 177, 196, 201, 202, 203, 209, 221, 222, 259, 271, 276, 280, 285, 286; critics of, 200; influence of, 199

Delirious (film), 157

Dexter, Wan, 178

Diamond, Neil, 272

Diamond, Selma, 237

Diary of a Mad Black Woman (film), 300

Dickerson, Dudley, 45

Diddy, P., 307

Different Strokes (television series), 123

A Different World (television series), 249, 251

Dilward, Thomas, 19

Dix, Lewis, 171, 174, 175, 176, 177

Dixon, George Washington, 15

DJ Pooh, 265, 266

D'Militant, 61, 70, 171, 177

Dolemite (film), 128

Dolphin Records, 128

Don't Make a Black Woman Take Off Her Earrings (Perry), 301

Dooto Records, 84, 85, 86

Do the Right Thing (film), 198

Doug, Doug E., 106

Down to Earth (film), 258, 260

Dr. Doolittle (film), 272

Dreamgirls (film), 234

Dreesen, Tom, 52, 86, 93, 101, 116, 131, 147, 153, 216, 258, 314; background of, 146; and black comedy, understanding of, 148, 149

Drew, Allen, 68, 69

Drozen, David, 87, 88, 89, 95, 137

Drozen, Louis, 87, 88, 89

Dr. Purvey, 169

Duff, Hillary, 318

Duke, Bill, 180

The Dutch Master Minstrels (radio program), 51

Dutton, Charles, 238

DysFunkTional Family (film), 262

Eagles, Greg, 264

Earthquake, 35, 190, 277; style of, 317

Easy-E, 266

Ebert, Roger, 231

Edelstein, Mike, 268

The Ed Sullivan Show (television series), 133

Edwards, David, 309

Edwards, Ian, 25, 84, 154, 188, 257, 260, 308–9

Ellis, Derrick, 69, 70, 108, 219, 295

Emperor Jones (film), 78

Epps, Mike, 203, 208, 267, 288; background of, 307–8; influences of, 308

Ethiopian Delineators, 15

Europe: minstrelsy in, 14

Evans, Damon, 119

Evans, Mike, 119

Evening at the Improv (television program), 199, 221

Everybody Hates Chris (television series), 258, 259

Farrakhan, Louis: on *Arsenio Hall Show*, 241, 242, 244, 245

Farrell, Bob, 15

Farrell, Colin, 234

Fat Albert and the Cosby Kids (television series), 105

Fat Doctor, 190

Fat Joe, 319

Father of the Pride (television series), 304

Feet and Brains, 68

female comedians: and pay, equity in, 283

Ferrell, Lamont, 302–3

Fetchit, Stepin (Lincoln Theodore Monroe Andrew Perry), 43, 70, 76; background of, 42

Field, Darren, 131

Fields, W. C., 32

First Kid (film), 249

Fishburne, Lawrence, 266

The Five Heartbeats (film), 180, 182, 261

Flack, Roberta, 77

Fletcher, Dusty, 70, 78

Fletcher, Tom, 21

Flex, 221

The Flip Wilson Show (television series), 114, 115, 134

Flood, Hope, 47, 57, 71, 178, 201, 214, 216, 225

Florian Slappery, 44

Floyd, Monica, 171

Flynn, Rory, 171

Fontaine...Why Am I Straight? (television special), 161

Foolish (film), 262, 263

Ford, Tommy, 239

For the Love of Money (film), 307

Forrest, Edwin, 14, 15

48 Hours (film), 156

Foxx, Jamie (Eric Bishop), 171, 178, 195, 208, 252, 257, 258; background of, 232, 233, 234; as comedian, as underrated, 235

Foxx, Redd (John Elroy Sanford), ix, 72, 87, 93, 114, 116, 117, 128, 138, 157, 158, 219, 220, 250, 259, 284, 315; background of, 84, 85, 86; bankruptcy of, 86; nightclub of, 86; and Slappy White, 95, 96

Foxworthy, Jeff, 187

Franklin, Aretha, 309

Frank's Place (television series), 149, 238

Frazier, Craig, 230

Frazier, Drew, 283

Free Clinic Players, 169

Freedom and Peace Party, 101

Freeman, Morgan, 234, 258

Fresh Hare (animated short), 61

The Fresh Prince of Bel-Air (television series), 252

Fresh Prince & DJ Jazzy Jeff, 252

Friday (film), 219, 265, 266, 268, 271, 272

Friday After Next (film), 267, 272, 285, 308

Fritz the Cat (film), 63

Fullerton, Sandy, 240

Gadson, Curtis, 205, 208, 214, 215, 220, 221

game shows, 95

Garcia, Jeff, 306

Garroway, Dave, 191

Gaynor, Joey, 264

Georgia Minstrels, 20

Gerard, 81, 84, 142, 301

Gershon, Gina, 291

Ghost (film), 161, 232

Gibbs, Marla, 36, 121, 181, 184, 206, 219; background of, 120; and Marla's Memory Lane, 120; Vision Theater, founder of, 120

Gibson, Josh, 282

Gilliam, Stu, 114, 150, 154

Gimme a Break (television series), 251, 252

Givens, Adele, 35, 48, 72, 163, 182, 189, 202, 203, 207, 277, 278, 280, 283, 286, 287, 295; background of, 285

Gleason, Jackie, 93

Glover, Danny, 234

Glover, Savion, 231

Goldberg, Whoopi (Caryn Johnson), 26, 214, 232, 244, 284, 309, 315; background of, 161; and Comic Relief, 161; tenacity of, 161

The Golden Child (film), 157

Gone with the Wind (film), 41, 45, 126

Gooding, Cuba Jr., 266

Good Times (television series), 117, 118, 119, 272

Gorshin, Frank, 97

Gosden & Correll, 34

Gosden, Freeman F., 51, 55

Gossett, Lou Jr., 161

Grant, Red, 179, 240

Graves, Teresa, 114

Gray, F. Gary, 180

Greased Lightning (film), 134

The Great White Hype (film), 229

Green, Al, 242

Green, Dannon, 81, 89

Gregory, Dick, ix, 52, 56, 59, 103, 108, 114, 291; as activist, 101, 104; background of, 98–99; humor and black church, connection between, 102; and Jack Paar, 99, 100; as overnight success, 99; social satire of, 98

Grier, David Alan, 197

Grier, Pam, 127

Griffin, Eddie, 42, 44, 69, 71, 89, 116, 117, 120, 126, 130, 159, 164, 181, 183, 191, 206, 218, 263, 295, 310; background of, 260, 261, 262

Griffin, T. Faye, 59, 216, 221, 276, 317

Griffith, D. W., 39, 40, 41; black film industry, as responsible for, 70

Gross, Bill, 169

Guilliame, Robert, 238

Guy, Jasmine, 251

Hackford, Taylor, 234

Hackley, Crackshot, 78

Half Baked (film), 310

Hall, Arsenio, 36, 157, 167, 197, 214, 243, 247, 248, 256, 305, 315; background of, 240, 241, 242; and Louis Farrakhan, backlash against, 241, 242, 244, 245

Hall, Vondie Curtis, 180

Halop, Florence, 237

Hangin' with Mr. Cooper (television series), 251, 252

Hanks, Tom, 310

Hannah, James, 71, 108, 217, 286

Hardison, Kadeem, 251

Harlem Nights (film), 138, 157, 219

Harris & Company (television series), 150

Harris, Ricky, 77, 158, 169, 170, 171, 174, 175, 176, 195, 202–3, 217, 285

Harris, Robin, 130, 138, 157, 167, 168, 169, 170, 173, 174, 175, 176, 178, 179, 180, 182, 212, 227, 292; background of, 172; death of, 172; disciples of, 171

Harry, Jackee, 120

Hart, Kevin, 25, 63, 183, 207, 237, 284, 294, 319, 321, 322; background of, 320

Hartman, Phil, 249

Harvey, Steve, 190, 195, 207, 242, 276; background of, 277, 278

Haverly, J. H., 20

Hayes, Isaac, 114, 125

Hayes, "Miss Laura," 184, 212, 214, 216, 269, 277, 283, 287, 313; background of, 213

Hayes, Spanky, 17, 119, 126, 216, 262, 271, 313

Head of State (film), 258

Hearn, T. P., 206

Hearst, Patty, 140

Heath, Darryl, 89, 183

Hefner, Hugh, vii, 94; color line, breaking of, viii, 99, 102

Hefron, John, 303, 305

Height, Bob, 20, 21

Held Up (film), 214, 233

Hemphill, Shirley, 122, 315

Hemsley, Sherman, 119

Henton, John, 169

Here and Now (film), 137

Hey, Hey—It's Fat Albert (television program), 64

Hicks, Charles, 20

Hoffman, Dustin, 138

Hogan, Ernest, 30; background of, 31

Holcomb, Corey, 304

Hollywood Shuffle (film), 179, 180, 272, 315; inspiration for, 181–82

Hollywood Squares (television series), 95, 161

Homeboys from Outer Space (television series), 260

Honest John, 59, 71, 163, 261, 272, 316–17

Hope, Bob, viii, 93, 131

Horatio, 221

Horn, Roy, 304

Hoskins, Alan "Farina," 43

House Guest (film), 249

House Party (film), 198, 268

House Party 3 (film), 271

Howard, Daran, 90, 110, 132, 282

Howard, Marc, 14, 25, 106, 162, 207, 216–17, 256, 259–60, 271–72, 284, 301, 315, 316

Howell, Kenny, 189, 280

How to Be a Player (film), 307

Hudlin brothers, 180

Hudlin, Reginald, 221

Hudson, Jennifer, 234

Hughes brothers, 180

Hughley, D. L., ix, 120, 176, 177, 178, 195, 208, 218, 258, 269, 276, 277, 286; background of, 206, 207

The Hughleys (television series), 207, 258, 285

Humphrey, Hubert, 101

Hung, Sammo, 242

Hutcherson, Warren, 303

Ice Cube (O'Shea Jackson), 211, 219, 307, 308; background of, 265, 266, 267; black comedy, contribution to, 267–68; as professional, 267

I Know I've Been Changed (play), 300

I'm Gonna Git You Sucka (film), 227

Independence Day (film), 252

In Living Color (television series), 226–27, 230, 233, 235, 238, 245, 315; cast of, 231, 232; and racism, 232

The Interrupted Card Game (film), 40

Irrera, Dom, 180

Is It Something I Said? (recording), 135

I-Spy (television series), 105

It's Your World (television series), 264–65

The Jack Benny Show (television series), 53

Jackie Gleason Show (television series), 96

The Jack Paar Show (television series), 119

Jackson, Erroll, 208

Jackson, Jesse, 101

Jackson, Michael, 16, 231

Jamal, A. J., 25, 89, 127, 144–45, 189, 221, 222, 242

Jamal-Warner, Malcolm, 262

James, Rick, 312

The Jamie Foxx Show (television series), 139, 233, 235

Janus, Samuel, 67

Jason's Lyric (film), 262

The Jazz Singer (film), 272

The Jeffersons (television series), 119, 120, 122

Jemmerio, 83, 176, 229, 295

Jim Crow laws, 23

Jingle All the Way (film), 249

Johnson, A. J., 268

Johnson, Billy, 33

Johnson, Don, 131

Johnson, Earvin "Magic," 169, 231, 241, 245, 248, 265

Johnson, J. R., 33

Johnson, T. J., 230

Jo Jo Dancer, Your Life Is Calling (film), 138

joke thieves, 69, 71

Jolson, Al, 33, 62

Jones, James Earl, 130, 135

Jones, Jedda, 264

Jones, Jenny, 256

Jones, Quincy, 240, 245, 246, 247, 248

Jones, Shaun, 43, 90

Joyner, Mario, 221, 259

Joyner, Tom, ix, 264

Judd, Naomi, 305, 306

Julia (television series), 113, 155

Julian, Max, 135

Juvenile Court (television series), 120

Kabush, Bill, 147

Kahn, Madeline, 106

Katz, Barry, 308

Kay, Monty, 114, 115

Keenan (television series), 245, 247

Keith, B. F., 77

Kelley, David E., 291

Kelly, Gerald, 283

Kelly, R., 319

Kersands, Billy, 20, 21, 24

Keyes, Alan, 101

Keymah, T'Keyah "Crystal," 106, 226, 227, 229, 231, 232, 315, 318

Kid Power (television program), 64. *See also* Wee Pals

King, Alan, 250

King, Mabel, 122

King, Marcus, 208

King, Regina, 176

Kings of Comedy tour, 207, 276, 277, 278, 281; imitators of, 283; urban comedy, as destroyer of, 282, 283

Kings of New York tour, 283

Kinison, Sam, 315

Kirby, George: background of, 97–98

Klein, Robert, 141

Knight, Gladys, 115

Knowles, Beyoncé, 183, 234

Kool Bubba Ice, 24, 47, 110, 296

Koppel, Ted, 244

Kravitz, Lenny, 119

Ku Klux Klan (KKK), 23, 39

Kutcher, Ashton, 319

Lady Sings the Blues (film), 134

Laff Records, 87, 88, 89

Lambert, Ray, 189

Lamont, Jay, 127

Lane, William Henry "Juba," 19

Lange, Ted, 123

Lapowski, Ray, 216

Las Vegas (Nevada), 79; and Moulin Rouge Agreement, 80; Rat Pack Summit in, 80; segregation in, 80

Last Comic Standing (television series), 303, 304

The Late Show (talk show), 240

Latham Entertainment Presents (film), 277

Latham, Walter, 276, 277, 282, 283

Lathan, Stan, 197, 202–3

Latin Kings of Comedy tour, 283

Lavelle, Andre, 280

Law, Bobby, 108, 115, 315

Lawford, Peter, 80

Lawrence, Martin, 122–23, 130, 143, 171, 177, 190, 201, 202, 203, 238, 239, 242, 247, 252, 257, 272, 280, 291, 292, 310; background of, 197, 198, 199

Lear, Norman, 115, 118, 119

Lee, Bruce, 160

Lee, Johnny, 34

Lee, Spike, 180, 229, 231, 277, 315

Leiber, Carol, 306

Leno, Jay, 119, 145, 240, 241

Leonard, Sugar Ray, 231

Leroi, Ali, 227, 259

Leroy & Skillet, 87, 116, 117, 140

Leslie, 46, 59, 71, 81, 90, 161, 164, 216

Let's Do It Again (film), 119, 130

Letterman, David, 119, 241

Lewis, Buddy, 47, 72, 110, 171, 197, 264

Lewis, Dawnn, 251

Lewis, Jerry, 283

Lewis, Willie, 95

Life (film), 199, 272

Lily (television special), 134

Lindsey, Mary, 189

Lionel, Evan, 25, 32, 47, 71, 163, 201, 216, 280

Lister, Tiny, 168

Little JJ, 317, 318

The Little Rascals (television series), 44. *See also* Our
    Gang

Little, Rich, 97

Live and Smokin' (recording), 134

Live on the Sunset Strip (film), 137

Living Single (television series), 232, 238

LL Cool J, 199, 233

Lockhart, Calvin, 130

Lohan, Lindsey, 318

Long, Johnny Lee, 78

Long, Nia, 199

Louis, Joe, 76, 80

Love, Faizon, 173, 268

Love, Loni, 21, 161, 255, 305, 306–7

Love Thy Neighbor (television series), 123

Lucas, Sam, 24; as transitional, 21

A Lucky Coon, 31

Luenell, 71, 117, 252, 307, 314

Lunceford, Jimmie, 84

Lyles, Aubrey, 33

Lynch, Jimmy, 87

Mabley, Jack, 78

Mabley, Moms (Loretta Mary Aiken), 43, 45, 67, 93;
    background of, 78; party records of, 79; persona of, 79

Mac, Bernie, 47, 57, 162, 183, 189, 202, 207, 240, 263, 272,
    276, 277, 286; background of, 280, 281

The Mack (film), 135

MacLachlan, Janet, 123

Madd Marv, 16, 94, 106, 113, 138, 160, 309–10

Madea's Family Reunion (film), 301

The Magic Hour (talk show), 231, 247

Magic Johnson Theaters, 265

Magnotti, Rob, 221

Major Payne (film), 229

Malcolm & Eddie (television series), 260

Malcolm X, 84, 134

Mann, Michael, 234

Marin, Cheech, 131

Markham, Pigmeat (Dewey Markham), 52, 55, 70, 78,
    114, 250; background of, 76–77

Marquez the Greatest, 69, 72, 90

Martial Law (television series), 242

Martin (television series), 198, 200, 202, 213, 238, 239

Martin, Dean, 80

Martin, Steve, 139

Masada, Jamie, 246

Masak, Ron, 123

Mason, John "Spider Bruce," 78

Master Piece (recording), 316

Match Game (television series), 95

Mathews, Charles James, 14, 15

Maude (television series), 117, 119

Maybelle, Harold, 87

McClain, Billy, 21

McClain, Stacy, 171, 174

McDaniel, Hattie, 39, 40, 161; background of, 41

McDonald, Rushion, 277

McGee, T. J., 171

McGruder, Aaron, 64

McIntosh, Tom, 21, 24

McMahon, Ed, 248, 305

McQueen, Butterfly, 41, 45, 52

Means, Angela, 47, 71, 173–74, 221, 257–58, 268, 270,
    285, 287, 291, 292

Me & the Boys (television series), 277

Me and Mr. B (play), 120

Men in Black (film), 252

Merritt, Teresa, 123

Meteor Man (film), 180, 262

Method Man, 139

Miami Vice (film), 234

Michaels, Lorne, 156

Michaels, Marilyn, 97

Midnight and Daybreak, 76

Milch, David, 144

Miller, Dennis, 256

Miller, F. E., 34

Miller, Flournoy, 33, 55

Miller & Lyles, 33, 34

Million Dollar Baby (film), 258

minstrelsy, 13, 14, 15, 17, 22, 67; African Americans, popularity among, 24; decline of, 25, 26; image of, 25; and minstrel troupes, 16, 25; and pantomime, 29

Mitchell, Joni, 141

Mitchell, Norman, 25, 63, 173, 176, 190, 216, 309

Mitchell, Scoey, 154

Moesha (television series), 260, 281, 303

Mohr, Jay, 305

Mo Money (film), 229

Money Talks (film), 271

Mo'Nique (Mo'Nique Imes-Jackson), 195, 277, 283; background of, 284

Monte, Eric, 117, 122

Monteith, Kelly, 145

Moody, Lynne, 123

Mooney, Darryl, 59, 133, 136, 262, 310, 315

Mooney, Dwayne, 136

Mooney, Paul, vii, 116, 135, 136, 167, 196, 197, 291, 313; as angry, 314, 316; background of, 314, 315, 316; as intimidating, 317; as uncompromising, 315

Moonves, Les, 307

Moore, Rudy Ray, ix, 43, 58, 79, 85, 94, 95, 96, 97, 114, 126, 129, 130, 173, 217, 219, 295; background of, 127, 128; persona of, 127

Moore, Tim, 56, 78

Moore, U. S., 178

Moreland, Mantan, 34, 52, 70, 78, 200; background of, 45

Morgan, Tracy, 221

Morris, Garrett: background of, 139

Morris, Keith, 16, 59, 69, 81, 86, 90, 129, 171, 217

Mosley, Brandonn, 171, 172, 174

Moss and Frye, 76

Murphy, Charlie, 155, 156, 157, 158, 235, 238, 266, 313

Murphy, Eddie, 58, 138, 143, 154, 155, 158, 159, 167, 197, 199, 212, 214, 219, 234, 240, 257, 272, 317; background of, 156; as breakout talent, 156; crossover appeal of, 161; influences of, 160

Murray, John "Rastus," 78

Myers, Lou, 251

My Little Margie (television series), 46

Myra J., 169, 171, 264, 283

My Wife and Kids (television series), 229

Nash Bridges (television series), 131

Negro baseball league, 282

Nelson, Heywood, 122

Newman, Lorraine, 139

Next Friday (film), 267, 307–8

Nicholas, Denise, 130

Nicholas, Harold, 130

Nichols, George, 15

Nigger (Gregory): reaction to, 100

Nigger in the Woodpile (film), 40

Night Court (television series), 237

The Nine Lives of Fritz the Cat (film), 63

Nixon, Richard, 101

Nolte, Nick, 156

Nunez, Miguel, 272

The Nutty Professor (film), 159, 272, 310

NWA (Niggaz with Attitude), 266

Ocean's 11 (film), 281

Ocean's 12 (film), 281

O'Connor, Carroll, 86

O'Donnell, Rosie, 187, 256

Of Black America (television series), 42

Okeh Records, 84

The Original Kings of Comedy (film), 277

Our Gang (film shorts), 43, 44. See also The Little Rascals

Ovitz, Mike, 241

Owen, Gary, 214, 215, 218

Paar, Jack, 99, 100

Pace, Harry, 84

Pacino, Al, 233, 318

Page, Harrison, 123

Page, LaWanda, 29, 87, 116, 239; background of, 117

Paige, Satchel, 282

The Parent 'Hood (television series), 181, 260

Parker, Dave, 171

Parker, J. Stafford, 116

Parker, Paula Jai, 238, 261–62, 265, 288, 291, 292

The Parkers (television series), 252, 284, 285

Partners in Crime (television progam), 179, 180, 230; inspiration for, 182

Parton, Dolly, 156

party records, 84

Passions (television series), 120

Pataki, George, 94

Paul, Reuben, 16, 71, 110, 162–63, 177, 206, 216, 242, 257, 270, 295

Payne, Allen, 262

Payne, Carl, 239

Peace and Freedom Party, 101

Pen & Ink, 76

Perry, Rodney, 25, 47, 57, 62, 71, 102, 158, 209, 235, 278, 291

Perry, Tyler: as brand, 300, 301

Phan, Dat, 303, 305

Phillips, Jay, 47, 57, 63, 81, 84, 90, 115, 130–31, 164, 190, 263

Picasso, Pablo, 141

A Piece of the Action (film), 130

Pierre, 59, 90, 110, 162, 181, 183, 230, 296, 307

Pietro, 32

Pinkett, Jada, 262

The P.J.'s (television series), 159

Plantation Party (radio program), 51

Player's Club (film), 233, 267

Poetic Justice (film), 176

Poitier, Sidney, 106, 119, 130, 137, 161, 200, 234

Politically Incorrect with Bill Maher (talk show), 256, 285

Pootie Tang (film), 258, 260

Pot, Pans, & Skillet, 76

Presley, Elvis, 160

Primrose, George, 20

Prince, Mark, 23, 43, 63, 78, 90, 118, 120, 217, 296

The Princess Bride (film), 161

Prinze, Freddy, 187

Pryor, Richard, vii, ix, 47, 59, 88, 94, 104, 116, 125, 129, 130, 140, 143, 149, 157, 158, 160, 187, 196, 212, 219, 243, 250, 263, 277, 286, 288, 309, 314, 315, 316; background of, 131–32; and Bill Cosby, as inspiration, 132; death of, 139; disciples of, 167; drug addiction of, 137, 138, 153; mainstream, turning back on, 133, 134; movie career of, 134, 135, 137, 138; as wild, 133; as writer, 135, 136

Quaid, Dennis, 233

Queen Latifah, 232

Queens of Comedy tour, 277, 283, 284, 285, 286, 291

Race (recording), 316

race films, 53, 70

racism: within black community, 111; in comedy, 107–11

radio: and black performers, 51, 53

Radner, Gilda, 139

Randolph, Lillian, 120

Rashad, Phylicia Ayers, 106

Raw (film), 157, 167, 227

Rawlins, Donnell, 190, 313

Ray (film), 234, 258

Reagan, Ronald, 153

reality shows, 304; and comedy, as disruptive force, 302

The Redd Foxx Show (television series), 86

Redemption (television film), 234

Redman, 139

Reed, Don, 169, 180

Reed, Leonard, 68, 76, 78

Reed, Rico, 177

Reed, Robi, 174, 176

Reed, Tracy, 130

Reese, Della, 114, 138, 157

Reese, Roxanne, 264

Reid, Tim, 147, 148, 149, 238, 315; background of, 146

Reiser, Paul, 187

Rey, Reynaldo, 83, 115, 116, 150, 157, 162, 163, 173, 205, 214, 215, 217, 220, 266; background of, 218–19

Rhodes, Tom, 142

Rhone, Eric, 210, 211, 300

Rhymes, Busta, 285, 319

Rice, Thomas D., 15

Richard Pryor (recording), 132

Richard Pryor in Concert (film), 137

Richard Pryor Meets Richard & Willie and the SLA (recording), 140

The Richard Pryor Show (television series), 237, 272

Richard & Willie, 87, 109, 140, 141

Rich, Matty, 180

Riperton, Minnie, 259

Rivers, Joan, 240

Roach, Hal, 43, 44

Robbins, Tollin, 319

Robinson, Holly, 251

Robinson, Jackie, 33

Robinson, Smokey, 149

Roc (television series), 238

Rock, Chris, 58, 59, 130, 188, 189, 203, 284; background of, 256, 257, 258, 259; socially relevant material of, 259

Rock, Tony, 131, 259, 295, 313

Rodd, Roger, 24, 98, 162, 188–89, 226, 256, 316

Rodman, 294

Rogers, Timmie: background of, 96–97; as groundbreaker, 96

Rogers, Will, 42, 68, 69–70

Roker, Roxie, 119

Rolle, Esther, 117, 118

Rollins, Howard, 181

Roney, Tony, 189

Rose, Anika Noni, 234

Ross, Diana, 114, 134

Rossi, Steve, 96, 149–50

Roundtree, Richard, 125

Rowan & Martin's Laugh-In (television series), 76, 114, 150

Roy, John, 305, 306

The Royal Family (television series), 86

Runnin' Wild, 34

Rush Hour (film), 271

Rush Hour 2 (film), 271

Rush, Rudy, 195

Russell, Nipsey, 70, 114; background of, 95

Salley, John, 241

Sam 'n Henry (radio program), 51. *See also* Amos 'n Andy

Sanders, Ajai, 47, 105, 159, 170, 171, 172, 174, 197–98, 206, 249, 270, 291, 292, 310

Sanders, Brad, 48, 62, 63, 75, 76, 93, 101, 105, 133, 162, 170–71, 264

Sanford (television series), 86, 117

Sanford Arms (television series), 117

Sanford, Isabel, 119

Sanford and Son (television series), 86, 117, 119, 134, 136; and *Steptoe and Son*, 116

Saturday Night Live (television series), 136, 139, 154, 156, 159, 228, 257, 315

Scarface (film), 318

Schiffman, Frank, 77

Schlesinger, Leon, 61

Schwarzenegger, Arnold, 249

Scott, Emmet J., 70

Scott-Heron, Gil, 141

Sculfield, Tony, 280

Seinfeld (television series), 199

Seinfeld, Jerry, 187

Shaft (film), 125

Shakur, Tupac, 176, 238

Shang, 24, 55, 71, 94, 163, 192–93, 195–96, 225, 272, 295, 315

Sharpton, Al, 101

Sheen, Charlie, 271

Shepherd, Sherri, 47, 70, 89, 260, 288, 291, 292, 293, 294

Shore, Mitzi, 169

Showtime at the Apollo (television series), 195, 196, 221, 232, 277

Shuckey Duckey, 316

Shuffle Along, 34

Siegfried and Roy, 304

Silver Streak (film), 137

Simmons, Russell, 197, 200, 202, 203

Simply Marvelous, 171

Sinatra, Frank, 80, 149

Sinbad (David Adkins), 22, 35, 56, 58, 70, 89–90, 106, 111, 114, 126, 127, 144, 163, 168, 169, 175, 179, 195, 232, 246, 247, 250, 251; background of, 248, 249

Sinbad (television series), 238

The Sinbad Show (television series), 249

Singleton, John, 176, 180, 266

Sissle, Noble, 34

Sister Act (film), 161

Sister Act 2 (film), 161

Sister, Sister (television series), 149

Sivad, Darryl, 206

Six Degrees of Separation (film), 43

Six Feet Under (television series), 253

Skelton, Red, viii

Skinny Women Are Evil (film), 284

Slocomb, Jonathan, 249, 257

Smiley, Rick, 218, 277

Smith, Bessie, 76

Smith and Watson, 171

Smith, Will, 43, 199, 234, 252

Smoove, J. B., 43, 63, 171, 196, 217, 234, 258, 260, 316

Snipes, Wesley, 169

Snoops, 291

Soap (television series), 238

A Soldier's Story (film), 180, 181

Sommore (Lori Rambo), ix, 17, 35, 41, 48, 69, 72, 161, 163, 183, 190, 213, 277, 283, 286, 287, 295; background of, 285

Soul Plane (film), 305

Soul Train (television series), 255

Speedy, 25, 58, 71, 128, 171, 208, 234, 296

Spencer, Chris, 23, 156, 207, 234, 235, 245, 246, 247, 261, 281

Spencer, Danielle, 122

Spielberg, Steven, 183

Spires, Tony, 33, 41, 117, 200, 206, 208, 269, 275–76, 282–83, 284

Spo-Dee-O-Dee, 78

Stallone, Sylvester, 156

Stanfield, Richard, 56, 58, 77, 79, 87, 88, 94, 96, 107, 163, 172; background of, 140, 141

stand-up comedy, 68; and comics, mentality of, 67; origins of, 29

Stanis, Bernadette, 117

Stapleton, Rob, 283

Starks, Doug, 264

Star Search (television series), 242, 248, 249, 256, 305, 306

The Starting Line Up (DVD series), 210

stereotypes: and mammy, image of, 40

Sterling's Black & White Minstrel Show (television program), 26

Steve Harvey's Big Time (television series), 278

The Steve Harvey Show (television series), 210, 277

Stewart, Jon, 241, 245

Stewart, Nicodemus, 45

Stir Crazy (film), 137

St. Jacque, Raymond, 107

Stone, Oliver, 233

Straight Outta Compton (recording), 266

Strays (film), 307

Strictly Business (television program), 231

Studdard, Ruben, 305

The Stu Erwin Show (television series), 46

Stump and Stumpy, 76

Suddenly Susan (television series), 291

Sugarhill Times (television series), 96

Sullivan, Ed, 55, 76, 97

Summer, Cree, 251

Sumner, Bob, 154, 155, 188, 197, 199, 200, 203, 225–26, 232, 259, 270–71, 277, 309

The Sunday Comics (television program), 199

Sunshine Sammy (Ernie Morrison), 43

Sussman, Morris, 77

Suter, Suzanne, 159, 238

Sweat, Keith, 284

Sweeney, J. W., 15

Sykes, Wanda, 256; background of, 259–60

Symone, Raven, 318

Talent, 58, 71, 89, 109, 116, 118, 122, 283, 286, 295, 314–15

Taylor, Curt, 116

Taylor, Montanna, 214, 218

television: as Golden Age, for African Americans, 113

That Nigger's Crazy (recording), 88, 135, 243

That's My Mama (television series), 123

That '70s Show (television series), 131

That's So Raven (television series), 318

Thea (television series), 252

Theatre Owners Booking Association (TOBA), 75, 76, 77

A Thin Line Between Love and Hate (film), 198

Thomas, Alex, 48, 58, 63, 69, 71, 76, 109, 128, 135, 164, 183, 199, 267, 268, 295

Thomas, Ernest, 122

Thomas, William, Jr., 44

Thoroughly Modern Millie (musical), 161

Tim & Tom, 146, 147, 148, 149

Toast of the Town (television series), 76, 97

Tolbert, Belinda, 119

Tomlin, Lily, 134, 187

Tone, Tony, 108, 162, 210, 216

The Tonight Show (talk show), 114, 149, 241, 247

Toomer, Al, 14, 25, 42, 47, 57, 70, 81, 83, 109, 193, 207, 214, 295

Toones, Fred "Snowflake," 45

Torry, Guy, 176, 190, 207, 271, 272, 276, 278–79, 301

Torry, Joe, 19, 51, 130, 171, 174, 177, 178, 190, 202, 203, 257, 264, 285; background of, 175, 176

To Tell the Truth (television series), 95

Townsend, Robert, 35, 58, 104, 134, 141, 158, 162, 167, 168, 183, 227, 230, 238, 260, 261, 315; career of, 179–80, 181, 182

Townsend Television (television series), 167, 181, 238, 261

Trading Places (film), 156

Travalena, Fred, 97

True Colors (television series), 238

Tucker, Chris, 16, 178, 190, 219, 284, 291, 307; background of, 268–71; persona of, 270

Tucker, Sophie, 97

Turman, Glynn, 251

Turner, Morrie, 64

227 (television series), 120, 219

Two Can Play that Game (film), 284

Two Zephyrs, 95

Tyler, Willie, 114

Tyson, Mike, 169

Uggams, Leslie, 247

Uncle Tom's Cabin: film version of, 21; stage production of, 21

Undercover Brother (film), 262, 263

Underwood, Sheryl, 218, 292

Unpredictable (recording), 234

UPN: and black comedies, 303

Uproar Records, 88

The Uptown Comedy Club (television series), 221

Uptown Comedy Express (television program), 257

Uptown Saturday Night (film), 130, 135

Vance, Norman Jr., 303

Van Peebles, Melvin, 107

vaudeville: and blacks, shunning of on, 33

Vibe (television series), 245, 246, 247

Victory at Entebbe (television movie), 107

Vidale, Thea, 23, 40, 41, 42, 44, 69, 89, 116, 117, 118, 119, 122, 184, 237, 252

Vince D., 63, 164, 171, 271, 312

Virginia Minstrels, 16

Voodoo Child (television program), 262

Walker, Aida O., 32

Walker, George, 31, 32, 34

Walker, Jimmie, 117, 130; background of, 119; negative image of, 118

The Walking Dead (film), 262, 263

Wallace, George, 130, 189, 291

Waller, Fats, 84

Walters, Barbara, 244

Wanda at Large (television series), 260

Warfield, Marsha, 169, 237, 284

Washington, Booker T., 32

Washington, Denzel, 169, 181, 234

Washington, Dinah, 95

Washington, Keith, 196

Watermelon Man (film), 107

Waters, Ethel, 55

Watkins, Royale, 98, 144, 180, 252; on black television shows, quality of, 253

Watson, Johnnie "Guitar," 219

The Wayans Bros. (television series), 260, 291

Wayans, Damon, 167, 168, 179, 180, 227, 248; background of, 228, 229

Wayans, Keenan Ivory, 141, 157, 167, 180, 181, 230, 235, 248; background of, 227

Wayans, Kim, 227, 232

Wayans, Marlon, 260

Wayans, Shawn, 227, 230, 260

Webster (television series), 123

Wee Pals (comic strip), 64. *See also* Kid Power

Wells, Joey "J-Dub," 17, 24, 25, 41, 43, 63, 69, 215

Wertimer, Ned, 119

What's Happening!! (television series), 117, 122, 123, 197, 272

Which Way Is Up? (film), 134, 315

White, Edwonda, 57, 71, 158, 163, 196, 201, 206, 218, 291, 293, 317

White, Slappy, 84, 87, 93, 114, 116, 149–50, 220, 250, 275; background of, 95–96; Catskills, booking in, 96; and Redd Foxx, 95, 96

Whitfield, Lynn, 198

Whitley, Kym, 70, 157, 241, 267, 271

Wilborn, George, 189, 214, 280

Wilder, Gene, 137

Wildman Steve, 87

Williams, Bert, 31; background of, 32; death of, 33

Williams, Billy Dee, 135

Williams, Damon, 25, 47, 71, 164, 189, 195, 277, 280, 307

Williams, Dootsie, 85, 86, 87

Williams, Doug, 211–12, 281, 295

Williams, Hal, 120

Williams, Joe, 77

Williams, Katt, 46, 72, 107, 156, 157, 258, 262, 267, 291, 308, 310

Williams, Michael, 167, 174, 175, 176, 177, 178, 251, 283, 288, 292

Williams, Robin, 139, 160, 161, 187, 212, 315

Williams, Sharon, 284, 292

Williams, Spencer, 44, 56

Williams & Walker, 31, 200

Willis, Bruce, 271

Wilmore, Larry, 264

Wilmore, Mark, 264

Wilson, Debra, 221

Wilson, Flip, 42, 130, 158; career of, 114, 115; characters of, 115

Wilson, Nancy, 77, 140, 240

Wilson, Teddy, 123

Wilson, Yvette, 171, 252, 268

Wilson, William, 171

Wilson, Woodrow, 39

Winfield, Rodney, 190, 191

Winfrey, Oprah, 285
Winninger, Charles, 46
Witherspoon, John, 15, 21, 57, 71, 84, 109, 162, 180, 266, 268, 299, 315; background of, 272
The Wiz (film), 134
WKRP in Cincinnati (television series), 149
Woman Thou Art Loose (play), 301
Wonder, Stevie, 177
Won Ton Ton the Wonder Dog (film), 43
Woodard, Alfre, 183

Wright, Carl, 189
Wright, Steven, 144

Yorkin, Bud, 119
Young, Andrew, 104
Young, Walter, 104

Ziegfeld, Florence, 32
Ziegfeld Follies, 32, 33